A Laboratory Manual of Human Anatomy and Physiology

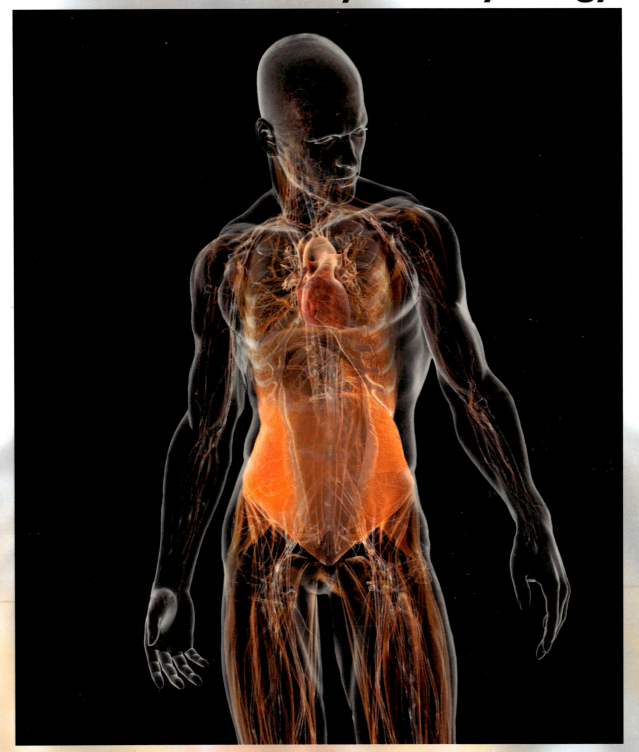

Donald R. Ferruzzi

Suffolk County Community College

BIOMATERIA

Contributing Editors: Erikka O. Mendez and Stanley Lamberg
Cover Art: Bryan Christie Design
Graphic Design: Stu Suchit
Printing: Printers 3 • Hauppauge, New York

A Laboratory Manual of Human Anatomy and Physiology

Volume One

Twenty-Eighth Printing

BIOMATERIA BOOKS

Post Office Box 503
Stony Brook, New York 11790

Printed in United States of America

ISBN 978-09896177-5-8

Contents

Preface

"What a piece of work is a man!" And in no other learning environment are the incredible architecture and precise operation of the body more strikingly apparent than in the laboratory. It is here that students take a firsthand look at the anatomy of cells, tissues and organs. It is here that they dismantle the body's complex of systems, investigate their anatomy and physiology, and reconstitute them into a more meaningful whole. It is through laboratory experience that they broaden their understanding of human design and gain a true appreciation of the interrelationship between form and function.

This manual provides a series of exercises which focus on basic principles of human anatomy and physiology. Its content has been selected to include subject matter that is most suitable for laboratory presentation and which lends itself to direct student involvement. The exercises are grouped according to fundamental concepts and major organ systems. It is hoped that each segment is not perceived as separate and autonomous, but rather as part of an interdependent group of systems within a wholly integrated organism.

To derive the greatest benefit from the laboratory, the student is urged to review pertinent background material and read through each exercise beforehand. Note that required anatomy within each particular illustration, photograph and electron micrograph is labeled in **boldface** type. The unlabeled diagrams in the Review Section are intended as self-tests and should be completed after mastery of laboratory models and specimens.

A number of procedures involve experimentation, and on occasion, require original test methodology on the part of the student. It is essential that complete and accurate records be kept and that all data be entered directly into the laboratory manual. When a procedure yields unexpected results, an attempt at a reasonable explanation often helps to understand the problem. Interpretation of information gathered in the laboratory is an important step toward independent and critical thinking.

All the laboratory work you undertake has one general purpose in mind: to present body form and function in a manner that is accessible, informative and stimulating. Thorough preparation and conscientious performance of the exercises will make the laboratory experience meaningful and rewarding.

August, 2015   D.R.F.

Acknowledgments

Secretarial support laid the foundation for the manuscript and I am indebted to Rosemarie Cherry, Janet Fuentes, and Jaidy Acosta for their unfailing reliability. Those on the Grant Campus biology faculty whose critical feedback shaped the final draft included George Fortunato, Nancy Penncavage, Hope Sasway, and Jim Remsen. Adjunct instructors who shared their comments were Mary Ellen Calitri, Stanley Lamberg, and Joel Reicherter. Silvia Montemurro of the English Department generously contributed her time and expertise. I am also indebted to Stephen Greenberg, MD, of North Shore Eye Care, who brought his considerable ophthalmic expertise to bear on the vision section of Special Senses, and to Howard Sussman MD, of Stony Brook Family Medicine, who reviewed the Clinical Applications with clinical precision.

On the technical side, Stu Suchit greatly influenced the quality of page layouts, including table and chart design and original illustrations.

Among those reviewers whom I had the pleasure of teaching was Liana Chin, who took on several chapters with unbridled enthusiasm. She was ably assisted by Lisa Novatney. They both have my gratitude for bringing a sharp editorial eye and a student perspective to *A Laboratory Manual of Human Anatomy and Physiology*.

Isabella Cosentino's critical appraisal drew upon her expertise as a linguist and award-winning teacher of foreign languages. Days before I was about to hand over the manual for publication, my sister came through with "just-in-timely" revisions backed by impeccable logic — and a tacit reminder that collaboration is key to any project of this magnitude.

And finally, to my Mom and Dad for their guidance and inspiration throughout my formative years and beyond.

Credits

The staff at Wiley's Higher Education division in Hoboken, NJ was instrumental in providing most of the illustrations featured in this manual. They were reproduced from Tortora and Derrickson's *Principles of Anatomy and Physiology*, 13th edition, with permission kindly granted by Anna Melhorn, Senior Illustration-Production Editor. Photomicrographs not derived from the Tortora text were graciously provided by Victor Eroschenko, Professor Emeritus of Anatomy at the University of Idaho from his stellar collection in DiFiore's *Atlas of Histology with Functional Correlations*. The modern and Neanderthal skull comparisons were furnished by the American Museum of Natural History in New York. My sincere gratitude to Mark Nielsen and Shawn Miller of the University of Utah for graciously allowing reproduction of cadaver images from *Atlas of Human Anatomy*, an extraordinary compilation of gross and microscopic human morphology. Figure study photographs were obtained mostly through copyright-free stock image agencies with the exception of the males pictured on pages 170 and 230. They were supplied courtesy of Chris Ferruzzi and Mikael Häggström, respectively. (For anyone concerned about Christopher's condition after contorting for the camera in the manner you will witness in Exercise 8, rest assured that he's doing rather well, thanks in no small part to the ministrations of photographer Kara Roberts.) Images of wet mount technique, dye-in-agar diffusion, the Beauchene skull, multiple axial and appendicular bones, and the ergometer were skillfully rendered by Victoria Sinacori.

Safety in the Laboratory

1. On the first day of laboratory, determine the location of fire extinguishers, fire blankets, eyewashes, first-aid kits, and evacuation exits. If your clothes or those of a lab partner ignite, remember: Stop, drop and roll! (See the illustrations in Figure F-1 demonstrating proper use of eyewash, fire extinguisher and fire blanket.)

2. Dress appropriately for the laboratory. Wear a lab coat or apron and gloves when called for. Tie back long hair and remove dangling jewelry. Avoid wearing open shoes and sandals.

3. Do not consume or store food and beverages in the laboratory.

4. Be mindful of where you place glassware containing solutions or collected specimens. Immediately inform the instructor of a spill or other accident in the laboratory.

5. Never pipet by mouth. Mechanical pipettes will be provided for all fluid transfers.

6. When you have finished your experiments, wash your bench top. (Rotate cleaning responsibility. One person from each table could be assigned each week.) Wash your hands with soap and water.

7. Do not place any object in mouth and keep hands away from face. Eyes, mouth, nose and skin are all points of entry for chemicals of one kind or another.

8. If you are pregnant; if you have allergies; or if you have a medical condition which may be affected or triggered by substances or procedures used in the laboratory please inform the instructor.

9. Do not work alone in the laboratory or perform any unauthorized experiments.

10. Please read and sign the Laboratory Safety Rules Acknowledgment form. Submit this form to your instructor during the first laboratory session.

ring

hand grip

flared hose end

a

b

c

STOP!   DROP!   ROLL!

d

FIGURE F-1. Laboratory safety equipment and procedures. (a) Eyewash technique: depress plunger to cleanse eyes; (b) fire extinguisher: grasp ring and pull out pin, point hose end at flames and squeeze hand grip to release foam; (c) fire blanket: envelop body by rotating counterclockwise; (d) If a fire blanket is not close by, stop, drop, and roll.

Laboratory Safety Rules Acknowledgment

I have read the rules in the Safety in the Laboratory section and will observe them during all laboratory activities.

Signature: _____

Print name: _____

Date: _____

Course: _____

Section: _____

Instructor: _____

Introduction to Anatomy: Terminology & Body Planes

Speaking the native language when touring a foreign country is a valuable asset. Likewise, familiarity with anatomical terms before embarking on a tour of the body is a practical step toward mastery of human form and function.

The Anatomical Position

The study of anatomy is facilitated by a reference posture, the **anatomical position** (Figure F-2). In this position, the body is erect and facing forward; upper limbs are fully extended, slightly more than shoulder width apart with palms facing forward; lower limbs are fully extended, hip width apart, the feet squarely on the ground.

Applying the terminology of the human body is made simpler and less confusing using the anatomical position. For example, the radius bone of the forearm is properly described as lateral to the ulna, that is, farther from the body midline. This assumes that the body is in the anatomical position. Without this reference position, standard directional terminology would not be feasible since the radius can rotate over the ulna and relocate to the opposite side of the forearm.

Regional Terms

- **cervical**   refers to the neck

- **thoracic**   the region between neck and abdomen; commonly referred to as the chest (thorax)

- **lumbar**   the back region between thorax and pelvis

- **plantar**   pertaining to the sole of the foot; opposite the plantar surface is the dorsum

- **palmar**   the anterior surface of the hand; the opposite side is the dorsum

- **axilla**   the armpit

- **inguinal**   refers to the groin, where abdominal wall meets thigh

- **arm**   the part of the upper limb between shoulder and elbow

- **forearm**   the part of the upper limb between elbow and wrist

- **thigh**   the part of the lower limb between hip and knee

- **leg**   the part of the lower limb between knee and ankle

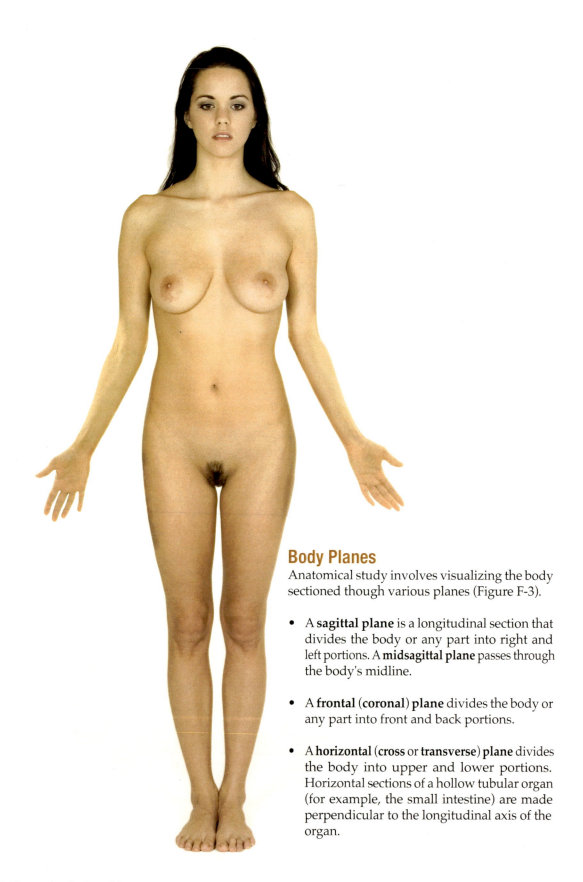

Body Planes

Anatomical study involves visualizing the body sectioned though various planes (Figure F-3).

- A **sagittal plane** is a longitudinal section that divides the body or any part into right and left portions. A **midsagittal plane** passes through the body's midline.

- A **frontal** (**coronal**) **plane** divides the body or any part into front and back portions.

- A **horizontal** (**cross** or **transverse**) **plane** divides the body into upper and lower portions. Horizontal sections of a hollow tubular organ (for example, the small intestine) are made perpendicular to the longitudinal axis of the organ.

FIGURE F-2. The anatomical position.

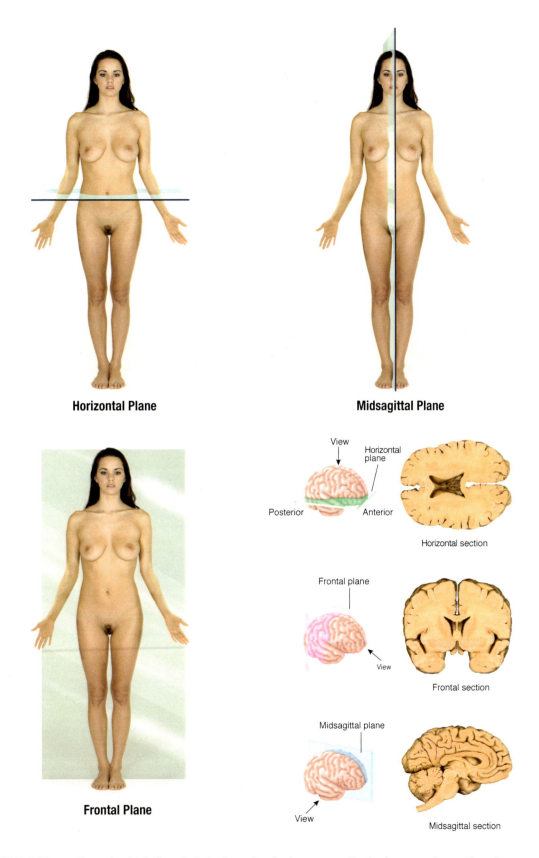

Horizontal Plane

Midsagittal Plane

Frontal Plane

View
Horizontal plane
Posterior
Anterior
Horizontal section

Frontal plane
View
Frontal section

Midsagittal plane
View
Midsagittal section

FIGURE F-3. Planes through which the whole body and a single organ — the brain — can be sectioned.

Term	Definition	Example
Anterior (ventral)	Toward or on the front of the body	The chest is anterior to the spine.
Posterior (dorsal)	Toward or on the back of the body	The buttocks are on the posterior surface of the body.
Superior (cranial)	Toward the head; relatively higher in position	The eyebrows are superior to the eyes.
Inferior (caudal)	Away from the head; relatively lower in position	The chin is inferior to the mouth.
Medial	Toward the midline of the body	The breast is medial to the armpit.
Lateral	Away from the midline of the body	The hip is lateral to the groin.
Proximal	Closer to the origin of a structure	The arm is proximal to the forearm.
Distal	Farther from the origin of a structure	The hand is distal to the wrist.
Superficial (external)	Located relatively closer to the body surface	The scalp is superficial to the cranium.
Deep (internal)	Located relatively farther from the body surface	The muscles are deep to the skin.

TABLE F-1. Directional Terms.

The Microscope

Exercise 1

O B J E C T I V E S

1. To identify the parts of the *compound light microscope* and describe the function of each.
2. To demonstrate proper microscope handling and focusing technique.
3. To define *magnification* and *resolution*.
4. To calculate total magnification.
5. To estimate the diameter of the low and high power fields.
6. To estimate the diameter of an actual cell.
7. To define *depth of focus* and compare depth of focus in low and high power lenses.
8. To identify the parts of the *stereomicroscope* and describe the function of each.

M A T E R I A L S

Compound microscope
Lens paper
Immersion oil (optional)
Prepared slide of letter *e*
Ruled stage micrometer
Prepared slide of oöcytes (egg cells)
  within an ovary
Prepared slide of colored threads
Biohazard bag

Physiologic saline, 0.9% NaCl
Microscope slides
Toothpicks, flat
Coverslips
Methylene blue stain
Disposable pipettes
Stereomicroscope
Specimens for stereomicroscope

P R E - L A B   Q U I Z

1. All observations under the microscope begin with a low power / high power objective lens positioned over the specimen. (Circle one.)
2. The _____ focus knob should never be used with a high power objective lens in place.
3. To clean the ocular or objective lenses, use:
   a. a soft cloth.   c. lens paper.
   b. a paper towel.   d. Any of these can be used.
4. Moving the iris diaphragm lever to the _____(direction) will allow more light to enter the objective lens.
5. Describe a technique that optimizes resolution.

The microscope is an indispensable tool for the study of cells and tissues in the laboratory. It extends the limits of anatomical observation to permit visualization of structures too small to be seen by the unaided eye. The ability of a microscope to reveal the structural details of a specimen depends on **magnification** and **resolution**.

Magnification

In a compound light microscope, magnification (magnifying power) is achieved by the interaction of two lenses: the **ocular (eyepiece) lens** and the **objective lens**. Magnification by the objective produces a real image that is projected to the ocular. The ocular adds further magnification as it transmits a virtual image to the eyes of the observer.

Each lens has a designated power of magnification; for the ocular, it is usually 10 diameters (10X). The objectives are commonly 4X (scanning lens), 10X (low power), 40X (high power), and 100X (oil immersion). *The total magnification is expressed as the product of the ocular and objective magnifications.* For example, a 10X ocular coupled with a 40X objective would enlarge the specimen 400 times.

Resolution

Resolution (resolving power) is the capacity of the microscope to distinguish two points that are a small distance apart. The optical systems of compound microscopes have a resolving power whose limit is approximately 0.2 micrometer (μm). This means that two objects will appear as distinct and separate entities if they are 0.2 μm or more apart. If they are closer than the resolution limit, the two objects will be seen as a single fused image. The resolving power of the human eye is about 100 μm (1/250 inch).

Resolution is limited by both the physical properties of light and the numerical aperture (N.A.) of the lens. (N.A. refers to the light-gathering ability of the lens.) The N.A. value for each of the objectives is printed on the lens; the higher the N.A. number, the more light enters the lens, and the greater the resolution.

Resolving power is strongly influenced by the angle of light entering the objective. In the exercises that follow, you will understand how the substage condenser and immersion oil direct light rays toward the objective and maximize resolution.

Introduction to the Compound Light Microscope

The proper use of the microscope will be a critical step in your exploration of human design. To use your time in the laboratory effectively, follow all operational guidelines and safety precautions to the letter. Mastery of microscopic technique will be the key to understanding the microanatomy you will soon encounter.

To begin, carefully remove the microscope from its cabinet and place it so that its base is comfortably set back from the table's edge. *Be sure to grasp the instrument securely with both hands, making certain that one hand always supports the base.* Unravel the power cord and plug it into a nearby outlet.

When moving the microscope on the lab table, always lift — *never drag* — the instrument from one place to another.

> **SAFETY PRECAUTION**
> Carefully position the microscope power cord at your workstation so that it cannot become entangled or tripped over.

PROCEDURE 1

Identifying the Parts of the Microscope

Study the parts of the compound microscope listed below. Each is pictured in Figure 1-1 and described in Table 1-1.

1. Ocular (eyepiece) lens
2. Head
3. Arm
4. Revolving nosepiece
5. Objective lens
6. Mechanical stage
7. Lever of iris diaphragm
8. Condenser
9. Coarse focus adjustment
10. Fine focus adjustment
11. Base
12. Illuminator
13. Stage travel knobs
14. Stage (slide) clip
15. Diopter ring

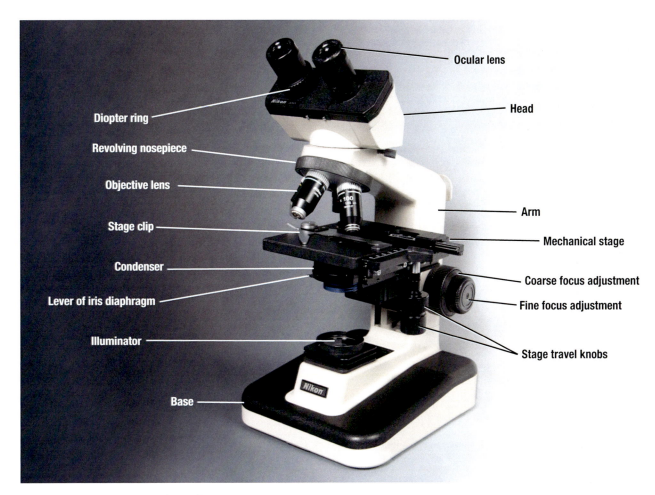

FIGURE 1-1. The compound light microscope.

PROCEDURE 2

Operating Instructions for the Microscope

Care of the Lenses

To ensure optimal performance from your microscope, the lenses must be periodically checked and cleaned if necessary. Usually, all that is needed to remove dust and smudges is the specially treated lens paper provided in the laboratory. These tissues are lint-free and low in abrasion. *They are not, under any circumstances, to be replaced by ordinary tissue paper or paper towels or fabric of any kind.*

To test the ocular for cleanliness, rotate it between your fingers while looking through it. If the dirt rotates with the ocular, then this lens should be wiped clean. For fixed oculars, simply wipe the lenses with lens paper.

Dirt that is on the objective — or on the slide itself — should be cleaned next. (Be sure to handle slides on the edges as you would a photograph to avoid smudges.) When a lens does not come clean with lens paper, a cleansing solvent should be applied. Consult your instructor or technical assistant should a solvent be required or if the problem warrants removal of an ocular or objective lens.

Examination with the Scanning Objective

To learn basic microscope technique and to recognize how an image is oriented by a compound lens system, a prepared slide of the letter *e* will serve as your first specimen. The instructions which follow will enable you to view the slide first with the scanning lens, then under low power, and finally using the high power objective. Adhere to these guidelines each time you use the microscope.

1. After plugging in your microscope, turn on the illuminator using the dial power switch.

TABLE 1-1. A Practical Guide to the Compound Microscope.

Part	Function
Ocular or eyepiece	The lens through which the image is viewed. The magnification (which is engraved on the rim) is usually 10X. A thin wire may be included within the ocular for pinpointing selected details of a specimen.
Diopter ring	A rotatable ring at the base of the left ocular that brings this lens into focus simultaneously with the right ocular.
Head	The region which attaches the ocular tube to the microscope. The head of some microscopes may be swiveled to facilitate viewing by someone other than the primary user.
Arm	A vertical support member between the head and the base.
Revolving nosepiece	A plate to which the objectives are attached. It rotates so that objectives of different magnifications can be used.
Scanning objective	The objective lens with the least magnification, usually 4X.
Low power objective	The objective lens with a magnification of 10X.
High power objective	The objective lens with a magnification that is usually 40X; also known as the high-dry objective.
Oil immersion objective	The objective lens whose tip is immersed in clear mineral oil to enhance resolution. This objective has the highest magnification, usually 100X.
Mechanical stage	The platform directly beneath the objective that is used to position a slide for viewing. A slide may be moved side to side or forward and backward in small increments by rotating two travel knobs on the stage's underside.
Iris diaphragm	A substage instrument whose aperture diameter can be adjusted with a lever to limit or increase the amount of light reaching the objective.
Condenser	A substage lens that directs a narrow beam of concentrated light to the objective to enhance resolution.
Coarse focus adjustment	A large knob on either side of the arm or base that brings an image into focus by moving the stage upward or downward in relatively large increments.
Fine focus adjustment	A small knob on either side of the arm or base that focuses by moving the stage upward or downward in relatively small increments.
Base	The horizontal support member of the microscope.
Illuminator	An electric light source in the base that provides illumination for the compound lens system.

2. If the scanning objective is not already in place, rotate the nosepiece so that the 4X lens clicks into position. *Never grasp the objective itself.* When properly aligned, the objective will be perpendicular to the stage.

3. Swing the stage clip out to the left and place your slide so that it lies flat on the mechanical stage. Center the letter *e* directly beneath the scanning objective by rotating the stage travel knobs. The *e* should be in the light path at this point. (Do not look into the ocular lenses until instructed to do so.)

4. Turn the coarse focus knob to raise the stage to its maximum height.

5. Now look through the oculars. Partially open the iris diaphragm by moving its lever to the left. Adjust the condenser lever so the condenser is one or two millimeters below its highest position. The circle of light you see is the microscopic **field of view**, or simply, the **field**. To ensure that the field appears as a single, distinct circle, grasp the oculars at their base and adjust the space between them as necessary. This interpupillary distance will now be tailored to your eyes.

6. With your eyes on the field, slowly rotate the coarse focus knob to lower the stage. When the letter *e* comes into view, use the fine focus knob to sharpen the image. Note the amount of space between slide and objective when the specimen is in focus. This is known as the **working distance**.

If the *e* does not appear, one of two problems may exist:

(a) You have exceeded the working distance. Solution: Return To Step 4 and repeat the focusing procedure.
(b) Your *e* is not aligned with the objective. Solution: Readjust the mechanical stage.

7. Adjust the light intensity with the iris diaphragm control lever. Ideally, light intensity should be about the same as the room lighting.

8. Once the *e* is clearly in view, observe how the orientation of the image differs from the orientation of the specimen on the slide. To

further appreciate how the lens system affects the image, move the slide from side to side and up and down using the mechanical stage. Is the direction of movement of the slide the same as that of the image?

_____

This technique of scanning the slide with the 4X objective is one you will frequently use to get an overall picture of a specimen, a kind of panoramic view.

9. Sketch the image of the *e*, exactly as it appears under the microscope in Table 1-2.

What has the optical system of the microscope done to the orientation of the *e*? Is it inverted (upside down)? Reversed (backward)?

_____

_____

Examination with the Low Power Objective

1. Rotate the nosepiece until the lower power lens click into position. *With your eyes at stage level, turn the coarse focus knob to raise the stage up to its maximum height.* (Although a braking mechanism should prevent contact between slide and objective, it is a good practice to keep an eye on the stage when it approaches an objective. Looking through the ocular while "up focusing" invites a collision between slide and objective if the safety mechanism fails.) Your goal at this point is to have the slide and objective close together, but not touching.

2. With your eyes on the field, slowly rotate the coarse focus knob to lower the stage. When the letter *e* comes into view, use the fine focus knob to sharpen the image.

If the *e* does not appear, one of two problems exists:

   (a) You have exceeded the working distance. Solution: Return to Step 1 and repeat the focusing procedure.
   (b) Your *e* is not aligned with the objective. Solution: Readjust the mechanical stage.

3. To ensure that the image is sharply focused in both eyes, a diopter ring adjustment is necessary.
   (a) Close your left eye and readjust the fine focus knob as needed so the right eye sees a sharp image.
   (b) Now close your right eye and rotate the diopter ring at the base of the left ocular until the image is sharp.

4. Sketch the image of the *e*, exactly as it appears, in Table 1-2.

High Power Examination

To view the specimen under the high power objective:

1. Make sure the image is sharply focused under low power.

2. Using the travel knobs, position the letter *e* in the center of the field. Since the high power objective has four times the magnification of the low power objective, its field will be only one-fourth the area of the low power field. Therefore, an image on the periphery of the low power field may be lost under high power unless it is first centered.

3. Change objectives by revolving the nosepiece to the click point of the high power lens. Since the microscope is *parfocal*, the letter *e* should remain nearly focused. (Parfocal lens systems ensure that the image is at least partly focused when objectives are switched.)

4. Sharpen the focus by adjusting the fine focus knob only. *Never attempt to focus under high power using the coarse adjustment since the working distance of this objective is small.* Moving the stage upward in large increments may endanger both slide and objective, so reserve coarse focus for low power work only.

5. Adjust the iris diaphragm and condenser controls as necessary. As a rule, high power viewing requires an increase in light intensity and an upward adjustment of the condenser.

TABLE 1-2. Summary of Microscope Findings								
	Scanning		**Low Power**		**High Power**		**Oil Immersion**	
Magnification of ocular lens	10	X	10	X	10	X	10	X
Magnification of objective lens		X		X		X		X
Total magnification		X		X		X		X
Orientation of letter e image								
Field diameter		μm		μm		μm		μm

Oil Immersion Technique (Optional)

In light microscopy, optimal magnification and resolving power are achieved with the oil immersion objective. Beyond high magnifying power, a key advantage of this objective is its high numerical aperture rating. (Recall that higher N.A. equates to greater light-gathering ability and higher resolution.)

The magnifying power of this objective is 100X. Resolving power is further enhanced by the addition of clear mineral oil between the objective and the slide. Because the oil has a refractive (light-bending) index similar to glass, it reduces the light scattering that ordinarily occurs with air between slide and objective. As the light rays are concentrated, the resolving power is increased.

When using the oil immersion objective, follow the sequence below:

1. Start with the specimen centered under high power focus. The extremely limited working distance of the oil immersion objective would make focusing this objective directly a difficult and risky procedure.

2. Revolve the nosepiece so that the oil immersion objective is about halfway to its click position. Place a drop of immersion oil in the middle of the slide.

3. Complete the rotation of the oil immersion objective to the vertical position. As it clicks into place, it should be in contact with the oil.

4. Turn the fine focus knob to sharpen the image.

5. Increase illumination with the iris diaphragm, and if necessary, the illuminator dial.

6. After completing your observations, swing the 100X objective back to a halfway position. Carefully wipe the oil from the objective with lens paper. Removing any residue is best accomplished by folding the lens paper in half lengthwise, then widthwise. Now dip a corner of the paper into liquid lens cleaner and, starting at the center, wipe the lens in a circular motion toward the periphery. Repeat as needed until all oil is removed.

Measurement of the Microscopic Field

During your microscopic observations, it is advantageous to know the approximate size of the specimens under consideration. To be able to estimate specimen size, it is necessary to measure the diameter of the low power field (LPF). This is accomplished by placing a ruled stage micrometer slide on the mechanical stage.

Stage Micrometer Technique

The stage micrometer is 2 mm long with 0.1 mm subdivisions (Figure 1-2). Once on the stage, rotate the low power (10X) objective to its click position.

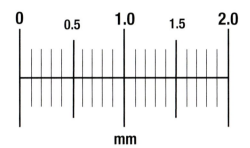

FIGURE 1-2. A ruled stage micrometer.

1. Estimate the low power field diameter in millimeters (mm) to the nearest tenth. Convert the diameter to micrometers (μm). (One mm = 1000 μm. See Table 1-3 for a comparison of linear metric units.)

Estimated LPF diameter = _____ μm

2. Now estimate the diameter of the high power field (HPF). For the high power field, the diameter can be measured directly or it can be calculated from the low power field diameter as follows:

$$\text{Diameter of HPF} = \frac{\text{LPF diameter X low power magnification}}{\text{high power magnification}}$$

Calculated HPF diameter = _____ μm

Record your estimate in Table 1-2.

TABLE 1-3. Metric Units of Length Commonly Used in the Anatomy/Physiology Laboratory.

Unit	Symbol	Equivalent
Meter *	m	10^0 (or 1) m
Centimeter	cm	10^{-2} m
Millimeter	mm	10^{-3} m
Micrometer	μm	10^{-6} m

* The English system equivalent of 1 meter is about 40 inches.

Estimating the Diameter of Actual Cells

1. Obtain a prepared slide of a mammalian ovary (Figure 1-3) and focus it under high power. Approximate the diameter of an **oöcyte** (egg cell) within an ovarian follicle by dividing the number of cells you estimate would fit end-to-end across the middle of the field into your high power field diameter number.

Estimated oöcyte diameter = _____ μm

2. The smallest of human cells — known as **spermatozoa** — are difficult to size up under the microscope. Rather than count an extremely large number of sperm cells across the field diameter to determine their width, assume the diameter of the head is about 1/25 that of an oöcyte.

Estimated sperm head diameter = _____ μm

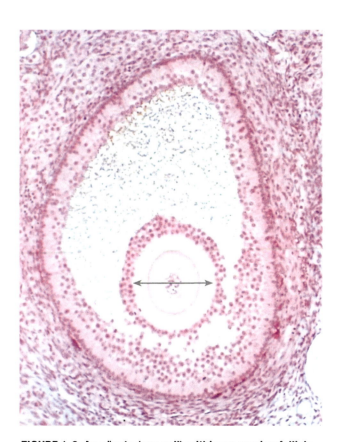

FIGURE 1-3. An oöcyte (egg cell) within an ovarian follicle. The cell's diameter is indicated by the arrows.

PROCEDURE 3

Observation of Cheek Cells (Optional)

SAFETY PRECAUTIONS

- **Obtain your own cheek cells and prepare only your own wet mount.**
- **Dispose of used toothpicks in the biohazard bag.**
- **Dispose of used slides and coverslips in the designated receptacle.**
- **Disinfect contaminated work surfaces.**

The cells lining the oral cavity are excellent living specimens. Since cheek tissue consists of layer upon layer of cells, those on the surface can be conveniently removed for microscopic examination. Figure 1-4 illustrates a basic technique for preparing a "wet" specimen for viewing under the microscope.

Preparation of a Wet Mount

1. Obtain two clean microscope slides.

2. Gently scrape the inside of the cheek several times with the flat end of a toothpick. Transfer the scraping to the first slide. Add one drop of the physiologic sodium chloride solution (Figure 1-4A), and mix thoroughly with the toothpick. Spread the mixture into a thin smear and preserve it with a coverslip. (Hold the coverslip by its edges at a 45°angle to the slide and gently lower it onto the specimen as in Figure 1-4B.) The specimen is now a **wet mount** (Figure 1-4C).

3. Repeat the scraping procedure and place your second sample on the other slide. Add a drop of methylene blue stain and mix thoroughly. Top with a coverslip.

4. Observe the two wet mounts under the microscope at both low and high power. Compare the cell features of the stained and unstained specimens under high power. Identify the nucleus, cytoplasm, and plasma membrane* of the most clearly defined cells.

5. Sketch the basic features of several stained cheek cells under high power. Flat cells of this type are known as **squamous cells**.

* Since the fine details of the plasma membrane are invisible under the light microscope, the membrane will appear simply as the outer boundary of the cytoplasm.

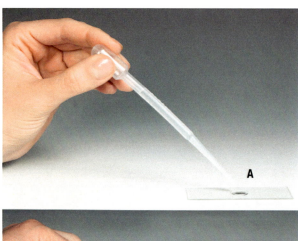

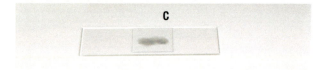

FIGURE 1-4. Basic wet mount technique. (A) Adding fluid medium to a specimen. (B) Applying a coverslip at a 45° angle. (C) The wet mount ready for viewing under the microscope.

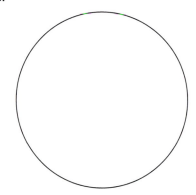

Sketch of Cheek Cells

PROCEDURE 4

Depth of Focus
The **depth of focus** (sometimes called **depth of field**) of a lens determines how much foreground and background area is simultaneously in focus. A good example of great depth of focus is a long-distance photograph, like a panoramic view of the Grand Canyon. Everything in the foreground and background

is clearly seen. By contrast, in a close-up photograph, like that of an emerging flower bud, the subject is in focus, but little else in front of or behind it is clear.

Microscope lenses, like camera lenses, vary in their depths of focus. You will soon notice that the depth of focus depends upon the particular objective in use.

Using the prepared slide of crossed colored threads, compare the depth of focus of the low and high power objectives. Focus initially with low power on the middle of the three threads. Move up and down through the focal field with the fine focus adjustment. How many threads are in simultaneous focus?_____

Now switch to high power. How many threads come into focus simultaneously?_____

Which lens has the greater depth of focus?

_____

Proper Storage of the Compound Light Microscope

1. Move the scanning (4x) objective into position.
2. Be sure the mechanical stage does not extend past the plane of the stage.
3. Turn dial power switch off.
4. Unplug the power cord by grabbing the plug housing and removing it from the outlet.
5. Carefully wrap the cord around the caddy on the back of the microscope arm. (If there is no cord caddy, wrap the cord around the base.)
6. *With both hands securing the microscope*, return it to the storage cabinet.

PROCEDURE 5

The Stereomicroscope (Dissecting Microscope)

The **stereomicroscope** (Figure 1-5) is used primarily to visualize gross specimens. These specimens may be studied intact or dissected while under observation. The stereoscopic design of this microscope creates an image with great depth of focus that appears three-dimensional.

Stereomicroscopes have a zoom objective lens. The zoom feature permits the user to continuously vary magnification throughout the range of the lens without loss of focus. Thus, no refocusing is necessary and no image blackout occurs when changing magnification. The range of magnifying power for the objective is printed on the magnification knob.

Total magnification is equal to ocular power (10X) multiplied by objective power (usually from 1X to 7X) for a maximum magnification of 70X. This is low by conventional microscope standards, but more than sufficient when the specimen is three-dimensional.

Although this microscope can provide light from beneath the stage for a wide-angle view of tissues and organs on prepared slides, its greatest asset lies in its capacity to reflect light from the surface of gross specimens. These specimens are illuminated from above the stage to dramatic effect.

The capabilities of the stereomicroscope make it a valuable complement to the conventional light microscope and you should take full advantage of its flexibility as an analytical tool whenever practical.

Identifying the Parts of the Stereomicroscope

1. Obtain a stereomicroscope and identify the following parts in Figure 1-5.

Oculars. Eyepieces that magnify the image transmitted by the objective lens.

Objective. A large single lens that enlarges the specimen through a range of magnifications.

Magnification knob. An adjustable knob on the head that changes the magnification of the objective through a continuous range with no image blackout.

Stage plate. A circular plate of glass above the base for placement of the specimen.

Base. The supportive platform of the microscope.

Arm. The region that connects the base to the head.

Head. The support for the ocular and objective lenses.

Focus knob. A circular knob on either side of the arm that provides coarse focus.

2. Get acquainted with your microscope by focusing on specimens provided by your instructor and those of your own choosing. (Hairs, fingernails, and other features of one's surface anatomy are good for starters. The nuances of coins and paper currency are also worth exploring.) What can you conclude about the depth of focus?

_____

_____

Focus Technique for the Stereomicroscope

1. Place the illuminator in the porthole: upper for reflected light, lower for transmitted light.

2. Set the magnification knob to its lowest power. Center the specimen within the field and adjust the focus knob until the best image is obtained.

3. To change magnification, rotate the magnification knob to any value between the lowest and highest settings.

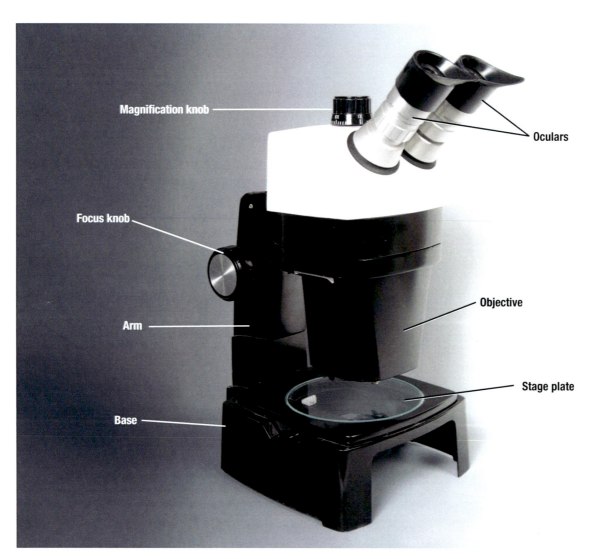

FIGURE 1-5. The stereomicroscope.

The Microscope

NAME _____

LAB TIME/DATE _____

The Parts of the Microscope

Label the indicated microscope parts.

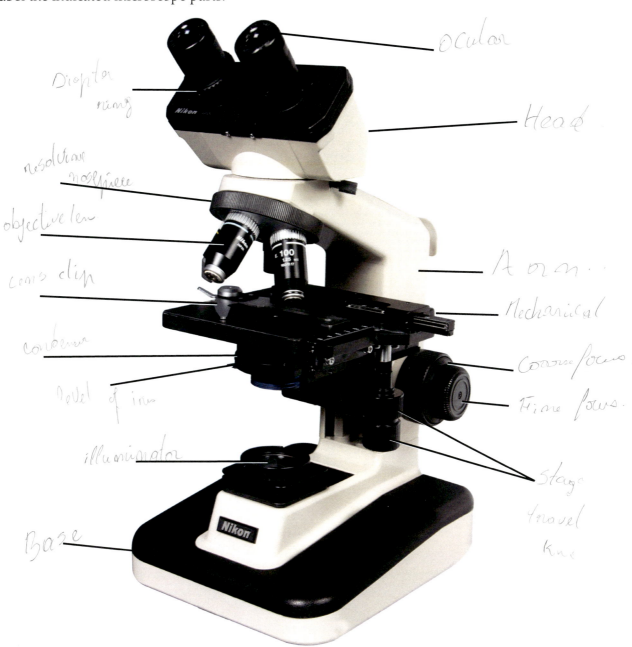

ocular

Diopter ning

resolving nosepiece

objective lens

lens clip

condenser

level of iris

illuminator

Base

Head

Arm

Mechanical

Coarse focus

Fine focus

Stage travel knob

Multiple Choice

_____   1.   Compared with the actual specimen, the image through the microscope is (a) inverted. (b) reversed. (c) inverted and reversed. (d) neither inverted nor reversed.

_____   2.   Advantages of the scanning objective include (a) high magnification. (b) high resolution. (c) depth of focus. (d) a panoramic view of the specimen. (e) Both c and d are correct.

_____   3.   Resolution is best explained as (a) magnifying and clarifying an image. (b) contrasting light and dark images within the same field of view. (c) focusing foreground, subject, and background simultaneously. (d) clearly distinguishing objects set a small distance apart.

_____   4.   Advantages of the stereomicroscope include all but which of the following? (a) great depth of focus (b) high magnification (c) no image blackout when changing objective magnification (d) a three-dimensional image (e) accommodates gross specimens.

Matching

a. condenser

b. diaphragm

c. objective

d. ocular

e. mechanical stage

___b___ Its adjustable aperture controls light entering objective.

___e___ Platform on which slide is placed and moved.

___a___ Improves contrast and resolution by delivering a concentrated beam of light to the specimen.

___d___ The lens through which the observer views the image.

___c___ Lens attached to nosepiece.

Completion

1. With increasing magnification, depth of focus _____.

2. The _____ ring ensures that once a specimen is clearly focused for a particular observer's right eye, it will also be in focus for the left eye.

3. If a low power field diameter were estimated to be 1600 μm, and about 8 of a certain cell could fit side-by-side across the diameter of the high power field, what is the estimated diameter of the cell in μm?

4. Using a 10X ocular with a 100X oil immersion lens yields a total magnification of _1000_ X.

5. A live ameba seen moving to the left under the microscope, is actually moving _to the right_.

Review Questions

1. Describe how immersion oil enhances resolution.

    _____

    _____

    _____

2. How does an objective's numerical aperture relate to resolution?

    _____

    _____

3. How much smaller is the high power field diameter compared to the low power field diameter?

_____

_____

4. Explain how a sharply focused structure under low power can disappear after switching to the high power objective.

_____

_____

_____

5. What is meant by *working distance*?

_____

_____

6. What happens to the working distance with increasing magnification?

_____

7. Which objective should you place in the vertical position when storing the compound microscope?

_____

The Cell

O B J E C T I V E S

1. To identify the structural features of a composite cell.
2. To observe cell specialization in a variety of human specimens.
3. To describe the processes of mitosis and cytokinesis.

M A T E R I A L S

Prepared slides:
  Ciliated columnar cells
  Spermatozoa
  Nerve cells (neurons)
  Smooth muscle cells (teased)
  Simple squamous epithelium
  Blood smear
  Blood cell models

Model or chart of a composite cell
Compound microscope
Video of mitosis
Models of mitosis
Prepared slide of whitefish embryo
Neuron model
Video: *Internal Defenses*

P R E - L A B   Q U I Z

1. In the cell's internal architecture, which organelle is known as a membranous transportation network? _____.
2. The bulk of a cell's energy currency (ATP) is generated by the
   _____.
3. True or False (Correct the statement if it is false). Lysosomes are readily visible under the light microscope.
4. During which stage of mitosis are chromosomes pulled by spindle fibers toward opposite ends of a dividing cell? _____.
5. Mitosis creates two daughter cells from a single parent cell. Cite one instance when a cell would undergo mitotic division. _____.

The Anatomy of the Cell

The cell is the fundamental structural and functional unit of living organisms. In the human body, cells exhibit a multitude of shapes, sizes and internal environments that are geared to their specific functions. All cells, however, must be able to perform basic functions essential to life. They must metabolize to use nutrients and dispose of wastes, respond to stimuli, and grow and reproduce. This requires that cells have certain basic structural characteristics in common. As you will soon discover, there is a clearly recognizable population of subunits — the **organelles** — that are common to many different cells.

The study of cells is a necessary prelude to further investigation of human anatomy and physiology. A thorough understanding of cell form and function will be an important asset as you progress to the tissue, organ, and organ system levels of structural organization.

PROCEDURE 1

Using the available models and charts of a typical cell, identify the structures corresponding to those in Figure 2-1. (This drawing is designed to illustrate characteristics common to most, but not all cells. It is a composite, or "generalized" cell, and does not represent any differentiated cell type in particular.)

The Plasma Membrane (Cell Membrane)

The cell is surrounded by a flexible **plasma membrane** that separates its contents from the extracellular fluid. Its basic structure is a double layer of lipids interspersed with large globular protein molecules (Figure 2-2).

The lipids are mostly phospholipids. About 25% are *glycolipids* and *cholesterol*. ("*Glyco*" refers to attached sugar chains.) One part of the phospholipid molecule is hydrophilic (water soluble, or *polar*), and the other is hydrophobic (fat soluble, or *nonpolar*). The hydrophobic

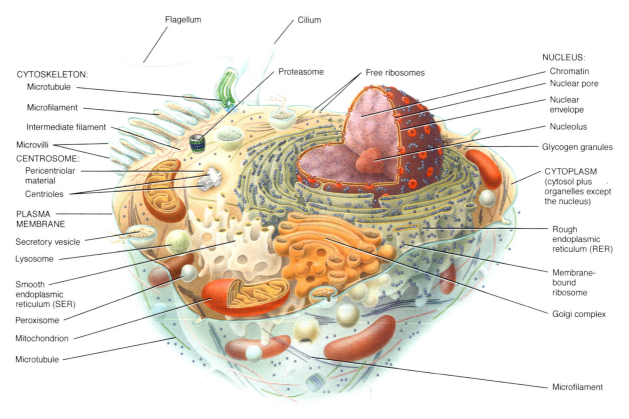

Sectional view

FIGURE 2-1. A composite human cell.

portions — the "tails" — face one another in the center of the membrane, while the hydrophilic portions — the "heads" — face outward and comprise the inner and outer membrane surfaces. The phospholipids easily permit the transport of nonpolar substances, such as other lipids, oxygen and carbon dioxide, but are a barrier to polar substances like ions, proteins and carbohydrates.

The protein molecules float in the phospholipid bilayer. The proteins (mostly glycoproteins) provide structural channels — **membrane pores** — for the passage of small polar substances.

Together, the components of the plasma membrane are fluid - like and always moving, yet form a protective barrier for the cell. (The term *fluid mosaic model* is often used to describe the dynamic interaction of the membrane's proteins and phospholipids.) The control membrane molecules have over what enters and exits the cell is of utmost importance. The fundamental property of the plasma membrane that regulates which ions and molecules are granted passage — and in what measure — is known as **selective permeability**.

In cells where absorption is the principal function, the plasma membrane exhibits tiny finger-shaped folds known as **microvilli.** These projections greatly increase the cell's absorptive surface area. They are integral to the functions of the small intestine and kidneys where absorption is a high priority.

Cytoplasm

Cytoplasm consists of the contents of a cell between the nuclear envelope and the plasma membrane. It contains the organelles and the **cytosol**, or **intracellular fluid**. The cytosol is an aqueous medium that contains dissolved solutes and various suspended components.

The Nucleus

The **nucleus** (Figure 2-3) is the coordinator of cellular activity. It is surrounded by a relatively porous double membrane, the **nuclear envelope**. It contains nucleoplasm that includes **DNA (deoxyribonucleic acid)**. The **genes** of the cell are subunits along the length of this DNA, which organizes itself into rod-shaped **chromosomes** during cell division.

Each chromosome contains a single DNA molecule that is coiled together with proteins called histones. This combination of DNA and proteins is known as **chromatin**. When the cell is not dividing, the chromatin decondenses, that is, becomes thin and thread-like. The chromatin remains loosely arranged in the nucleus until the next division when it condenses back into chromosomes.

In the nuclei of all human cells except sex cells (sperm and oöcytes or egg cells), there are 46 chromosomes (23 from each parent). The sum of all the genetic information contained in a cell is its **genome.**

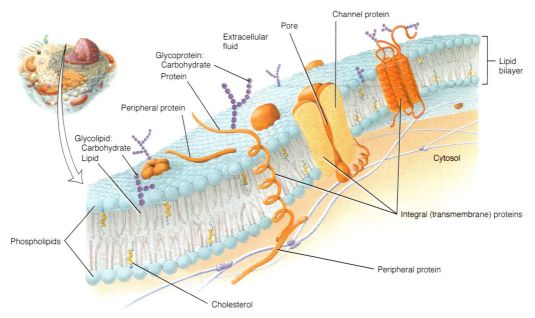

FIGURE 2-2. The plasma membrane.

The Nucleolus

The **nucleolus** (noo-KLEE-uh-lus) is a spherical body within the nucleus consisting of proteins, **RNA (ribonucleic acid)** and some DNA. Its RNA is destined to leave the nucleus and form subunits of ribosomes (ribosomal or rRNA) in the cytoplasm. Unlike the nucleus and other organelles, the nucleolus is not bound by a membrane (Figure 2-3). A cell may contain more than one nucleolus, in which case the plural **nucleoli** (noo-KLEE-uh-lye) will apply. (Note the TEM abbreviation in this and other figures. It signifies an image seen through a **t**ransmission **e**lectron **m**icroscope. Any micrograph labeled SEM was taken through a **s**canning **e**lectron **m**icroscope.)

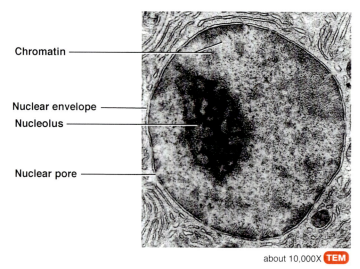

Chromatin

Nuclear envelope
Nucleolus

Nuclear pore

about 10,000X **TEM**

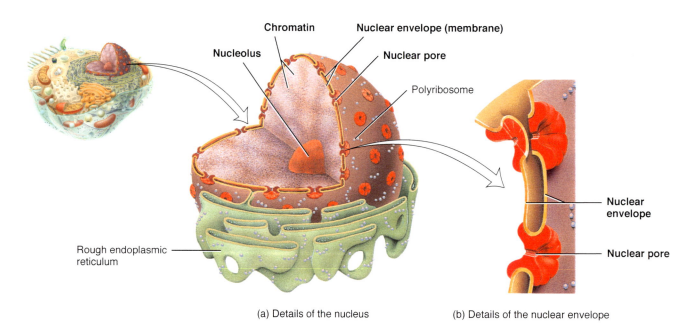

(a) Details of the nucleus

(b) Details of the nuclear envelope

FIGURE 2-3. The nucleus.

Endoplasmic Reticulum

Similar in structure to the plasma membrane, the **endoplasmic reticulum (ER)** is an interconnecting network of membranous channels and vesicular (sac-like) structures (Figure 2-4). The ER serves as an internal system of roadways, transporting molecules from place to place within the cell. **Rough (granular) ER** is studded with ribosomes, which are sites of protein synthesis. **Smooth (agranular) ER**, which has no ribosomes, functions in lipid synthesis and other enzymatic processes.

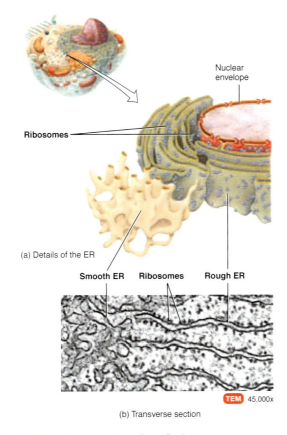

(a) Details of the ER

Smooth ER   Ribosomes   Rough ER

Ribosomes

Nuclear envelope

TEM 45,000x

(b) Transverse section

FIGURE 2-4. The endoplasmic reticulum.

Lysosomes

The **lysosome** (Figure 2-5) is a membrane-bound organelle containing digestive enzymes derived from the Golgi complex. Lysosomes recycle worn-out cell parts, and supply microbe-destroying enzymes within white blood cells and scavenger cells called **macrophages**. The microbes enter these cells by a process known as **phagocytosis** and are presented to the lysosome packaged in a **phagocytic vesicle**. The merger of the vesicle and lysosome is followed by the controlled release of *proteases*, enzymes that break down proteins. (See pages 41 and 42 for more on phagocytosis.)

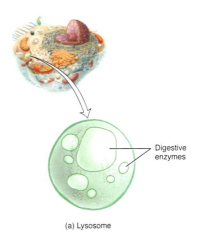

Digestive enzymes

(a) Lysosome

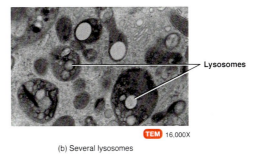

Lysosomes

TEM 16,000X

(b) Several lysosomes

FIGURE 2-5. The lysosome.

Peroxisomes

Peroxisomes are structurally similar to lysosomes, but smaller (hence their alternative name, microbodies.) The enzymes contained within peroxisomes are classified as *oxidases*. These enzymes routinely oxidize fatty acids and amino acids as part of a cell's normal metabolism. They also oxidize, and thus detoxify, alcohol in the liver. The greater number of peroxisomes in liver cells (hepatocytes) correlates well with the liver's role as a major organ of detoxification.

Clinical Application
Impaired Phagocytosis

Any medical condition that impairs the phagocytic activity of white blood cells leads to increased susceptibility to infection. This is a complication for some diabetics and those suffering from chronic kidney failure.

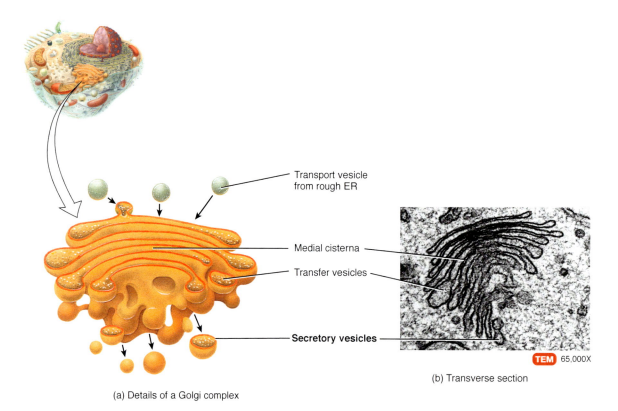

Transport vesicle from rough ER

Medial cisterna

Transfer vesicles

Secretory vesicles

TEM 65,000X

(b) Transverse section

(a) Details of a Golgi complex

FIGURE 2-6. The Golgi complex.

Golgi Complex

Most numerous in secretory cells, the **Golgi complex** or **Golgi body** is an ER-derived organelle responsible for packaging cell products, such as enzymes, into discrete, membrane-bound sacs (Figure 2-6). These sacs, or **secretory vesicles**, can be used in the cell or exported via exocytosis to another part of the body. (Cells of the pancreas, for example, produce hydrolytic enzymes destined to digest food molecules in the small intestine.)

Ribosomes

Ribosomes are organelles composed of RNA subunits whose surfaces serve as the sites of protein synthesis. It is here that the protein blueprints encoded in the genes within DNA are translated. Ribosomes exist in the cytoplasm singularly or in clusters known as **polyribosomes**, or they may be part of rough endoplasmic reticulum.

Proteasomes

The recently discovered **proteasomes** are barrel-shaped organelles that destroy unneeded or faulty proteins in the cytosol. They are named for the many proteases they contain. Proteasomes, aided by other enzymes, degrade proteins into amino acids that can be reused as building blocks of new proteins.

Centrioles

Centrioles are associated with packaging microtubules into the formation of spindle fibers, a prerequisite for mitosis. Centrioles are part of an organelle known as a **centrosome**. (Mitosis is discussed in Procedure 3.)

Microtubules

Microtubules are minute tubular structures of protein which function in the formation of the cytoskeleton and spindle fibers, and in cell repair. They are also the key elements within (1) **cilia**, hair-like extensions on the free surface of cells lining the airways and uterine (Fallopian) tubes; and (2) **flagella**, the whip-like "tails" of sperm cells.

Mitochondria

Mitochondria (my-tuh-KON-dree-uh) (Figure 2-7) use oxygen to form 95% of the cell's ATP (adenosine triphosphate), its energy currency. The double-membrane structure of a mitochondrion (singular) includes an inner membrane arranged into many folds known as **cristae**. These folds create a large internal surface area upon which lie the enzymes that make the oxidation of food-derived molecules and ATP synthesis possible. Mitochondria also contain DNA, which gives them the potential to replicate when needed.

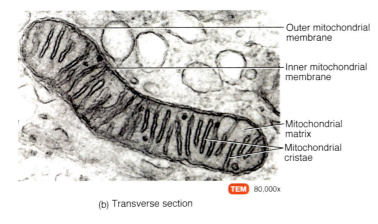

Outer mitochondrial membrane
Inner mitochondrial membrane
Mitochondrial matrix
Mitochondrial cristae
Ribosome
Enzymes

(a) Details of a mitochondrion

Outer mitochondrial membrane
Inner mitochondrial membrane
Mitochondrial matrix
Mitochondrial cristae

TEM 80,000x

(b) Transverse section

FIGURE 2-7. A mitochondrion.

PROCEDURE 2

A Study of Diversity Among Human Cells.

To perform the diverse activities essential to life, cells must be highly specialized. While incorporating many similar internal features, cells display considerable anatomical variations.

The guiding principle here is that *form follows function*, that is, a cell's architecture reflects its functional specialty. For example, nerve cells communicate via long wiry extensions; ciliated cells are equipped for propelling mucus and particles across their surface; and muscle cells — thin and elongated — are structurally adapted for contraction.

Each of the cell types that follow possesses at least one distinguishing structural characteristic. Before attempting to view prepared slides on your own, study the specific structural details of cells at a demonstration microscope or using cell models or charts.

After you have some idea of what you will be looking for, set up your microscope and observe the slides, noting in particular each cell's anatomical specialization described below. Then sketch the cells and provide leader lines and labels for the special features in *italicized* type. Keep in mind that your compound light microscope can only reveal a cell's nucleus, nucleolus, plasma membrane, and those marvels of microtubules, cilia and flagella.

1. **Ciliated Columnar Epithelial Cells (trachea)**
   Note the *cilia* on the exposed cell surfaces of the trachea. These projections are designed to move debris trapped in mucus across adjacent cell surfaces toward the throat.

2. **Spermatozoa**
   Note the *flagellum*, the whip-like extension of the cell which propels it forward.

3. **Smooth Muscle Cells (uterus)**
   Note the elongated, spindle-shaped cells (also known as muscle fibers) that contract (shorten) to produce movement. The *nucleus*, located in the center of the cell, appears as a flattened oval.

4. **Nerve Cells (Neurons) (spinal cord)**
   Nerve cells, or neurons, feature long *cytoplasmic processes* (projections) that branch out to communicate with other nerve cells.

5. **Blood Smear**

   A blood smear is a stained film of blood containing red and white cells. **Red blood cells** — also known as **red blood corpuscles**, or **erythrocytes** — are *biconcave disks* without nuclei. The shape of the RBCs increases their surface area and facilitates the loading and unloading of oxygen. The absence of a nucleus and other organelles allows more room for oxygen-binding hemoglobin, a red pigment molecule. The diverse **white blood cells**, or **leukocytes,** are distinguished by their distinctive *nuclei* and differential staining characteristics.

6. **Simple Squamous Epithelial Cells (mesothelium)**

   In the language of tissues, *simple* means having a single layer of cells. Note the rounded *nucleus* located near the center of the cell. In capillaries, a single layer of flat squamous cells forms an ultra thin membrane for the rapid movement of oxygen, carbon dioxide, nutrients, and waste products across their walls in the service of surrounding cells. This tissue also lines the true body cavities where it is the inner layer of a lubricating membrane. Simple squamous epithelium that lines true body cavities is known as **mesothelium**.

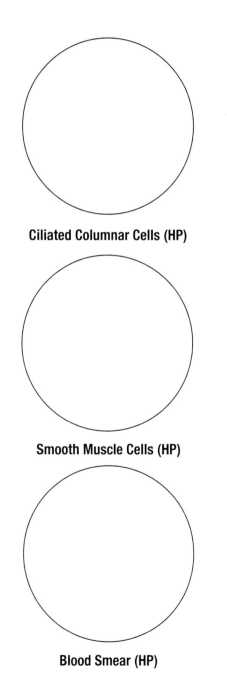

Ciliated Columnar Cells (HP)

Smooth Muscle Cells (HP)

Blood Smear (HP)

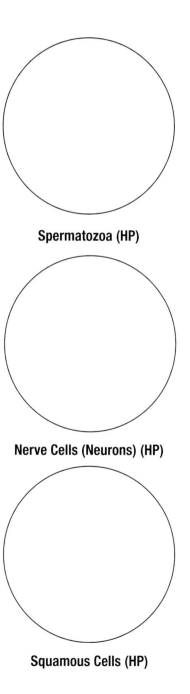

Spermatozoa (HP)

Nerve Cells (Neurons) (HP)

Squamous Cells (HP)

PROCEDURE 3

Cell Division: Mitosis and Cytokinesis

Cells divide to increase their number within a tissue to enable the tissue to grow. Cells also divide to replace worn out or injured cells. **Mitosis** is the division of the nucleus in somatic (non-sex) cells. **Cytokinesis** is the division of the cytoplasm and occurs during the final stage of mitosis. Once initiated, mitosis is a continuous process. It is usually divided into four steps for convenience — **prophase, metaphase, anaphase,** and **telophase** — with each stage having a particular appearance under the microscope. It is not always possible, however, to determine the precise beginning and end points of each stage. Mitosis is a phase, the M phase, within the cell cycle (Figure 2-8).

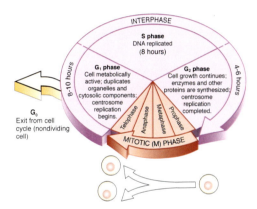

FIGURE 2-8. The cell cycle.

When a cell is not dividing, it is in **interphase.** In this period, the cell continues to perform its routine metabolic functions and grows. It duplicates DNA and organelles (such as centrioles) before dividing in two. The duplicated chromosomes will not, however, be visible under your microscope until mitosis has begun.

Stages of Mitosis

Prophase. Mitosis begins. The chromatin shortens and thickens, forming visible rod-shaped chromosomes. Each of the duplicated chromosomes is composed of two strands of sister **chromatids** that are joined in their center at a constricted region known as a **centromere**. Each chromatid is attached to a bundle of microtubules, the **spindle fiber**. These **mitotic spindles** originate in the centrioles, and with these organelles, gradually make their way toward opposite poles of the cell. During prophase, the nuclear envelope and nucleolus disappear. The *pro* in prophase denotes this stage as the first of a series.

Metaphase. At this point, the centrioles have completed their migration to opposite ends of the cell. You may see a star-shaped arrangement of microtubular rays (an "aster") surrounding each centriole. The prefix *meta* means middle and is indicative of what the chromatids are doing at this stage: they organize themselves in the middle of the cell. The sister chromatids are aligned on opposite sides of the midline, a region known as the cell's **equator**, or **metaphase plate**.

Anaphase. In this stage, the chromatids separate from one another, each being drawn backward to its respective pole by a spindle fiber. (*Ana* translates as backward.) Once separated, chromatids are once again called chromosomes.

Telophase. This phase begins as the two sets of chromosomes reach their poles. Once at the poles, the chromosomes gradually become longer and thinner and invisible. Meanwhile, the nuclear envelope and nucleolus reappear. This signifies the end of mitosis. (*Telo* means end.) During telophase, cytokinesis takes place. This occurs at a **cleavage furrow** that first appears late in anaphase. Approximately half the original cytoplasmic contents is apportioned to each new daughter cell. Once cytoplasmic division has been completed, the daughter cells enter interphase, grow to the same size as the original cell, and then enter mitosis again.

The result of mitosis is the even distribution of the species number of chromosomes — 46 in humans — to each of the two daughter cells.

Identifying the Stages of Mitosis

1. Watch a video of animal mitosis.

2. Obtain a prepared slide of animal cells undergoing mitosis. Embryonic cells are ideal for this purpose because the embryo is a rapidly growing stage during which many cells are dividing mitotically. The slide will include several whitefish embryos at an early stage of development known as the **blastula**.

3. As you observe the slide under the microscope, scan it for cells undergoing mitosis. Search out cells which provide an especially good example of each stage of mitosis, referring to the demonstration models as needed.

4. Sketch your findings in the spaces provided on page 25. Label any chromosomes, spindle fibers and other structures involved in mitosis that you have observed.

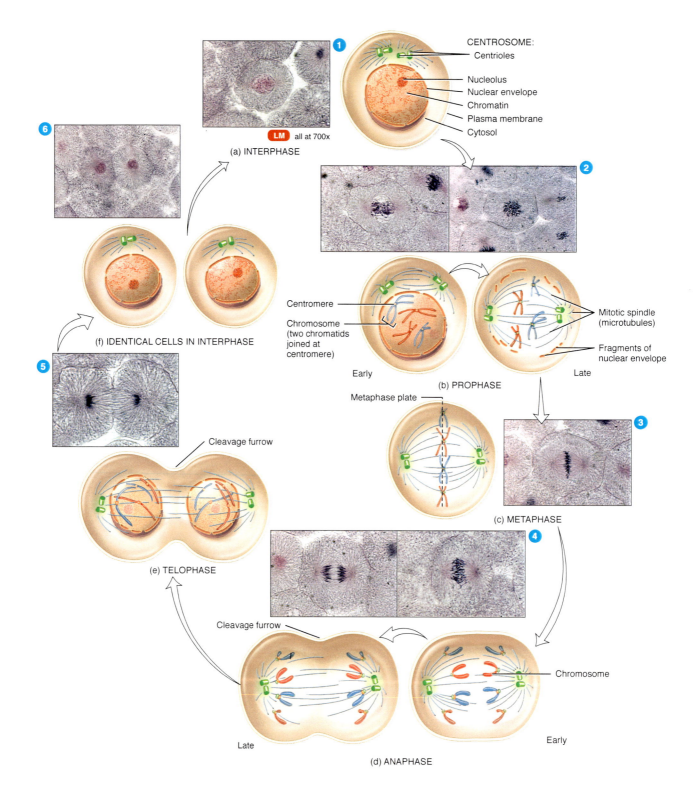

CENTROSOME:
Centrioles
Nucleolus
Nuclear envelope
Chromatin
Plasma membrane
Cytosol

LM all at 700x

(a) INTERPHASE

(f) IDENTICAL CELLS IN INTERPHASE

Centromere
Chromosome
(two chromatids
joined at
centromere)

Early

Mitotic spindle
(microtubules)

Fragments of
nuclear envelope

Late

(b) PROPHASE

Metaphase plate

(c) METAPHASE

Cleavage furrow

(e) TELOPHASE

Cleavage furrow

Chromosome

Late

Early

(d) ANAPHASE

FIGURE 2-9. Cell division: mitosis and cytokinesis in a whitefish blastula. Begin the sequence at ❶ the top of the figure and read clockwise to complete the process.

The Stages of Mitosis

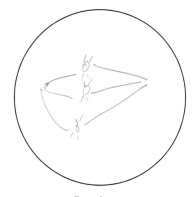

Prophase

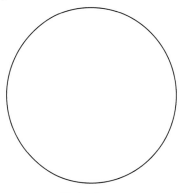

Metaphase

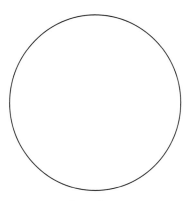

Anaphase

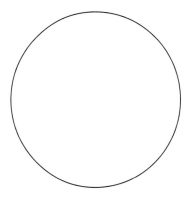

Telophase

The Origins of Cancer

Uncontrolled mitosis is the underlying cause of cancer. A tumor begins to develop when a cell experiences a mutation within the genetic material in its nucleus. This mutation leads the cell and its descendants to divide more often than a normal cell, resulting in a mass of cells that forms a tumor. One of these altered cells then mutates again. This causes not only a greater-than-usual number of cells, but cells whose appearance has changed. These cells are now malignant. Further mutations then endow these cancerous cells with the ability to spread to other organs, a process known as *metastasis*. Metastatic cancer is more ominous than *in situ* cancer, a form of the disease that has not spread.

The Cell

NAME _____

LAB TIME/DATE _____

The Anatomy of the Cell

Label the indicated cell structures.

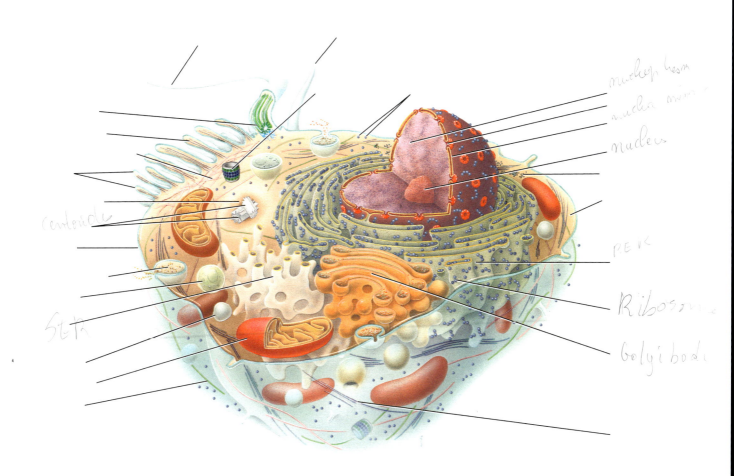

nuclear plasm
nuclear mem
nucleus

centriole

REK

Ribosom

StTn

Golgi bodi

Matching

_b_ Microtubules ✓   a. Packages cellular secretions for export
_c_ Ribosome ✓   b. Of primary importance in cilia and flagella
_d_ Nucleus   c. Protein assembly site
_e_ Lysosome   d. Stores informational molecules
_a_ Golgi complex ✓   e. Vehicle for hydrolytic enzymes

Completion

1. Two organelles that are clearly visible under your microscope are the _____ and the _____.

2. The Golgi complex is derived from another membranous intracellular structure, the _____.

3. Peroxisomes produce enzymes known as _____.

4. Rod-shaped nuclear structures which contain DNA and are visible only during mitosis are the _____.

Review Questions

1. State the functions of the following organelles:

   (a) endoplasmic reticulum _____

   _____

   (b) mitochondria _____

   _____

A Study of Diversity Among Human Cells

1. Some cells are capped with _____, folds of plasma membrane that greatly increase absorptive surface area.

2. Give three examples of how structural specialization has adapted a cell to a particular region of the body.

   _____

   _____

   _____

3. What is the importance of cilia?

_____

_____

_____

4. The number of Golgi complexes within a cell is variable: Cells specializing in exporting secretions, such as enzymes, have the greatest number of these organelles. Using secretory activity as the key function, identify a cell type likely to be endowed with many Golgi.

_____

_____

_____

Cell Division: Mitosis and Cytokinesis

1. In general, mitosis occurs in _____ (non-sex) cells.

2. While a cell does not divide during interphase, it is clearly not idle. What is occurring during this stage of the cell cycle?

_____

_____

_____

3. Mitosis makes its debut about 24 hours after the union of sperm and egg cells produces a single fertilized ovum. If this first pair of embryonic daughter cells then divides at a rate of about once every 18 hours, how many cells would the embryo have after four days (96 hours)? Assume all dividing cells split into two at the same time.

_____

4. During which stage does cytokinesis occur and what is the end result?

_____

_____

Notes

Cell Physiology: Transport Mechanisms

OBJECTIVES

1. To distinguish *passive* from *active transport* processes.
2. To define *diffusion* and determine the variables that affect the diffusion rate of ions and molecules.
3. To define *osmosis* and *osmotic pressure*.
4. To define *hypotonic*, *hypertonic*, and *isotonic* solutions and to determine what osmotic changes occur when artificial cells and red blood cells are placed within them.
5. To define *vesicular transport*, *phagocytosis*, *pinocytosis*, and *exocytosis*.

MATERIALS

Passive Processes

Diffusion of a Dye in Agar
  Agar gel in petri dishes
  Potassium permanganate solution
    in dropper bottles
  Methylene blue solution
    in dropper bottles
  Cork hole borer (or 13-mm test tube)
  Wax pencils
  Metric ruler
  Water bath or incubator at 37°C
  Ice bath

The Osmometer
  Thistle tube
  Sucrose solution, 20%, or molasses
  Dialysis tubing (synthetic selectively
    permeable membrane), 10-cm length
  Ring stand
  Beaker (250-ml)
  Rubber band

(continued on next page)

PRE-LAB QUIZ

1. The movement of substances from a region of higher concentration to one of lower concentration is termed _____.
2. _____ is the movement of water molecules down their concentration gradient across a selectively permeable membrane.
3. _____ energy causes ions and molecules to move randomly within the body's fluid compartments.
4. Penetrating solutes are those small enough to pass through membrane channels known as _____.
5. Which of the following represents an active process?
   a. diffusion of sodium ions
   b. phagocytosis of a bacterium
   c. water molecules entering cells lining the stomach
   d. dye molecules moving through an agar gel

M A T E R I A L S   (continued)

Osmosis in Artificial Cells
Dialysis tubing, 10-cm length
String or dialysis tubing clamps
Solutions of 10%, 20% and 30%
sodium chloride (NaCl)
Pipettes (10ml) and pipettors
Balance
Beakers (100ml)

Red Blood Cell Experiment
Sheep blood
Slides and coverslips
Sodium chloride (NaCl) solution, 10%
Physiologic saline solution, 0.9%
Distilled water
Disposable pipettes
Compound microscope
Disposable gloves
Biohazard bag
Disinfectant solution

The Effects of a Selectively Permeable
Membrane on the Movement of Solutes
Down Their Concentration Gradients
Glucose solution, 5%
Starch solution, 1%
Egg albumen suspension
Silver nitrate solution, 2.9%
Benedict's solution
Biuret reagent
Spot plates
IKI solution
Distilled water

Active Processes
Video of phagocytosis

The survival of cells depends on obtaining nutrients and oxygen from their external environment and expelling waste products. To satisfy these metabolic imperatives, cells interact with their fluid environment through the plasma membrane.

The plasma membrane has the all-important task of regulating what — and when — substances enter or leave the cell. To function effectively, it must be a **selectively (differentially) permeable membrane**. This property allows the membrane to act as a gatekeeper, controlling the passage of whatever travelers come its way. These travelers are ions and molecules dispersed in the intracellular and extracellular fluids. Transport across the plasma membrane may occur via passive or active processes.

Passive Processes: Diffusion

Due to their inherent kinetic energy, ions and molecules are constantly moving in random fashion through the body fluids. When a difference in solute concentration exists — termed a **concentration gradient** — the molecules move faster toward the region of lower concentration. This physical process of substances moving down a concentration gradient from a region of higher concentration to one of lower concentration is known as **diffusion**. Diffusion is a form of **passive transport**. It is driven by kinetic energy, which tends to evenly disperse molecules within their environment. The uniform distribution of molecules is known as **equilibrium**. In this state, molecules will move in all directions with equal frequency and diffusion no longer occurs.

Within the body, diffusion plays a significant role in absorption and excretion and is also responsible for gas exchange between the bloodstream and tissues. *In passive transport, the cell expends no energy; movement is by purely physical means.*

PROCEDURE 1

The Effect of Molecular Weight on the Diffusion Rate of a Dye in Agar Gel

Molecular weight is a variable that influences how fast particles move and consequently how fast they diffuse.

To compare the diffusion rates of different sized molecules, you will use an agar medium and two solutions containing crystals of different molecular weight. Agar is a gelatinous extract from algae and has colloidal properties similar to those of cytoplasm. In this experiment, you will observe the movement of the molecules through the water channels of the agar. All variables will be controlled with the exception of molecular weight (the experimental variable). The hypothesis: *At a given temperature, smaller molecules move faster than larger ones.*

1. Using the cork hole borer (or a test tube) as you would a cookie cutter, punch out, remove, and discard two circular plugs of agar from the petri dish.

   Using Figure 3-1 as a reference, note that the wells should be equidistant from the sides of the plate and from each other. With a wax pencil, label each well on the underside of the plate: KP for potassium permanganate; MB for methylene blue.

2. Obtain solutions of potassium permanganate (molecular weight 158) and methylene blue (molecular weight 374) in dropper bottles. Carefully fill one well with potassium permanganate and the other with methylene blue. (Do not allow any dye to spill over the top of the well into the agar.) Add the same number of drops of each. Record the time when the dyes are added: _____

3. Measure the diameters of the diffusion rings at 15-minute intervals for one hour with a millimeter ruler. Record your data in Table 3-1.

How would you explain the outward movement of the dye molecules?

_____

_____

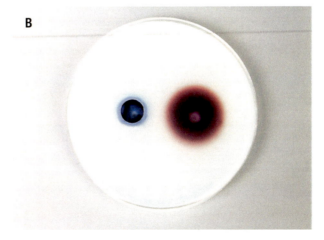

A

B

FIGURE 3-1. Diffusion of dyes in agar gel. (A) wells immediately after addition of dye solutions; (B) diffusion rings after one hour.

_____

_____

Calculate the diffusion rate for potassium
permanganate: _____mm/min

Calculate the diffusion rate for methylene blue:
_____mm/min

Which of the two dyes moved faster?

_____

Was the hypothesis relating molecular weight to
diffusion rate supported?_____

The Effect of Temperature on the Diffusion Rate of a Dye in Agar Gel

Increasing the temperature of diffusing molecules will increase their kinetic energy. This experiment will control all variables except the temperature at which dye molecules will diffuse. The hypothesis: *Dye molecules will move and diffuse faster at higher temperatures*.

1. Obtain two petri dishes containing agar gel.

2. Using the cork hole borer as outlined in Procedure 1, create a well in the center of each dish. Place one dish in an ice bath, the other in an incubator at 37°C for 15 minutes. This will bring the agar medium to desired temperature.

3. After the 15-minute pre-incubation period, fill each well with potassium permanganate.

4. Return the petri dishes to their water baths. Record the moment the dishes are returned to the baths as time zero.

5. Measure the diameters of the diffusion rings at 15-minute intervals for one hour. Record your data in Table 3-2.

TABLE 3-1. Diffusion Rates of Potassium Permanganate and Methylene Blue in Agar Gel

Diffusion Ring Diameter (mm)		
Time (min)	Potassium Permanganate	Methylene Blue
0		
15		
30		
45		
60		

TABLE 3-2. The Effect of Temperature on the Diffusion Rate of Potassium Permanganate in Agar Gel

Diffusion Ring Diameter (mm) for Potassium Permanganate		
Time (min)	0°C	37°C
0		
15		
30		
45		
60		

How would you explain the outward movement of the dye molecules?_____

_____

_____

Calculate the diffusion rate for potassium permanganate at 0° C: _____mm/min

Calculate the diffusion rate for potassium permanganate at 37° C: _____mm/min

At which temperature did the dye move faster? _____

Was the hypothesis relating temperature to diffusion rate supported?_____

Passive Processes: Osmosis

Osmosis *is the diffusion of water molecules across a selectively permeable membrane.*

A solution is comprised of a solute dissolved in a solvent. Water is the universal solvent. As the solute concentration rises, the relative concentration of water decreases. Conversely, the lower the solute concentration, the greater the concentration of water.

When solutes cannot cross the plasma membrane, they are classified as *non-penetrating*. If two solutions containing non-penetrating solutes were separated by a membrane, water would move down its concentration gradient across the membrane by osmosis. The membrane will select against these solutes, but permits free passage of water. In living systems, water's passage into and out of cells is a passive process solely dependent upon the gradient of water molecules. Water will move preferentially from where there is more of it to where there is less.

PROCEDURE 3

Measuring Osmotic Pressure

This demonstration is designed to show what happens when two fluids differing in solute concentrations — and therefore water content — are separated by a membrane.

- The fluid with the higher solute concentration or **tonicity**, must have relatively fewer water molecules.

- The fluid with the lower solute concentration must have relatively more water molecules. The hypothesis: *Water molecules will therefore move down their concentration gradient across the membrane from lower tonicity to higher tonicity.*

- When water crosses a membrane by osmosis and enters a compartment (such as a cell or the intercellular space), it exerts a force within that compartment known as **osmotic pressure**. Osmotic pressure is directly related to solute concentration: the greater the number of solute particles, the greater the tendency to attract water, and the higher becomes the osmotic pressure. This pressure can be measured in the laboratory with an **osmometer**.

If you need to assemble an osmometer, follow Steps 1 to 4 and consult Figure 3-2. If an osmometer has already been assembled, proceed to step 5.

1. Obtain a thistle tube and partially fill the wide end with a solution of 20% sucrose, a disaccharide whose size exceeds the molecular weight cutoff of cell membrane pores. The sucrose molecules are larger than the membrane pores and therefore cannot diffuse through them. Molasses contains sugar that is likewise non-penetrating and may be substituted for sucrose.

2. With a rubber band, tightly cover the wide end of the tube with a synthetic selectively permeable membrane.

3. Invert the tube and secure it to a ring stand.

4. Immerse the membrane side of the tube into a beaker of distilled water. Mark the starting point at the *meniscus* — the curved surface of the fluid column — with a wax pencil.

5. Record as time zero when the tube is lowered into the beaker of water._____

Water will move osmotically until equilibrium is reached, at which time the rate of water molecules moving across the membrane is equal in both directions. At this point, the **hydrostatic pressure** (the force of the fluid column that pushes water out of the tube though the membrane) equals osmotic pressure (the force created by solute molecules that draws water across the membrane into the tube).

6. Measure the height of the solution in the tube at the end of the lab session: _____mm

Was the hypothesis supported? _____

Given the solute concentrations on both sides of the membrane, how would you explain how water molecules moved from the beaker into the thistle tube against the opposing forces of hydrostatic pressure and gravity?

_____

_____

PROCEDURE 4

Osmosis in Artificial Cells

As demonstrated in Procedure 3, the osmotic movement of water molecules depends on the relative concentrations of solutions on both sides of a selectively permeable membrane. The following key terms are used to describe the concentration of the extracellular fluid relative to the intracellular fluid.

- A fluid environment **hypertonic** to the cell has a greater solute concentration (and therefore less water) than the intracellular fluid.

- A fluid environment **hypotonic** to the cell has a lower solute concentration (and consequently more water) than the intracellular fluid.

- If both the intracellular and extracellular fluids contain solutions of equal concentration, they are said to be **isotonic**.

To explain biological phenomena such as osmosis, scientists frequently construct models that imitate life processes, but without all the complexities of a living system. By clarifying basic principles, models can convey the essence of a concept.

Methodology

In this experiment, you will be asked to design a method to determine the effects hypertonic, hypotonic and isotonic solutions have on model cells made from artificial membranes. The intracellular and extracellular solutions contain sodium chloride, a common solute. Keep in mind that your model system will simulate osmosis that takes place among the various fluid compartments of the body. (While the selectivity of both living and laboratory membranes depends on pore size, the lipids within a living membrane represent another level of selectivity.) The hypothesis: *Water molecules will move down their concentration gradient.*

For this procedure, the class will be divided into groups. Each group is responsible for the experimental protocol and should analyze the objectives and read through all relevant procedures in advance. While the lab instructor will be available as a technical advisor, it is up to each group to properly plan and conduct the experiment. *Check in with your instructor for final approval before proceeding.*

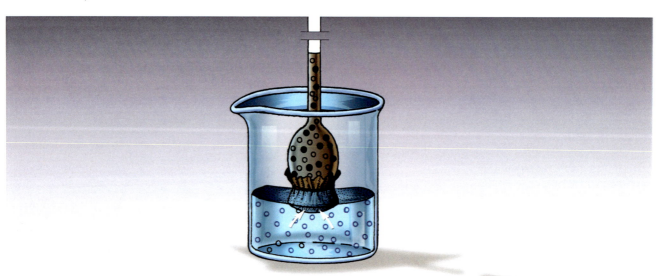

FIGURE 3-2. An osmometer showing the preferential movement (arrows) of water molecules (○) toward the fluid compartment of greater solute (●) concentration.

1. Each group will be provided with:
    Three pieces of tube-shaped dialysis membrane
    Three beakers of 100-ml capacity
    String or clamp to close open end of tubing
    A balance, for weighing simulated cells.
    Pipettes
    Sodium chloride solutions of 10%, 20% and 30%

2. Each group should determine which of three salt solutions: 10%, 20% or 30%, would be the only intracellular fluid choice to enable these same salt solutions to serve as hypotonic, hypertonic, and isotonic extracellular environments. All three "cells" will have the same intracellular fluid.

   Which is your intracellular fluid choice?_____%

   On what basis did you eliminate the other two solutions from consideration?_____

   _____

   _____

3. Obtain three lengths of 10-cm dialysis tubing. Tie a tight overhand knot at one end of the membrane. Once the intracellular solution has been selected, pipet 8 ml of the solution into each membrane sac and tie a tight string knot around the open end (or clamp it). Cut off any excess string.

4. Carefully dry the simulated cells thoroughly with a paper towel and weigh each to the nearest 0.1 gram using a laboratory balance.

5. Obtain three 100-ml beakers and label them 1, 2 and 3. Position each cell vertically in an empty beaker. Pour just enough solution into each beaker to exceed the fluid level of the cell; add 10% salt solution to Beaker 1, 20% to Beaker 2, and 30% to Beaker 3. *Do not get the strings wet or an inaccurate weight will be obtained when the cell is re-weighed later.*

6. Record as time zero is the exact moment your cells are immersed._____

7. Since time is a controlled variable in this experiment, all three simulated cells should stay immersed for the same interval: 60 minutes. After 60 minutes, carefully and completely dry off each cell and reweigh. Be especially mindful of fluid clinging to membrane folds.

8. Record the new weights, weight changes, and percentage changes from initial weights in Table 3-3.

TABLE 3-3. Data: Osmosis in Artificial Cells

	Cell in Hypotonic Medium	Cell in Isotonic Medium	Cell in Hypertonic Medium
Weight (g) at Time Zero			
Weight (g) at 60 Minutes			
Weight Change (g)			
% Change *			

* To calculate the weight change as a percentage:
$$\frac{\text{Final weight - Initial weight}}{\text{Initial weight}} \times 100\%$$
Signify a weight loss by placing a minus sign before the % change.

PROCEDURE 5

The Effect of Hypertonic, Hypotonic, and Isotonic Environments on Red Blood Cells (Erythrocytes)

Red blood cells (**RBCs** or **erythrocytes**) can be markedly altered by environments that are not isotonic to their cytoplasm. A hypertonic medium will cause **crenation**, the shrinkage of a red blood cell from a net loss of water via osmosis. Note the irregular plasma membrane of crenated cells in Figure 3-3. Red blood cells swell in a hypotonic medium from an osmotic gain of water and may undergo

hemolysis. Hemolysis is the rupture of an RBC, resulting in the loss of hemoglobin from the cell (and a transparent membrane remnant known as an RBC "ghost").

1. Obtain two clean test tubes and, with a glass-marking pencil, label them 1 and 2. Place the tubes in a test tube rack.

2. Into Tube 1, add 2 ml physiologic saline solution. To this, add three drops of sheep blood. Swirl the tube gently to mix the contents and to create a suspension. (*Physiologic* or *normal saline* — 0.9% NaCl — is isotonic to erythrocytes.)

3. Prepare a wet mount of a drop of the suspension and examine it under the microscope using the high dry objective.

4. Deliver 2 ml 10% NaCl into Tube 2. Add three drops of sheep blood and swirl gently.

5. Prepare a wet mount of this preparation and observe under the microscope. Note the effects of a hypertonic medium on the erythrocytes.

6. Place a very small drop of sheep blood on a slide and overlay it with a coverslip. Slowly add a large drop of distilled water to the blood sample at edge of the coverslip. (The tip of the dropper should be resting on the slide/coverslip junction while the water is gently squeezed in.)

7. Place your wet mount under the microscope *immediately* and observe the effects of a hypotonic medium on the erythrocytes.

Why must the cells in a hypotonic medium be observed immediately after preparation?

_____

_____

_____

_____

Sketch and describe your observations on the following page.

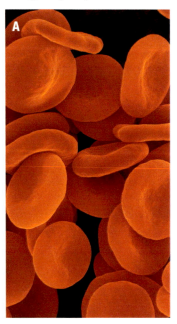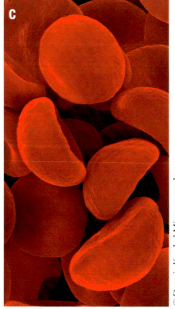

© Dennis Kunkel Microscopy, Inc

FIGURE 3-3. Red blood cells in various saline solutions: (A) normal cells in physiologic saline; (B) crenated cells in a hypertonic solution; (C) swollen cells in a hypotonic solution.

In the space below, sketch your observations of red blood cell in various saline solutions. Write a concise summary of your findings.

Sheep Red Blood Cells Under the Microscope

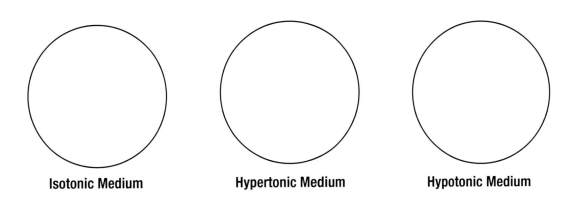

Isotonic Medium   Hypertonic Medium   Hypotonic Medium

Describe the appearance of the red blood cells in each of the three environments.

Hypertonic: _____

_____

_____

Hypotonic: _____

_____

_____

Isotonic: _____

_____

_____

The Effects of a Selectively Permeable Membrane on the Movement of Solutes Down Their Concentration Gradients

The separation of substances in solution by means of a selectively permeable membrane is known as **dialysis**. This experiment will emphasize how membranes select particles according to size.

1. Construct an artificial cell using a section of dialysis tubing and 5 ml of a prepared mixture of 0.9% NaCl, 5% glucose, 1% starch, and egg albumen. Shake the reagent bottle before pipetting. Once the mixture has been added, tie a knot to tightly close the open end of the tube.

2. Immerse the bag in a beaker containing distilled water and set aside for one hour.

3. At the end of the hour, test for the presence of each solute in the beaker fluid.

a. Chloride: On a black spot plate, mix five drops of beaker fluid and one drop of 2.9% silver nitrate. A white precipitate is a positive test for the chloride ion.

b. Glucose: Into a test tube, pipet 5 ml of beaker fluid. Add 5 ml Benedict's solution and heat in the 100°C water bath for two minutes. A positive test is indicated by a color change from blue to green, yellow, orange or rust.

c. Starch: On a white spot plate, mix 3 drops of beaker fluid with 3 drops of IKI solution. A positive test is indicated by a dark blue or purple color.

d. Albumen: Into a test tube, pipet 3 ml of beaker fluid. Add biuret reagent dropwise and shake well after each drop. A violet color is a positive test for protein.

Table 3-4. The Effects of a Selectively Permeable Membrane on the Movement of Solutes Down Their Concentration Gradients (Indicate your test results below with a check mark in the appropriate column.)

Solute	Penetrating	Nonpenetrating
Chloride		
Glucose		
Starch		
Albumen		

Active Processes

Any transport across the plasma membrane that requires ATP is classified as an active process. This includes substances that must move "uphill" against a concentration gradient and those that cannot penetrate the membrane due to size limitations or solubility characteristics. Active processes include active transport and vesicular transport.

Active Transport

Active transport of ions and molecules into or out of a cell requires a **carrier (transporter) protein** within the plasma membrane. Moving dietary amino acids into the cells lining the small intestine is a classic example of active transport. These molecules must move against their concentration gradient toward a higher intracellular concentration. Because the hydrophilic amino acids cannot penetrate the hydrophobic phospholipid bilayer or pass through the protein channels, an energy-dependent carrier molecule is necessary to continuously replenish these vital nutrients.

Vesicular Transport

Proteins and other substances of considerable molecular weight can negotiate the plasma membrane via **vesicular transport**. The two forms of vesicular transport are **exocytosis** — transport out of the cell — and **endocytosis** — transport into the cell.

Exocytosis

Exocytosis is an active process employed when large, hydrophilic molecules must exit the cell. Pancreatic cells exemplify exocytosis when they routinely export enzymes — which are high-molecular weight proteins — bound for the small intestine.

Phagocytosis

One form of endocytosis is **phagocytosis**, literally, cell eating. A phagocytizing human cell will expand a portion of its plasma membrane and cytoplasm around a large, solid substance, such as a bacterial cell, and engulf it. The protrusions of the phagocyte that engulf microbes and other solid substances are called **pseudopods**. A portion of the pseudopods' membrane separates from the whole, forming a **phagosome**, which then merges with a lysosome (Figure 3-4A). Phagocytosis and the digestion of a phagosome's contents by lysosomal enzymes are a key defensive strategy of white blood cells. (For a realistic look at a white blood cell moving toward its bacterial prey, see the electron microscope image in Figure 3-5.)

Pinocytosis

When a cell's membrane forms a vesicle by engulfing small droplets of liquid (usually containing proteins), the process is called **pinocytosis**.

PROCEDURE 7

Observe a video of time-lapse photography showing cells undergoing phagocytosis.

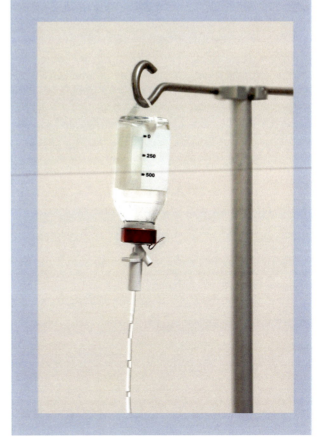

Clinical Application
Intravenous Saline

Isotonic saline solution is often administered intravenously (IV) to restore fluid volume lost after severe dehydration or to offset hemorrhagic fluid loss before a blood transfusion can be given. It is also used IV to maintain the body's water and salt balance when oral intake is contraindicated (for example, before or after surgery). This *normal* or *physiologic saline* is non-insulting to blood cells and can therefore be infused directly into the bloodstream.

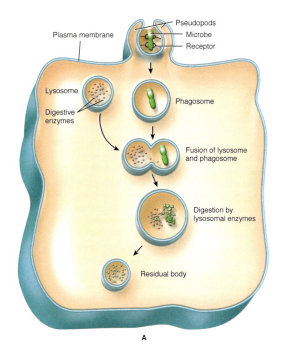

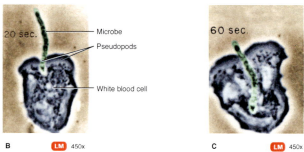

FIGURE 3-4. Phagocytosis. (A) A phagocytic cell (phagocyte) surrounds a microbe, and a phagosome (phagocytic vesicle) is formed. The phagosome fuses with a lysosome, whose enzymes destroy the microbe. (B) A white blood cell engulfing a microbe. (C) The white blood cell destroying the microbe.

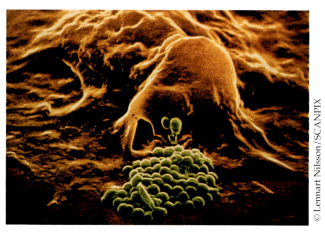

FIGURE 3-5. A human white blood cell about to phagocytose bacterial cells (spheres in foreground). Note that this active white blood cell (taken with a scanning electron microscope and magnified several thousand times), has left the bloodstream and appears amorphous. It bears little resemblance to the passive white blood cells seen in blood smears under light microscopy (as in Figure 4-5M).

Cell Physiology: Transport Mechanisms

NAME _____

LAB TIME/DATE _____

1. Observe the red blood cells in the three microscopic fields depicted below. The single arrows represent the net movement of water molecules by osmosis.

Field 1 illustrates RBCs in a(n) _____ solution. How would you describe the changes

occuring in these cells? _____

_____

Field 2 shows cells in a(n) _____ solution. What does the equal and opposite movement of water molecules indicate about the relative concentration of solutes on both sides of the plasma membrane?

_____

_____

Field 3 represents cells undergoing _____ in response to the _____ solution surrounding them. How would you describe the changes occuring in these cells?

_____

_____

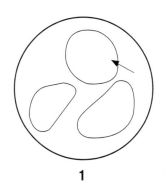

1

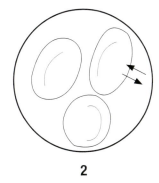

2

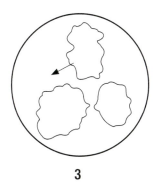

3

2. The rate at which particles will diffuse will be increased by all but which variable?
   a. increased temperature
   b. increased molecular weight
   c. greater concentration gradient
   d. increased kinetic energy

Review Questions

1. Define diffusion. _____

   _____

   _____

2. If Solution A were separated by a selectively permeable membrane from Solution B and A demonstrates greater osmotic pressure, what can you conclude regarding the solute concentration in A?

   _____

   _____

   In which direction would there be a net movement of water? _____

3. In an osmometer, no net movement of water molecules into the thistle tube occurs when the hydrostatic pressure of the tube equals its osmotic pressure. How would you describe this condition?

   _____

4. What specific feature of a synthetic selectively permeable membrane permits or blocks the passage of various substances?

   _____

   What characteristics of a human plasma membrane allow it to be more selective than an artificial membrane?

   _____

   _____

   _____

5. Suppose that in the man-on-a-deserted-island scenario, there were only salt water to drink. Should he drink from the sea or hold out for an ocean liner? Support your answer.

_____

_____

_____

_____

_____

6. In what way is active transport fundamentally different from passive transport?

_____

_____

_____

_____

_____

Notes

Histology: The Study of Tissues

OBJECTIVES

1. To name the four *primary tissues* of the human body and their major subtypes.
2. To identify the form and organization of the four primary tissues.
3. To relate the structure of a tissue to its specific function.
4. To relate the primary tissues to their locations in the body.

MATERIALS

Prepared slides:
   Epithelial Tissue
     Simple squamous
     Simple cuboidal

Simple columnar
Pseudostratified ciliated columnar
Stratified squamous
Transitional epithelium

(continued on next page)

PRE-LAB QUIZ

1. Which is *not* a hallmark of epithelial tissues?
   a. a free surface
   b. closely-spaced cells
   c. a rich blood supply
   d. a basal lamina

2. Stratified epithelial tissue is *least* likely to be found
   a. in the epidermis of the skin.
   b. in the mouth.
   c. lining the esophagus.
   d. in the walls of capillaries.

3. Collagenous fibers form an integral part of
   a. dense regular connective tissue.
   b. gastrointestinal epithelium.
   c. adipose tissue.
   d. nervous tissue.

4. All the following are features unique to skeletal muscle *except*
   a. peripheral nuclei.
   b. long, cylindrical cells.
   c. striations.
   d. multinucleated cells.

5. Which is *not* found in osteons?
   a. a central canal
   b. reticular fibers
   c. canaliculi
   d. lamellae

MATERIALS (continued)

Connective Tissue
    Areolar
    Adipose
    Reticular
    Dense regular
    Dense irregular (optional)
    Elastic (optional)
    Hyaline cartilage
    Fibrocartilage
    Elastic cartilage
    Compact bone
    Blood smear

Muscular Tissue
    Skeletal (l.s. and c.s.)
    Smooth (l.s. and c.s.)
    Cardiac (l.s. and c.s.)

Nervous Tissue
    Neurons (multipolar, smear)

Compound microscope
Lens paper

Human architecture is inspiring at any level of structural organization. To fully appreciate its anatomical complexity and how anatomy relates to physiology, **histology** is essential. *Histology is the study of tissues, groups of cells that together accomplish what cells in isolation could not.* The human body consists of four primary tissues: **epithelial, connective, muscular**, and **nervous**. These tissues perform specialized functions that enable different organs of the body to carry out specific tasks. For example, the epithelial tissue lining the small intestine is well adapted for the absorption of nutrients.

A tissue is made up of cells and the medium in which the cells reside. The cells of a particular tissue are similar to one another in both form and function. The medium, or **extracellular matrix (ECM)***, contains **intercellular fluid** and may also include various cell products, such as fibers, that define the matrix.

To understand how a tissue functions, one must first appreciate the morphology (form) and organization of its components.

* Extracellular matrix is sometimes called **intercellular substance (ICS)**.

General Guidelines for Studying Tissues

The histology laboratory is an important step toward understanding human anatomy. Equipped with a microscope and a battery of prepared slides, students can discover what they are really made of. But as exciting a prospect as this may be, finding one's way around an unfamiliar tissue specimen can be frustrating. Many of the pitfalls beginning students encounter can be avoided if a few simple guidelines are followed.

1. *Have some idea of what you are looking for.* Become familiar with how tissues within an organ are organized (Figure 4-1).

2. *Know the orientation of the tissue slice.* In preparing histological specimens, three-dimensional organs are sectioned into two-dimensional slices. Labels such as "cross section" (c.s.) and "longitudinal section" (l.s.) are included to explain how the tissue is presented.

3. *When placed under the microscope, the human body is visualized for the most part as cells, fibers, and fluid.* Although almost everything you see

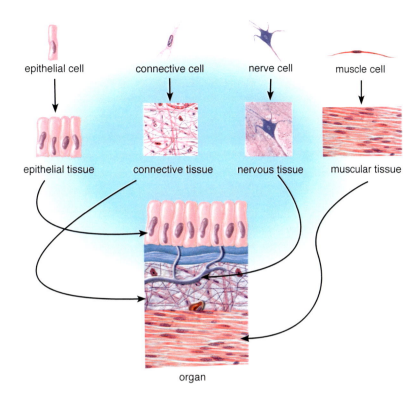

epithelial cell   connective cell   nerve cell   muscle cell

epithelial tissue   connective tissue   nervous tissue   muscular tissue

organ

FIGURE 4-1. Structural organization at the tissue and organ levels.

falls into one of these three categories, not every feature of your specimen is unmistakable. Elongated cells, especially those of muscle tissue, are often confused with fibers. Nuclei may be interpreted as whole cells, particularly when the cytoplasm or plasma membrane is ill defined.

4. *Examine each slide first under the scanning or low power objective, then with high power.* Under low magnification, you will get a panoramic view of the section. This is especially helpful when two or more tissue types share the stage. Once you have seen the anatomical relationships among different tissues, choose a particular region and focus it under high power.

5. *Try to ascertain the function(s) of each tissue,* such as absorption or protection. To study tissue structure is to appreciate its function. Think of the tissue's anatomy in relation to the special function that tissue performs and where in the body it would be located.

6. *After carefully observing the slides, label the photomicrographs in the Review Section.* Whenever in doubt, refer to the resource materials in the laboratory and to your textbook.

7. *Persevere!* Learning to "read" tissue slides demands considerable time and patience, but is well worth the effort. Observing human design through tissue study underscores the relationship between form and function.

Epithelial Tissue

Epithelial tissue — or simply **epithelium** — covers the outer surface of the body and all organs, and lines all tubes, cavities and most organs.* Epithelial tissues share several features in common (Figure 4-2).

• All epithelial tissues are characterized by an **apical (free) surface,** that is, the cells border on open space, such as those facing the **lumen** (interior space) of hollow organs. The apical surface anatomy is specialized according to location. For example, cilia cover the epithelial cells that line the airways of the respiratory system.

• The cells are closely packed with very little extracellular material.

*Covering and lining epithelia are distinguished from glandular epithelia, which will not be covered here.

- There is a complete absence of blood vessels. Epithelium is thus described as **avascular.** The underlying connective tissue contains numerous capillaries whose blood plasma is released to form tissue fluid. This intercellular fluid is a medium for the exchange of nutrients and wastes between connective and epithelial tissues.

- Epithelial tissue lies upon a membrane known as the **basal lamina.** Coupled with a second layer (the reticular lamina), it comprises the **basement membrane**. Beneath the basement membrane, there is always a layer of connective tissue.
  The numerous types of epithelial tissues are classified according to the shape and arrangement of the cells (Figure 4-3).

Epithelial Cell Shapes

- **Squamous cells** are flat and thin.

- **Cuboidal cells** are roughly cube-shaped. In a two-dimensional view, they appear almost square.

- **Columnar cells** are taller than they are wide and take on a rectangular appearance when cut lengthwise.

- **Transitional epithelium**, found exclusively in the urinary system, contains cells whose shape varies from columnar to squamous. The shape of the cells in this multilayered tissue changes as the bladder, for example, is distended by urine (Figure 4-4G).

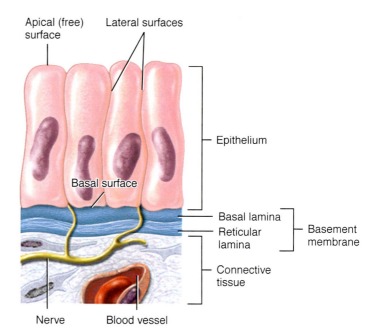

FIGURE 4-2. Epithelial cells in relation to underlying connective tissue.

FIGURE 4-3. Cell shapes and arrangement of layers for covering and lining epithelia.

Arrangement of Epithelial Cell Layers

- If an epithelial tissue consists of a single layer of cells, it is called **simple epithelium**.
- If it has two or more layers of cells, it is **stratified epithelium**.
- If the tissue appears to have several layers, but is actually composed of a single layer, with all cells touching the basal lamina, it is termed **pseudostratified epithelium**.

PROCEDURE 1

Microscopic Examination of Epithelial Tissue

From the demonstration table, obtain slides of simple squamous, simple cuboidal, simple columnar (ciliated and nonciliated), pseudostratified ciliated columnar, stratified squamous, and transitional epithelia. As you view each specimen, note how the cells are arranged as continuous sheets with no noticeable intercellular space. This organizational scheme is ideal for lining and covering organs. For example, tightly fitting epithelial cells ensure that the outer layer of skin (the epidermis) acts as a protective barrier.

As you navigate through the epithelial slide set, refer to Figure 4-4 for a look at common epithelial tissues, their locations, and their functions. Consult the Review Section regularly for relevant questions as you examine the epithelia and the other primary tissues.

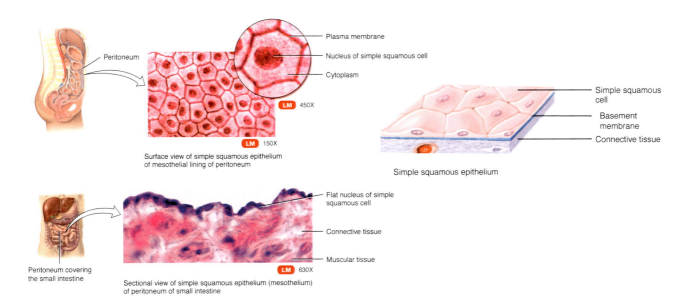

Plasma membrane

Nucleus of simple squamous cell

Cytoplasm

LM 450X

LM 150X

Surface view of simple squamous epithelium of mesothelial lining of peritoneum

Peritoneum

Simple squamous cell

Basement membrane

Connective tissue

Simple squamous epithelium

Flat nucleus of simple squamous cell

Connective tissue

Muscular tissue

LM 630X

Peritoneum covering the small intestine

Sectional view of simple squamous epithelium (mesothelium) of peritoneum of small intestine

Histology Hints	The surface view reveals cells that resemble irregular floor tiles. The nucleus lies in the center of each cell and is circular or oval in outline. In a sectional view, the single layer of flat cells exhibits a low profile.
Location	Simple squamous epithelium (1) lines the heart and all blood and lymphatic vessels where it is called **endothelium**, and (2) forms the outer layer of the serous membranes of the heart (pericardium), lungs (pleura), and abdominopelvic viscera (peritoneum). Here it is known as **mesothelium**. It is also found in the walls of air sacs (alveoli) of the lungs and the glomerular capsules of the kidney.
Function	The single layer of flat cells is well adapted to rapid transfer of fluids and solutes (filtration and absorption through the single-celled walls of capillaries) and diffusion (as of respiratory gases through air sac walls into and out of the bloodstream).

FIGURE 4-4A. Simple squamous epithelium.

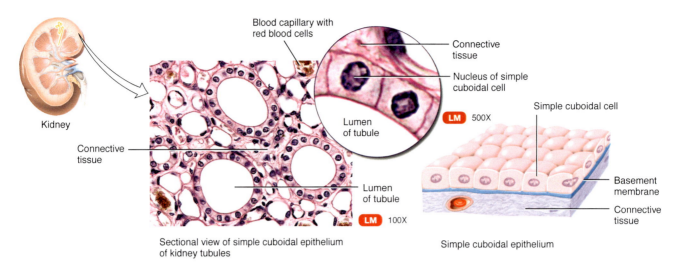

Sectional view of simple cuboidal epithelium
of kidney tubules

Simple cuboidal epithelium

Histology Hints	This tissue displays a single layer of cells resembling cubes whose nuclei are round and centered. In section, look for cells that appear square or like triangles whose apex is cut off. (This narrower apical surface allows cuboidal epithelium to assume a tubular form.)
Location	Lines kidney tubules and ducts of glands; forms secretory cells of thyroid gland; covers surface of ovary.
Function	Secretion and absorption

FIGURE 4-4B. Simple cuboidal epithelium.

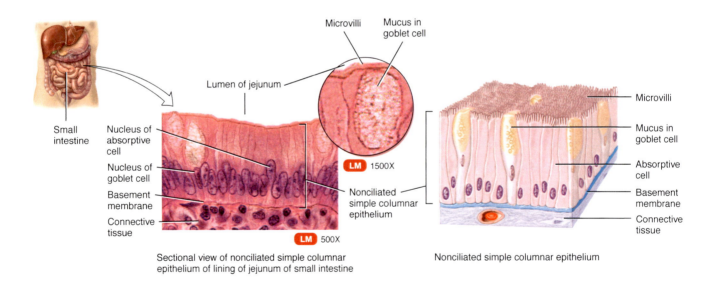

Sectional view of nonciliated simple columnar
epithelium of lining of jejunum of small intestine

Nonciliated simple columnar epithelium

Histology Hints	Note the single layer of columnar-shaped cells having single oval nuclei near the basal surface. The apical surface contains **microvilli** that appear as a "brush border" under the light microscope. (Microvilli dramatically enhance absorptive surface area.) **Goblet cells** — modified columnar cells whose specialty is mucus production — resemble miniature champagne glasses due to accumulated mucus in the upper part of the cell.
Location	Lining of gastrointestinal tract (beginning at the stomach) and the walls of ducts of many types of glands.
Function	Secretion (of digestive juices) and absorption (of nutrients, water, and salts). Mucus, via goblet cells, and the mucous membrane formed by the epithelium and underlying connective tissue, lubricates and protects.

FIGURE 4-4C. Nonciliated simple columnar epithelium.

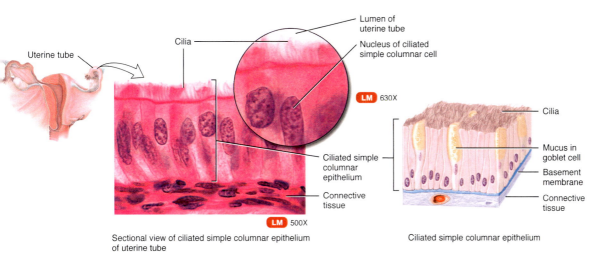

Histology Hints Note a single layer of column-shaped cells with dark oval nuclei and prominent hair-like cilia. Goblet cells are found between the columnar cells.

Location Uterine (Fallopian) tubes, uterus, and some of the small airways (bronchioles) of the lungs.

Function Sweeping action of cilia moves egg cells (oöcytes) through uterine tubes after ovulation into uterus. In the airways, ciliary action is a major part of the immune response to inhaled particles, moving them — along with the mucus that traps them — away from the lungs and into the throat.

FIGURE 4-4D. Ciliated simple columnar epithelium.

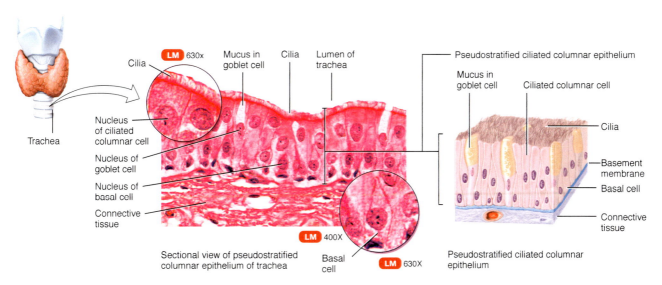

Histology Hints A single-layered epithelium that appears stratified, hence the name (*pseudo* = false). Illusion of stratification is created by nuclei located at different levels — lower nuclei in shorter cells, higher nuclei in taller, ciliated cells that reach the free surface. Goblet cells are also present.

Location Most airways of the upper and lower respiratory tracts; nonciliated variety lines part of the male urethra and the larger-diameter ducts of numerous glands.

Function Ciliated form sweeps away mucus-bound debris in the respiratory tract.

FIGURE 4-4E. Pseudostratified ciliated columnar epithelium.

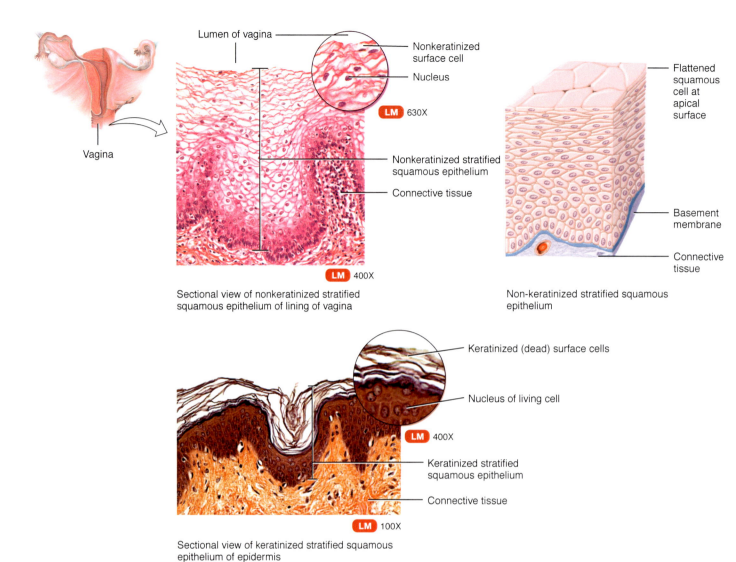

Vagina

Lumen of vagina

Nonkeratinized surface cell

Nucleus

LM 630X

Nonkeratinized stratified squamous epithelium

Connective tissue

LM 400X

Sectional view of nonkeratinized stratified squamous epithelium of lining of vagina

Flattened squamous cell at apical surface

Basement membrane

Connective tissue

Non-keratinized stratified squamous epithelium

Keratinized (dead) surface cells

Nucleus of living cell

LM 400X

Keratinized stratified squamous epithelium

Connective tissue

LM 100X

Sectional view of keratinized stratified squamous epithelium of epidermis

Histology Hints	Look for many layers of cells of various shapes. Those on the free surface are squamous, those deeper range from cuboidal in middle layers to short columnar near the basement membrane. Dead cells on the free surface lose their connection to one another and may appear loosely attached to the layer below.
	Keratinized stratified squamous epithelium, found in the epidermis, is named for a tough, protective protein (keratin) that develops in several layers of superficial cells. The predominant epidermal cell, the keratinocyte, dies as it migrates farther from the nutritive tissue fluid in the basal layers. The nonliving keratinized cells near the free surface appear scaly and loosely connected to one another and to the degenerating but intact cells below.
Location	Keratinized form of stratified squamous: skin (epidermis); non-keratinized form: mucous membrane lining of mouth, pharynx, esophagus, vagina and anus.
Function	Protection against water loss, mechanical stress, and microbial invasion.

FIGURE 4-4F. Stratified squamous epithelium.

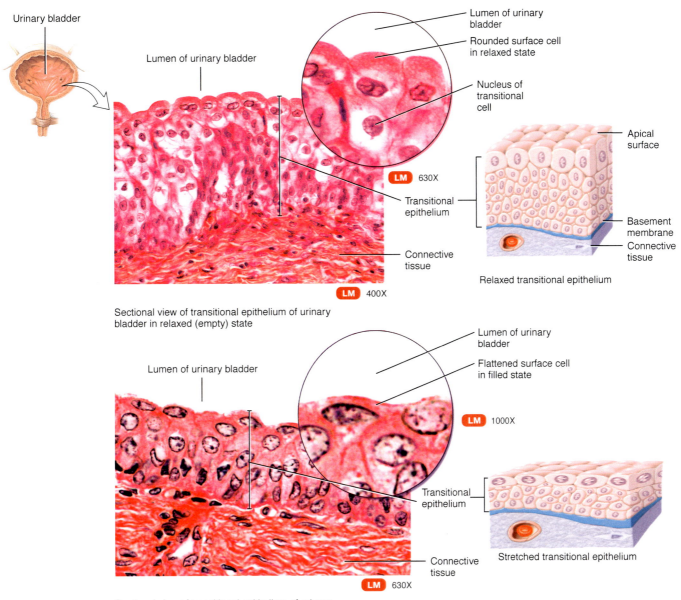

Sectional view of transitional epithelium of urinary bladder in relaxed (empty) state

Sectional view of transitional epithelium of urinary bladder in stretched (filled) state

Histology Hints   In the unstretched (relaxed) condition, transitional epithelium is six to eight layers thick, with mostly cuboidal cells. The cells on the free surface are larger and dome-shaped in the apical region when viewed from the side. As urine stretches the tissue, cells slide past one another and become flatter. The thickness of the epithelium is reduced to three or four layers when stretched and the free surface cells are lower in profile.

Location   Lining of bladder and ureters and proximal urethra.

Function   Transitional epithelium allows urinary organs to expand without rupturing.

FIGURE 4-4G. Transitional epithelium.

Connective Tissue

Connective tissue is the most abundant primary tissue in the body and appears in many diverse forms. Its primary functions are to provide a supportive and protective internal framework and to bind one type of tissue to another, as well as organ to organ.

Bone, or **osseous tissue**, makes up the rigid infrastructure that supports the body as a whole and protects internal organs. Its attachment to muscles makes body movements possible. **Ligaments** and **tendons** are dense connective tissues. Ligaments bind bones together at joints and tendons connect muscles to bone. **Areolar tissue** (Figure 4-5) is a soft packing material that surrounds and cushions organs. It includes cells and noncellular fibers common to many connective tissues. **Adipose tissue** insulates and cushions organs and is a storage depot for fat. **Hemopoietic**, or blood-forming tissue, produces blood cells.

The general characteristics of connective tissues include:

• cells that are spaced relatively far apart.

• a rich blood supply (excepting certain poorly vascularized tissues such as tendons and cartilage).

• an abundance of **extracellular matrix**, or intercellular material. In most connective tissues, the matrix is a semisolid gel, but it may also be fluid (blood), semirigid (cartilage) or rigid (bone). A product of connective tissue cells known as **ground substance** is primarily responsible for the consistency of the extracellular matrix and acts as a medium for nutrient and waste exchange. Ground substance consists mainly of intercellular fluid and proteins. Fibers deposited within this ground substance form an important part of the matrix.

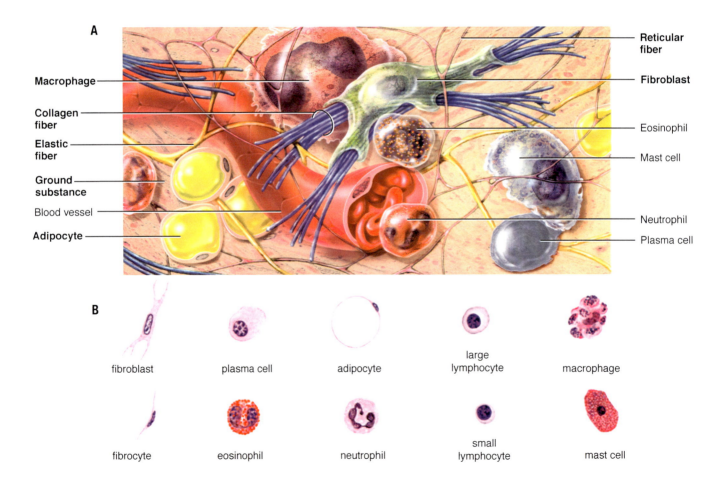

FIGURE 4-5. Areolar tissue, a model of connective tissue proper. (A) Cell and fiber types common to many connective tissues. (B) Isolated cells found in connective tissues. (Note: The macrophage contains material ingested by phagocytosis. The fibrocyte is a mature fibroblast.)

Classification of Connective Tissue

Adult connective tissues have been classified into five major groups, each with subdivisions. The first two groups are considered "connective tissue proper." Groups three, four and five are designated specialized connective tissues.

1. Loose Connective Tissue
   A. Areolar tissue
   B. Adipose tissue
   C. Reticular connective tissue

2. Dense Connective Tissue
   A. Dense regular connective tissue
   B. Dense irregular connective tissue
   C. Elastic connective tissue

3. Cartilage
   A. Hyaline cartilage
   B. Fibrocartilage
   C. Elastic cartilage

4. Bone (osseous) tissue
   A. Compact bone
   B. Spongy (cancellous) bone

5. Fluid Connective Tissue
   A. Blood
   B. Lymph

The predominant cell type found in connective tissue proper is the **fibroblast**. This cell on surface view is multipolar; viewed from the side, it is spindle shaped. It has a centrally placed oval nucleus. It produces the fibers and ground substance found within the matrix. **Collagenous fibers** are tough and inelastic due to the presence of collagen protein. Under the microscope they appear as relatively thick bundles of wavy fibers in a parallel arrangement. **Elastic fibers** possess elasticity because of the protein elastin. These fibers are yellow and appear as thin, branching structures. **Reticular fibers** are similar to collagenous fibers in composition, but are arranged in delicate net-like configurations. All connective tissues are derived from embryonic tissue known as **mesenchyme**.

PROCEDURE 2

Microscopic Examination of Connective Tissue

From the demonstration table, obtain slides of areolar, adipose, reticular, dense regular, dense irregular, and elastic connective tissue; of hyaline cartilage, fibrocartilage, and elastic cartilage; of compact bone; and of blood.

Histology Hints   Note the elements in areolar tissue common to many diverse connective tissues: collagenous and elastic fibers, fibroblasts, and macrophages surrounded by a semifluid ground substance.

Location   Areolar connective tissue is part of subcutaneous (beneath-the-skin) tissue and is found as a packing material around internal organs.

Function   Strong (due to presence of collagenous fibers) and elastic (due to fibers containing elastin) support.

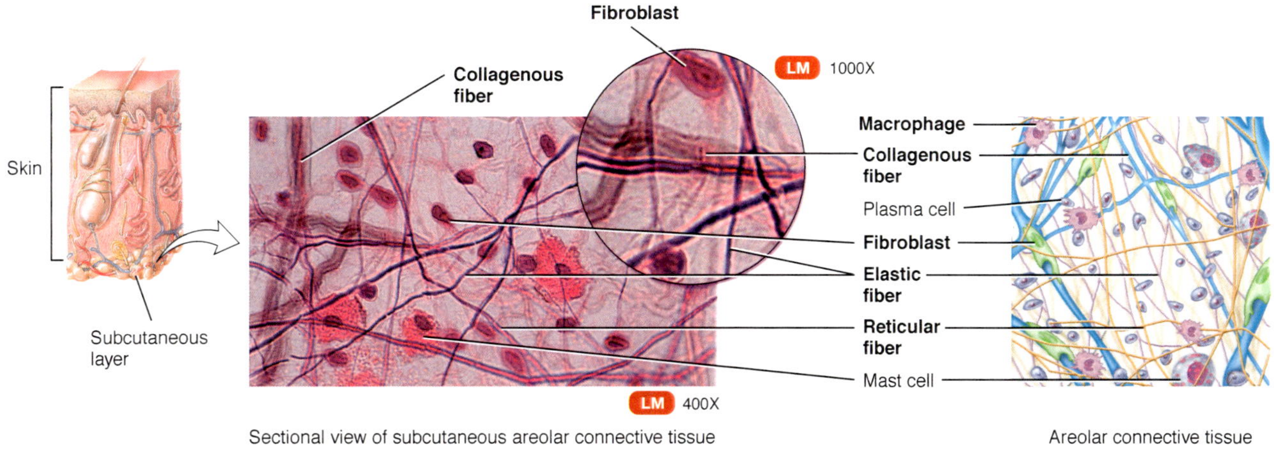

FIGURE 4-5C. Areolar connective tissue.

Histology Hints   Note cells — **adipocytes** — whose nucleus and cytoplasm are pushed to the periphery by a droplet of fat
(triglyceride).

Location   Adipose follows distribution pattern of areolar connective tissue: subcutaneous and as
a shock-absorbing pad around organs such as the heart, kidneys, and eyeball. It is also found in membranes
external to the stomach and intestines.

Function   Supports and protects organs; insulates against heat loss through the skin; acts as an energy reserve.

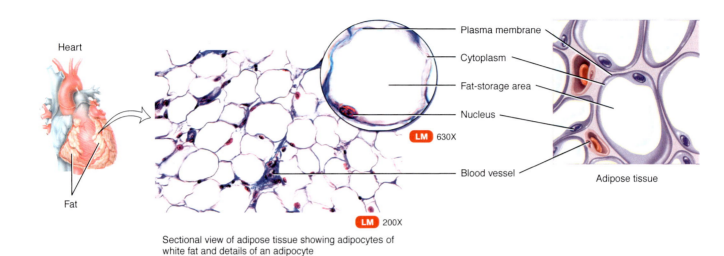

Sectional view of adipose tissue showing adipocytes of
white fat and details of an adipocyte

FIGURE 4-5D. Adipose tissue.

Histology Hints   Look for a network of fine, interconnecting reticular fibers with cells residing in spaces between the fibers.

Location   Reticular fibers form a supportive framework (stroma) in lymph nodes, the spleen, the liver, and red bone
marrow, and comprise the reticular lamina of basement membranes.

Function   Reticular tissue supports organs internally. Fibers filter microbes in lymph nodes and dead or worn-out
blood cells in spleen. (Phagocytes destroy filtered blood cells to remove them from the
circulation.)

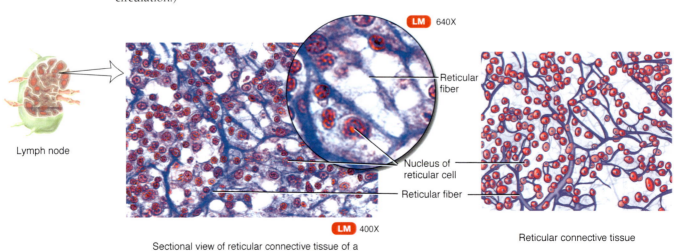

Sectional view of reticular connective tissue of a
lymph node

FIGURE 4-5E. Reticular tissue.

Histology Hints   This tissue is a relatively simple combination of (mainly) collagen fibers arranged in parallel bundles and the fibroblasts that make them. The fibroblasts are arranged in rows between the collagen fibers. Commonly, only the fibroblast nuclei are visible.

Location   This tissue forms tendons (which are inelastic), ligaments (which are more stretchable due to the greater presence of elastic fibers), and aponeuroses (broad, flat tendons for wide muscles of the abdomen and back).

Function   Dense regular connective tissue provides a strong connection between muscle and bone (tendons) or between bones at their joints (ligaments).

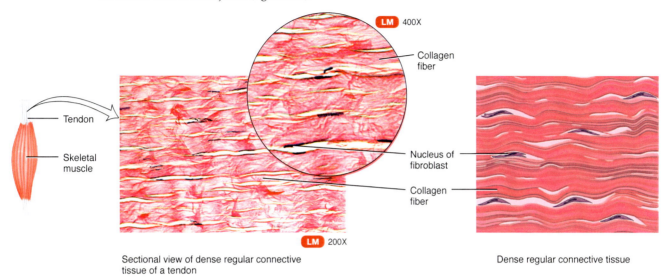

Sectional view of dense regular connective tissue of a tendon

Dense regular connective tissue

FIGURE 4-5F. Dense regular connective tissue.

Histology Hints   Note the irregularly arranged collagen fibers interspersed with fibroblast nuclei.

Location   Reticular region of the skin's dermis, periosteum of bone, perichondrium of cartilage, fibrous layer of pericardium, and fascia (a sheet-like covering of muscles).

Function   The nonparallel arrangement of collagen fibers strongly resists pulling forces in many directions.

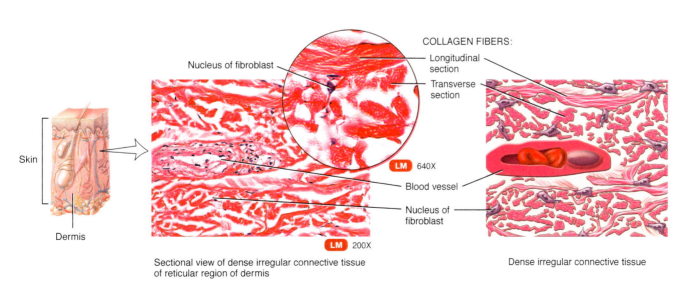

Sectional view of dense irregular connective tissue of reticular region of dermis

Dense irregular connective tissue

FIGURE 4-5G. Dense irregular connective tissue (optional).

Histology Hints   Look for wavy parallel bundles of predominantly elastic fibers which are naturally yellow, but stain black. Nuclei of fibroblasts are visible between the fibers.

Location   Lung tissue and the walls of arteries.

Function   Elastic fibers allow the lungs and arteries to stretch, then recoil, an important aspect of their physiology.

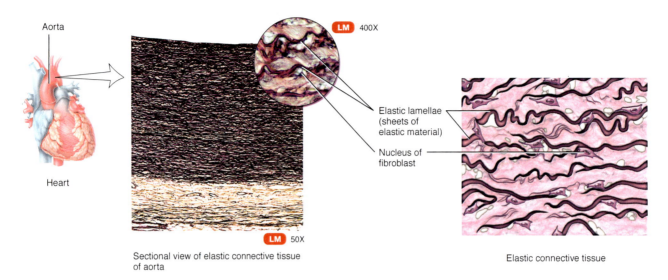

FIGURE 4-5H. Elastic connective tissue (optional).

Histology Hints   The extracellular matrix of this shiny cartilage — named from the Greek word for "glassy" — will appear as purple or pink in a stained specimen. Cartilage cells, or **chondrocytes**, are readily visible within **lacunae**, bubble-like enclosures surrounded by a ground substance with the consistency of a semirigid gel. (Collagenous fibers within the matrix are not usually visible.) Look for a surrounding membrane, the **perichondrium**. (The perichondrium is absent in the articular cartilage of joints.)

Location   Respiratory tract (nose, larynx, trachea, bronchi); ends of bones at joints; embryonic and fetal skeleton.

Function   Provides support, protection, and flexibility, as exemplified by the costal cartilage of the rib cage; provides joints with a smooth, slippery surface during movement.

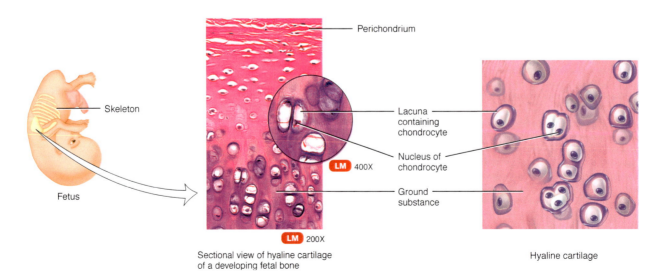

FIGURE 4-5I. Hyaline cartilage.

Histology Hints   Look for chondrocytes in lacunae (usually in rows) on a backdrop of clearly visible collagenous fibers arranged in thick bundles within the matrix. No perichondrium is present.

Location   Intervertebral discs, menisci (pads of cartilage in the knee joint), and the pubic symphysis (where the two hip bones meet anteriorly).

Function   The strongest of cartilage types, fibrocartilage provides rigid support for the joints it holds together.

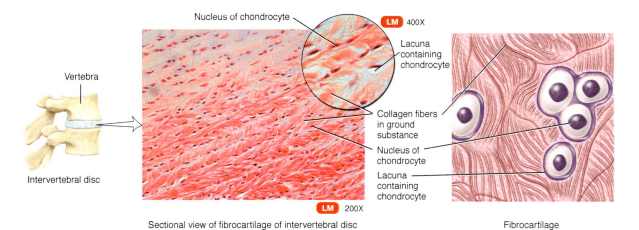

FIGURE 4-5J. Fibrocartilage.

Histology Hints   The lacunae and chondrocytes are surrounded by thread-like elastic fibers within the matrix. Note the surrounding perichondrium.

Location   Epiglottis, the protective leaf-like lid over the glottis (part of which is the air space of the larynx), and part of the external anatomy of the ear.

Function   The fiber-reinforced matrix provides strength and elasticity.

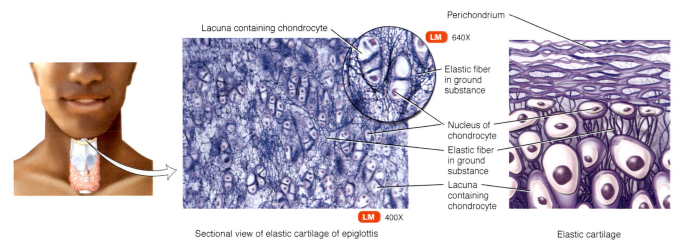

FIGURE 4-5K. Elastic cartilage.

Histology Hints In **compact bone** you will observe numerous subunits known as **osteons**. Each osteon (formerly known as a Haversian system) consists of lacunae containing mature bone cells, the **osteocytes**. (The tissue is usually presented as a dry specimen whose osteocytes were lost in preparation; the lacunae are therefore empty.) A **central canal** containing vascular structures provides tissue fluid to each lacuna via tiny passageways – the **canaliculi** – which radiate from the center like spokes in a wheel. The lacunae and canaliculi are arranged in concentric layers called **lamellae**.

Spongy bone differs dramatically in its microscopic (and gross) appearance. Thin bars of bone — the **trabeculae** — make up the interior; no osteons are present. In the spaces between the trabeculae is red marrow.

Location Compact and spongy bone tissue are found together in all bones of the skeleton.

Function Bone tissue's rigid matrix provides protection (as in the cranium) and support (the body's internal framework). Bones act as levers for movement via skeletal muscle contraction. Bone tissue is also a storage site for red marrow and minerals such as calcium and phosphorus.

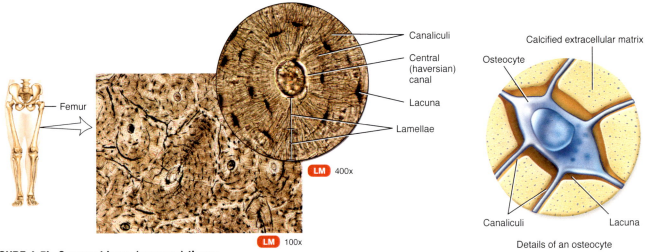

FIGURE 4-5L. Compact bone (osseous) tissue.

Histology Hints **Red blood cells** (**erythrocytes**) are pink or reddish biconcave discs whose center is less concentrated in hemoglobin pigment and therefore appears lighter. There is no nucleus in a mature red cell. **White blood cells (leukocytes)** are nucleated and are divided into two groups based on the presence of visible cytoplasmic granules: The granulocytes (whose nuclei are segmented) and the agranulocytes (whose nuclei are not segmented). **Platelets (thrombocytes)** are fragments of a large marrow cell, which, like red cells, do not meet the criteria of true cells.

Location Within an extracellular matrix known as plasma, blood cells are found in the blood vessels and heart chambers.

Function Red blood cells transport oxygen (and some carbon dioxide) throughout the body. White blood cells are indispensable players in immune responses. Among their immunologic functions are phagocytosis and antibody production. Platelets are necessary for blood clotting.

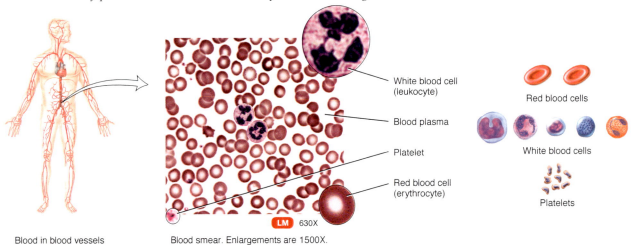

FIGURE 4-5M. Blood smear.

Muscular Tissue

Muscular tissue (Figure 4-6) consists of cells that are specialized for contraction and expansion. During contraction, a muscle cell — or **muscle fiber** — condenses and shortens. At the tissue level, the contraction of many cells creates movement. Following its contraction period, a muscle relaxes and expands. The elastic properties of muscular tissue allow it to return to its original shape once its length has changed.

Muscular tissue exists in three forms: skeletal, cardiac, and smooth. In each case, the cells are elongated. This enables muscle cells to shorten enough during contraction to produce movement and force.

- **Skeletal muscle** makes up the fleshy part of our anatomy and is the only muscle type that is voluntary: It can be contracted through conscious effort. Skeletal muscle is named for its attachment to bones and produces limb, trunk, facial, and other body movements. Its cells are the longest muscle fibers and are characterized by prominent **striations** (transverse bands resembling stripes) and multiple peripheral nuclei.

- **Cardiac muscle** is unique to the heart. It is the only muscular tissue whose cells form a branching pattern. The cells have faint striations and usually a single central nucleus. They are separated from each other by **intercalated discs**, thickenings on the plasma membranes where cell-to-cell contact is made. These discs facilitate impulse conduction and permit cardiac muscle cells to contract as a unit.

- **Smooth muscle** is located within the walls of internal organs and blood vessels and is nonstriated, hence its name. Given its location, it is also known as **visceral muscle**. The cells of smooth muscle are thin, and spindle shaped, with tapered ends and a single, central nucleus.

PROCEDURE 3

Microscopic Examination of Muscular Tissue

From the demonstration table, obtain slides of cardiac, smooth, and skeletal muscle tissue in cross and longitudinal sections. In your microscopic observations, and with the aid of Figure 4-6, compare the structural features of each muscle type.

Histology Hints Unique features: Skeletal muscle fibers are long and cylindrical with several nuclei on the periphery. Striations are prominent.
Location Attached to bones via tendons. (Exceptions are the soft-tissue attachments of facial muscles.)
Function Body movements, maintaining posture, protection of underlying structures, and generation of heat.

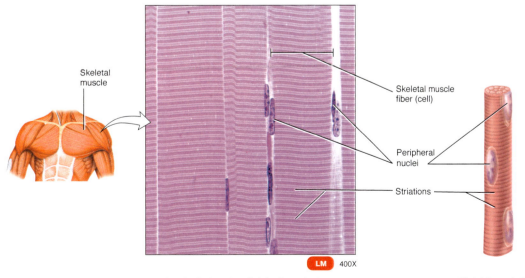

Longitudinal section of skeletal muscle tissue

Skeletal muscle fiber

FIGURE 4-6A. Skeletal muscle tissue.

Histology Hints Unique features: Cardiac muscle fibers are branched with **intercalated discs** (which hold adjacent fibers together during contraction and facilitate conduction of cardiac impulses). Cardiac muscle is striated like skeletal; there is a single, central nucleus in most cells, although binucleated cells may be seen.

Location The walls of the heart

Function Contraction forces blood from heart to all parts of the body.

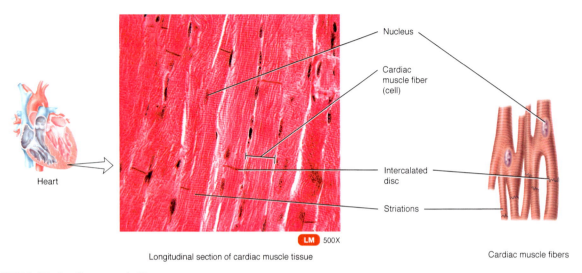

Heart

Longitudinal section of cardiac muscle tissue

LM 500X

Nucleus

Cardiac muscle fiber (cell)

Intercalated disc

Striations

Cardiac muscle fibers

FIGURE 4-6B. Cardiac muscle tissue.

Histology Hints The spindle shape of a smooth muscle cell and the absence of striations are unique. The single nucleus is in the center of the cell.

Location Wall of the stomach, intestines, urinary bladder, uterus, blood vessels, and airways; iris of the eye.

Function Movement (as in propulsion of food through the alimentary canal and expulsion of urine from the bladder). Constriction of blood vessels and airways.

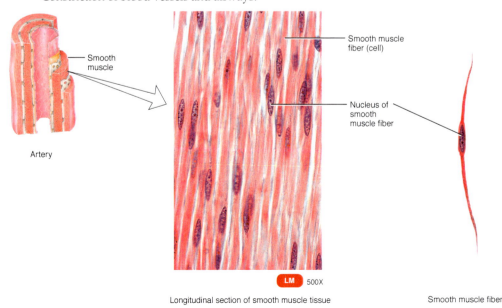

Artery

Smooth muscle

Longitudinal section of smooth muscle tissue

LM 500X

Smooth muscle fiber (cell)

Nucleus of smooth muscle fiber

Smooth muscle fiber

FIGURE 4-6C. Smooth muscle tissue.

Nervous Tissue

Nervous tissue is specialized for conducting nerve impulses. It is composed of nerve cells, or **neurons**, and **neuroglia**, cells that support, protect, and help nourish the neurons (Figure 4-7). Neurons are highly excitable cells which, when stimulated, send their electrical messages from one part of the body to another. A **nerve** is a composite of many neurons bound together by connective tissue.

Although neurons exist in a variety of forms, they all possess a **cell body** and **cytoplasmic processes**. Typically, a singular, elongated process, the **axon,** extends from one side of the cell body. It is often referred to as a **nerve fiber**, but should not be confused with the fibers of connective tissue. The terminal branches of axons contain bulb-like swellings that store transmitter chemicals to influence other neurons, muscles, or glands. Projecting from the cell body on the opposite side are one or more shorter, highly branched processes, the **dendrites**. Dendrites provide receptive surface area that enables interaction with other nerve cells.

Neurons may or may not possess **myelin**, a fatty material that envelops the axon. Myelin insulates neurons within nerves to prevent cross stimulation and increases impulse conduction velocity. When present, the myelin sheath is interrupted at regular intervals by **neurofibral nodes** (the nodes of Ranvier). These nodes maintain continuity between the neuron and the extracellular fluid.

PROCEDURE 4

Microscopic Examination of Nervous Tissue

From the demonstration table, obtain a slide of multipolar neurons. Note the nucleus and nucleolus and the cytoplasmic processes. Identify the neuroglial cells.

Histology Hints   Note the central **cell body** which gives rise to cytoplasmic processes: a singular **axon**, and many, highly-branched **dendrites**. (In some neurons, there is a singular dendrite, but the specimens you will likely encounter in the laboratory are "multipolar" cells with many dendrites.) The **neuroglia** appear as dark dot-like cells in the background.

Location   Nervous system

Function   Neurons generate nerve impulses that influence muscles, glands, and other neurons. Neuroglia provide neurons with nutritional, antimicrobial, and physical support.

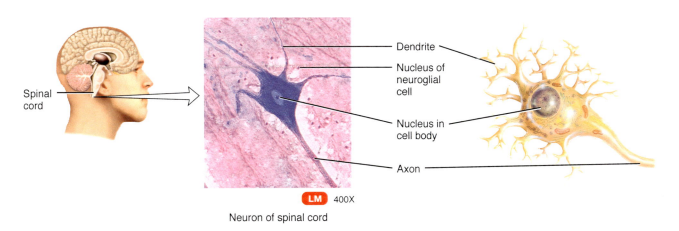

LM 400X

Neuron of spinal cord

FIGURE 4-7. Nervous tissue, showing neurons and neuroglial cells.

Histology: The Study of Tissues

NAME _____

LAB TIME/DATE _____

General Review Questions

Match the primary tissue on the left with its corresponding features on the right.

_____ epithelium

_____ nervous tissue

_____ muscular tissue

_____ connective tissue

a. elongated cells, some of which are striated

b. closely spaced cells found on body surfaces

c. extracellular matrix includes ground substance

d. includes supportive glial cells

Epithelial Tissue

1. As a group, the epithelia are characterized by 1) a _____ surface

    and 2) an underlying _____ membrane.

2. Where is pseudostratified ciliated columnar epithelium found? _____

    _____

    What is its function? _____

    _____

3. Mucus-producing one-celled glands that are interspersed among columnar epithelial cells

    of the digestive and respiratory tracts are known as _____ cells.

4. How does the arrangement of simple squamous epithelium relate to its role in human physiology? Give two specific examples of how form complements function.

_____

_____

_____

_____

_____

5. How is the function of stratified epithelial tissue different from that of simple epithelium?

_____

_____

_____

_____

6. In the absence of blood vessels, how are epithelial cells nourished?

_____

_____

_____

_____

7. What characteristics of transitional epithelium allow it to expand as the urinary bladder fills with urine?

_____

_____

_____

_____

8. Match the epithelial tissue to its location.

_____ simple squamous   a. lining of digestive tract

_____ stratified squamous   b. kidney tubules

_____ simple columnar   c. serous membranes

_____ simple cuboidal   d. lining of mouth

Connective Tissue

1. The cartilage that supports airways in the respiratory system is _____.

2. The radially arranged components of bone histology that are analogous to an irrigation system are the _____.

3. Compare the extracellular matrix of bone, cartilage, and blood.

    _____

    _____

    _____

    _____

    _____

4. Using the word list, identify the connective tissues described below. Tissue names may be used more than once.

    a. adipose tissue, b. areolar tissue, c. dense regular connective tissue, d. hyaline cartilage, e. fibrocartilage, f. elastic cartilage, g. bone tissue, h. hemopoietic tissue

    _____ 1. Organized into osteons

    _____ 2. Provides flexibility for the epiglottis

    _____ 3. Attaches muscles to bones

    _____ 4. Tough component of intervertebral discs

    _____ 5. A heat-retaining insulator

(continued on next page)

_____ 6. Forms the embryonic skeleton

_____ 7. Fat storage tissue

_____ 8. A soft packing material around internal organs containing numerous white and
yellow fibers

_____ 9. Blood-forming connective tissue

_____ 10. Its matrix is hardened by calcium salts.

Muscular Tissue

Compare the three muscle types by placing a check mark in the appropriate box.

Feature	Skeletal	Cardiac	Smooth
Long cylindrical cells			
Striations			
Single nucleus			
Many nuclei per cell			
Nucleus near center of cell			
Nucleus on cell periphery			
Intercalated discs			
Cells show branching pattern.			
Voluntarily controlled			
Involuntarily controlled			

Nervous Tissue

1. To receive input from other nerve cells, highly branched _____ afford neurons receptive surface area.

2. The_____ is a long, singular cytoplasmic process that enables neurons to conduct nerve impulses across relatively long distances.

3. Although they are highly specialized, neurons share certain structural characteristics with other cells. Identify two of these common attributes.

   _____

   _____

   _____

   _____

Visual Identification of Tissues

For each of the photomicrographs, identify the tissue by name and the highlighted structures. (Word list is on page 74.)

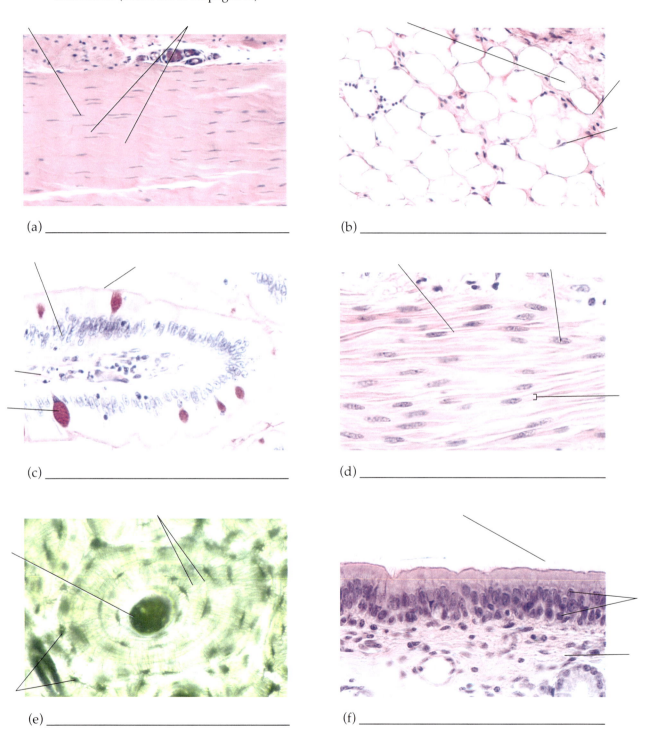

(a) _____

(b) _____

(c) _____

(d) _____

(e) _____

(f) _____

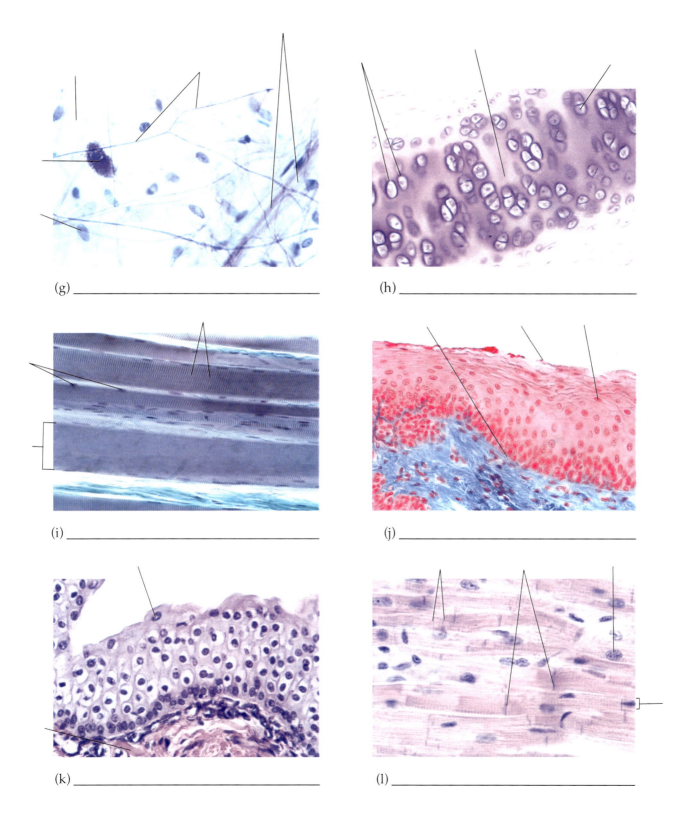

(g) _____

(h) _____

(i) _____

(j) _____

(k) _____

(l) _____

Visual Identification of Tissues: Word List

1. cardiac muscle fiber
2. adipocyte nucleus
3. extracellular matrix of areolar tissue
4. intercalated discs
5. canaliculi
6. fat droplet
7. lacunae of hyaline cartilage
8. fibroblast nucleus of regular dense connective tissue
9. adipocyte plasma membrane
10. nucleus of cardiac muscle fiber
11. striations of skeletal muscle fiber
12. extracellular matrix of hyaline cartilage
13. nucleus of chondrocyte
14. basement membrane of stratified squamous epithelium
15. nucleus of transitional epithelium surface cell
16. connective tissue of transitional epithelium
17. nucleus of squamous cell
18. mast cell of areolar tissue
19. nuclei of skeletal muscle fiber
20. stratified squamous surface cell
21. goblet cell
22. smooth muscle fiber
23. collagenous fibers of dense regular connective tissue
24. elastic fibers of areolar tissue
25. nuclei of pseudostratified columnar epithelium
26. cilia
27. brush border (microvilli) of simple columnar epithelium
28. collagenous fibers of areolar tissue
29. lacunae of bone tissue
30. nucleus of simple columnar epithelium
31. central canal
32. nucleus of smooth muscle fiber
33. connective tissue of simple columnar epithelium
34. cytoplasm of smooth muscle fiber
35. connective tissue of pseudostratified columnar epithelium
36. striations of cardiac muscle fiber
37. skeletal muscle fiber
38. fibroblast nucleus of areolar tissue

Introduction to the Skeletal System

OBJECTIVES

1. To describe the functions of the skeletal system.
2. To identify cartilages associated with the skeletal system.
3. To describe the four major anatomical classifications of bones.
4   To identify bone markings (surface features) and their functions.
5. To identify the gross anatomy of a sectioned dry long bone and a fresh beef bone.
6. To review the microanatomy of compact bone.
7. To explain how physical characteristics of bone relate to its organic and inorganic constituents

MATERIALS

Articulated skeletons
Prepared slides of compact and
    spongy bone tissue (c.s.)
Compound microscope
Baked and acid-treated bone
    specimens

Human long bone in longitudinal section
Fresh beef bone, sectioned horizontally and
    longitudinally
Disposable examination gloves
Three-dimensional model of bone
    microanatomy

PRE-LAB QUIZ

1. Which of the following is not part of the axial skeleton?
    a. the vertebral column
    b. the ribs
    c. the sternum
    d. the clavicle

2. True or False. (Correct if false.)
    Compact bone is concentrated in the diaphysis of a long bone while spongy bone predominates in the epiphyses.

3. The bone marking best suited for joint formation is a
    a. foramen.
    b. condyle.
    c. spine.
    d. meatus.

4. The fibrous connective tissue that surrounds bones and attaches to muscles via their tendons is part of the_____.

5. The type of cartilage whose strength and durability make it an ideal component of intervertebral discs is
    a. elastic.
    b. hyaline.
    c. fibrocartilage.

Skeletal System Overview

The skeletal system — a complex of bone and cartilage that is at once strong and lightweight — comprises the rigid framework of the body. Its varied functions include:

- structural support
- protection of internal organs
- leverage for body movement
- storage of calcium and other minerals
- housing for blood-forming (hemopoietic) tissue

The bones — and to a lesser extent, cartilages — connect to one another at joints, or **articulations**. The skeleton consists of two divisions: the **axial** and **appendicular skeletons** (Figure 5-1). The axial skeleton includes the skull, vertebral column, and rib cage and forms the body's axis of support. The upper appendicular skeleton consists of the pectoral (shoulder) girdles and upper limbs. The lower division consists of the pelvic girdles (hip bones) and lower limbs. The girdles secure the limbs to the axial skeleton and, in the shoulder region, provide mobility. As you study skeletal anatomy, note how form — a framework of strong, interlocking bones — follows function: protection of internal organs while allowing us to freely move about the planet.

Cartilages of the Skeleton

Most of the cartilage found in our fetal and childhood skeleton is replaced with bone tissue by adulthood. The cartilage that remains includes:

- **articular cartilage:** Hyaline cartilage persists where bones unite to form movable joints.
- **costal cartilage:** Hyaline cartilage acts as a go-between the ribs and sternum (breastbone) to add greater flexibility during breathing.
- **meniscal cartilage:** These crescent-shaped fibrocartilaginous pads, the **menisci**, provide shock absorption within the knee joint.
- **intervertebral discs:** These oval pads are enclosed in fibrocartilage and separate and cushion vertebrae (backbones) in the spine.

Classification of Bones

Bones of the adult skeleton are classified into **compact (cortical) bone** and **spongy (cancellous) bone.** Compact bone is the denser, heavier form that covers the outside of all bones and comprises most of the shaft of long bones. Its concentration in the shaft of thigh and leg bones, for example, endows them with resistance to stress from torsion and weight bearing. (*Torsion* is a force that tends to twist the shaft around its long axis.)

Spongy bone is found at the ends of long bones (and to a small degree within their marrow cavities) and is the major component of the interior of other bone types. Its architecture is a complex of tiny bars and struts — the **trabeculae**. While seemingly random, trabeculae are oriented along lines of stress and comprise a highly effective weight-bearing infrastructure. The spaces within spongy bone store red marrow.

Bones are also classified according to their shape: long, short, flat, and irregular. Sesamoid bones constitute a special fifth category (Figure 5-2).

- **Long bones** have greater length than diameter and consist of a shaft, or **diaphysis**, and an **epiphysis** at either end. The shaft is slightly curved to evenly distribute body weight and better absorb its forces. Long bones include the humerus (arm bone), the ulna and radius (forearm bones), the femur (thighbone) and the tibia and fibula (leg bones).

- **Short bones** have nearly the same length and width. A thin layer of compact bone surrounds a spongy bone interior, as in the carpals (wrist bones) and most tarsals (ankle bones).

- **Flat bones** are relatively thin for their length with spongy bone sandwiched between two thin plates of compact bone. Examples of flat bones — and their protective nature — are the cranial bones that create a vault around the brain, and the ribs and sternum, which safeguard organs within the thorax.

- **Irregular bones** are those with variable shapes that do not fall into the previous categories. Examples include the vertebrae, the hip bones, and the calcaneus (heel bone).

- **Sesamoid bones** are formed in tendons prone to mechanical stress (as in the soles of the feet). They are usually small (several millimeters in diameter) and unnamed. The notable exceptions are the patellae (kneecaps), which protect the knee and confer a mechanical advantage to movements at the knee joint.

Axial

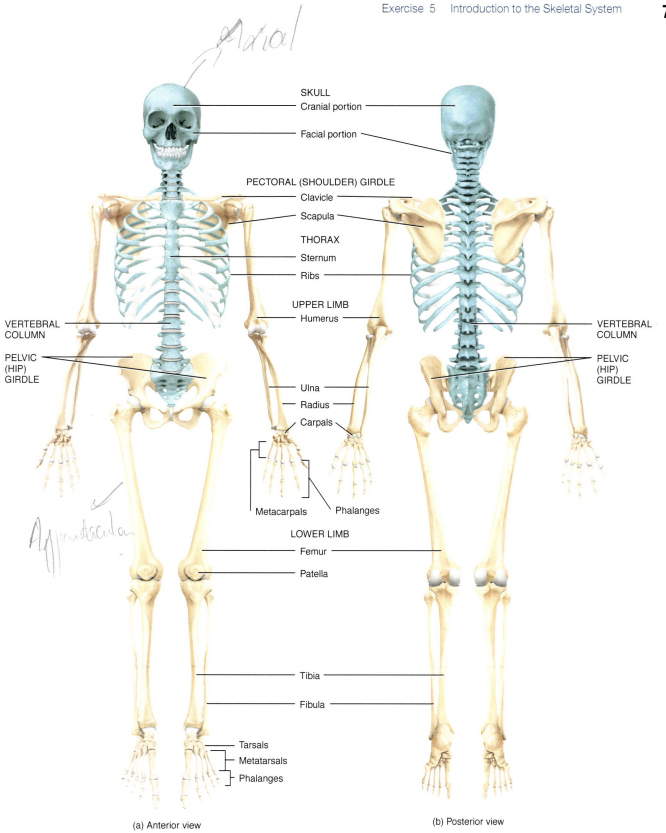

SKULL
Cranial portion
Facial portion

PECTORAL (SHOULDER) GIRDLE
Clavicle
Scapula
THORAX
Sternum
Ribs

UPPER LIMB
Humerus

VERTEBRAL
COLUMN

PELVIC
(HIP)
GIRDLE

VERTEBRAL
COLUMN

PELVIC
(HIP)
GIRDLE

Ulna
Radius
Carpals

Appendicular

Metacarpals   Phalanges

LOWER LIMB
Femur
Patella

Tibia

Fibula

Tarsals
Metatarsals
Phalanges

(a) Anterior view

(b) Posterior view

FIGURE 5-1. Axial and appendicular divisions of the skeletal system. The axial skeleton is indicated in blue.

Proximal → closer to the origin.
distal → away from the origin.

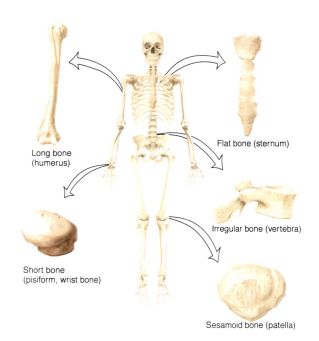

Long bone
(humerus)

Short bone
(pisiform, wrist bone)

Flat bone (sternum)

Irregular bone (vertebra)

Sesamoid bone (patella)

FIGURE 5-2. Bone classification based on shape. (The bones are not drawn to scale.)

Identification of Bone Markings

Bone markings, such as holes, cavities, projections and other surface features, are described in Table 5-1. Many bony projections — known as **processes** — are part of our surface anatomy and can be felt beneath the skin. Examination of surface anatomy with the hands is referred to as **palpation**. Palpate whenever possible to reinforce your understanding of human skeletal anatomy.

Gross Anatomy of a Long Bone

A sectioned long bone, such as a humerus or femur, is a study in functional anatomy. The shape of bones, as well as the balance of spongy to compact tissue, allow bones to effectively fill their functional niche.

Marking	Description
Processes (Projections)	
Processes that form joints:	
Condyle	A usually rounded, knoblike enlargement at an articular end
Head	An enlarged, rounded articular projection set apart from the shaft by a narrower portion (neck)
Facet	A nearly flat articular surface
Processes that attach to ligaments and tendons:	
Tuberosity	A large, usually roughened projection
Trochanter	A large, blunt projection (found only on the femur)
Tubercle	A small, somewhat rounded process
Epicondyle	A projection lying above a condyle or similar process
Crest	A prominent ridge
Line	A slight ridge
Spinous process (spine)	A usually sharp, slender process
Depressions	
Fossa	A basin-like depression
Groove (sulcus)	A furrow designed to accommodate a soft-tissue structure, such as a blood vessel
Notch	An indentation near the edge of a bone
Openings	
Foramen	A hole designed to admit blood vessels or nerves; plural: foramina
Meatus	A tubelike passageway
Sinus	An air-filled cavity lined with a mucus-secreting membrane. Sinuses also lighten the skull.

TABLE 5-1. A Summary of Bone Markings

PROCEDURE 1

1. Obtain an adult human long bone that has been sawed longitudinally from end to end. A fresh butcher bone, if available, will complement the human bone and include cartilage and other connective tissues missing from a dry specimen. (Always use examination gloves when handling fresh material.)

2. Note the **epiphyses**, one at each end, that are sculpted to articulate to other bones (Figure 5-3a). Beneath a thin veneer of compact bone in the epiphysis lies a spongy bone interior. Note the **trabeculae** which form the bulk of the epiphyseal anatomy.

The fresh bone will contain **red marrow**, blood-forming tissue in the spaces of epiphyseal spongy bone. The fresh preparation also retains the **articular cartilage** that caps each epiphysis.

3. The **metaphysis** is the region between the epiphysis and shaft, or **diaphysis**. During the growth years, each metaphysis is bordered by an **epiphyseal growth plate**. This disk of hyaline cartilage is where the diaphysis grows in length. Once the bone reaches its maximum length, the growth plate is replaced by an **epiphyseal line** (Figure 5-3a and b). This usually occurs by age 18, but lengthwise growth may continue until age 21.

4. Focus now on the diaphysis, the relatively long shaft that is predominantly compact bone. Almost all the spongy bone that formed in the center of the diaphysis during its early development has been removed by osteoclasts (bone matrix-dissolving cells) in favor of a **medullary (marrow) cavity**. The fresh specimen will contain **yellow marrow**, a reserve of adipose tissue.

5. On the surface of the fresh bone, note the tough, fibrous **periosteum**, whose outer layer anchors tendons and thereby transmits the force of skeletal muscle contraction to the bone. If permissible, peel back a small section of periosteum to reveal its fibrous nature. Note that the periosteum does not extend to the articular surface of the epiphyses.

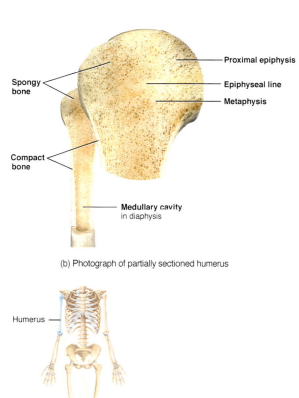

Articular cartilage

Spongy bone (contains red bone marrow)

Proximal epiphysis

Metaphysis

Epiphyseal line

Compact bone

Endosteum (lines medullary cavity)

Nutrient artery

Diaphysis

Medullary (marrow) cavity (contains yellow bone marrow in adults)

Periosteum

Metaphysis

Distal epiphysis

Articular cartilage

(a) Partially sectioned humerus (arm bone)

Spongy bone

Proximal epiphysis

Epiphyseal line

Metaphysis

Compact bone

Medullary cavity in diaphysis

(b) Photograph of partially sectioned humerus

Humerus

FIGURE 5-3. Parts of a long bone, the humerus.

Microscopic Anatomy of Bone

Compact Bone. To the naked eye, compact bone appears uniformly dense. Microscopic examination tells a different story: a landscape of repeating cavity-filled **osteons**. Osteons are structural subunits of compact bone. Within the osteons are tiny chambers that house bone cells. These cells are serviced by a system of minute canals that convey blood vessels (central canals) and tissue fluid (canaliculi).Within each **osteon** (Figure 5-4a) are:

- **lacunae**, the bubble-like chambers that contain mature bone cells called **osteocytes**.
- **canaliculi**, the thread-like passageways that ferry tissue fluid to nourish osteocytes. Within the canaliculi, the cytoplasmic processes of the osteocytes interconnect, increasing their total surface area and facilitating the flow of mineral ions (such as calcium) between the extracellular fluid and bone matrix.
- **a central canal**, which contains blood vessels (along with lymphatics and nerves). The blood vessels supply tissue fluid to the canaliculi, which radiate from the central canal like spokes of a wheel.
- **concentric lamellae**, circular plates of extracellular matrix that resemble the growth rings of a tree. They add considerable strength to bone tissue.
- **circumferential lamellae,** found at the outer and inner borders of compact bone.
- **interstitial lamellae,** which represent areas where bone has been replaced by newer bone growth.

Other key features of compact bone include the:

- **periosteum**, a dense, vascular collagenous connective tissue that is protective and, as previously noted, attaches to tendons. The inner osteogenic layer contains **osteoblasts**, young bone-forming cells that secrete an osseous matrix, and **osteoclasts** that secrete enzymes to break down bone tissue during remodeling. The periosteum is secured to the bone surface by collagenous **perforating (Sharpey's) fibers.**
- **perforating canals**, located perpendicular to the osteon, and which convey blood vessels from the periosteum.

Spongy Bone. Spongy bone is lattice-like in appearance, with its trabeculae and the spaces between them large enough to be grossly visible (Figure 5-4b). Under the microscope, the trabeculae evidence lamellae, lacunae, canaliculi, osteocytes, but no osteons.

PROCEDURE 2

Comparison of Compact and Spongy Bone

Obtain slides of compact and spongy bone tissue. Identify lacunae, canaliculi, and concentric lamellae in both samples. Note the trabecular pattern in spongy bone and the osteons in compact bone. Sketch your observations below. (The compact bone slide in most cases is a dry ground specimen whose lacunae no longer contain osteocytes.)

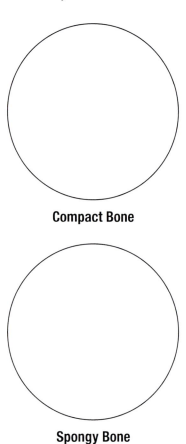

Compact Bone

Spongy Bone

Chemical Components of Bone Tissue

Adult bone tissue is about 65% inorganic salts. These calcium compounds confer hardness, a characteristic which resists compression.

The organic constituents are the osteocytes and collagen fibers. The collagen is necessary for the deposition of calcium salts and gives bone added strength. Although collagen fibers themselves are inelastic, they confer flexibility ("give") to ensure bones are not easily broken. *Analogy: Collagen fibers are to bone as steel rods are to reinforced concrete.*

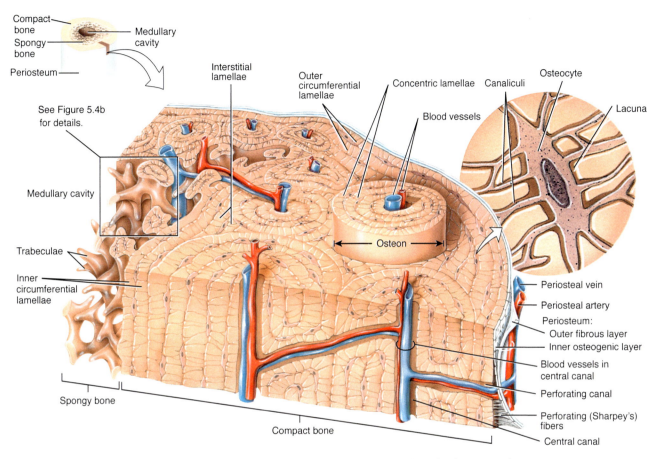

Compact bone
Spongy bone
Periosteum
Medullary cavity

See Figure 5.4b for details.

Medullary cavity

Trabeculae

Inner circumferential lamellae

Spongy bone

Compact bone

Interstitial lamellae

Outer circumferential lamellae

Concentric lamellae

Blood vessels

Osteon

Canaliculi

Osteocyte

Lacuna

Periosteal vein
Periosteal artery
Periosteum:
 Outer fibrous layer
 Inner osteogenic layer
Blood vessels in central canal
Perforating canal
Perforating (Sharpey's) fibers
Central canal

(a) Osteons (Haversian systems) in compact bone and trabeculae in spongy bone

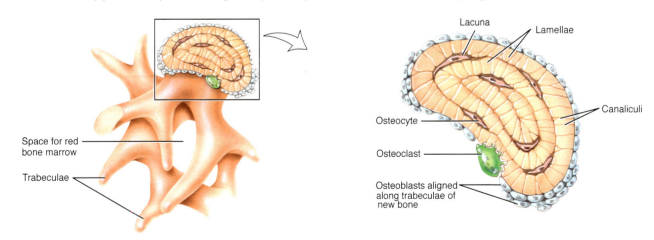

Space for red bone marrow

Trabeculae

(b) Enlarged aspect of spongy bone trabeculae

Lacuna
Lamellae
Canaliculi
Osteocyte
Osteoclast
Osteoblasts aligned along trabeculae of new bone

(c) Details of a section of a trabecula

FIGURE 5-4. Histology of compact and spongy bone.

PROCEDURE 3

Organic and inorganic components of bone are uniformly integrated. Baked and acid-treated bones that selectively remove organic and inorganic components, respectively, outwardly appear no different from untreated bones. Their physical characteristics, however, are markedly different as you will see in this exercise.

1. Don examination gloves and obtain an untreated long bone from a chicken (or other source). For this and all specimens to follow, grab both ends and gently bend the specimen.

2. Obtain a chicken bone baked in an oven for several hours to remove all organic components.
What do you notice about the consistency of a baked bone compared to the untreated specimen?

_____

_____

3. Obtain a chicken bone soaked in acetic acid.
What do you notice about the consistency of an acid-treated bone?

_____

_____

In conclusion, what are the physical characteristics conferred by organic and inorganic constituents of bone tissue?

Organic: _____

_____

_____

_____

_____

Inorganic: _____

_____

_____

_____

_____

Clinical Application
Osteoporosis

With advancing age — and decreased hormone secretion and physical activity — comes a greater risk for osteoporosis. The hallmark of this condition is progressively weakened bones whose organic and inorganic components have been diminished.

Note the comparison between the normal and osteoporotic electron micrographs below. With the loss of bone mass, the spongy architecture of the osteoporotic bone appears more "porous" than that of the normal specimen.

From a medical perspective, there is a clear correlation between osteoporosis and a greater incidence of traumatic and spontaneous fractures.

Normal Bone   **Osteoporotic Bone**

Introduction to the Skeletal System

NAME _____

LAB TIME/DATE _____

Cartilages of the Skeleton

Enter the letter of the matching cartilage in the space to the left of the statement indicating where it is found.

Key: A = hyaline cartilage; B = elastic cartilage; C = fibrocartilage

_____ 1. intervertebral disks

_____ 2. articular surfaces of movable joints

_____ 3. menisci

_____ 4. between ribs and sternum

Classification of Bones

Match the bone with its shape name.

_____ 1. femur

_____ 2. rib

_____ 3. vertebra

_____ 4. patella

_____ 5. wrist bone

_____ 6. sternum

_____ 7. radius

_____ 8. calcaneus

a. short

b. irregular

c. long

d. flat

e. sesamoid

Bone Markings

Match the bone marking on the left to its description on the right.

_____ 1.   fossa   a. a prominent ridge

_____ 2.   foramen   b. a hole for nerves and vessels

_____ 3.   spinous process   c. a knuckle-like articular surface

_____ 4.   condyle   d. a usually sharp, slender projection

_____ 5.   crest   e. a depression

Microscopic Anatomy of Bone

Enter the numbers of the structures listed beneath the illustration.

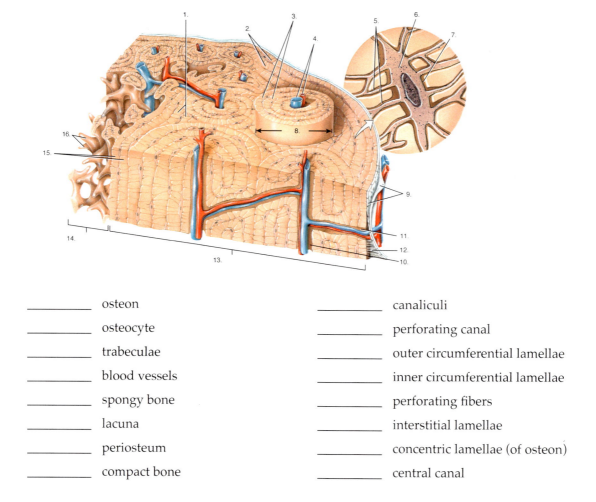

_____ osteon   _____ canaliculi

_____ osteocyte   _____ perforating canal

_____ trabeculae   _____ outer circumferential lamellae

_____ blood vessels   _____ inner circumferential lamellae

_____ spongy bone   _____ perforating fibers

_____ lacuna   _____ interstitial lamellae

_____ periosteum   _____ concentric lamellae (of osteon)

_____ compact bone   _____ central canal

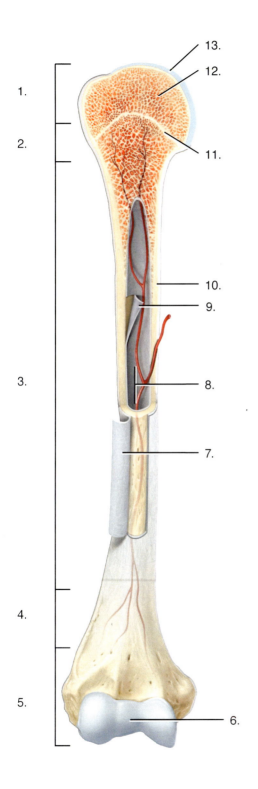

13.

12.

1.

2.

11.

10.

9.

3.

8.

7.

4.

5.

6.

Parts of a Long Bone

_12_	spongy bone
_7_	endosteum
_10_	compact bone
_3_	diaphysis
_8_	medullary (marrow) cavity
_11_	epiphyseal line
_9_	periosteum
_1, 5_	epiphysis (2 places)
_13, 6_	articular cartilage (2 places)
_2, 4_	metaphysis (2 places)

Critical Thinking

1. Bones are marvels of human engineering. The distribution of compact and spongy bone is ideally balanced to ensure that form follows function.

   Imagine if long bones, such as the femur or tibia, were composed only of compact bone tissue. What functional compromises would result?

   _____

   _____

   _____

   _____

2. Are these the x-rayed bones of an adult or adolescent? Justify your answer.

   _____

   _____

   _____

   _____

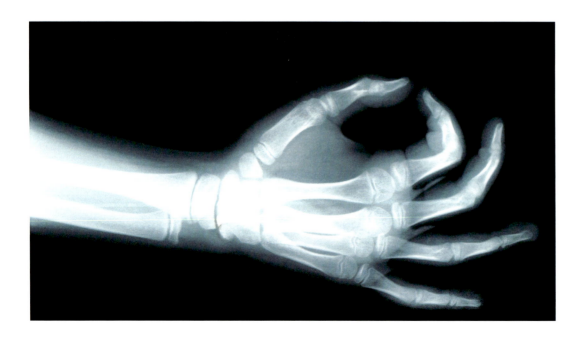

The Axial Skeleton

OBJECTIVES

1. To identify the bones comprising the skull, vertebral column, and thorax of the adult axial skeleton.
2. To name the markings on each axial bone.
3. To distinguish among the various types of vertebrae.
4. To identify the spinal curvatures and name three types of abnormal curvatures.

MATERIALS

Articulated skeletons
Articulated and Beauchene (exploded) skulls
Articulated vertebral column

Isolated cervical, thoracic, and lumbar vertebrae, sacrum, and coccyx
X rays of the axial skeleton (optional)
X rays of abnormal spinal curvatures (optional)

PRE-LAB QUIZ

1. The axial skeleton includes the vertebral column, bony thorax, and
    a. shoulder bones.
    b. hip bones.
    c. cranial bones.
    d. thigh bones.

2. The central portion of a vertebra that directly faces the anterior side of the spinal column is the
    a. spinous process.
    b. body.
    c. articular process.
    d. vertebral arch.

3. True or False. Intervertebral disks have a tough external ring-like layer of hyaline cartilage. _F_

4. The ___Cervic___ vertebrae contain flat articular surfaces known as facets to facilitate attachment to the ribs.

5. The mandible articulates to the _____ bone to form the only movable joint of the skull.
    a. temporal
    b. zygomatic
    c. lumbar
    d. Both a and b are correct.

The axial skeleton is protective of the vital organs and serves as attachment points for the limbs. It is comprised of the skull, vertebral column, and thorax (the thoracic or rib cage). There are 80 axial bones, which are highlighted in blue in Figure 5-1 on page 77.

PROCEDURE 1

Identification of Skull Bones

The Skull

The skull is divided into the **cranium** — designed to protect the delicate tissues of the brain and eye and attach to muscles that move the head — and the **face**. The facial bones protect the eye and enable mastication and facial expression through their attachment to skeletal muscles. Facial anatomy also provides openings to the respiratory and digestive systems.

The bones of the skull are fused together by fixed interlocking joints, or **sutures**, with one exception: The mandible (lower jaw) is attached by a pair of freely movable joints.

The Cranium

The cranium is divided into the **cranial vault** — comprising the walls of the skull — and the **cranial floor**, or **base**. The cranial floor has three recesses within which the brain lies: the **anterior, middle**, and **posterior fossae**.

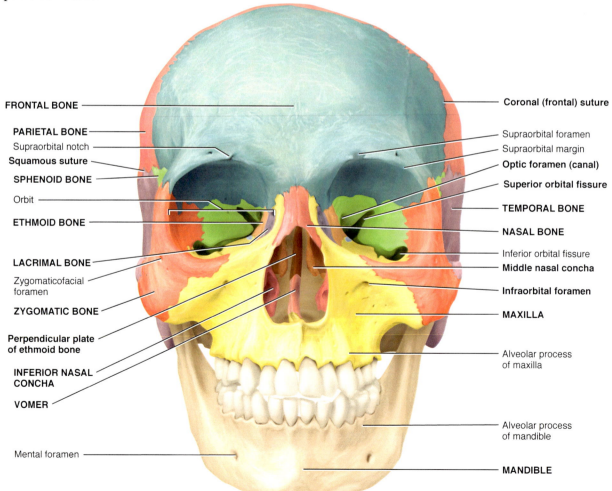

FRONTAL BONE

PARIETAL BONE
Supraorbital notch
Squamous suture
SPHENOID BONE
Orbit
ETHMOID BONE

LACRIMAL BONE
Zygomaticofacial foramen
ZYGOMATIC BONE

Perpendicular plate of ethmoid bone
INFERIOR NASAL CONCHA
VOMER

Mental foramen

Coronal (frontal) suture
Supraorbital foramen
Supraorbital margin
Optic foramen (canal)
Superior orbital fissure
TEMPORAL BONE
NASAL BONE
Inferior orbital fissure
Middle nasal concha
Infraorbital foramen
MAXILLA
Alveolar process of maxilla
Alveolar process of mandible
MANDIBLE

FIGURE 6-1. Anterior view of the skull.

The eight individual cranial bones and their principal markings are:

Frontal Bone
A single bone that forms the
- forehead
- upper margin of the **orbit** (eye socket)
- floor of the anterior cranial fossa (Figures 6-1, 6-2 and 6-4.)

Parietal Bone
One of a pair of bones that forms the lateral wall of the cranium posterior to the frontal bone.
- The **sagittal suture** joins the two parietal bones in the midline of the skull (Figure 6-3).
- The **coronal suture** unites the parietals with the frontal bone (Figure 6-2).

Temporal Bone
One of a pair of irregular (although mostly flat) bones of the lateral wall of the skull behind the orbits and inferior to the parietal bone. Each temporal bone is subdivided into a **squamous region** adjacent to the parietal bone, the **tympanic region** surrounding the external ear opening, the **mastoid region** just behind the tympanic region, and the **petrous region** that forms the lateral portion of the cranial floor (Figures 6-2 and 6-4). Squamous region markings include:

- the **squamous suture** at the junction with the parietal bone.
- the **mandibular fossa**, a depression that joins with the **mandible** on each side to form the only movable articulation as is in the skull: the **temporomandibular joint.**
- the **zygomatic process**, a sharply pointed projection that fuses to the **zygomatic (cheek) bone** to form the bridge-like **zygomatic arch**.

Tympanic region markings include the:
- **external auditory meatus**, a canal that conducts sound vibrations to the tympanic membrane (eardrum) and middle ear.
- **styloid process**, a sharply pointed projection below the external auditory meatus that attaches to neck muscles.

The tympanic region also includes tiny middle-ear bones that transmit sound vibrations from the tympanic membrane to the internal ear, the **auditory ossicles**: the **malleus**, **incus**, and **stapes**.

Mastoid region markings include the:
- **mastoid process**, a nipple-shaped projection posterior and inferior to the external acoustic meatus. It attaches to muscles that rotate the head. *Palpation: Place an index finger just medial to your earlobe.*

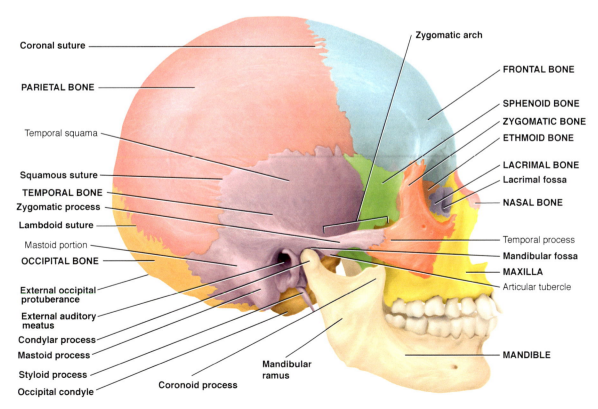

FIGURE 6-2. Right lateral view of the skull.

Petrous region markings include the:
- **internal acoustic meatus**. This opening permits the passage of cranial nerves (VII and VIII) (Figures 6-4 and 6-6).
- **jugular foramen**. An opening medial to the styloid process named for the internal jugular vein passing through it, it also accommodates cranial nerves (IX, X, and XI) (Figure 6-4).
- **carotid foramen** (canal), an opening medial to the styloid process. It is named for the internal carotid artery passing through it (Figure 6-6).

Occipital Bone

A single bone that forms part of the posterior wall and base of the skull (Figures 6-3 and 6-4). Locate the
- **external occipital protuberance**, a muscle attachment site.

Palpation: Slide the middle and index fingers upward along the midline of your neck until you feel a bony "overhang".

- **foramen magnum**, a large circular opening on the inferior aspect through which the spinal cord passes from the base of the brain (Figures 6-4 and 6-6).
- **occipital condyles**, a pair of rounded processes that straddle the foramen magnum and articulate the skull to the first cervical vertebra (Figure 6-6).

- **lambdoid suture**, the union of the occipital and parietal bones that is shaped like the Greek letter lambda (Figure 6-3).

Sphenoid Bone

A single compound bone at the base of the cranium toward the anterior side. *The sphenoid articulates to all other cranial bones and is therefore known as the keystone of the cranium.* Find the:
- **optic foramina** (**canals**), openings for the two optic nerves visible in the back wall of the orbits (Figure 6-1 and 6-4b).
- **greater wings**, which form the lateral and posterior walls of the orbit. The lateral portion can be seen on both sides of the skull just anterior to the temporal bones. Within each greater wing is a **foramen ovale** through which a cranial nerve (V) passes (Figures 6-4a and 6-6).
- **lesser wings**, anterior and lateral to the sella turcica. They contain the optic foramina (Figure 6-4b).
- **sella turcica**, named for its resemblance to a Turkish saddle. Its **hypophyseal fossa** is a depression that houses the hypophysis, a synonym for the pituitary gland (Figure 6-4a).

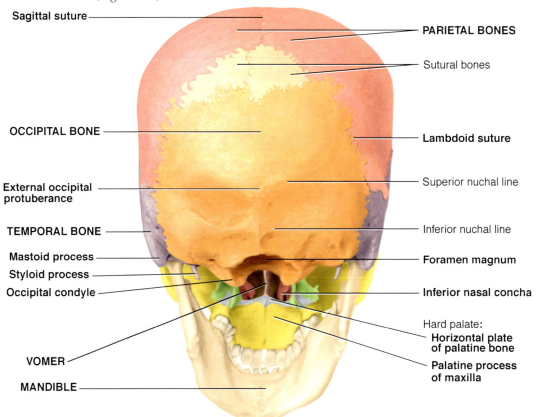

Sagittal suture — PARIETAL BONES

Sutural bones

OCCIPITAL BONE — Lambdoid suture

External occipital protuberance — Superior nuchal line

TEMPORAL BONE — Inferior nuchal line

Mastoid process — Foramen magnum

Styloid process

Occipital condyle — Inferior nasal concha

Hard palate:
Horizontal plate of palatine bone

VOMER — Palatine process of maxilla

MANDIBLE

Posteroinferior view

FIGURE 6-3. Posterior view of the skull.

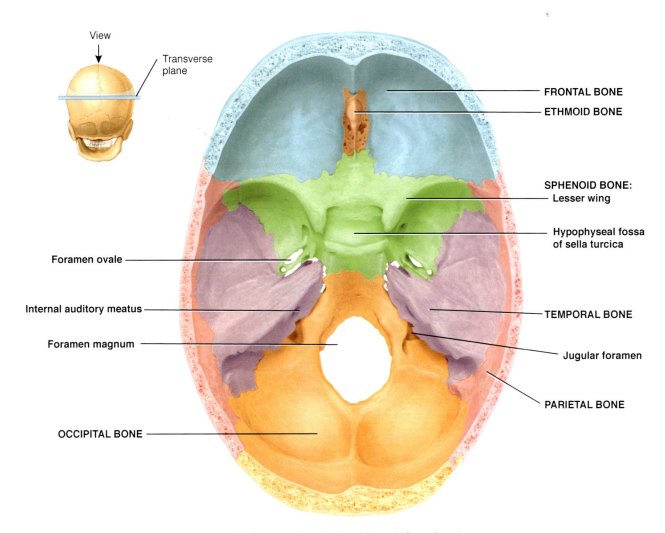

View

Transverse plane

FRONTAL BONE

ETHMOID BONE

SPHENOID BONE:
Lesser wing

Hypophyseal fossa
of sella turcica

Foramen ovale

Internal auditory meatus

Foramen magnum

TEMPORAL BONE

Jugular foramen

PARIETAL BONE

OCCIPITAL BONE

(a) Superior view of sphenoid bone in floor of cranium

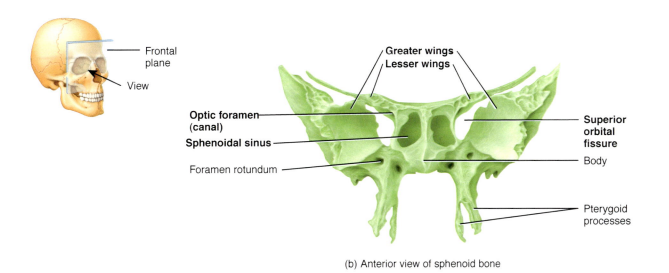

Frontal plane

View

Greater wings

Lesser wings

Optic foramen
(canal)

Sphenoidal sinus

Foramen rotundum

Superior orbital fissure

Body

Pterygoid processes

(b) Anterior view of sphenoid bone

FIGURE 6-4. The sphenoid bone.

- **superior orbital fissure**, an irregular opening between the greater and lesser wings that allows passage of cranial nerves (III, IV, V, and VI) to and from the eye (Figures 6-1 and 6-4b).

Ethmoid Bone

An irregular bone in the midline of the skull located in the anterior region of the cranial floor (Figure 6-5). It lies anterior to the sphenoid bone. Note the

- **perpendicular plate**, which forms the superior portion of the bony nasal septum.
- **cribriform plate**, which forms the roof of the nasal

cavity and is perforated by **olfactory foramina** to enable nerve endings for the sense of smell to reach the brain.

- **crista galli**, an anchor point for a membrane that protects the brain. It projects vertically from the center of the cribriform plate.
- **middle and superior conchae** (KON-kee, plural, KON-ka, singular), bones shaped like conch sea shells located on the lateral walls of the nasal cavity. The conchae, like the entire nasal cavity, are draped with mucous membrane. They enhance the warming, humidifying, and cleansing of inhaled air by increasing the surface area to which air is exposed.

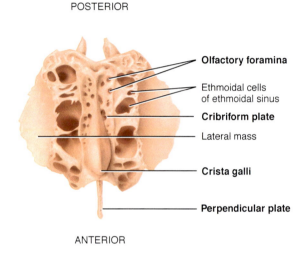

POSTERIOR

- Olfactory foramina
- Ethmoidal cells of ethmoidal sinus
- Cribriform plate
- Lateral mass
- Crista galli
- Perpendicular plate

ANTERIOR

(a) Superior view of isolated ethmoid bone

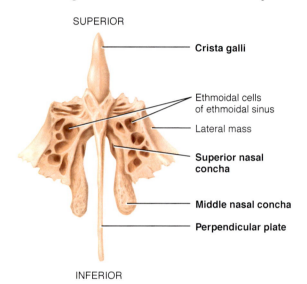

SUPERIOR

- Crista galli
- Ethmoidal cells of ethmoidal sinus
- Lateral mass
- Superior nasal concha
- Middle nasal concha
- Perpendicular plate

INFERIOR

(b) Anterior view of isolated ethmoid bone

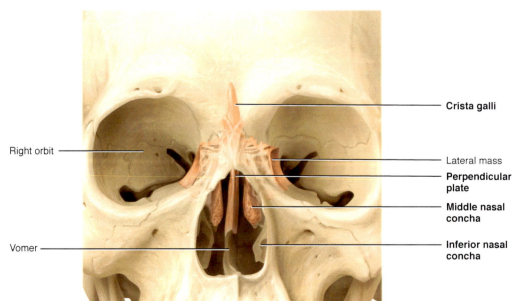

Crista galli

Right orbit

Lateral mass

Perpendicular plate

Middle nasal concha

Inferior nasal concha

Vomer

(c) Anterior view of position of ethmoid bone in skull (projected to the surface)

FIGURE 6-5. The ethmoid bone.

Facial Bones

There are 14 facial bones, six of which are paired. Though not a facial bone, the hyoid bone in the neck region is usually presented with facial anatomy.

Maxillae

The two **maxillae** (max-ILL-ee), or maxillary bones (Figures 6-1 and 6-2), are the keystones of the face: They articulate to all other facial bones with the exception of the lower jaw. The midline suture where the maxillae are fused can be seen in the roof of the mouth.

Locate the:
- **palatine processes**, the part of each maxilla that forms the anterior portion of the hard palate (Figure 6-6).
- **alveoli** (al-VEE-uh-lye), the tooth sockets, which are arranged as the upper dental arch. There are 16 teeth in a complete upper set (Figure 6-6).

- **infraorbital foramen**, an opening beneath each eye socket for blood vessels and nerves supplying the nasal region (Figure 6-1).

Palatine Bones

The paired **palatine** (PAL-uh-tyne) bones make up the posterior portion of the hard palate. They also contribute to the floor of the nasal cavity and a small part of the orbit (Figure 6-6).

Zygomatic Bones

The **zygomatic bones**, or cheekbones (Figures 6-1), are lateral to the maxillae and anterior to the temporal bones. Besides their prominent role in determining facial appearance, they form the lateral margin of the orbit. Recall that the zygomatic bone articulates with the temporal bone to form the **zygomatic arch** (Figures 6-2 and 6-6).

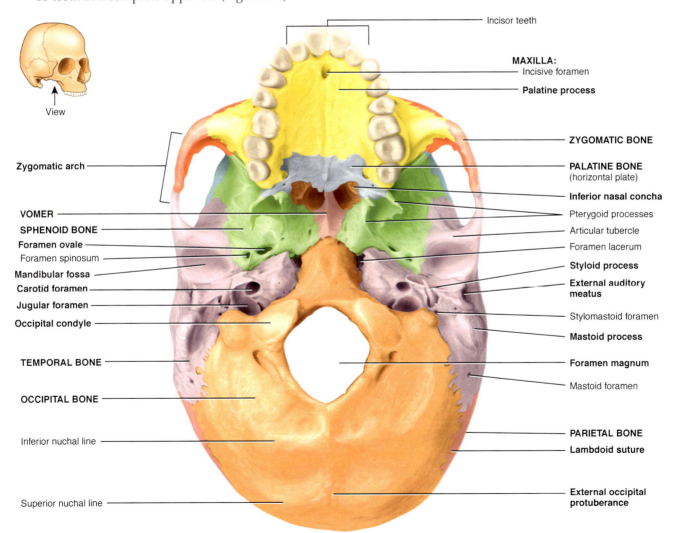

FIGURE 6-6. Inferior view of the skull.

Mandible

The **mandible**, or lower jaw, is the largest and strongest bone of the face (Figure 6-1, 6-2 and 6-9). Identify the:

- **condylar** (KON-dih-lar) **processes**, also known as the **mandibular condyles** (Figure 6-2). These are convex projections on the posterior ends that articulate with each temporal bone to form the temporomandibular joint. Abbreviated TMJ, it is the only movable joint of the skull.
  Palpation: Gently, but snugly, place your pinky finger into the external auditory meatus. Lower and raise the mandible to feel the action of the temporomandibular joint.
- **body**, the horizontal portion, the anterior region of which forms the chin. (Curiously, the anatomical adjective pertaining to the chin is *mental*.)
- **mandibular ramus** (RAY-mus), the upward extension of the body on either side (Figure 6-2).
- **coronoid** (KOR-uh-noyd) **process**, a thin wave-shaped projection anterior to the condylar process (Figure 6-2). It is a muscle attachment site.
- **alveoli**, the tooth sockets of the lower dental arch. There are 16 teeth in a complete lower set (Figures 6-1 and 6-2).

Lacrimal Bones

The thinnest bone of the face, each **lacrimal** (LAK-rih-mul) helps form the medial wall of the orbit between the maxilla and the ethmoid bone. Identify the:

- **nasolacrimal fossa**, which in life contains the nasolacrimal duct that tunnels into the nasal cavity, draining tears from the eye (*lacrima* = tear). (Figures 6-1 and 6-2).

Vomer

The **vomer** (VOE-mur), a triangular bone named for its resemblance to a plowshare, comprises the inferior portion of the nasal septum. It articulates with the perpendicular plate of the ethmoid above and the maxillae below where they meet in the midline. The nasal cavity is thus divided into two chambers (Figures 6-1 and 6-5).

Nasal Bones

The paired nasal bones (Figures 6-1 and 6-2) are roughly rectangular bones situated on either side of the midline at the nose's superior margin. Variable in size and form — they may be flattened, concave, or convex — the nasal bones form and define the "bridge" of the nose. Most of the external nasal anatomy consists of subcutaneous cartilage. (Note the nasal cartilage in Figure 6-8b depicted in light blue.)

Inferior Nasal Conchae

The **inferior nasal conchae** are a pair of bones inferior to the middle conchae of the ethmoid. The inferior conchae duplicate the function of other conchae: They increase surface area and the efficiency of conditioning the airstream within the nasal cavity. (The conchae are also known as the **turbinates**.) (Figures 6-1 and 6-5.)

Hyoid

The **hyoid** is a U-shaped bone designed to support the tongue and other muscles of the throat region. It is customarily included among the skull bones, but has no articulation to any other bone.
Palpation: Encircle your larynx with your thumb and index finger and slide upward until your fingers naturally come to rest at the base of the mandible. Squeeze medially.

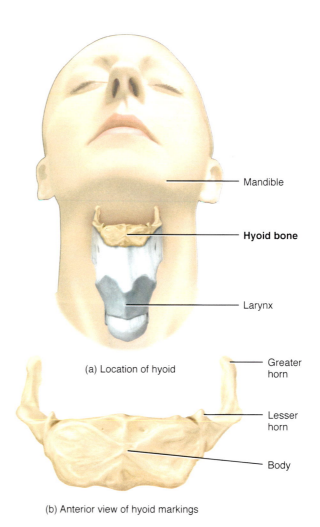

(a) Location of hyoid

— Mandible

— **Hyoid bone**

— Larynx

— Greater horn

— Lesser horn

— Body

(b) Anterior view of hyoid markings

FIGURE 6-7. The hyoid bone.

Paranasal Sinuses

Four of the skull bones — the ethmoid, sphenoid, maxillary, and frontal — contain **paranasal sinuses**, air-filled cavities that lighten the skull and make the voice more resonant. Note the largest sinuses are in the maxillae.

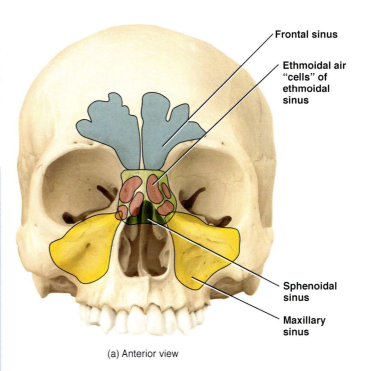

Clinical Application
Sinusitis

The sinuses are lined with mucous membrane that is continuous with that of the nasal chamber. Bacterial infections of the nose can thus spread to the sinuses, causing *sinusitis*. This condition is characterized by membrane swelling and accumulation of mucus, both of which may block the passageways leading out of the sinus cavity. This sets the stage for a headache near the inflamed sinus. In severe cases, surgical intervention widens the narrowed path from sinus to nasal cavity to promote drainage of excess mucus and infectious fluid. This procedure will also reduce the risk for future occurrences.

(a) Anterior view

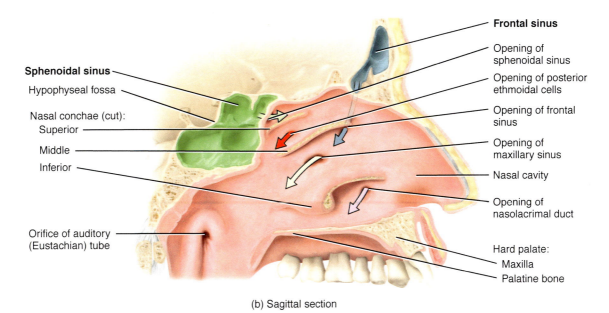

(b) Sagittal section

FIGURE 6-8. The paranasal sinuses.

Refer to the disarticulated skull on the demo table to review individual skull bones in a unique configuration (Figure 6-9). (Given the delicate arrangement of these bones, ask your instructor for assistance.)

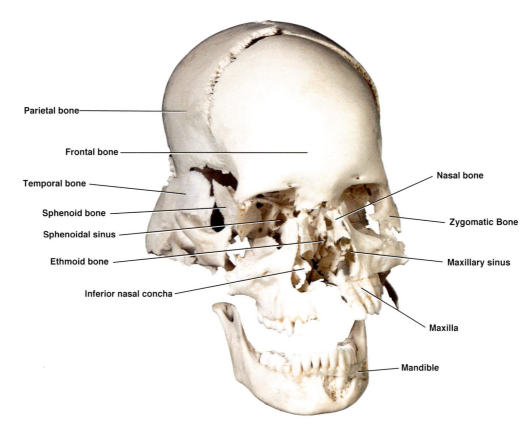

FIGURE 6-9. Anterior lateral view of a disarticulated (Beauchene) skull.

The Fetal Skull

The skull of an embryo is composed of cartilage and mesenchyme (embryonic connective tissue). During the fetal period — from the third through ninth months of pregnancy — ossification replaces much of the embryonic skull, but is incomplete at birth. Persisting between nascent skull bones are fibrous membranes derived from the mesenchyme. These "soft spots" are known as **fontanels** (fon-tuh-NELZ) (Figure 6-10). Fontanels are critically important for two reasons: They (1) provide flexibility during the skull's passage through the birth canal, and (2) allow for enlargement of the cranial bones during rapid brain growth in fetal and early postnatal life.

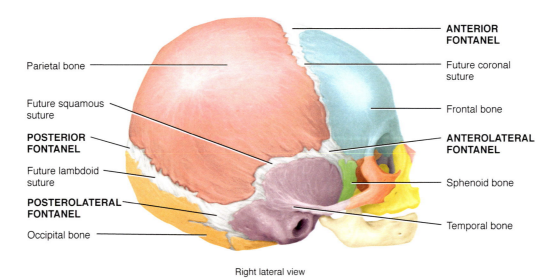

Right lateral view

FIGURE 6-10. The fetal skull, illustrating fontanels. The largest fontanel (the anterior) persists for 18 to 24 months after birth.

Obtain a model of a fetal skull and identify the fontanels and adjacent cranial bones.

The Vertebral Column

The **vertebral** or **spinal column** provides the body's principal axial support. The architecture of the vertebral column is such that body weight is distributed efficiently from the skull to the pelvis. It is a marvelously engineered series of interlocking bones that works together with muscles and ligaments to:

- support the head, upper limbs, and trunk.
- enable movement of the back in several directions.
- provide a point of attachment to the rib cage.
- protect the spinal cord.

A remarkable feature of the vertebral column is its ability to shield the delicate spinal cord while permitting a relatively wide range of motion. Think of the supple and fluid maneuvers of an Olympic gymnast to appreciate the spine's extraordinary flexibility.

The adult spine has 26 **vertebrae** (VER-tuh-bree; singular is **vertebra**) as shown in Figure 6-11. (The total during childhood is usually 33, a difference explained by the fusion of several lower vertebrae where the spine reinforces the pelvis.) The vertebrae are organized into regions as follows:

- Seven are neck, or **cervical** vertebrae (C1-C7).
- Twelve are chest-level, or **thoracic** vertebrae (T1-T12).
- Five are lower-back, or **lumbar** vertebrae (L1-L5).
- One is the **sacrum**, which consists of five fused sacral vertebrae (S).
- One is the **coccyx**, which consists of three to five, but usually four, fused coccygeal vertebrae (Co).

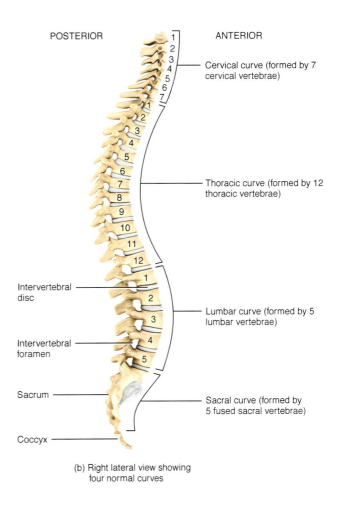

(a) Anterior view showing regions of the vertebral column

(b) Right lateral view showing four normal curves

FIGURE 6-11. The adult vertebral column.

Note: Our normal spinal curvature is far superior for weight bearing and flexibility than a straight spinal column.

Intervertebral Discs and Foramina

Intervertebral discs are found between vertebrae. These discs absorb shock and permit some degree of movement. The cushioning properties result from a gelatinous core, the **nucleus pulposus**, and a tough outer layer of fibrocartilage, the **annulus fibrosus** (Figure 6-12a). The annulus encapsulates the nucleus and maintains the integrity of the disc under mechanical stress.

A major function of intervertebral discs is to bear weight through compression — a feature that protects vertebral bone from wear-and-tear forces (Figure 6-12b). These discs also add flexibility to the spinal column.

The **intervertebral foramina** — spaces framed by a pair of adjacent vertebrae — allow for passage of the spinal nerves to and from the spinal cord.

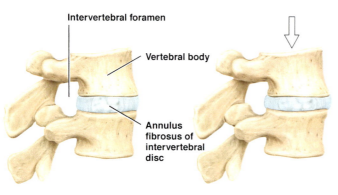

(a) Normal intervertebral disc

(b) Compressed intervertebral disc in a weight-bearing situation

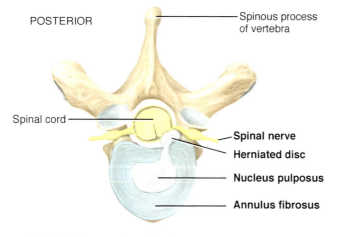

(c) A herniated intervertebral disc. Note the impingement of the disc on the root of a spinal nerve and on the cord.

FIGURE 6-12. The intervertebral disc.

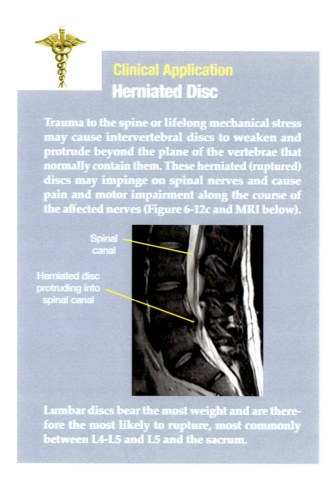

Clinical Application
Herniated Disc

Trauma to the spine or lifelong mechanical stress may cause intervertebral discs to weaken and protrude beyond the plane of the vertebrae that normally contain them. These herniated (ruptured) discs may impinge on spinal nerves and cause pain and motor impairment along the course of the affected nerves (Figure 6-12c and MRI below).

Lumbar discs bear the most weight and are therefore the most likely to rupture, most commonly between L4-L5 and L5 and the sacrum.

PROCEDURE 2

Examine a vertebral column on an articulated skeleton. Identify the cervical, thoracic, lumbar, sacral, and coccygeal regions.

In which region, cervical, thoracic, or lumbar, are the vertebrae — and discs — the largest?

_____

How does the size of a vertebra and its disc relate to the physical load it bears?

_____

_____

_____

_____

Spinal Curves

Normal Spinal Curves

The four curves of the normal spine create an S-shaped configuration (Figure 6-11b) that acts as a highly effective shock absorber.

A strictly vertical design would accelerate the degeneration of discs and vertebral bone.

At birth, there is a single curve in the vertebral column that is convex in the posterior direction (Figure 6-13a). This is the **primary curve**. As the infant begins to pick up its head at about three months, a concave curve is accentuated in the cervical region. Once the child sits up, then begins to walk, a concave lumbar curve develops. These are the **secondary curves**. Note the progression to the adult spinal curves (Figure 6-13b).

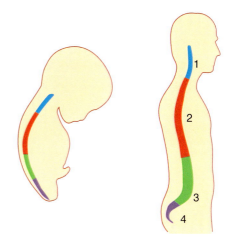

(a) Single (primary) curve in fetus.   (b) Four curves in adult.

FIGURE 6-13. Fetal and adult spinal curves.

PROCEDURE 3

Obtain an articulated vertebral column (or an entire skeleton) and study the four spinal curves. In which spinal region are there convex curves facing posteriorly?

_____

_____

Where are the curves concave posteriorly?

_____

_____

Taken as a whole, what is a key advantage of these curves?

_____

_____

curves, is a lateral bend in the vertebral column, usually in the thoracic region. Compare a normal laboratory spinal column to the abnormal curves in Figure 6-14.

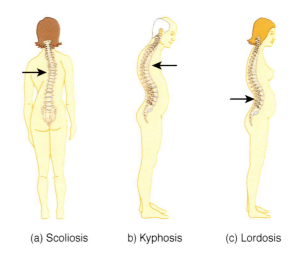

(a) Scoliosis   b) Kyphosis   (c) Lordosis

FIGURE 6-14. Abnormal spinal curves.

Abnormal Spinal Curves (Optional)

Observe X rays of abnormal spinal curves, if available. An exaggerated thoracic curve is known as **kyphosis**. The term **lordosis** refers to a greater-than-normal lumbar curve. **Scoliosis**, the most common of the abnormal

PROCEDURE 4

Structure of a Typical Vertebra

The vertebrae share several features in common (Figure 6-15): Note that a typical vertebra has a:

- **body (centrum)**: the round, spool–like central portion located on the anterior side, and a

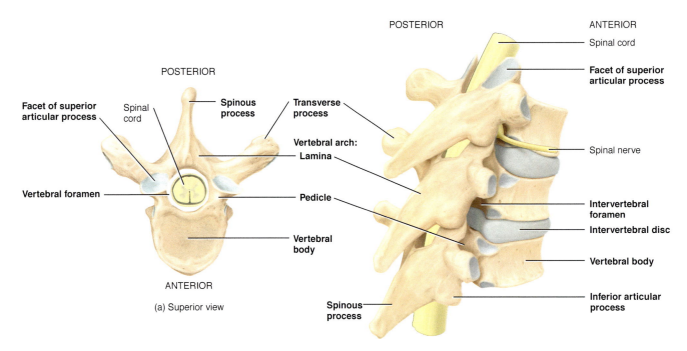

(a) Superior view

(b) Right posterolateral view of articulated vertebrae

FIGURE 6-15. Structure of a typical vertebra (a). Several articulated vertebrae are shown overlapping articular processes (b).

- **vertebral arch**: a posterior extension from the body consisting of:

  pedicles (PED-ih-kuls; *pediculus* = little foot). Two short, thick processes (right and left) that connect the arch to the body. Each has a superior and inferior notch. The notches of two adjacent vertebrae form an intervertebral foramen on either side. Through this opening pass the roots of a spinal nerve.

  laminae (LAM-uh-nee; *lamina* = thin layer). Thin, flat segments on the posterior side of the arch.

  vertebral foramen: The passageway — immediately behind the body — through which passes the spinal cord. Together, all the vertebral foramina comprise the vertebral canal.

- **processes**: Seven processes arise from the vertebral arch for muscular and articular attachments:

  spinous process (spine): A single midline projection posterior to the vertebral foramen where the laminae-unite.

  transverse processes: Two lateral projections from the vertebral arch at the junction of the laminae and pedicles.

  articular processes: Four vertical projections from the vertebral arch — two **superior articular processes** and two **inferior articular processes** — lateral to the vertebral foramen. The superior articular processes are overlapped by the inferior pair of the vertebra above. These processes form the foundation for the joints that enable the vertebral column to move back and forth and side to side. The flat joint surfaces of the articular processes are called **facets**. These facet joints are freely moveable and add considerable flexibility to the vertebral column.

As you examine each vertebra, look for anatomical features that make it ideally suited for its particular location within the spine.

Simulating Movements of the Spinal Column

Obtain a model of two vertebrae coupled to a simulated intervertebral disc from the demo table or find a pair of thoracic vertebrae from the bin of disarticulated bones. Join the free vertebrae in a way that simulates their natural relationship and place a plastic model of an intervertebral disc between the vertebral bodies.

Hold the pair at eye level with the spinous processes to your left as in Figure 6-15b. Now gently maneuver the top vertebra slightly forward and upward while holding the bottom bone steady. This simulates flexion of the vertebral column.

Which pair of articular processes on the top vertebra glides upward over the articular processes on the bottom vertebra during flexion?

_____

_____

Name the articular processes on the bottom vertebra involved in this movement.

_____

_____

What is the name given to the flat joint surfaces on the articular processes?

_____

_____

Cervical Vertebrae

In the neck region, the concave curvature makes the cervical spine stronger and easier to support the head. There are seven cervical vertebrae; as the lightest and smallest of the vertebrae, they bear the least weight.

On a spinal column model and with disarticulated cervical vertebrae, refer to Figure 6-16. Identify the anatomy detailed in the *Structure of a Typical Vertebra* section and specialized cervical features, including the:

- **atlas**. This atypical first vertebra lacks a body and has transverse processes modified to receive the skull. The articulation between the atlas and the skull (the atlanto-occipital joint), along with other intervertebral joints in the neck, permit nodding of the head, as in the "yes" movement.

- **axis**, the second cervical vertebra. Its tooth-like **dens** projects superiorly from the body to serve as an axis of rotation (at the atlanto-axial joint) as in the "no" movement of the head.

- **transverse foramina**, openings in the transverse processes to accommodate the vertebral arteries and veins. These foramina are unique to the cervical vertebrae.

Clinical Application
The Cervical Vertebrae

Our upright posture allows the head to sit on top of the spinal column in near–perfect balance, a fact that allows the bones — and their accompanying muscles — to be smaller.

On the downside, the relatively large human head in proportion to the cervical vertebrae and supporting tissues, coupled with great range of motion, make the neck especially vulnerable to whiplash injuries and disc degeneration.

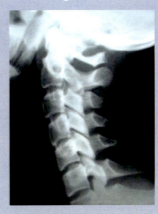

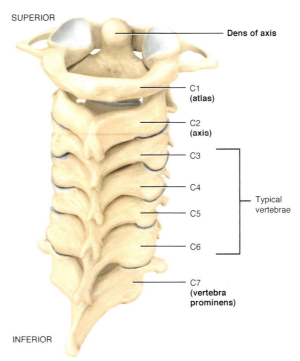

Posterior view of articulated cervical vertebrae

FIGURE 6-16. The cervical vertebrae.

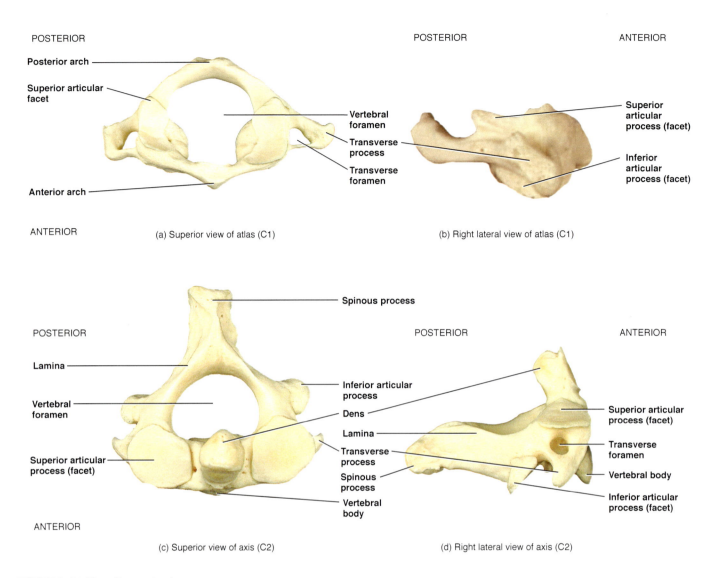

POSTERIOR

Posterior arch

Superior articular facet

Vertebral foramen

Transverse process

Transverse foramen

Anterior arch

ANTERIOR

(a) Superior view of atlas (C1)

POSTERIOR   ANTERIOR

Superior articular process (facet)

Inferior articular process (facet)

(b) Right lateral view of atlas (C1)

Spinous process

POSTERIOR

Lamina

Vertebral foramen

Superior articular process (facet)

ANTERIOR

Inferior articular process

Dens

Lamina

Transverse process

Spinous process

Vertebral body

(c) Superior view of axis (C2)

POSTERIOR   ANTERIOR

Superior articular process (facet)

Transverse foramen

Vertebral body

Inferior articular process (facet)

(d) Right lateral view of axis (C2)

FIGURE 6-17. The atlas and axis.

- **vertebra prominens**, the seventh cervical vertebra, whose spinous process is an anatomical landmark: It is the only cervical spinous process that can be palpated. This process, unlike C2 through C6, is not *bifurcated* or *bifid*, that is, divided into two branches.
  Palpation: Beginning at the nape of the neck, run a finger down the midline until you feel the spinous process of C7.

Thoracic Vertebrae

Compared to the cervical vertebrae, the twelve **thoracic** (thuh-RA-sik) **vertebrae** are larger and stronger.

The thoracic vertebrae form the spinal support of the **thoracic** or **rib cage**. This distinguishing feature requires articulations between the vertebrae and ribs known as **vertebrocostal joints**. This anatomical relationship limits movement of the thoracic spine (and makes the discs of thoracic vertebrae least likely to herniate).

On a spinal column model and with disarticulated thoracic vertebrae, refer to Figure 6-18. Identify the anatomy detailed in the *Structure of a Typical Vertebra* section and the following specialized thoracic features, including the:

- **costal facets** (*costa* = rib) on the transverse processes to facilitate articulation to the tubercle of each rib.

- **facets** and **demifacets** on the vertebral bodies for articulation to the head of each rib. These fortify the attachment of ribs to the vertebral column. A vertebral facet is the articulation site of a single vertebra to the head of a rib. When a rib connects to two vertebral bodies simultaneously, each articular surface is called a demifacet. See Figure 6-18.

- **spinous processes**, which are long, sharp, and point downward. Due to their length and shape, these processes can be recognized in the midline of the back as part of our surface anatomy.

Note: Most thoracic vertebral bodies have a pair of demifacets — one superior, one inferior — for rib articulation. However, the pattern of demifacets and of singular facets on these vertebrae is not uniform, as illustrated in Figure 6-18.

T1: On each side of the vertebral body is a superior facet for the first rib and an inferior demifacet for the second rib.

T2-T8: On each side of the vertebral body is a superior and inferior demifacet. Ribs two through nine thus articulate with two vertebrae.

T9: On each side is a superior demifacet to complement the inferior demifacet of T8 for attachment to rib nine.

T10 -T12: On each side of the vertebral body is a single facet for attachment to ribs ten through twelve.

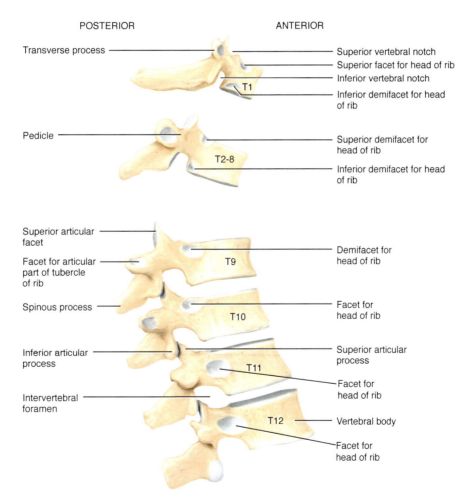

POSTERIOR   ANTERIOR

Transverse process — Superior vertebral notch
Superior facet for head of rib
Inferior vertebral notch
T1
Inferior demifacet for head of rib

Pedicle —
Superior demifacet for head of rib
T2-8
Inferior demifacet for head of rib

Superior articular facet
Demifacet for head of rib
Facet for articular part of tubercle of rib
T9
Spinous process —
Facet for head of rib
T10
Inferior articular process
Superior articular process
T11
Facet for head of rib
Intervertebral foramen
T12
Vertebral body
Facet for head of rib

Right lateral view of several articulated thoracic vertebrae

FIGURE 6-18. The thoracic vertebrae.

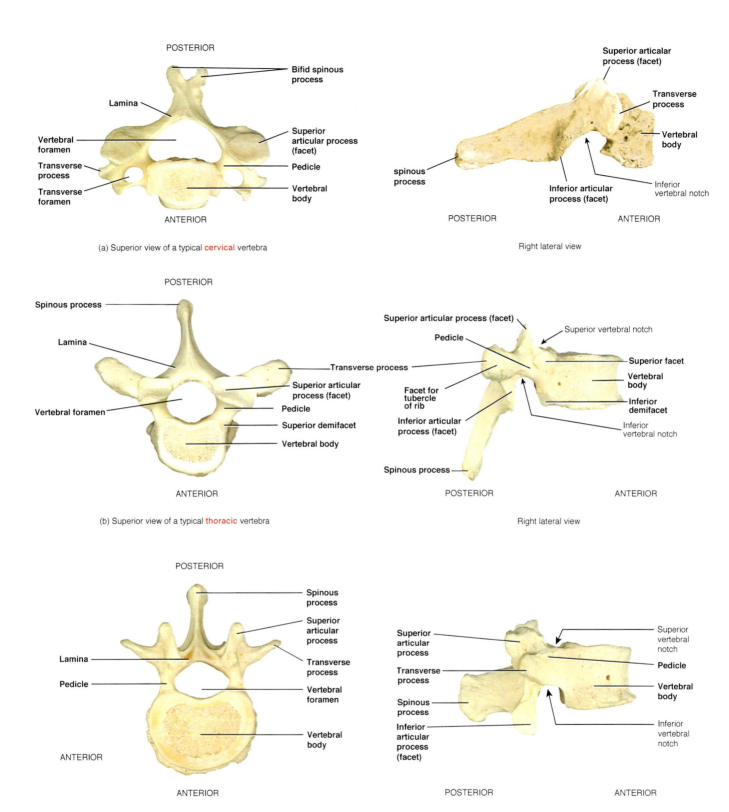

POSTERIOR

Bifid spinous process

Lamina

Vertebral foramen

Transverse process

Transverse foramen

Superior articular process (facet)

Pedicle

Vertebral body

ANTERIOR

(a) Superior view of a typical **cervical** vertebra

Superior articalar process (facet)

Transverse process

Vertebral body

spinous process

Inferior articular process (facet)

Inferior vertebral notch

POSTERIOR   ANTERIOR

Right lateral view

POSTERIOR

Spinous process

Lamina

Vertebral foramen

Transverse process

Superior articular process (facet)

Pedicle

Superior demifacet

Vertebral body

ANTERIOR

(b) Superior view of a typical **thoracic** vertebra

Superior articular process (facet)

Pedicle

Facet for tubercle of rib

Inferior articular process (facet)

Spinous process

Superior vertebral notch

Superior facet

Vertebral body

Inferior demifacet

Inferior vertebral notch

POSTERIOR   ANTERIOR

Right lateral view

POSTERIOR

Spinous process

Superior articular process

Transverse process

Vertebral foramen

Vertebral body

Lamina

Pedicle

ANTERIOR

ANTERIOR

(c) Superior view of a typical **lumbar** vertebra

Superior articular process

Transverse process

Spinous process

Inferior articular process (facet)

Superior vertebral notch

Pedicle

Vertebral body

Inferior vertebral notch

POSTERIOR   ANTERIOR

Right lateral view

FIGURE 6-19. Comparison of cervical, thoracic, and lumbar vertebrae.

Lumbar Vertebrae

The lumbar spine is subject to more mechanical stress than the cervical or thoracic regions due to the greater accumulated weight in the lower back. Lumbar vertebrae are thus larger and stronger. On a spinal column model and with disarticulated lumbar vertebrae, refer to Figures 6-19 and 6-20. Identify the anatomy detailed in the *Structure of a Typical Vertebra* section and the following specialized lumbar features:

- **vertebral bodies**, which are very large to provide sufficient mass for weight bearing.

- **spinous processes**, which are thick and shaped like hatchet blades. They extend directly backward.

- **transverse processes**, which are straight and extend perpendicular to the spinous processes.

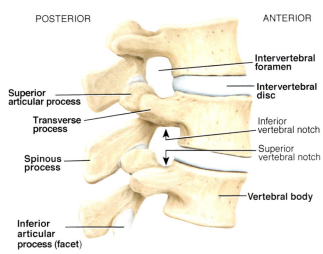

Right lateral view of articulated lumbar vertebrae

FIGURE 6-20. Lumbar vertebrae.

The Sacrum

The sacrum is a wedge-shaped composite bone that is formed from five vertebrae that fuse together primarily during the teen years. Its superior articulation is with L5; inferiorly, it attaches to the coccyx. Its concave surface forms the posterior border of the pelvis. Note the location of the sacrum and coccyx in relation to the pelvic and gluteal anatomy in Figure 6-21. Refer to Figures 6-21 and 6-22 and identify the:

- **base**, which articulates to the body of L5. Its anterior border is the **sacral promontory**.

- wing-like **alae**, fused transverse processes that articulate laterally with the two hipbones at the sacrum's **auricular surfaces**. This union of the sacrum with the iliac region of each hipbone is the **sacroiliac joint**.

- **sacral foramina** — four each on the anterior and posterior sides — allow blood vessels and nerves to pass through.

- **median sacral crest**, the fused spinous processes on the posterior side.
  Palpation: Begin at the upper end of the intergluteal cleft and move superiorly in the midline. (Refer to Figure 6-21.)

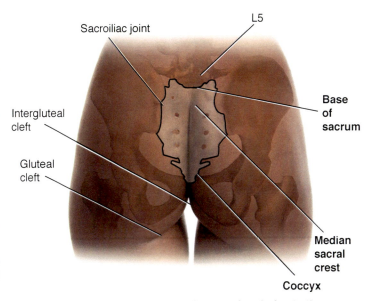

FIGURE 6-21. The sacrum and coccyx in relation to the pelvic and gluteal anatomy.

- **sacral canal**, a continuation of the vertebral canal.

- **sacral hiatus** (hi-AY-tus; *hiatus* = opening), the inferior end of the vertebral canal near the coccyx.

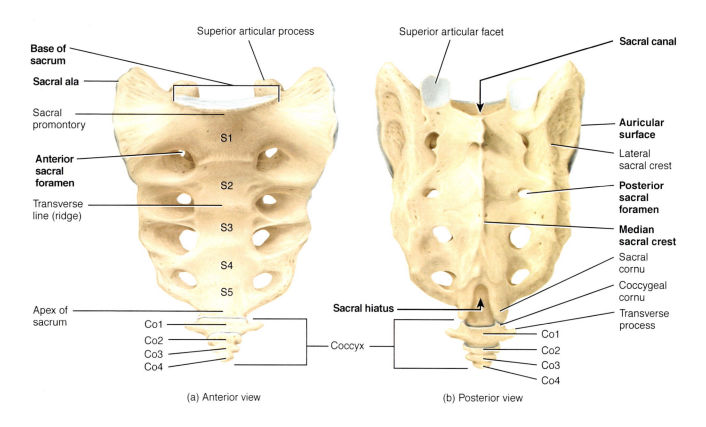

(a) Anterior view   (b) Posterior view

FIGURE 6-22. The sacrum and coccyx.

The Coccyx

The coccyx (KOK-sicks) (Figure 6-22) is our triangular "tailbone", a fusion of three to five, but usually four, odd-shaped vertebrae. The coccygeal vertebrae fuse between the ages of 20 and 30 and attach to the sacrum by ligaments. The remnants of individual vertebrae are abbreviated as Co1, Co2, etc.

The male coccyx points anteriorly. In females, it points inferiorly, allowing more anteroposterior (front-to-back) space for childbirth.

Palpation: Starting at the top of the intergluteal cleft, slide a finger downward until you reach the lowermost tip of the coccyx. Refer to Figure 6-21. (Palpate discreetly, that is, in private!)

The Thoracic Cage

The **thoracic (rib) cage** comprises the sternum, ribs, and thoracic vertebrae. It is protective of the vital organs in the thoracic cavity and is of critical importance in breathing. The cartilages that connect the ribs to the sternum provide flexibility that (1) allows the rib cage to expand and contract during respiration, and (2) reduces the likelihood of fractures from chest trauma.

PROCEDURE 5

Examining the Thoracic Cage

The Sternum

The **sternum**, or breastbone (Figure 6-23), is comprised of three flat bones that fuse together by about age 25. Obtain an isolated sternum and one that is part of an articulated skeleton. Identify the:

• **manubrium** (muh-NOO-bree-um), the superior segment.

• **body**, the middle and largest segment.

• **xiphoid** (ZY-foyd) **process** (*xiphos* = sword), the lower, often pointed, and smallest segment.

Sternal landmarks include the:

• **suprasternal (jugular) notch**, a depression on the sternum's superior end.
Palpation: Place your index finger at the top of your sternum between your clavicles (collarbones).

• **sternal angle**, a ridge at the joint between the body and manubrium. It is clinically useful because it indicates the location of the second rib. (The spaces between the second/third ribs and fifth/sixth ribs are key sites for listening to heart sounds.)
Palpation: From the suprasternal notch, move an index finger an inch or two inferiorly until a bump is felt.

The Ribs

All ribs articulate posteriorly with their corresponding vertebrae via their heads and tubercles. Note their downward slant from back to front. During inhalation, intercostal muscles between the ribs contract, elevating the ribs toward the horizontal and enlarging the chest cavity.

On an articulated skeleton and referring to Figure 6-23, identify the:

• **true ribs**, the first seven pairs. These ribs attach directly to the sternum via their costal cartilages and are thus known as **vertebrosternal ribs**.

• **false ribs**, the last five pairs. Ribs 8 through 10 connect indirectly to the sternum by cartilage and are called **vertebrochondral ribs**. Ribs 11 and 12 have no attachment to the sternum and are called **vertebral** or **floating ribs**.

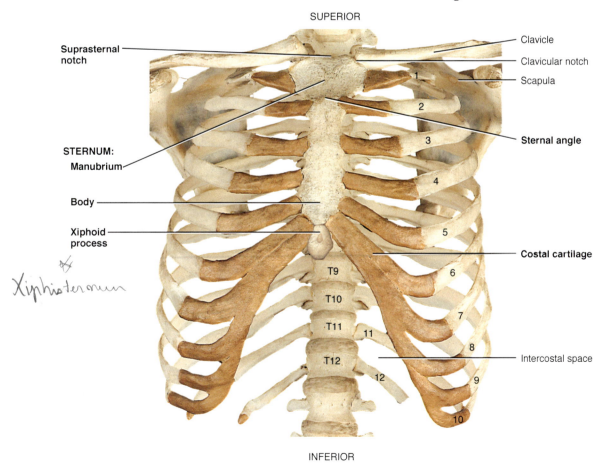

SUPERIOR

Suprasternal notch

Clavicle

Clavicular notch

Scapula

Sternal angle

STERNUM:
Manubrium

Body

Xiphoid process

Xiphisternum

T9

T10

T11

T12

1
2
3
4
5
6
7
8
9
10
11
12

Costal cartilage

Intercostal space

INFERIOR

Anterior view of skeleton of thorax

FIGURE 6-23. The thoracic (rib) cage.

The most posterior portion of a rib is its **head**, which articulates to a vertebral body via its **superior** and **inferior facets**. Just lateral to the head is the **neck**, a constricted region that is continuous with the **body**, or shaft. At the junction of neck and body is the knoblike **tubercle**. The tubercle attaches to a vertebral transverse process through its **articular facet** and by ligaments. Where a rib meets the vertebral body and transverse process is a **vertebrocostal joint**.

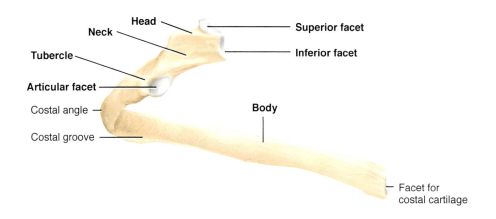

(a) Posterior view of a typical (third through ninth) left rib.

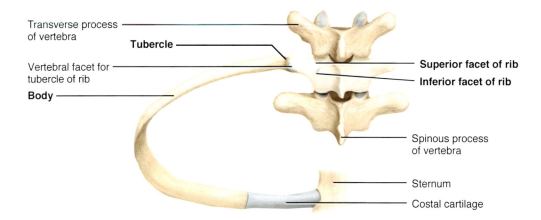

(b) Posterior view of left true rib articulated with thoracic vertebrae. Anteriorly, true ribs connect directly to the sternum via costal cartilage.

FIGURE 6-24. The structure of a rib and its articulation to a vertebra.

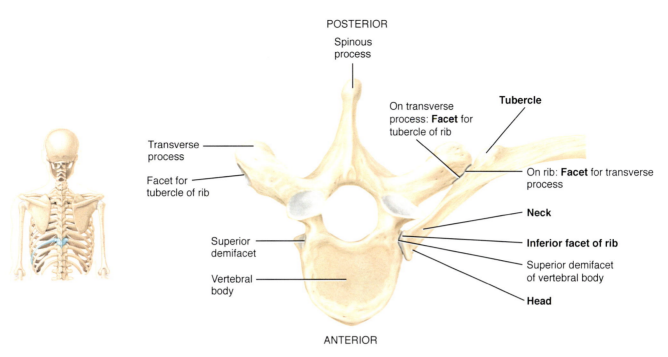

POSTERIOR

Spinous process

Transverse process

Facet for tubercle of rib

On transverse process: **Facet** for tubercle of rib

Tubercle

On rib: **Facet** for transverse process

Neck

Superior demifacet

Inferior facet of rib

Superior demifacet of vertebral body

Vertebral body

Head

ANTERIOR

(c) Superior view of left rib articulated with thoracic vertebra

FIGURE 6-24. (continued)

PROCEDURE 6

Rib Cage Movements during Respiration

While palpating your xiphoid process, inhale as deeply as you can. Notice how the intercostal muscles elevate the rib cage as they pull the ribs upward. Now (breathing naturally) place your palm horizontally along the sternum with your index finger lying across the sternal angle. Inhale deeply once again and observe your hand moving forward as the chest expands front to back.

The Axial Skeleton

Exercise

NAME _____

LAB TIME/DATE _____

The Skull

Matching

Match the bone in column B with its description in column A.
(The B bones may be used more than once.)

Column A

_____1. Site of mastoid process

_____2. Delicate bone with groove for tear duct

___f___3. Teeth-bearing pair

___a___4. Site of sella turcica

___e___5. Contains largest paranasal sinus

___f___6. "Back-of-head" bone, literally

___n___7. Face-defining cheekbone

___c___8. U-shaped muscle anchor

___g___9. Articulates with condyle from lower jawbone

___i___10. Lower part of nasal septum

_____11. Cribriform plate is porous "roof" of this bone.

___f___12. Site of foramen magnum

___e___13. Perforated by optic foramen (canal)

___e___14. One of a pair forming cranial wall

___k___15. Forehead bone

Column B

a. Sphenoid

b. Vomer

c. Hyoid

d. Zygomatic

e. Temporal

f. Maxilla

g. Mandible

h. Ethmoid

i. Lacrimal

j. Occipital

k. Frontal

l. Parietal

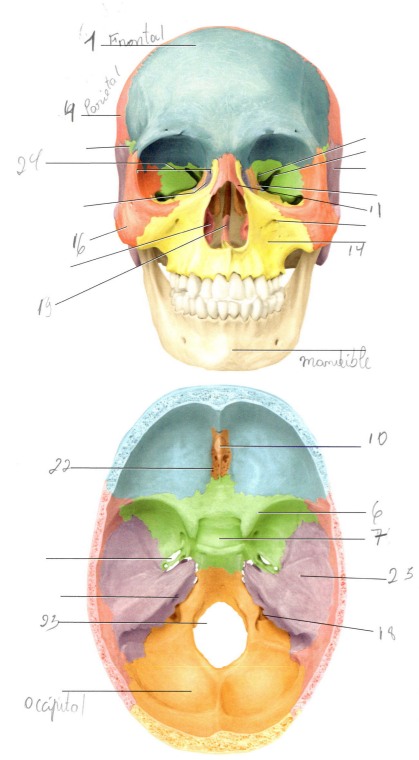

Handwritten annotations on diagram:
- 1 Frontal
- 4 Parietal
- 24
- 16
- 19
- 11
- 14
- mandible
- 10
- 22
- 6
- 7
- 2 5
- 18
- 93
- Occipital

Diagram Self-Test

For each of the next three illustrations, place the number of the corresponding key label next to the leader line.

Key

1. Frontal

2. Optic foramen (canal)

3. Foramen ovale

4. Parietal

5. Superior orbital fissure

6. Lesser wing of sphenoid

7. Sphenoid (anterior view)

8. Hypophyseal fossa of sella turcica

9. Cribriform plate of ethmoid

10. Ethmoid (anterior view)

11. Nasal

12. Internal auditory meatus

13. Lacrimal

14. Maxilla

15. Foramen magnum

16. Zygomatic

17. Inferior nasal concha

18. Middle cranial fossa within temporal

19. Vomer

20. Mandible

21. Occipital

22. Crista galli of ethmoid

23. Jugular foramen

24. Orbit

25. Temporal (anterior view)

26. Infraorbital foramen

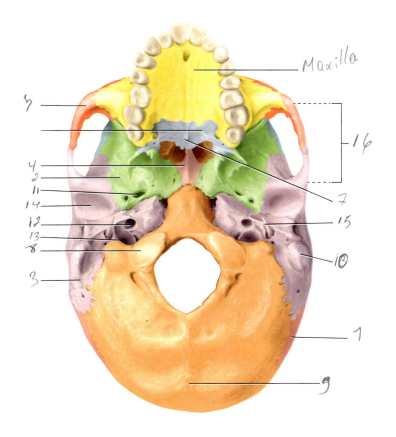

Maxilla

Key

1. Parietal bone
2. Sphenoid bone
3. Temporal bone
4. Vomer
5. Zygomatic bone
6. Maxilla
7. Palatine bone
8. Occipital condyle
9. External occipital protuberance
10. Mastoid process
11. Foramen ovale
12. Carotid canal
13. Jugular foramen
14. Mandibular fossa
15. Styloid process
16. Zygomatic arch

1. Name the eight bones that comprise the cranium.

   2 Parietal, 1 occipital, 1 Frontal, 1 Sphenoide,
   2 temporal , 1 ethmoid

2. Why is the sphenoid considered the keystone of the cranial floor?

   _____

   _____

   _____

3. Which bone is the keystone of the facial anatomy?

    _____

4. Which bones meet at the coronal suture?

    _____

    _____

5. Which bones meet at the lambdoid suture?

    _____

6. Besides the palatine, there are six other bones that contribute to the orbit. Name them.

    _____

    _____

7. The hyoid is unique among axial bones in that it does not articulate with any other bone. What is one function of this bone?

    _____

    _____

8. Name the only movable ("unsutured") bone of the skull.

    _____

9. What is the function of the paranasal sinuses?

    _____

    _____

10. Cite two reasons why fontanels in the skull are important.

    _____

    _____

    _____

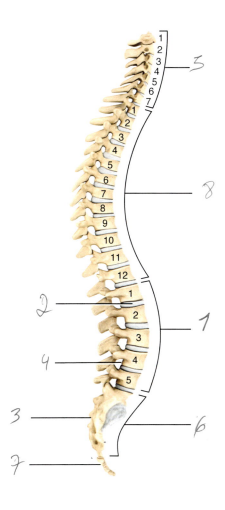

The Vertebral Column

Place the number of the corresponding key label next to the leader line.

Key

1. lumbar curve ✓
2. intervertebral disc ✓
3. sacrum ✓
4. intervertebral foramen ✓
5. cervical curve ✓
6. sacral curve ✓
7. coccyx ✓
8. thoracic curve ✓

Structure of a Vertebra

I. Match the structure in column B with its description in column A. (More than one answer may apply.)

II. Label the illustration by placing the letters of column B structures next to their matching leader lines.

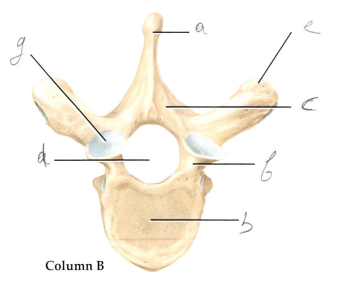

Column A

_____ d 1. Opening for spinal cord

_____ e 2. Anchor point for muscle attachment

_____ b 3. Principal weight-bearing region

_____ b 4. Faceted surface where adjacent vertebrae connect

_____ c 5. Part of the vertebral arch on its posterior aspect

_____ f 6. Short process between body and vertebral arch

_____ a 7. Posterior projection, sometimes forked

Column B

a. spinous process

b. body

c. lamina

d. vertebral foramen

e. transverse process

f. pedicle

g. articular process

1. Through which passageways do spinal nerves communicate with the spinal cord?

    _____

    _____

2. When an intervertebral disc herniates (ruptures), what specific parts of the disc are displaced?

    _____

    _____

    _____

    What are the consequences of a herniated disc when it compresses surrounding neuroanatomy?

    _____

    _____

    _____

    _____

3. Where in the vertebral column are there points of movement? (Describe the intervertebral anatomy responsible for flexibility of the spine.)

    _____

    _____

    _____

    _____

3. Identify the vertebra as cervical, thoracic, or lumbar. What is the rationale for your answer?

    cervical because

    the vertebrae have

    transverse foramen

    _____

    _____

The Thoracic Cage

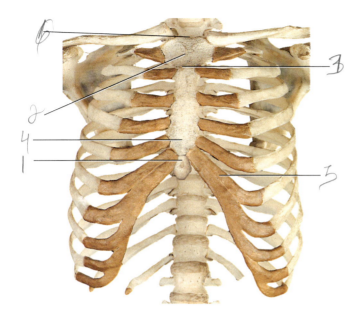

Diagram Self-Test

Place the number of the corresponding key label next to the leader line.

Key

1. xiphoid process

2. manubrium

3. sternal angle

4. sternal body

5. costal cartilage

6. suprasternal notch

1. Excluding the vertebral column, the anatomy of the thoracic cage is formed principally by the

    _____*Ribs*_____ and _____*Sternum*_____.

2. Cite two functions of the rib cage.

    _____

    _____

    _____

    _____

3. What is the significance of the sternal angle as an anatomical landmark?

    _____

    _____

    _____

Critical Thinking

Skeletal evidence of the Neanderthal species of humans can be traced to about 130,000 years ago. Although Neanderthal and modern human DNA is estimated to differ by only 0.3 %, there are marked differences in the anatomy of their skulls.

Observe the modern and Neanderthal skulls below. Note the Neanderthal's larger facial structure and greater overall volume.

Homo sapiens   *Homo neaderthalensis*

1. Which "keystone" bone of the face is significantly longer than that of modern humans?

2. In Neanderthals, which cranial bone determines the low-profile forehead with the exceptionally large browridge?

3. Name the bone which literally translates as "back of the head". How does this bone in Neanderthals differ from its modern counterpart?

4. In males, Neanderthal cranial volume was about 1450 cubic centimeters (cc). That of modern human males averages about 1345 cc. Thus, the brain of Neanderthals is considered to be larger. Brain size, however, is relative to body size, constituting 2% of body weight.

    Given an average Neanderthal male body weight of 77.6 kg (170.7 lb) and an average modern male weight of 72.7 kg (159.9 lb*), was the Neanderthal brain significantly larger in a relative sense? (Hint: Calculate the percent difference for cranial volume and for body weight and compare those percentages.)

* Modern weight is based on a *mesomorph* — a person who is neither too thin or too fat — of average height: 175.3 cm (5'9").

The Appendicular Skeleton

OBJECTIVES

1. To identify the bones comprising the appendicular skeleton.
2. To identify the surface markings on appendicular bones.
3. To compare the specialized functions of the pectoral and pelvic girdles.
4. To differentiate the anatomy of the male and female pelvic girdles.

MATERIALS

Articulated skeletons
Disarticulated appendicular bones

Isolated hand and foot skeletons
X rays of appendicular bones

PRE-LAB QUIZ

1. The pectoral/pelvic girdle (Circle one.) has more extensive bone-to-bone articulation to the axial skeleton.
2. Cite one function of the clavicle.
3. Which surface feature of the humerus joins the ulna to form the elbow joint?
4. The more lateral of the two forearm bones is the _____.
5. The _____ bones (Insert a number.) between the carpals and phalanges are called the _____.
6. The finger with the greatest range of motion is the _____.
7. How would you classify the pubic angle of the female pelvis?
8. The largest and strongest bone in the human skeleton is the _____.
9. The knee joint includes the
   a. tibia and fibula.
   b. femur and fibula.
   c. femur and tibia.
   d. tibia, fibula and femur.
10. Identify one specific connective tissue that maintains bones of the foot in an archlike configuration.

The appendicular skeleton (Figure 5-1, gold-shaded bones) consists of bones of the limbs and the girdles that attach the "appendages" to the axial skeleton. There are 126 bones in the adult appendicular skeleton, 64 in the upper division and 62 in the lower.

PROCEDURE 1

The Pectoral Girdle and Upper Limbs

Identify the bones and principal markings of the pectoral girdle and upper limbs on an articulated skeleton or using isolated specimens. For all appendicular bones, try to distinguished anatomical right from left.

The Pectoral Girdle

The paired **pectoral** (PEK-tuh-rul) **girdles**, also known as shoulder girdles, each consist of the anterior clavicle

- **sternoclavicular joint**, where the clavicle's rounded medial side meets the manubrium of the sternum. *Palpation: Place your left index finger on the suprasternal notch. Move it a centimeter (about half an inch) to the right to the medial end of the clavicle. With your right arm in the anatomical position, lift it overhead and back again (as in a jumping-jack exercise) to feel the sternoclavicular joint through its range of motion.*

- **acromioclavicular joint**, where the flattened lateral end of the clavicle joins the acromion of the scapula.

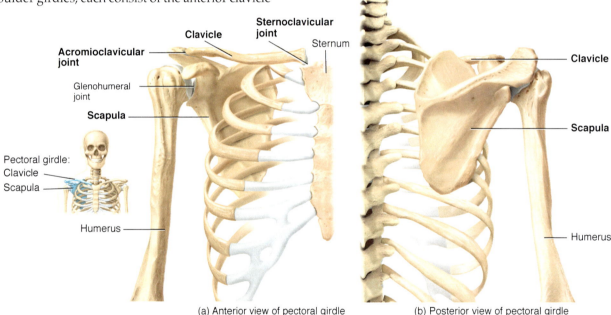

(a) Anterior view of pectoral girdle   (b) Posterior view of pectoral girdle

FIGURE 7-1. The pectoral (shoulder) girdle viewed from the right side.

and posterior scapula (Figure 7-1). Their primary function is to attach the upper limbs to the axial skeleton. They also serve as attachment sites for muscles of the neck, back and chest.

Clavicle

The **clavicle**, commonly called the collarbone (Figure 7-2), connects the rib cage to the upper limb by its articulation to the sternum and the scapula. It acts as a brace to protect the shoulder joint against dislocation while allowing free arm movement. It can easily be palpated along its entire length. Identify the:

Scapula

The **scapula**, commonly called the shoulder blade (Figure 7-3), is a flattened, triangular bone that articulates to the clavicle and humerus (arm bone). It rests on the superior, posterior aspect of the rib cage. Having no bony articulation to the axial skeleton, it is attached to the rib cage by muscles and is therefore highly mobile. It includes the:

- **spine**, which projects from the scapula's dorsolateral surface.

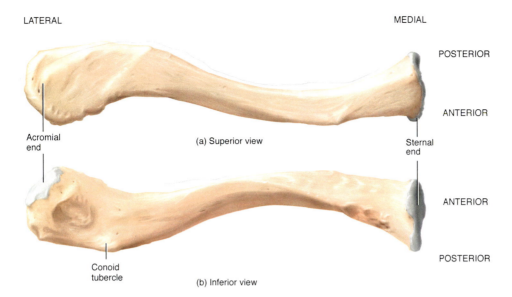

LATERAL

MEDIAL

POSTERIOR

ANTERIOR

Acromial
end

(a) Superior view

Sternal
end

ANTERIOR

ANTERIOR

POSTERIOR

Conoid
tubercle

(b) Inferior view

FIGURE 7-2. The right clavicle viewed from above and below.

- **acromion** (uh-KRO-mee-un), literally the high point of the shoulder, at the lateral end of the spine.

- **coracoid** (KOR-uh-koyd) **process**, a projection whose name reflects its bird-beak shape. It is below the acromion, points anteriorly, and is an attachment site for upper limb muscles.
  Palpation: Starting at the acromion, place your middle and index fingers about 8 centimeters (roughly 3 inches) inferiorly and just medial to your arm. Swing your arm forward and backward and feel for a rounded anterior process.

- **glenoid cavity** (*glene* = socket) which articulates to the humerus to form the shoulder joint.

- **supraspinous fossa**, a depression lying just above the spine.

- **infraspinous fossa**, a depression lying just below the spine.

- **lateral** and **medial borders**, the lateral and medial edges of the scapular blade.

- **superior** and **inferior angles**, where the blade assumes a roughly triangular shape on the uppermost and lowermost edges.

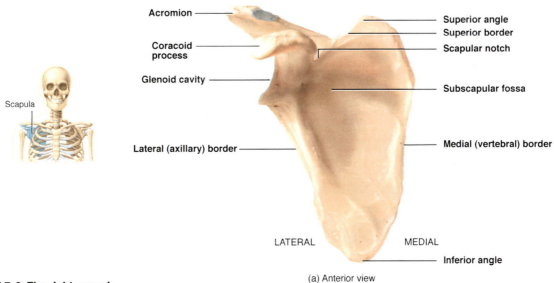

Acromion

Coracoid
process

Glenoid cavity

Scapula

Lateral (axillary) border

Superior angle

Superior border

Scapular notch

Subscapular fossa

Medial (vertebral) border

LATERAL

MEDIAL

Inferior angle

(a) Anterior view

FIGURE 7-3. The right scapula.

- **superior border**, the edge of the blade lateral to the superior angle.

- **scapular notch**, an indentation between the superior border and the coracoid process.

Functional Anatomy of the Shoulder

Human pectoral girdle anatomy is adapted for mobility and thus is not designed to be strong and rigid. It reflects our human *bipedalism*: locomotion on two feet — with no mandatory weight bearing on our upper limbs. Here's how form follows function:

- *Bony articulation to the axial skeleton is limited to the relatively small sternoclavicular joints.*

- *The shallow glenoid cavity permits great range of motion of the arm bone at the shoulder joint.*

- *The scapula has no bony attachment to the rib cage. It "floats" in soft tissue, thus permitting it — and the entire shoulder assembly — a high degree of flexibility, as in shrugging the shoulders.*

The Arm

The **humerus**, or *brachium*, is the singular bone of the arm (Figure 7-4). It articulates with the scapula at the shoulder and the two forearm bones in the elbow region. Locate the:

- **head**, a smooth, rounded process that joins the glenoid cavity to form the shoulder (glenohumeral) joint. Just inferior to the head is the **anatomical neck**, which lies directly above the more constricted **surgical neck**. ("Surgical" denotes this part of the humerus as a common fracture site.)

- **greater** (lateral) and **lesser** (medial) **tubercles**, two elevations on opposite sides of the humeral head. Between the tubercles is the **intertubercular sulcus** (bicipital groove). The tubercles are muscle attachment sites; the sulcus guides a tendon from the biceps muscle to its point of attachment above the glenoid cavity.

- **body (shaft)**, which is cylindrical for most of its length, but becomes triangular at its distal end.

- **deltoid tuberosity**, a ridge on the upper lateral aspect where the deltoid muscle attaches. Somewhat more posterior is the **radial groove**, which marks the path of the radial nerve.

- **trochlea** (TRA-klee-uh), a projection at the distal end that articulates to the ulna to form the elbow (humeroulnar) joint.

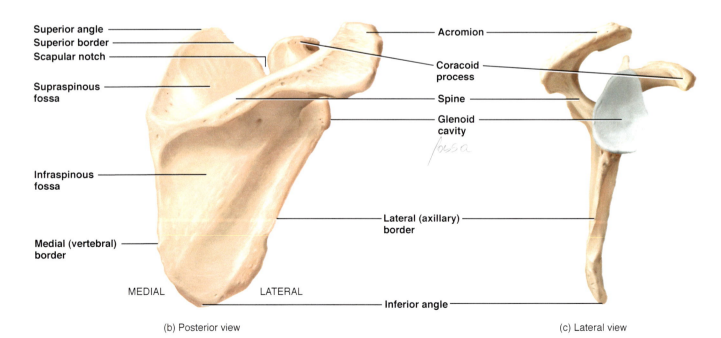

Superior angle
Superior border
Scapular notch
Supraspinous fossa
Infraspinous fossa
Medial (vertebral) border
MEDIAL
LATERAL
(b) Posterior view

Acromion
Coracoid process
Spine
Glenoid cavity
Lateral (axillary) border
Inferior angle
(c) Lateral view

FIGURE 7-3 (continued). The right scapula.

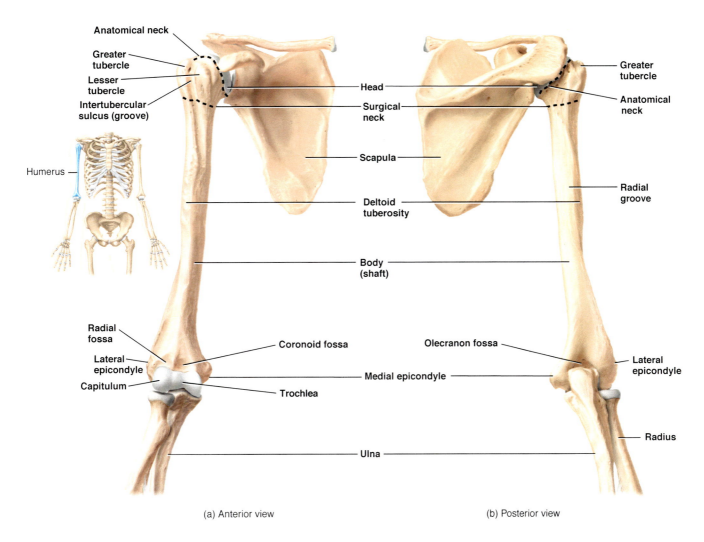

Anatomical neck
Greater tubercle
Lesser tubercle
Intertubercular sulcus (groove)

Humerus

Head
Surgical neck

Scapula

Deltoid tuberosity

Body (shaft)

Radial fossa
Lateral epicondyle
Capitulum

Coronoid fossa

Medial epicondyle

Trochlea

Ulna

Greater tubercle
Anatomical neck

Radial groove

Olecranon fossa

Lateral epicondyle

Radius

(a) Anterior view   (b) Posterior view

FIGURE 7-4. The right humerus.

- **capitulum** (kuh-PIH-chuh-lum; literally, small head), a spherical projection on the distal end that articulates to the radius laterally to form a pivot joint.

- **radial fossa**, an anterior depression just above the capitulum that receives the head of the radius when the forearm is bent during flexion.

- **medial** and **lateral epicondyles**, which are just proximal to the capitulum and trochlea. These projections are the origins of most muscles of the forearm.

Palpation: The epicondyles are prominent and visible subcutaneous projections. Using the "point" (olecranon) of your right elbow as a starting point, slide your left index finger toward the lateral aspect of the humerus for the lateral epicondyle, then back toward the medial aspect for the medial epicondyle.

- **coronoid fossa** (KOR-uh-noyd, crown-shaped), an anterior depression just above the trochlea that accommodates the coronoid process of the ulna during forearm flexion at the elbow's hinge joint.

- **olecranon fossa** (uh-LEK-kruh-non), a posterior depression at the distal end that receives the olecranon process of the ulna when the forearm is straightened during extension at the elbow's hinge joint.

The Forearm

The forearm, or *antebrachium* ("before the arm") is comprised of the radius and ulna (Figure 7-5). The two bones are parallel, and in the anatomical position, the radius is on the lateral aspect (thumb side) and the ulna is on the medial aspect (little-finger side) of the forearm. A mnemonic device for recalling the position of the ulna relative to the hand is "PU": the **p**inky finger is on the **u**lnar side.

On the radius, (Figure 7-5), locate the:
- **head**, a disc-like marking on the proximal end that articulates to the capitulum. This joint (the humeroradial), allows rotation of the forearm, during which an imaginary circle is described. The radius bone is at the center of the circle, and from it to the circumference is the circle's — no surprise here — radius!
- **radial tuberosity**, a bump on the medial aspect of the shaft, just distal to the head, that anchors the tendon of the arm's biceps muscle.
- **styloid process**, a lateral projection on the distal end of the radius (*styloid* means slender and pointed).

Palpation: Follow the shaft of the right radius with your left thumb to where it terminates about 2 centimeters (roughly an inch) proximal to the base of the thumb (Figure 7-6).

- **ulnar notch**, a small depression at the end of the radius that articulates to the end of the ulna.

On the ulna, (Figure 7-5), locate the:
- **trochlear notch** (TROK-lee-uh), a crescent–shaped curve that joins the trochlea of the humerus to form the elbow (humeroulnar) joint. During flexion and extension of the forearm, this joint moves like a pulley, a fact reflected in the translation of trochlea from the Greek *trochos*, wheel.

- **coronoid process**, a small projection below the trochlear notch.

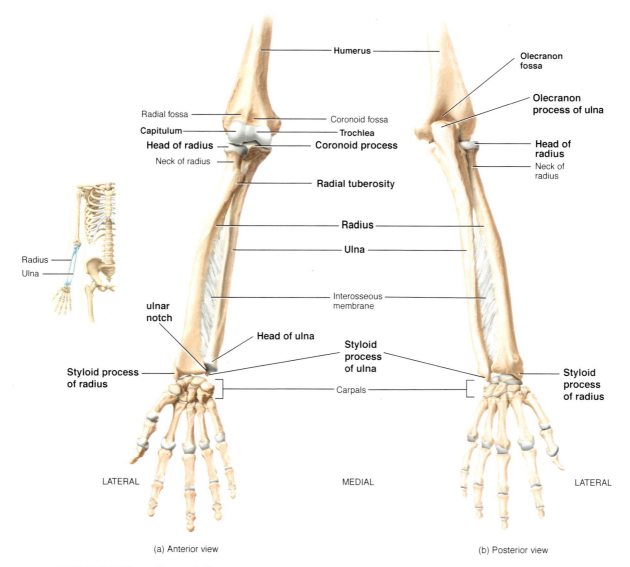

(a) Anterior view

(b) Posterior view

FIGURE 7-5. The radius and ulna.

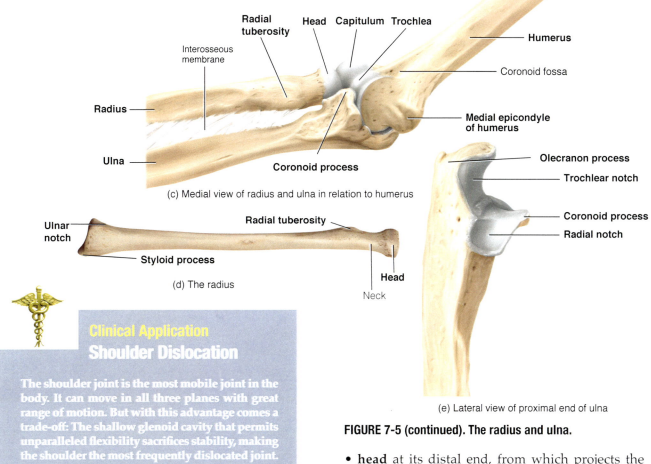

(c) Medial view of radius and ulna in relation to humerus

(d) The radius

(e) Lateral view of proximal end of ulna

FIGURE 7-5 (continued). The radius and ulna.

- **head** at its distal end, from which projects the **styloid process**. Although — unlike the radius — the distal end of the ulna has no bony attachment to the wrist, the styloid process connects to, and reinforces, the wrist via ligaments.

Palpation: With the palm of the right hand facing downward, place the thumb of your left hand on the styloid process of the radius. With the index finger of the palpating hand, feel for the ulna's styloid process on the medial side near the ulnar head about one centimeter (about half an inch) proximal to the radial styloid process (Figure 7-6).

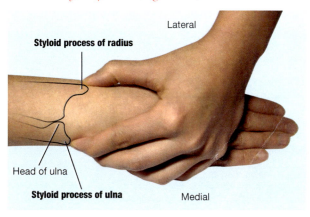

FIGURE 7-6. Palpating the styloid processes of the radius and ulna. (Note: The more prominent bump on the ulna is the head.)

- **olecranon process**, the prominent — and easily felt — elevation on the posterior ulna above and behind the trochlear notch. These structures cradle the trochlea and thus support the elbow joint.

- **radial notch**, a small concavity on the lateral side of the coronoid process named for its articulation to the radial head. This radioulnar joint is a second pivot point during rotation of the forearm.

The Hand

The bones of the hand are subdivided into three groups: the wrist, or carpus; the palm, or metacarpus; and the fingers, or phalanges.

Carpus (Wrist)

The eight **carpals** are named for their shapes and are arranged in two rows (Figure 7-7). The four bones in the proximal row (in lateral-to-medial order) are the:

- **scaphoid** (SKAF-oyd; *scaphos* = boat)

- **lunate** (LOO-nate; *luna* = crescent moon)
- **triquetrum*** (try-KWEE-trum; *triquetrus* = three-cornered)
- **pisiform** (PEEZ-ih-form; *pisum* = pea)

The four bones in the distal row (lateral-to-medial) are the:

- **trapezium** (truh-PEE-zee-um; *trapezion* = four-sided shape that has no parallel sides)

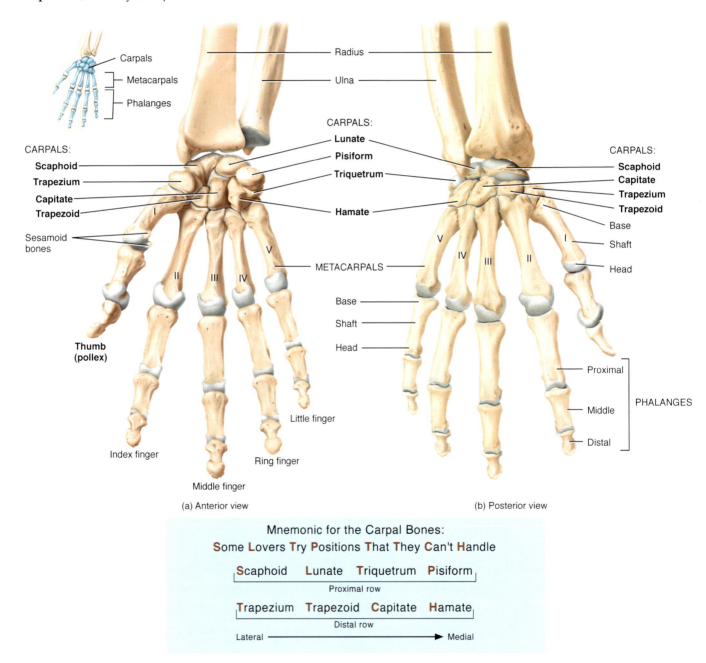

FIGURE 7-7. The carpals are named. The skeleton of the right hand. The metacarpals numbered, and the phalanges numbered and named.

* The triquetrum is also known as the *triangular*.

- **trapezoid** (TRA-puh-zoyd; *trapezoides* = four-sided shape that has two parallel sides)

- **capitate** (KA-puh-tate; *capitus* = head)

- **hamate** (HAY-mate; *hamatus* = hook)

Carpal Connections

- The capitate is the largest carpal, but despite its size, it is difficult to palpate as are most carpals due to their flat dorsal and ventral surfaces.

- The pisiform is the smallest carpal, but one of the easiest to palpate.
Palpation: With the palm of your right hand facing up, place the tip of your left index finger on the medial side of your hand at the distal wrist crease.

- The hook of the hamate can also be readily felt.
Palpation: Place the interphalangeal (IP) joint of your left thumb on the pisiform of your right hand. (The IP is marked as the most distal crease on the palmar side.) Point the distal end of your thumb toward the right index finger. When the wrist is flexed, the hamate can be felt with the tip of the thumb.

- The scaphoid is the carpal most commonly fractured. Picture someone falling and the natural inclination to break the fall with an outstretched hand. More often than not, the scaphoid takes the brunt of the impact.

Metacarpus

The five **metacarpals**, the skeleton of the palm (Figure 7-7), are numbered I to V (1 to 5) from the thumb to the little finger (lateral to medial). Each metacarpal has a **shaft** between a proximal **base** and a distal **head**. The bases articulate to the carpus, and except for the first, with adjacent metacarpals. Each head articulates with a proximal finger bone, and when the hand forms a fist, becomes a knuckle.

On the posterior aspect of the hand — which is the hand's *dorsum* — each metacarpal can be felt beneath tendons from muscles in the forearm.

Phalanges

The finger bones, or *digits*, are formally known as the **phalanges** (singular, **phalanx**) (Figure 7-7). Like the metacarpals, they are technically long bones and are numbered from I to V, starting with the thumb. The thumb has two phalanges (proximal and distal); each of the other fingers has three phalanges (proximal, middle, and distal).

Thumbs up. The thumb is by far the most mobile — and unusual — finger. Anatomists would submit that it is in a class by itself, so unlike the other fingers that it merits its own label: the *pollex*.

Although primates and other mammals may come close, humans hold the distinction of having the only fully *opposable* thumb: it can precisely touch all other digits fingertip to fingertip (Figure 7-8). A major reason for the thumb's extraordinary mobility is the saddle-shaped carpometacarpal joint between its metacarpal and the trapezium of the wrist.

The thumb's central role in the functional anatomy of the hand is usually taken for granted — until one tries to grasp a mug, pick up a coin, or close a zipper without it. (Try taping your thumb and index finger together for an exercise in manual futility!) Its evolution led to more accurate fine motor skills that in turn led to the development of tools, written language and other distinctly human attributes. It is safe to assume that civilization as we know it could not have been possible without our thumbs.

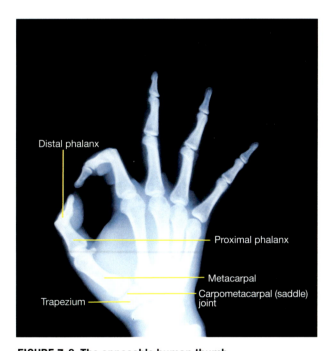

FIGURE 7-8. The opposable human thumb.

The lower appendicular skeleton is organized into four major components: a girdle formed by the hip bones, the thigh, the leg, and the foot. It's function is weight bearing and locomotion.

The Pelvic Girdle and Lower Limbs

The Pelvic (Hip) Girdle

The **pelvic (hip) girdle** consists of two **hip bones**, also known as **coxal bones**, or **os coxae** (Figure 7-9). The hip bones are joined anteriorly at the **pubic symphysis** (PYOO-bik SIM-fuh-sis). This girdle enables attachment of the lower limbs to the axial skeleton. The axial connection is a posterior union of the hip bones with the sacrum at the **sacroiliac joints**. The pelvic girdle and sacrum, along with the coccyx, thus form a ring of bone: the basin-like **pelvis**, or **bony pelvis**. It bears the weight of the upper body and transmits it to the ground through its articulation with the lower limbs.

Bottom Line: Compared to the pectoral girdle, the bones of the pelvic girdle are larger and heavier and are designed preferentially for weight bearing rather than mobility.

Each hip bone is commonly divided into three regions, representing three individual bones of a child: the ilium, ischium, and pubis (Figure 7-10). (Fusion into a single bone is usually complete by age 23.) Obtain specimens

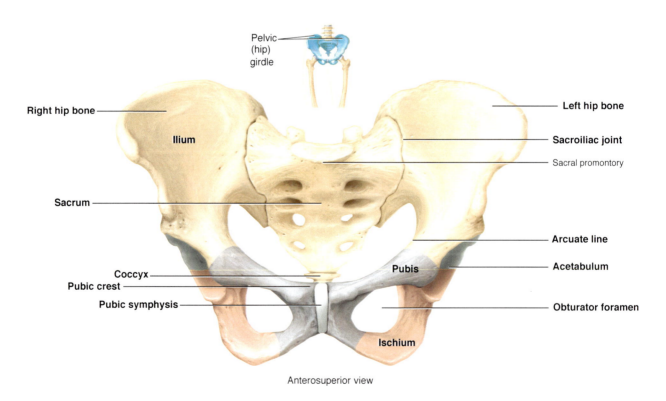

FIGURE 7-9. The pelvic girdle (hip bones) and sacrum form the bony pelvis.

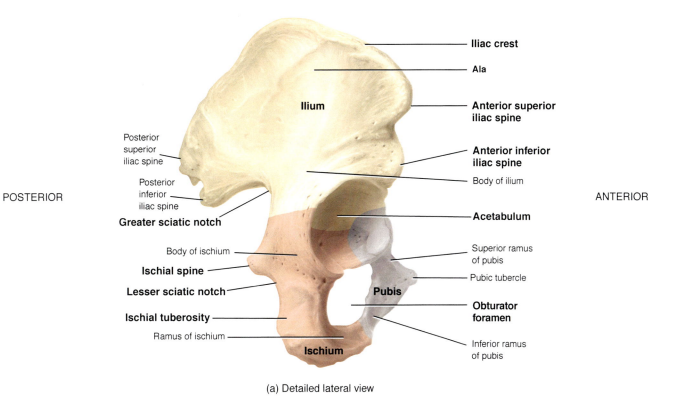

Iliac crest

Ala

Ilium

Anterior superior
iliac spine

Posterior
superior
iliac spine

Anterior inferior
iliac spine

Posterior
inferior
iliac spine

Body of ilium

POSTERIOR

ANTERIOR

Greater sciatic notch

Acetabulum

Body of ischium

Superior ramus
of pubis

Ischial spine

Pubic tubercle

Lesser sciatic notch

Pubis

Ischial tuberosity

Obturator
foramen

Ramus of ischium

Ischium

Inferior ramus
of pubis

(a) Detailed lateral view

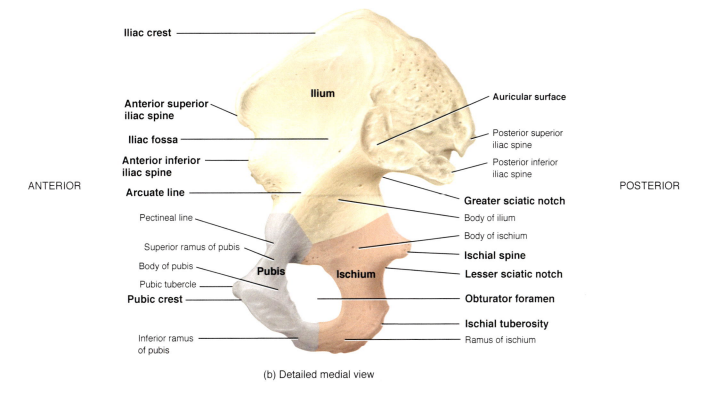

Iliac crest

Ilium

Anterior superior
iliac spine

Auricular surface

Iliac fossa

Posterior superior
iliac spine

Anterior inferior
iliac spine

Posterior inferior
iliac spine

ANTERIOR

Arcuate line

Greater sciatic notch

POSTERIOR

Pectineal line

Body of ilium

Superior ramus of pubis

Body of ischium

Body of pubis

Pubis

Ischium

Ischial spine

Pubic tubercle

Lesser sciatic notch

Pubic crest

Obturator foramen

Ischial tuberosity

Inferior ramus
of pubis

Ramus of ischium

(b) Detailed medial view

FIGURE 7-10. The right hip bone.

of individual hip bones and *pelves* (the plural of pelvis) to locate the following bones and their surface features.

Ilium

The **ilium** (IL-ee-um) is the largest portion of the coxal bone. Identify the:

- **iliac crest**, the upper margin of the ilium which can be felt by simply placing hands on hips.

- **ala** (AY-luh), the superior region of the ilium that extends from the iliac crest to the level of the greater sciatic notch posteriorly and the anterior superior iliac spine (ASIS) anteriorly; plural **alae** (AY-lee)

- **anterior superior iliac spine**, the anterior termination of the crest and an important landmark, abbreviated ASIS. It is the standard starting point for measuring lower limb length. Below is the **anterior inferior iliac spine**. The spines serve as points of attachment for muscles of the hip and thigh.
Palpation of ASIS: While standing, run your index finger from the crest forward to a point in line with the middle of your thigh.

- **iliac fossa**, a shallow depression on the medial surface.

- **greater sciatic notch** (*sciaticus* = relating to the hip), an indentation on the posterior aspect of the ilium through which the sciatic nerve passes.

- **arcuate line** (AR-kyoo-wut) (*arcus* = bow), a curved ridge on the lower ilium that helps define the pelvic brim (inlet).

Ischium

The **ischium** (ISS-kee-um) is the inferior and posterior region of the coxal bone. Identify the:

- **ischial tuberosity**, the ischium's most prominent surface feature, and the part of the pelvis that bears our weight when seated.
Palpation: In a sitting position, lean to one side and place your hand, palm side up, discreetly beneath the buttock not bearing your weight. Return to an upright sitting position and note the tuberosity.

- **ischial spine**, a prominent projection above the tuberosity, and an important landmark for its attachment site for pelvic muscles.

- **lesser sciatic notch**, an indentation below the ischial spine.

Pubis

The **pubis**, or **pubic bone**, is the most anterior portion of the coxal bone. Identify the:

- **pubic crest**, a ridge on the superior aspect of the pubis at its most medial point.

- **pubic symphysis**, where the two pubic bones come together in the midline of the pelvis. Sandwiched between them is a pad of fibrocartilage, forming a joint with somewhat more give than a bone-to-bone articulation. (This cartilaginous union has implications for women during childbirth, allowing slightly greater pelvic flexibility.)

- **obturator foramen**, an extremely large opening bounded by the pubis and ischium that allows the passage of blood vessels and nerves between the thigh and pelvic regions. (Its name is derived from the Latin *obturare*, meaning "to block". This refers to the fact that most of this large foraminal space is closed off by a membrane in life.)

Together the ilium, ischium, and pubis form the **acetabulum** (as-uh-TAB-yuh-lum), the socket of the hip joint. The size and shape of the acetabulum strongly resembles the vinegar cups of ancient Rome (*acetum* = vinegar), hence its name.

Functional Anatomy of the Pelvic Girdle

Architectural elements of the pelvic girdle reveal numerous adaptations for bearing weight. Note how form follows function:

- *The acetabulum is relatively deep to stabilize the hip bone/femur(thighbone) joint.*

- *The acetabulum is attached to the head of the femur by a special ligament to help secure the lower limb.*

- *The broad sacroiliac joints feature extensive bone-to-bone contact between the sacrum and ilium to effectively transmit weight from the trunk to the lower limbs.* (It is not surprising that the sacroiliacs are a focus of low back pain given the forces that bear down on them.)

The False and True Pelves

The **false (greater) pelvis** is that portion of the pelvis superior to the pelvic brim (Figure 7-11a). The **pelvic brim**, or **pelvic inlet**, is outlined by the arcuate lines, pubic symphysis and crests, and sacral promontory. The false pelvis is bordered laterally by the **alae** of the ilia, the lumbar vertebrae posteriorly, and anteriorly by the abdominal wall.

The **true (lesser) pelvis** is inferior to the pelvic inlet (Figure 7-11b). It is bordered by the lower ilia and ischia laterally, the pubic bones anteriorly, and the sacrum and coccyx posteriorly.

The pelvic inlet is the superior opening of the true pelvis; its inferior opening is the **pelvic outlet**. The boundaries are the ischia laterally, pubic arch anteriorly, and the sacrum and coccyx posteriorly.

The dimensions of the true pelvis, and most significantly, those of the inlet and outlet, are critical during childbirth because they define the space accorded the fetus during its passage through the birth canal.

Pelvimetry is the measurement of the pelvic inlet and outlet diameters, usually by sonography. A too-small pelvic cavity makes the case for a cesarean section.

How does the functional anatomy of the pelvic girdle compare with that of the pectoral girdle?

_____

_____

_____

_____

Comparison of Male and Female Pelves

The greatest differences between the male and female skeletons reside in the pelvis (Table 7-1). Using the laboratory models and human pelves, note the differences described and illustrated in Table 7-1.

• The angle of the **pubic arch** (**pubic angle**), measured between the pubic bones on their inferior aspect, is less than 90 degrees (acute) in males and greater than 90 degrees (obtuse) in females.

• The pelvic brim, is wider, more shallow, and elliptical (like a flattened circle) in females and narrower, deeper, and funnel-shaped in males.

• The distance between the ilia is greater in females *in relation to overall pelvic dimensions*.

• The sacrum and coccyx in females are less curved anteriorly, widening the pelvic outlet.

• The ischial spines in females are shorter and farther apart, also widening the pelvic outlet.

Bottom Line: With its proportionately larger dimensions, the female pelvis is better adapted to childbearing.

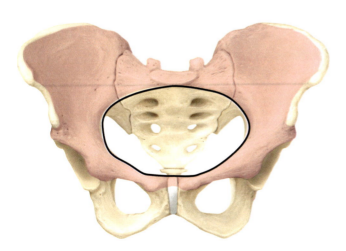

(a) Anterior view of false pelvis (pink)

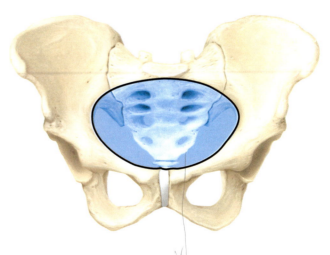

(b) Anterior view of true pelvis (blue)

internal os of the pelvis

FIGURE 7-11. False and true pelves. The pelvic brim (inlet) is outlined in black.

Table 7.1

Comparison of Female and Male Pelves

Point of comparison	Female	Male
Pelvic brim (inlet)	Wide and more oval.	Narrow and heart-shaped.
Acetabulum	Small and faces anteriorly.	Large and faces laterally.
Obturator foramen	Oval.	Round.
Pubic arch	Greater than 90° angle.	Less than 90° angle.

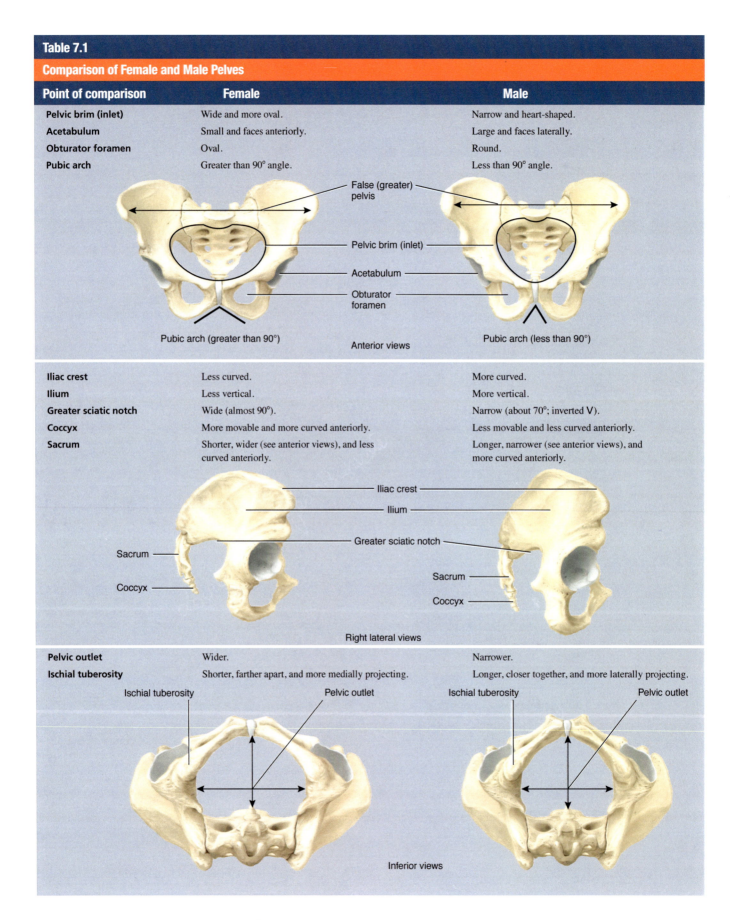

False (greater) pelvis

Pelvic brim (inlet)

Acetabulum

Obturator foramen

Pubic arch (greater than 90°)   Anterior views   Pubic arch (less than 90°)

Point of comparison	Female	Male
Iliac crest	Less curved.	More curved.
Ilium	Less vertical.	More vertical.
Greater sciatic notch	Wide (almost 90°).	Narrow (about 70°; inverted V).
Coccyx	More movable and more curved anteriorly.	Less movable and less curved anteriorly.
Sacrum	Shorter, wider (see anterior views), and less curved anteriorly.	Longer, narrower (see anterior views), and more curved anteriorly.

Iliac crest

Ilium

Greater sciatic notch

Sacrum

Coccyx

Sacrum

Coccyx

Right lateral views

Point of comparison	Female	Male
Pelvic outlet	Wider.	Narrower.
Ischial tuberosity	Shorter, farther apart, and more medially projecting.	Longer, closer together, and more laterally projecting.

Ischial tuberosity   Pelvic outlet   Ischial tuberosity   Pelvic outlet

Inferior views

The Thigh

Femur

The **femur**, commonly called the thighbone, is our longest and heaviest bone (Figure 7-12). As such, it is well suited for transmitting body weight from the hip bone to the leg in a standing position. Obtain a femur from the demo table and identify the:

- **head**, a ball-shaped projection at the proximal end that articulates with the acetabulum to form the hip joint. Find the **fovea capitis** (*fovea* = pit), a depression at its center. The fovea anchors a short ligament that helps bind the femur to the acetabulum. Place the head of your lab specimen into the acetabulum of a disarticulated hip bone to observe the relationship of femur to pelvic anatomy. (Be sure each bone is from the same side of the body).
Note the greater degree of bony overlap — and stability — compared with the ball–and–socket joint of the shoulder.

- **neck**, a constricted region distal to the head that joins it to the body.

- **greater** and **lesser trochanters**, two prominent processes that provide leverage for powerful hip and thigh muscles. The lesser trochanter is medial and inferior to its larger counterpart.
Palpation: The greater trochanter can be felt on the lateral aspect of the thigh about a hands-width below the iliac crest. As you palpate, swing your leg sideways like a pendulum.

- **gluteal tuberosity**, a vertical midline ridge on the posterior aspect that begins at the level of the lesser trochanter and blends into the **linea aspera**, literally a rough line, that occupies the middle third of the shaft. Both these elevations attach to thigh muscles.

- **medial** and **lateral condyles**, large "knuckles" at the expanded distal end, between which is the **intercondylar fossa**. These condyles articulate the femur to the tibia of the leg to form the knee joint.

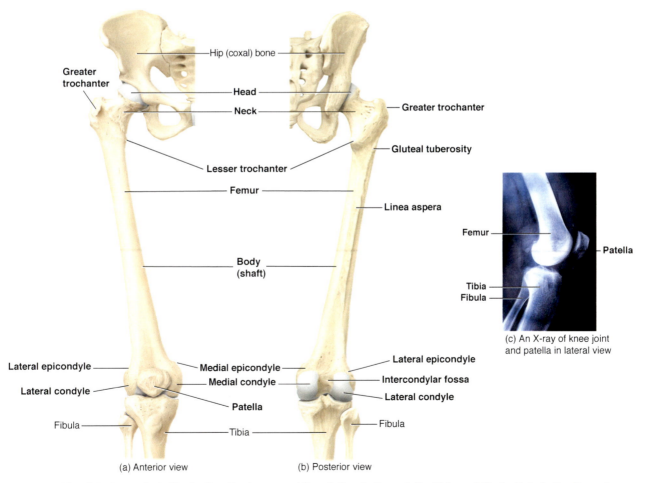

(c) An X-ray of knee joint and patella in lateral view

(a) Anterior view   (b) Posterior view

FIGURE 7-12. The right lower limb illustrating the femur and its relation to the patella, tibia and fibula. Note in the X-ray image (c) that the patella articulates to the femur in an unusual way because it is embedded in a tendon. As the knee is flexed and extended, the patella tracks within a groove between the femoral condyles.

- **medial** and **lateral epicondyles**, which are just superior to the condyles. They anchor ligaments that support the knee.

Femur Facts

- The length of the femur is about ¼ of one's height. In forensic investigations, discovery of an isolated femur can easily lead to an estimate of a missing person's height and an approximation of overall dimensions.

- To ensure the body is balanced while standing, the femur curves medially to align the knees with the body's *center of gravity* (the point, near the upper sacrum, where body weight is concentrated when in the anatomical position). The medial condyle bears more weight than the lateral condyle because the line of gravity is medial to the knee. There is therefore greater stress on the medial condyle and on the cushioning pad of cartilage — the *meniscus* — beneath it. This meniscus is consequently torn more frequently than its counterpart on the lateral side.

- The diagonal slant of the femur creates an obtuse lateral angle at the knee, which when exaggerated is termed "knock-knee".

- The neck is the part of the femur most vulnerable to fracture, especially in the elderly. Such an injury is commonly referred to as a "broken hip".

Patella

The **patella**, commonly called the kneecap, is a triangular bone tucked into the tendon connecting anterior thigh muscles to the tibia (Figure 7-13). This bone — the only named sesamoid — thus does not articulate directly to another bone. Between the apex and its attachment to the tibia, the tendon that encloses the patella is renamed the **patellar ligament.** The superior border of the patella is its **base**; the lateral and medial borders converge to the **apex**. Its borders and anterior surface are easily palpated, especially when the knee is extended (straightened). On its posterior surface, smooth facets glide over the femoral condyles during knee extension and flexion (bending).

Bottom Line: The patella's function is to protect the knee joint and add leverage to the thigh muscles that extend it. Without that leverage, these muscles would be functionally weaker, making routine activities such as stair climbing extremely difficult.

PROCEDURE 5

The Leg

The tibia and fibula form the skeleton of the leg. Observe these bones as individual specimens and on the articulated skeletons.

Tibia

The **tibia**, commonly called the shinbone, is the larger medial bone of the leg (Figure 7-14). In a standing position, it transmits weight from the femur to the foot. Identify the:

- **lateral** and **medial condyles** at its flared proximal end. They articulate to the respective condyles of the femur to form the knee (tibiofemoral) joint. The inferior surface of the lateral condyle presents a facet for articulation to the head of the fibula.

- **tibial tuberosity**, a roughened bump in the tibia's midline, just below its condyles. This protrusion — which can be felt one or two finger widths below the patella — anchors the patellar ligament (and indirectly, the anterior muscles of the thigh).

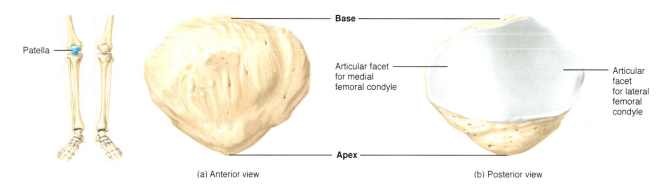

(a) Anterior view

(b) Posterior view

FIGURE 7-13. The right patella.

- **anterior border** (**crest**), the sharply sculpted "shin" of the leg. It is easily palpated down its length due to scant subcutaneous fat and the absence of underlying muscle.

- **medial malleolus** (muh-LEE-uh-lus), a prominent bump on the medial side of the tibia's inferior end. This highly visible landmark is named for its resemblance to a round hammer head and can easily be palpated. The malleolus helps stabilize the ankle joint as does the smooth inferior articular surface that slides over the talus bone of the ankle. (The tibia's inferior end also articulates with the fibula.) *The medial malleolus is the endpoint for leg length measurements, which begin at the anterior superior iliac spine.*

Fibula

The **fibula** is the lateral bone of the leg and the body's thinnest long bone. Its name harks back to the Latin word for a pin-like clasp, hence its modern nickname, the "pin bone". Unlike the more massive tibia, the parallel fibula does not bear weight. It is surrounded by muscles, and except for its proximal and distal ends, cannot be palpated. Identify the:

- **head**, the rounded proximal end that articulates with the tibia's lateral condyle just distal to the knee joint. *Palpation: From the tibial tuberosity, the head is about four finger widths toward the lateral side of the leg.*

- **lateral malleolus**, the distal termination of the fibula that bulges prominently — and is easily felt — on the lateral side. The malleolus articulates with the lateral side of the tibia and talus. It helps contain the ankle joint to keep it stable. The classic fracture of the ankle is at the fibula's lower end.

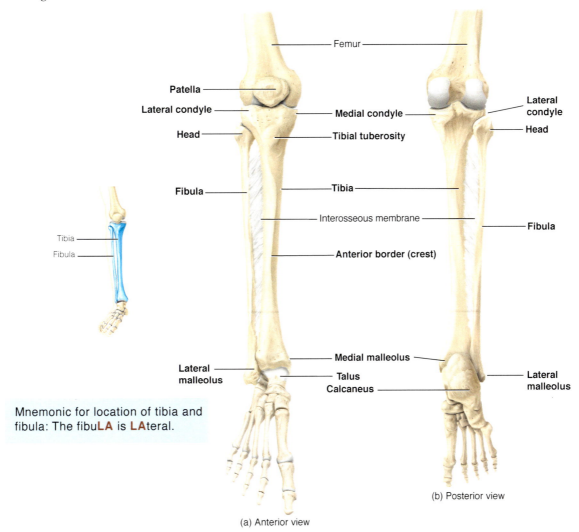

Mnemonic for location of tibia and fibula: The fibu**LA** is **LA**teral.

(a) Anterior view

(b) Posterior view

FIGURE 7-14. The right tibia and fibula in relation to the femur, patella and talus.

The Foot

The foot consists of three groups of bones: the ankle, or tarsus, the instep, or metatarsus, and the toes, or phalanges. Obtain a foot skeleton and note its components as described below.

Tarsus (Ankle)

There are seven **tarsals** in the ankle group (Figure 7-15). In the posterior foot, identify the:

- **talus** (TAY-lus = ankle bone), which is framed by the tibia and fibula. When the foot is viewed in profile, the talus is the most superior of the ankle bones. Mnemonic: The *talus* is the *tallest*.

- **calcaneus** (cal-KAY-nee-us = heel), the largest and strongest tarsal. It receives body weight via the talus above and transmits it to the ground.

Anteriorly, identify the:
- **navicular** (nuh-VIK-yuh-lar; *navicula* = boat)

- **cuneiforms** (kyoo-NEE-ih-forms; *cuneus* = wedge): **medial** (first), **intermediate** (second), and **lateral** (third) located between the navicular and cuboid.

- **cuboid** (KYOO-boyd = cube-shaped), just anterior to the calcaneus.

(Note the mnemonic for remembering the names of the tarsals accompanying Figure 7-15. The M, I, and L represent the medial, intermediate and lateral cuneiforms.)

Metatarsus

The five **metatarsals**, the bones of the instep (Figure 7-15), are numbered I to V, medial to lateral. Like the metacarpals of the hand, each metatarsal has a **shaft** between a proximal **base** and a distal **head**. The bases articulate proximally to the cuboid and cuneiforms and

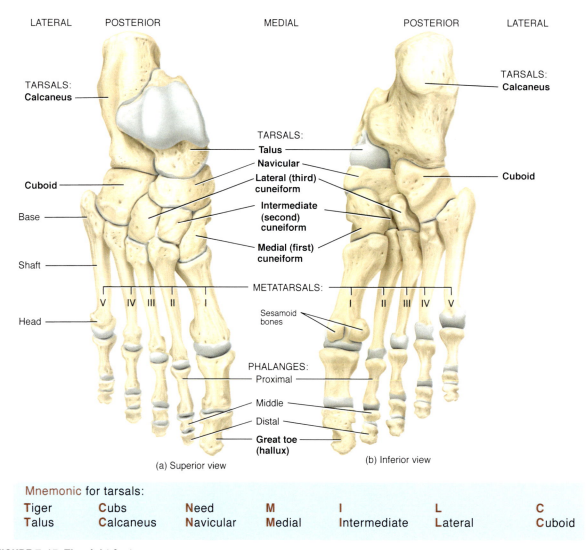

(a) Superior view

(b) Inferior view

Mnemonic for tarsals:						
Tiger	**Cubs**	**Need**	**M**	**I**	**L**	**C**
Talus	**Calcaneus**	**Navicular**	**Medial**	**Intermediate**	**Lateral**	**Cuboid**

FIGURE 7-15. The right foot.

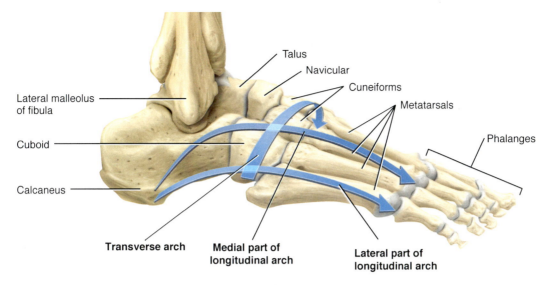

Lateral view of arches

FIGURE 7-16. The arches of the right foot.

FIGURE 7-17. An X-ray of the foot viewed from the side. Distribution of weight to the ground is via the calcaneus and heads of the metatarsals.

with adjacent metatarsals. Each head articulates distally with a proximal toe bone. Note the first metatarsal is the largest owing to the greater weight it bears.

Phalanges

The **phalanges** of the foot — the toe bones — are arranged like their counterparts in the hand. The great or "big" toe has two phalanges (proximal and distal) and is disproportionately large. Each of the other toes has three phalanges (proximal, middle, and distal). Only the great toe, the *hallux*, is named.

The Arches of the Foot

The bones of the foot are maintained in an archlike configuration, a shape that is the strongest and most efficient for weight bearing. The arches — two longitudinal and and one transverse — are held in place by ligaments and tendons and are flexible (Figure 7-16). The arches give under the stress of body weight and recoil (spring back) as downward force is diminished. They are usually fully developed by age 13. Flat feet, or *pes planus*, can be an inborn defect or acquired ("fallen arches"). Obtain a foot skeleton and observe the arches from both sides in an eye-level lateral view.

Functional Anatomy of the Foot

- *The arches not only confer greater strength, but are effective shock absorbers as well and provide leverage as we walk.*

- *The arches provide an ideal distribution of body weight to the foot, but while standing and during locomotion, body weight is transmitted to the ground via the calcaneus and the heads of the metatarsals, the "unarched" parts of foot anatomy. The calcaneus bears about 60% of the load and the metatarsal heads — the ball of the foot — about 40%.*

- *The great toe's outsize dimensions make mechanical sense: When walking or running, we push off the medial aspect of the foot, with much of the propulsive force centered on this largest toe.*

Clinical Application
Hip Fractures

The term *hip fracture* may apply to any break in the pelvic girdle or femur. Most commonly, it refers to a femoral fracture. There are an estimated 400,000 to 500,000 people who experience a hip fracture annually. This frequency appears to be rising, mainly due to increasing longevity. Those most vulnerable are the elderly, especially women. Post-menopausal women are particularly prone to developing osteoporosis with its attendant loss of bone mass and integrity.

Surgical intervention is the most common means of treating hip fractures. Surgery stabilizes the fracture and ensures a greater likelihood of healing completely and minimizing pain. In severe cases, a metal or plastic prosthesis may be indicated to replace markedly compromised bone tissue.

In the X-ray, note the longitudinal fracture in the shaft of the femur just distal to the lesser trochanter. The asterisk is on a portion of the femur that was displaced. Such a fracture would usually be stabilized with metal screws or a combination of screws, pins and plates.

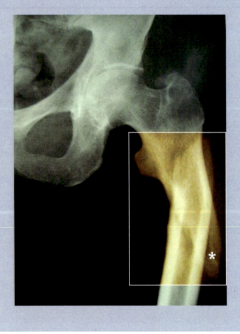

1. Which region of the femur is most vulnerable to fracture?

   _____

   _____

   _____

2. Assume the patella was fractured beyond repair and surgically removed. Without a normal patella, what noticable difference would there be as the knee joint is extended by muscles of the thigh? (Aside from its role in protecting the knee, discuss the biomechanical disadvantage of a missing kneecap.)

   _____

   _____

   _____

   _____

   _____

   _____

The Appendicular Skeleton

NAME _____

LAB TIME/DATE _____

The Pectoral Girdle and Upper Limb

Matching

Match the bone or marking in column B with its description in column A. (The B bone may be used more than once.)

Column A

_____1. the "point" of the elbow

_____2. the head of this bone is a knuckle

_____3. the collarbone

_____4. the forearm bone on the medial aspect

_____5. the forearm bone on the lateral aspect

_____6. the "socket" of the shoulder joint

_____7. the anterior brace of the pectoral girdle

_____8. This forearm bone is part of the elbow joint.

_____9. This bone of the pectoral girdle "floats" in soft tissue.

_____10. limb bone of the shoulder joint

_____11. cavity within arm bone that allows full extension of the forearm

_____12. the "high point" of the shoulder

_____13. beak-shaped muscle anchor on the pectoral girdle

_____14. "little head" at distal end of arm bone

_____15. wheel-like marking on proximal bone of elbow joint

_____16. most flexible phalanx

Column B

a. ulna

b. clavicle

c. acromion

d. coracoid process

e. trochlea

f. humerus

g. radius

h. glenoid cavity

i. metacarpal

j. olecranon process

k. scapula

l. olecranon fossa

m. capitulum

n. pollex

The Pectoral Girdle and Upper Limbs

Scapula

Place the number of the corresponding key label next to the leader line.

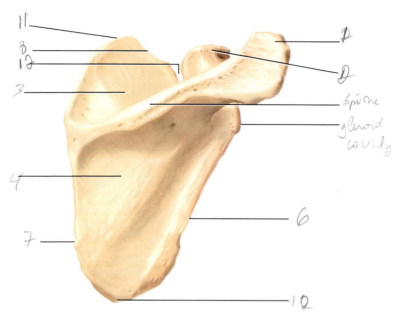

Key
1. acromion
2. coracoid process
3. supraspinous fossa
4. infraspinous fossa
5. spine
6. lateral border
7. medial border
8. superior border
9. glenoid cavity
10. inferior angle
11. superior angle
12. scapular notch

1. The mobility of the pectoral girdle depends directly on the anatomical relationship of the clavicle and scapula to the axial skeleton. Briefly describe these axial/appendicular connections.

   Clavicle: _____

   _____

   _____

   Scapula: _____

   _____

   _____

2. Aside from affording the pectoral girdle considerable mobility, what is another function of the clavicle?

   _____

   _____

   _____

3. Name the carpals in the proximal row from lateral to medial.

_____

Name the carpals in the distal row, lateral to medial.

_____

Humerus, Radius and Ulna

Place the number of the corresponding key label next to the leader line.

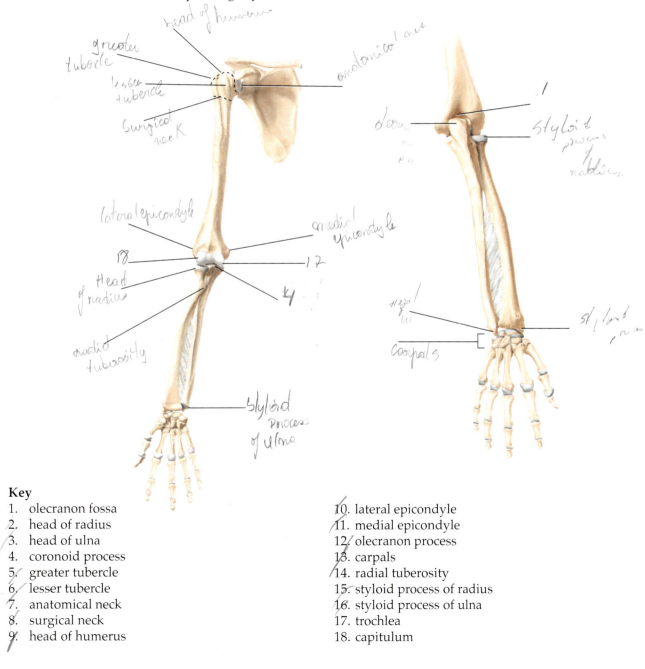

Key
1. olecranon fossa
2. head of radius
3. head of ulna
4. coronoid process
5. greater tubercle
6. lesser tubercle
7. anatomical neck
8. surgical neck
9. head of humerus
10. lateral epicondyle
11. medial epicondyle
12. olecranon process
13. carpals
14. radial tuberosity
15. styloid process of radius
16. styloid process of ulna
17. trochlea
18. capitulum

The Hand

Place the number of the corresponding key label next to the leader line.

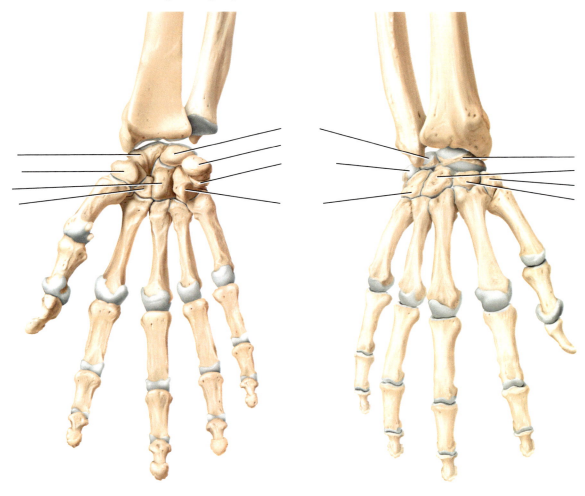

Key

1. trapezium
2. hamate
3. triquetrum
4. lunate

5. scaphoid
6. pisiform
7. trapezoid
8. capitate

1. Label metacarpals I-V.

2. Label a "knuckle".

3. Name a carpal that can be palpated without much effort.

_____

The Pelvic Girdle and Lower Limbs

Matching

Match the bone or marking in column B with its description in column A.

Column A

_____1. heel bone

_____2. in profile, tallest of tarsals

_____3. one of a trio of wedge-shaped tarsals

_____4. the "boat bone" of the foot

_____5. most medial toe

_____6. the thinnest long bone

_____C_____7. the longest bone

_____8. an instep bone

_____9. sesamoid bone of the knee

_____j_____10. the smaller "C" in, "Tiger Cubs Need MILC"

_____11. the shinbone

_____12. socket of hip joint

_____13. This transmits weight from derrière to chair.

_____K_____14. midline pelvic girdle union

_____15. where the patellar ligament attaches

_____16. This is palpated when hands are on hips.

_____17. large proximal femoral projection

_____e_____18. space on ilium for passage of a prominent nerve

_____19. winglike part of ilium

_____20. joint where hip bones meets axial skeleton

Column B

a. tibia

b. greater trochanter

c. femur

d. patella

e. ischial tuberosity

f. iliac crest

g. sacroiliac

h. navicular

i. hallux

j. calcaneus

k. pubic symphysis

l. greater sciatic notch

m. cuneiform

n. fibula

o. metatarsal

p. acetabulum

q. talus

r. cuboid

s. tibial tuberosity

t. ala

1. What is the difference between the pelvic girdle and the pelvis?

   _____

   _____

2. Compare the pelvic and pectoral girdles by matching them with their appropriate description (by letter) from the key.

Key	Pectoral Girdle	Pelvic Girdle
a. lighter weight		
b. heavier weight	_____	_____
c. greater emphasis on stability		
d. greater emphasis on flexibility	_____	_____
e. more bone-to-bone articulation to axial skeleton		
f. less bone-to-bone articulation to axial skeleton	_____	_____

3. a. How are the arches of the foot maintained?

   _____

   _____

   _____

   b. What is one consequence of flat feet (fallen arches)?

   _____

   _____

   _____

4. An anatomical difference between the male and female pelvis that is often cited by students is, "The female pelvis is wider." This is not always true; large men have wider pelves than petite women when compared using absolute measurements. How — in a *relative* sense — are the dimensions of the female pelvis wider? (Hint: Focus on the superior portion of the two hip bones.)

   _____

   _____

3. What is the sex of the pelvis in Figure 7-11?

   _____

   _____

   _____

Close your eyes and have your lab partner hand you a disarticulated bone of the extremities. Using the bone's dimensions and palpation of bony landmarks as clues, determine the identity of your specimen.

Pelvic Girdle and Pelvis

Place the number of the corresponding key label next to the leader line.

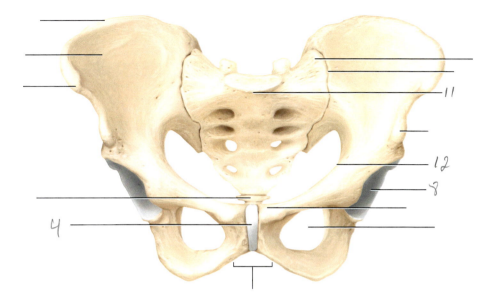

Key
1. iliac crest
2. iliac fossa
3. pubic crest
4. pubic symphysis
5. ala of sacrum
6. sacroiliac joint
7. anterior superior iliac spine
8. acetabulum
9. obturator foramen
10. anterior inferior iliac spine
11. coccyx
12. pubic arch
13. sacral promontory
14. arcuate line

Femur, Tibia and Fibula

Place the number of the corresponding key label next to the leader line.

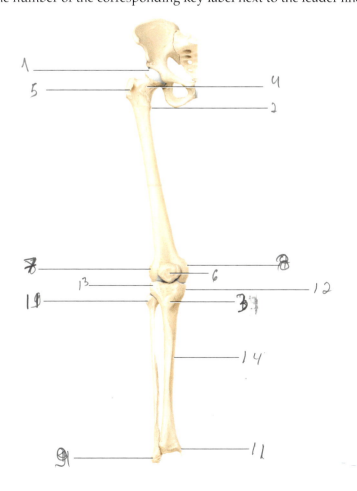

Key
1. head of femur
2. neck of femur
3. tibial tuberosity
4. greater trochanter
5. lesser trochanter
6. patella
7. lateral condyle of femur
8. medial condyle of femur
9. lateral malleolus
10. medial malleolus
11. head of fibula
12. lateral condyle of tibia
13. medial condyle of tibia
14. anterior border of tibia

1. In a kneeling position, what specific parts of the thigh and / or leg does the body rest on? (Cite specific bones and landmarks in your answer.)

    _____

    _____

2. Hip fractures involving the femur may occur in any of several regions in close proximity to the hip joint.

    Refer to the clinical application on p. 138. In his X ray-based diagnosis, an orthopedic surgeon wrote "subtrochanteric fracture of the femur" on the patient's record to pinpoint the location of the break. Further, the doctor is obligated to note on which side the break occurred. Is this a right or left femur? Justify your answer.

    _____

    _____

The Foot

Place the number of the corresponding key label next to the leader line.

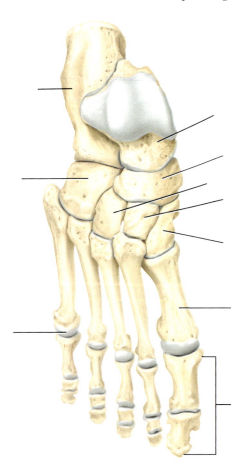

Key
1. calcaneus
2. cuboid
3. lateral (third) cuneiform
4. intermediate (second) cuneiform
5. medial (first) cuneiform
6. talus
7. navicular
8. hallux
9. first metatarsal
10. metatarsal head

1. In the anatomy of the foot, there are two focal points that transmit weight to the ground. Name them.

    _____

    _____

2. Wearing high-heel shoes tilts the back of the foot upward, causing imbalance and compromising the foot's ability to bear weight. Which of the two weight-transmitting focal points in the previous question is overburdened by high heels?

    _____

Summary of Skeletal Anatomy

Identify bones of the articulated, skeleton, singly or collectively (at asterisks), by inserting their names next to the leader lines.

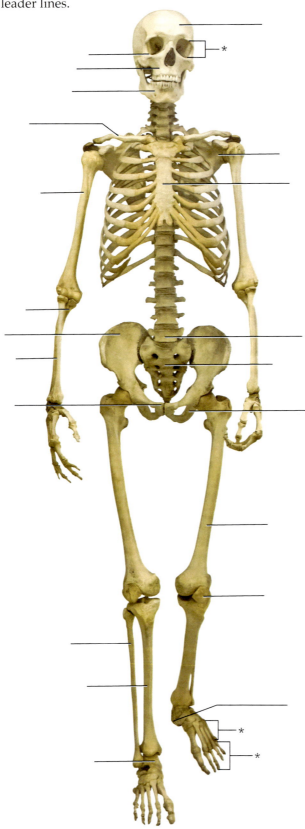

Critical Thinking

1. In the forelimb girdle of a quadriped (four-legged animal), what essential difference would you expect to see compared to the pectoral girdle of humans?

    _____

    _____

2. What is wrong with this illustration? (Hint: Focus on the carpal / forearm anatomy.)

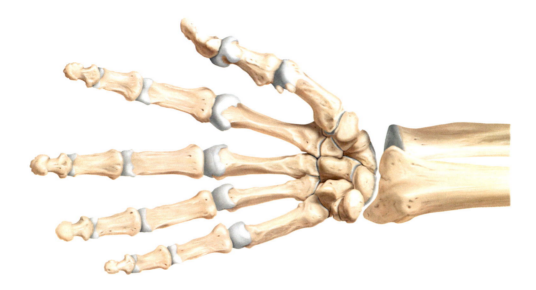

3. During an archaeological dig in Ethiopia, two human skeletons are unearthed. One shows evidence of epiphyseal lines in the femurs, an obtuse pubic angle, and an elliptical pelvic opening. The second skeleton shows epiphyseal cartilage plates in the femurs, an acute pubic angle, and a funnel-shaped pelvic inlet.

    What can you say about the age and gender of each of these human remains? (Describe the age as *adult* or *adolescent*.)

	First Skeleton	Second Skeleton
Age		
Gender		

4. What is missing from this hand skeleton? Try to determine which two bones are gone. (Hint: A bone count is a good starting point.)

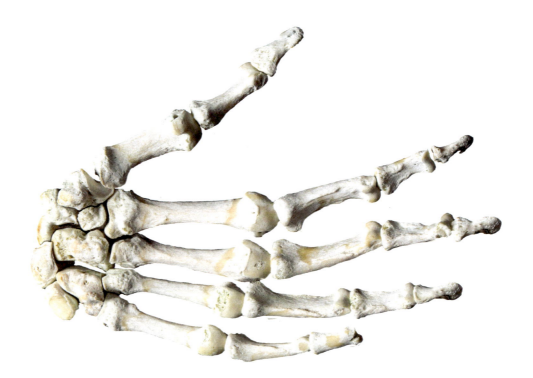

Articulations and Body Movements

Exercise 8

OBJECTIVES

1. To describe the structural and functional classifications of joints.
2. To describe the structure and function of fibrous joints.
3. To describe the structure and function of cartilaginous joints.
4. To describe the structure and function of synovial joints.
5. To distinguish among uniaxial, biaxial, and triaxial synovial joints.
6. To define the different body movements and identify those that occur at synovial joints.
7. To describe the structure and function of the knee joint as a special synovial joint.

MATERIALS

Articulated skeletons
Human skulls
Functional models of shoulder, hip and
  knee joints

Adult human femur in longitudinal section
  (optional)
X rays of arthritic joints (optional)
Human knee joint prosthesis (optional)

PRE-LAB QUIZ

1. A structural feature of all synovial joints is a fluid-filled _____.
2. The functional classification of joints is based on which criterion?
   a. the degree of movement permitted by the joint
   b. the type of connective tissue between articulating bones
   c. presence of a joint cavity
3. True or False (Correct the statement if false.) All diarthroses are synovial joints.
4. Synarthroses permit free/limited/no movement. (Circle one.)
5. An example of a fibrous joint is _____.
6. Bands of connective tissue external to joints that support and stabilize them are called _____.
7. Which is a joint found between vertebral bodies?
   a. gomphosis   c. suture
   b. syndesmosis   d. symphysis
8. True or False (Correct the statement if false.) The elbow joint is a plane joint.
9. The atlanto-axial joint is an example of a _____ joint.
   a. condyloid   c. ball-and-socket
   b. pivot   d. hinge
10. A movement that reduces the angle between two articulating bones is called

    _____.

Articulations, or joints, are points of connection between adjacent bones. Beyond holding bones together, joints allow for flexibility and gross body movements. The study of joints is known as *arthrology*.

Articulations are classified according to (1) structural, and (2) functional criteria. Depending on what tissue intervenes between articulating bones, the structural classifications are **fibrous**, **cartilaginous**, and **synovial joints**. Functional designations are based on joint mobility: **synarthroses** are generally immovable, **amphiarthroses** allow limited movement, and **diarthroses** are freely movable.

Fibrous Joints

Fibrous joints do not have a joint cavity between articulating bones and therefore permit little or no movement. Dense irregular connective tissue holds the bones together. Fibrous joints include sutures, syndesmoses, and interosseus membranes.

PROCEDURE 1

Examining Fibrous Joints

Sutures
Sutures, which are found only in the skull, are joints with dense irregular connective tissue occupying the space between articulating bones. In infants and children, there is some movement possible; the joint at this stage is functionally an amphiarthrosis. The "soft spots", or fontanels, which are present for up to two postnatal years, are relatively large areas of fibrous membrane. They, and smaller membrane remnants later in childhood, permit expansion of the brain and cranial volume. The adult brain and cranium are considered to be "full grown" at 18-20 years of age. (See page 100 for a more detailed discussion of fontanels.)

In adulthood, the intervening fibrous membranes are greatly diminished or absent altogether. Adult sutures are immovable (synarthrodial) joints with jagged, interlocking surfaces (Figure 8-1a). Such an arrangement secures the articulating bones tightly and is perfectly adapted to their location in the cranium and face. The joint between the frontal and parietal bones in Figure 8-1 you may recall as the coronal suture.

In some areas, separate skull bones fuse together as a single bone. This is a **synostosis** and is exemplified by the frontal bone, whose two lateral masses fuse into a single bone at about age six.

Obtain a human skull (rather than a plastic model whose sutures may be indistinct) to observe sutures in an adult specimen. Remove the calvarium to see the ridge demarcating the frontal synostosis on the inner cranial surface.

Syndesmoses
Syndesmoses (sin-dez-MOE-seez; *syndesmo-* = ligament) are fibrous joints with a greater distance and more dense irregular connective tissue between the articulating bones than sutures. The connective tissue is usually arranged as a ligament, whose bandlike fibers bridge joint bones together. This configuration

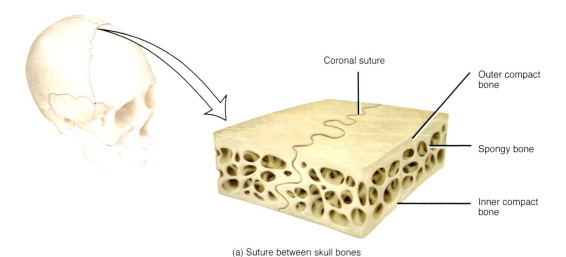

(a) Suture between skull bones

FIGURE 8-1. Fibrous joints.

allows limited movement. One example of a syndesmosis is the distal tibiofibular joint (Figure 8-1b).

A second example of a syndesmosis is a **gomphosis** (Figure 8-1b). This type of joint is found only between a tooth's cone-shaped roots and the sockets within the maxillae and mandible. A synonym for gomphosis — based on the combining form *dento-* for tooth and the noun *alveolus* for socket — is **dentoalveolar joint**. The dense irregular connective tissue binding a tooth to its socket is the **periodontal ligament**. A normal dentoalveolar joint is immovable and therefore classified as a synarthrosis. In cases of periodontal disease, the gums, periodontal ligament, and jawbone may degenerate to the extent that the tooth becomes loose. Periodontal disease is the most common cause of lost teeth in adults.

Interosseus Membranes

An interosseus membrane ("in-tur-AHSS-ee-us) is a sheet of dense irregular connective tissue that binds neighboring long bones and permits slight movement. This type of amphiarthrotic joint is found between the radius and ulna and between the tibia and fibula (Figure 8-1c).

Cartilaginous Joints

Cartilaginous joints (kar-tih-LAJ-ih-nus), like fibrous joints, lack a joint cavity. Cartilage — hyaline or fibrocartilage — intervenes between the articular surfaces, allowing limited or no movement.

Examining Cartilaginous Joints

Synchondroses

A **synchondrosis** (sin-kon-DROE-sus; *syn–* = together, *chondr–* = cartilage) is a joint wherein two bones are connected by hyaline cartilage. The epiphyseal growth plate — connecting the epiphysis and diaphysis of a growing bone — is a synchondrosis (Figure 8-2a). Once lengthwise growth is complete, the cartilage is replaced by bone, forming an **epiphyseal line** (a synostosis) (Figure 8-2b). In either life stage, these joints are immovable (synarthroses). A second example is the joint between the sternum and first rib.

If available, obtain an adult human femur in longitudinal section. Note the line where epiphysis and diaphysis fuse together after the cartilage growth plate disappears.

Symphyses

A **symphysis** (SIM-fih-sis = growing together) is a joint wherein a disc of fibrocartilage connects the bones. A symphysis is a slightly movable joint (amphiarthrosis). The two examples of *symphyses* (plural) are the:

- pubic symphysis, the junction of the two pubic bones in the midline of the pelvis (Figures 8-2c and 7-9).

- intervertebral joints between the vertebral bodies (Figure 6-12). Recall from Exercise 6 that the outer portion of the intervertebral disc is fibrocartilage.

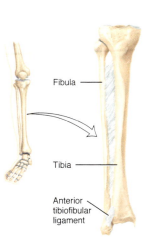

Fibula

Tibia

Anterior tibiofibular ligament

Syndesmosis between tibia and fibula at distal tibiofibular joint

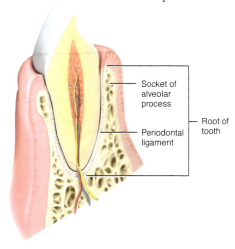

Socket of alveolar process

Root of tooth

Periodontal ligament

Syndesmosis between tooth and socket of alveolar process (gomphosis)

(b) Syndesmoses

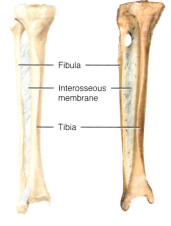

Fibula

Interosseous membrane

Tibia

(c) Interosseous membrane between diaphyses of tibia and fibula

On an articulated skeleton, review the anatomy of the pubic symphysis and the joints between vertebral bodies.

Functional Anatomy of the Fibrous and Cartilaginous Joints

Absent a joint cavity, fibrous and cartilaginous joints feature some form of connective tissue between articulating bones. This structural arrangement has the following functional implications:

- *These joints are far more stable than synovial joints.*

- *Stability equates with protection. Sutures create a strong, fracture-resistant bond between cranial and facial bones. Intervertebral discs — the shock absorbers of the spine — guard against wear on vertebral bodies while sparing torso anatomy from excessive jarring.*

- *Fibrous and cartilaginous joints are immovable or slightly movable, depending on location. Whereas movements of sutures and teeth are undesirable, intervertebral discs compress slightly to limit the impact of weight-bearing forces and to provide a measure of flexibility during body movements.*

Synovial Joints

Synovial joints, unlike fibrous and cartilaginous joints, have a space between articulating bones, the joint cavity. Within this **synovial cavity** is synovial fluid*. All synovial joints are freely movable and therefore classified as diarthroses.

The general features of a synovial joint (Figure 8-3) include:

- **articular cartilage** on the articulating surface of the bones. This hyaline cartilage is smooth and reduces friction as the bones move through their range of motion.

- an **articular capsule** comprised of an outer **fibrous membrane** that is a thickened continuation of the periosteum's dense irregular connective tissue. This fibrous layer permits some give during joint movement, but its mostly collagenous makeup fortifies the joint to hedge against dislocation. The capsule's inner layer is the **synovial membrane**, a connective tissue that secretes synovial fluid into the joint cavity. The fluid is a shock-absorbing lubricant that also serves the metabolic needs of the avascular articular cartilage that it bathes.

- **fibrocartilaginous discs** that act as additional shock absorbers. These discs are not typical; they are limited to certain weight-bearing joints.

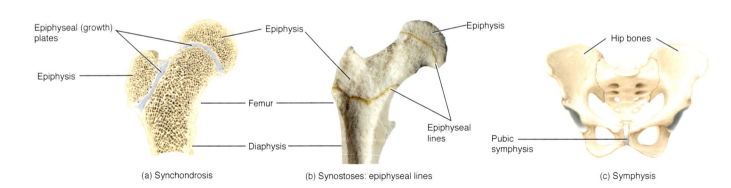

(a) Synchondrosis   (b) Synostoses: epiphyseal lines   (c) Symphysis

FIGURE 8-2. Cartilaginous joints.

* "Synovial" derives from *syn-*, the prefix meaning "with", coupled to the combining form *ovi-*, meaning "egg". This adjective was coined to reflect the fact that synovial fluid is a clear, viscous fluid similar to the appearance and consistency of raw egg white.

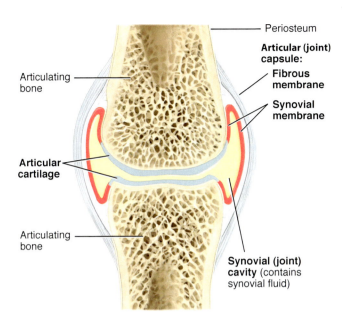

Periosteum

Articular (joint) capsule:

Fibrous membrane

Synovial membrane

Articulating bone

Articular cartilage

Articulating bone

Synovial (joint) cavity (contains synovial fluid)

Frontal section

FIGURE 8-3. Structure of a typical synovial joint.

• **accessory ligaments**. These ligaments are usually *extracapsular* (outside the articular capsule and synovial joint proper) to bind the articulating bones for greater stability. *Example*: the collateral ligaments on either side of the elbow joint. *Intracapsular* ligaments lie within the joint and also act as stabilizers. *Example*: the cruciate ligaments inside the knee joint.

PROCEDURE 3

Examining Synovial Joints

Obtain functional models for the shoulder, hip, and knee joints from the demo table. Try to identify the articular surfaces, the joint capsule, and the accessory ligaments.

Synovial Joint Types

There are six principal categories of synovial joints based on the shape of the articular surfaces. These surfaces determine (1) the structural classification of the joint, and (2) the type and degree of movement that can occur (Figures 8-4 through 8-9).

Synovial joints movements can be classified according to the number of axes of motion permitted. An axis is a straight line about which a bone moves. For our purposes in anatomy lab, an axis of motion refers to movement of a bone in one of the three anatomical planes: horizontal, sagittal, or frontal. Depending on

the degree of movement possible, synovial (diarthrotic) joints are grouped as follows :

• *uniaxial*: movement in one plane
• *biaxial*: movement in two planes
• *triaxial*: movement in three planes

The types of synovial joints are:

• **plane joints** (biaxial), in which the joint surfaces are flat or slightly curved (Figure 8-4). Plane (also called *planar* or *gliding*) joints permit gliding movements, that is, the sliding of articular surfaces past one another with no significant change in the angle between the articulating bones. (Although some textbooks submit that plane joints are "nonaxial" due to the absence of angular change, the interpretation here is that both back-and-forth and side-to-side movements are possible, thus classifying the movements as biaxial.) *Examples*: intercarpal, intertarsal, and sternoclavicular joints, and the joints between vertebral articular processes.

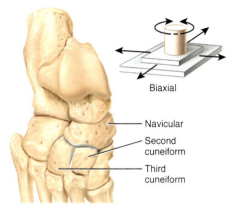

Biaxial

Navicular

Second cuneiform

Third cuneiform

(a) Intertarsal joint between navicular and second and third cuneiforms in foot.

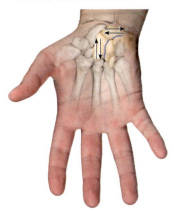

(b) Intercarpal joint showing gliding between carpals (arrows).

FIGURE 8-4. Plane joints.

- **hinge joints** (uniaxial), in which a cylindrical convex process fits into a concave surface of another bone (Figure 8-5). Hinge joints permit only flexion and extension and are named for movements that mimic a hinged door.
Examples: elbow, knee, ankle, and interphalangeal joints.

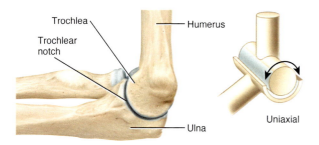

(b) Hinge joint—the humeroulnar—between trochlea of humerus and trochlear notch of ulna at the elbow.

FIGURE 8-5. Hinge joint.

- **pivot joints** (uniaxial), where a rounded surface articulates with a ring-shaped foramen or depression in another bone (Figure 8-6). A pivot joint permits rotation around its own longitudinal axis and is thus limited to a single plane of movement. *Examples*: the proximal radioulnar joint and the atlanto-axial joint: the dens of the axis within the vertebral foramen of the atlas. (To visualize rotation, imagine head move-ments while watching a tennis match.)

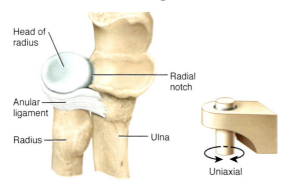

(c) Pivot joint—the radioulnar—between head of radius and radial notch of ulna.

FIGURE 8-6. Pivot joint.

- **condyloid joints** (biaxial), also called *ellipsoidal* joints, have a convex oval process of one bone that complements an oval (ellipsoidal) depression of another bone (Figure 8-7). A condyloid joint permits movement in two planes and can flex-extend and abduct-adduct a part of the body. *Examples*: radiocarpal (wrist) and metacarpophalangeal (knuckle) joints. For the latter, picture flexion and extension as clenching to make a

fist, then unclenching; abduction is when fanning out the fingers and adduction when returning them to the anatomical position.

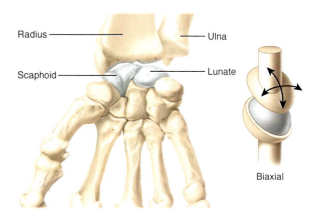

(d) Condyloid joint—the radiocarpal—between radius and scaphoid and lunate bones of wrist.

FIGURE 8-7. Condyloid joint.

- **saddle joints** (biaxial), wherein the articulating surfaces are saddle-shaped, or *sellar* (Figure 8-8). Like the condyloid joints, saddle joints are capable of movements in the planes of flexion and extension and abduction and adduction. *Example*: Saddle joints are unique to the carpometacarpal joints of the thumbs.

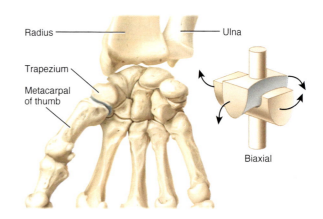

(e) Saddle joint between trapezium of wrist and metacarpal of thumb. This is a carpometacarpal joint.

FIGURE 8-8. Saddle joint.

- **ball-and-socket joints** (triaxial), also known as *spheroid* joints, consist of a ball-like process that joins a cup-like depression (Figure 8-9). This anatomical arrangement creates the most flexible of synovial joints, allowing flexion-extension, aduction-adduction, and rotation. *Examples*: shoulder and hip joints

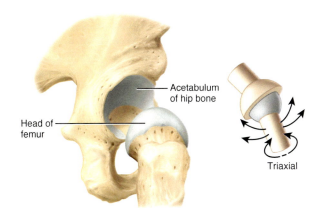

(f) Ball–and–socket joint between head of femur and acetabulum of hip bone. This is the hip (acetabulofemoral) joint.

FIGURE 8-9. Ball and socket joint.

Functional Anatomy of Synovial Joints

- *Synovial joints are all freely movable diarthroses.*

- *A joint cavity between articulating bones allows a range of motion that is not possible in fibrous and cartilaginous joints.*

- *To ensure that synovial joints are sufficiently stable, accessory ligaments buttress the joint anatomy to hedge against instability or dislocation.*

Types of Movements at Synovial Joints

Gliding

Gliding is a movement between relatively flat articular surfaces. Unlike most synovial joints, there is no angular change during gliding movements.

Angular Movements

Angular movements involve an increase or decrease in the angle between articulating bones. They include:
- **Flexion** (Figure 8-10), a movement that decreases the angle between two bones and brings them closer together. Flexion usually occurs in the sagittal plane. **Lateral flexion** applies to bending the trunk to either side in the frontal plane at the intervertebral joints.

- **Extension** (Figure 8-10), a movement that increases the angle between two bones. It is the opposite of flexion and brings a part of the body back to the

anatomical position after flexion. **Hyperextension** is extension that continues beyond the anatomical position.*

- **Abduction** (Figure 8-11), the movement of a bone away from the midline.

- **Adduction** (Figure 8-11), the movement of a bone toward the midline. It is the opposite of abduction.

- **Circumduction** (Figure 8-12), which is not a pure angular movement, but a combination of flexion, extension, abduction, and adduction. A familiar example is the windup of a softball pitcher.

- **Rotation** (Figure 8-13), the movement of a bone around its own longitudinal axis. If the movement is directed toward the midline, it is termed **medial (internal) rotation**. Rotation away from the midline is **lateral (external) rotation**.

Clinical Application
Rheumatoid Arthritis

Rheumatoid arthritis (RA) is an autoimmune disease. The immune system causes inflammation of the synovial membrane and erosion of articular cartilage. The joint cavity is progressively reduced and this results in a painfully enlarged and disfigured joint (arrow in photo below) with loss of mobility. In its worst form, the articulating bones fuse together (*ankylosis*). The onset of RA is usually in middle age, but it may occur in the 20s and 30s. It is more common in the joints of the hands than in larger joints.

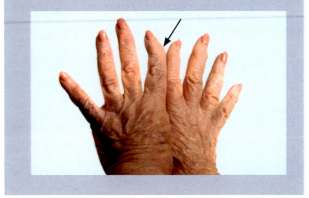

---

* *Hyperextension* as a normal joint movement should not be confused with clinical hyperextension, which is an abnormal degree of movement, usually at a hinge joint, beyond the anatomical limit of that joint. *Example:* When the knee joint is completely extended and then forced further, the joint is hyperextended and its supporting ligaments overstretched.

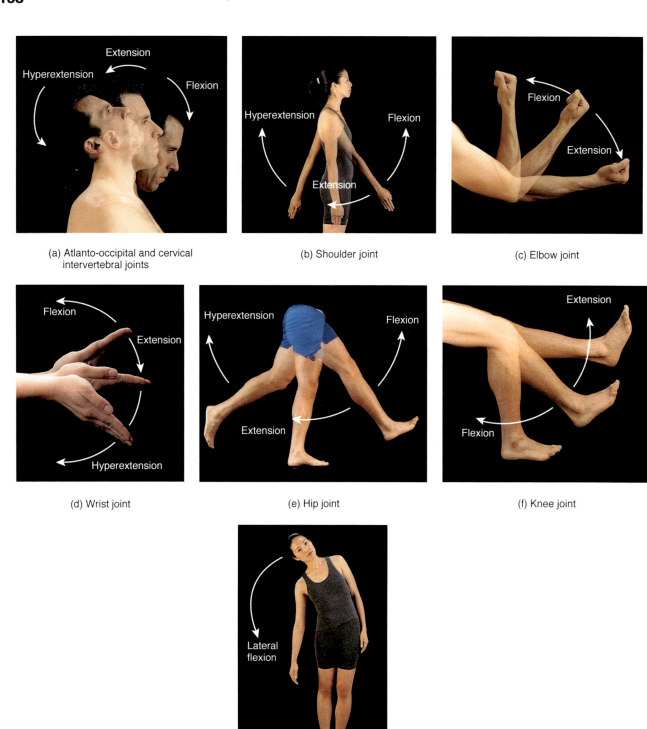

(a) Atlanto-occipital and cervical intervertebral joints

(b) Shoulder joint

(c) Elbow joint

(d) Wrist joint

(e) Hip joint

(f) Knee joint

(g) Intervertebral joints

FIGURE 8-10. Angular movements at synovial joint flexion, extension, hyperextension, and lateral flexion.

(a) Shoulder joint

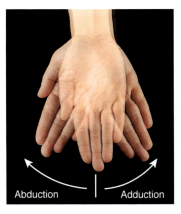

(b) Wrist joint

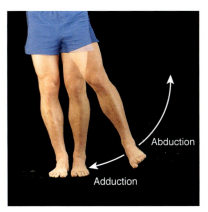

(c) Hip joint

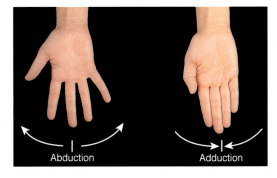

(d) Metacarpophalangeal joints of the fingers (not the thumb)

FIGURE 8-11. Angular movements at synovial joints: abduction and adduction.

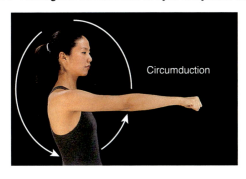

(a) Shoulder joint

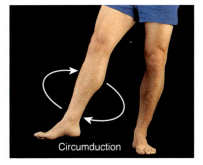

(b) Hip joint

FIGURE 8-12. Angular movement at synovial joints: circumduction.

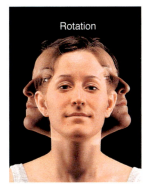

(a) Atlanto-axial joint

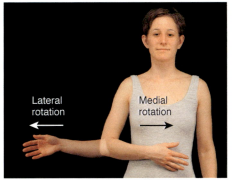

(b) Shoulder joint

(c) Hip joint

FIGURE 8-13. Angular movement at synovial joints: rotation.

TABLE 8.1

Summary of Movements at Synovial Joints

MOVEMENT	DESCRIPTION	MOVEMENT	DESCRIPTION
Gliding	Movement of relatively flat bone surfaces back and forth and side to side over one another; little change in angle between bones.	**Rotation**	Movement of bone around longitudinal axis; in limbs, may be medial (toward midline) or lateral (away from midline).
Angular	Increase or decrease in angle between bones.	**Special**	Occurs at specific joints.
Flexion	Decrease in angle between articulating bones, usually in sagittal plane.	Elevation	Superior movement of body part.
Lateral flexion	Movement of trunk in frontal plane.	Depression	Inferior movement of body part.
Extension	Increase in angle between articulating bones, usually in sagittal plane.	Protraction	Anterior movement of body part in transverse plane.
Hyperextension	Extension beyond anatomical position.	Retraction	Posterior movement of body part in transverse plane.
Abduction	Movement of bone away from midline, usually in frontal plane.	Inversion	Medial movement of sole.
Adduction	Movement of bone toward midline, usually in frontal plane.	Eversion	Lateral movement of sole.
		Dorsiflexion	Bending foot in direction of dorsum (superior surface).
Circumduction	Flexion, abduction, extension, adduction, and rotation in succession (or in the opposite order); distal end of body part moves in circle.	Plantar flexion	Bending foot in direction of plantar surface (sole).
		Supination	Movement of forearm that turns palm anteriorly.
		Pronation	Movement of forearm that turns palm posteriorly.
		Opposition	Movement of thumb across palm to touch fingertips on same hand.

(a) Temporomandibular joint   Elevation   (b) Depression

(c) Temporomandibular joint   Protraction   (d) Retraction

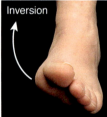

(e)   Intertarsal joints   Inversion

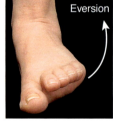

(f)   Eversion

(g) Ankle joint   Dorsiflexion   Plantar flexion

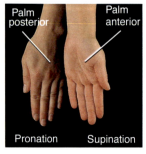

(h) Radioulnar joint   Palm posterior   Palm anterior   Pronation   Supination

(i) Carpometacarpal joint of thumb   Opposition

FIGURE 8-14. Special movements at synovial joints.

Special Movements at Synovial Joints

Special movements (Figure 8-14) apply to a limited number of joints and include:

- **Elevation** is moving a body part superiorly.

- **Depression** is moving a body part inferiorly.

- **Protraction** is the anterior movement of a body part in the anterior plane.

- **Retraction** is the posterior movement of a body part in the anterior plane.

- **Inversion** is moving the sole of the foot medially.

- **Eversion** is moving the sole of the foot laterally.

- **Dorsiflexion** (dor-sih-FLEX-shun), is bending the foot at the ankle joint upward toward its superior surface, or *dorsum*, as in standing on one's heels. The angle between the dorsum and the leg is thus reduced.

- **Plantar flexion** (PLAN-tar) is bending the foot at the ankle joint toward the plantar surface (sole), as in standing on tiptoes. (The flexion in this movement pertains to reducing the angle between the plantar side of the foot and the back of the leg.) Plantar flexion is the opposite of dorsiflexion.

- **Supination** (soo-pih-NAY-shun) is moving the forearm such that the palm faces anteriorly.

- **Pronation** (pro-NAY-shun) is moving the forearm such that the palm faces posteriorly. Mnemonic. The three Ps of pronation: Pronation has the Palm facing Posteriorly.

- **Opposition** is moving the thumb across the palm to the fingertips (Figure 8-14 and 7-8).

The Knee: A Special Synovial Joint

The knee joint is the body's largest and most complex joint (Figures 8-15). It can be viewed as three joints in a single synovial cavity:

- A **lateral tibiofemoral** joint is comprised of the lateral femoral condyle, lateral meniscus, and lateral tibial condyle.

Clinical Application
Total Knee Replacement

When the protective layer of articular cartilage has eroded to the point where bone tissue in the femur and tibia is in direct contact, a total knee joint replacement is indicated to prevent further damage and alleviate pain.

A common prelude to knee replacement surgery is *osteoarthritis*, also known as wear-and-tear arthritis. It results from accumulated stress on weight-bearing joints and is highly correlated with occupations that place heavy loads on the knee and hip joints. Given this backdrop, it is rarely seen before the age of forty.

The femoral and tibial condyles are replaced with a combination of titanium and plastic prostheses. The illustration on the left shows a single plastic component that substitutes for the tibial condyles (see asterisk), and metallic components to replace the other knee structures. On the right is a computer-enhanced X ray of the final result.

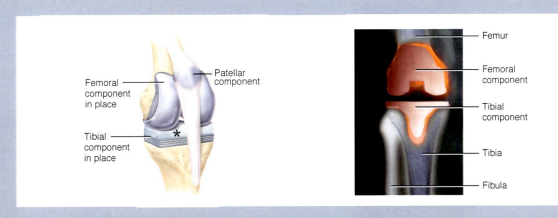

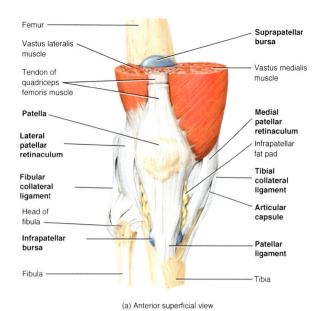

(a) Anterior superficial view

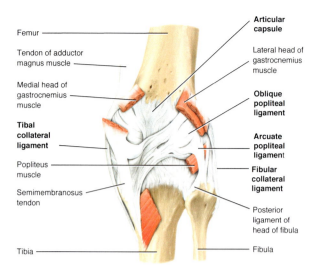

(b) Posterior deep view

- A **medial tibiofemoral** joint is comprised of the medial femoral condyle, medial meniscus, and medial tibial condyle.

- An intermediate **patellofemoral** joint between the patella and the anterior (patellar) surface of the femur between the condyles.

The knee joint is a modified hinge joint which allows flexion and extension and only slight rotation (when the knee is partially flexed). Rotation is counteracted by the menisci and surrounding ligaments. The anterior portion of the knee's articular capsule is incomplete, another unique feature of this highly specialized joint. Shoring up this anterior aspect are the:

- **patellar ligament** (Figure 8-15a), an extension of a tendon (from the quadriceps), which attaches the patella to the tibial tuberosity, and the

- **medial** and **lateral retinacula** (reh-tuh-NAH-kyuh-luh) (Figure 8-15a), which derive from the distal ends of thigh muscle tendons and merge with the tibia on either side.

Extracapsular ligaments include the:

- **fibular** and **tibial collateral ligaments** (Figures 8-15a, b and d), which stabilize the knee and prevent rotation during extension, and the

- **oblique popliteal** (pa-pluh-TEE-ul) and **arcuate** (AR-kyoo-wut) **ligaments** (Figures 8-15b).

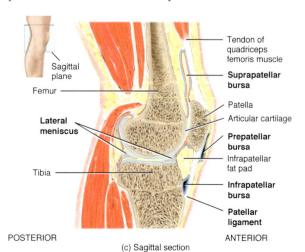

(c) Sagittal section

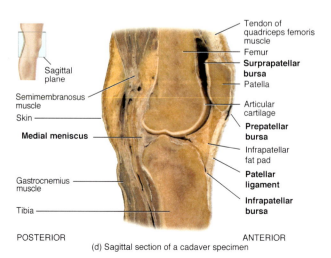

(d) Sagittal section of a cadaver specimen

FIGURE 8-15. The knee joint, accessory ligaments and bursae.

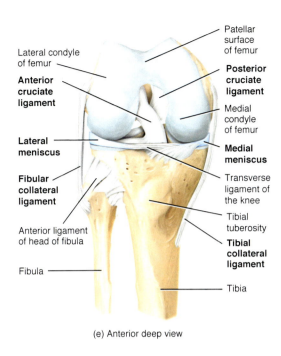

Lateral condyle of femur

Anterior cruciate ligament

Lateral meniscus

Fibular collateral ligament

Anterior ligament of head of fibula

Fibula

Patellar surface of femur

Posterior cruciate ligament

Medial condyle of femur

Medial meniscus

Transverse ligament of the knee

Tibial tuberosity

Tibial collateral ligament

Tibia

(e) Anterior deep view

FIGURE 8-15. (continued)

Intracapsular ligaments (Figure 8-15e) include the:

- **anterior cruciate** (KROO-shee-ate) (*cruciate* = cross–shaped) **ligament (ACL)** , which prevents hyperextension and anterior sliding of the tibia over the femur, and the

- **posterior cruciate ligament (PCL)**, which controls flexion by limiting the posterior sliding of the tibia. When walking down a staircase or an incline, the femur is forced forward. The PCL opposes this tendency and ensures a balanced and steady descent.

The Menisci

Beneath each femoral condyle is a disk of fibrocartilage known as a **meniscus** (muh-NISS-kus). The two **menisci** (muh-NIH-sky), which are semilunar in shape (*meniskos* = little moon), serve an important role as

Gray Matter Matchup
Common Body Movements, Technically Speaking

Organize teams of four to six students each. Each team will be given a randomly assigned action by the instructor from the list below, after which that team will explain their answer to the other teams within ten minutes. Anyone on another team may challenge an answer deemed inaccurate and provide an articulate rebuttal. (Consult your instructor when a disagreement over a "disjointed" answer cannot be resolved.) Record all movements in the table below.

Action	Joints Involved	Joint Movements
1. Standing erect from a sitting position	Hip Knee Trunk (two opposing movements)	
2. Kicking a football (consider lower limb joints only)	Hip (two opposing movements) Knee (two opposing movements) Ankle	
3. Rolling a bowling ball	Shoulder (two opposing movements) Elbow Wrist Interphalangeals (two opposing movements)	
4. Turning a doorknob	Metacarpophalangeals Interphalangeals Proximal radioulnar	
5. Shaking the hands of your classmates at the end of this exercise	Elbow (two opposing movements) Interphalangeals	

TABLE 8.2			
Summary of Structural and Functional Classifications of Joints			
STRUCTURAL CLASSIFICATION	DESCRIPTION	FUNCTIONAL CLASSIFICATION	EXAMPLE
FIBROUS No Synovial Cavity; Articulating Bones Held Together by Fibrous Connective Tissue.			
Suture	Articulating bones united by thin layer of dense irregular connective tissue, found between skull bones; with age, some sutures replaced by synostosis (separate cranial bones fuse into single bone).	Synarthrosis (immovable) and amphiarthrosis (slightly movable).	Coronal suture.
Syndesmosis	Articulating bones united by more dense irregular connective tissue, usually a ligament.	Amphiarthrosis (slightly movable).	Distal tibiofibular joint.
Interosseous membrane	Articulating bones united by substantial sheet of dense irregular connective tissue.	Amphiarthrosis (slightly movable).	Between tibia and fibula.
CARTILAGINOUS No Synovial Cavity; Articulating Bones United by Hyaline Cartilage or Fibrocartilage.			
Synchondrosis	Connecting material: hyaline cartilage; becomes synostosis when bone elongation ceases.	Synarthrosis (immovable).	Epiphyseal plate between diaphysis and epiphysis of long bone.
Symphysis	Connecting material: broad, flat disc of fibrocartilage.	Amphiarthrosis (slightly movable).	Pubic symphysis and intervertebral joints.
SYNOVIAL Characterized by Synovial Cavity, Articular Cartilage, and Articular (Joint) Capsule; May Contain Accessory Ligaments, Articular Discs, and Bursae.			
Plane	Articulated surfaces flat or slightly curved.	Many biaxial diarthroses (freely movable): back-and-forth and side-to-side movements. Some triaxial diarthrosis: back-and-forth, side-to-side, rotation.	Intercarpal, intertarsal, sternocostal (between sternum and second to seventh pairs of ribs), and vertebrocostal joints.
Hinge	Convex surface fits into concave surface.	Uniaxial diarthrosis: flexion–extension.	Knee (modified hinge), elbow, ankle, and interphalangeal joints.
Pivot	Rounded or pointed surface fits into ring formed partly by bone and partly by ligament.	Uniaxial diarthrosis: rotation.	Atlanto-axial and radioulnar joints.
Condyloid	Oval-shaped projection fits into oval-shaped depression.	Biaxial diarthrosis: flexion–extension, abduction–adduction.	Radiocarpal and metacarpophalangeal joints.
Saddle	Articular surface of one bone is saddle-shaped; articular surface of other bone "sits" in saddle.	Biaxial diarthrosis: flexion–extension, abduction–adduction.	Carpometacarpal joint between trapezium and metacarpal of thumb.
Ball-and-socket	Ball-like surface fits into cuplike depression.	Triaxial diarthrosis: flexion–extension, abduction–adduction, rotation.	Shoulder and hip joints.

cartilaginous cushions that diminish the impact of body weight as it is transmitted from femur to tibia. Recall that the menisci are an integral part of the tibiofemoral joints (p.166).

The Bursae

A **bursa** is a fluid-filled sac designed to resist mechanical pressure and ease friction between bones and tendons. Bursae are strategically placed near synovial joints to cushion bones during movement. In the knee, on the anterior aspect, are the **suprapatellar**, **infrapatellar** and **prepatellar bursae** (Figures 8-15c and d).

Articulations and Body Movements

Exercise

NAME _____

LAB TIME/DATE _____

Fibrous, Cartilaginous, and Synovial Joints

Matching

Match the joint on the left to its example on the right.

Column A

_____1. ball-and-socket

_____2. condyloid

_____3. suture

_____4. symphysis

_____5. gomphosis

_____6. syndesmosis

_____7. pivot

_____8. synostosis

_____9 hinge

_____10. synchondrosis

Column B

a. wrist joint

b. joint between parietal bones

c. epiphyseal plate

d. joint between vertebral bodies

e. coxal bone and femur

f. interphalangeal joint

g. distal tibiofibular joint

h. atlanto-axial joint

i. fusion of frontal bones

j. tooth in maxilla

1. Identify two variables that limit the movement of a joint.

   _____

   _____

2. Within the knee joint, identify two intracapsular ligaments that increase the joint's stability.

   _____

   _____

3. Beyond the articular cartilage that caps the femoral and tibial condyles, what other cartilages in the knee joint act as shock absorbers?

_____

_____

4. Observe the red, swollen area at X. The condition was diagnosed as *bursitis*, inflammation of a bursa. The photograph below documents a case of _____ bursitis. (Identify the protruding bone marking that is posterior to the joint in question.)

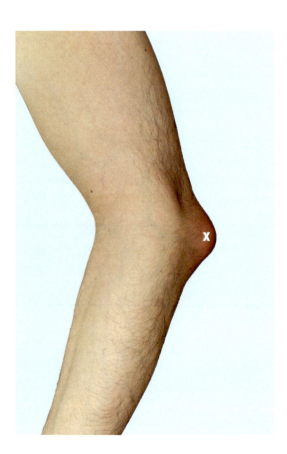

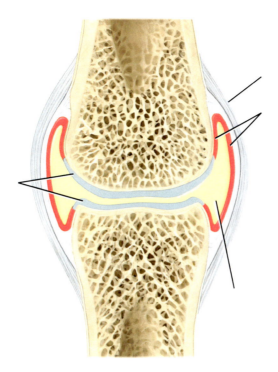

Add a label to each leader line in the diagram. Describe the function of the synovial joint features below. (The four terms provide the word list for the diagram.)

1. synovial fluid _____

   _____

2. articular cartilage _____

   _____

3. synovial membrane of articular capsule _____

   _____

4. fibrous membrane of articular capsule _____

   _____

Joint Identifications

Identify the eight joints by their names, structural classification and functional classification. Record your answers in the table on the next page.

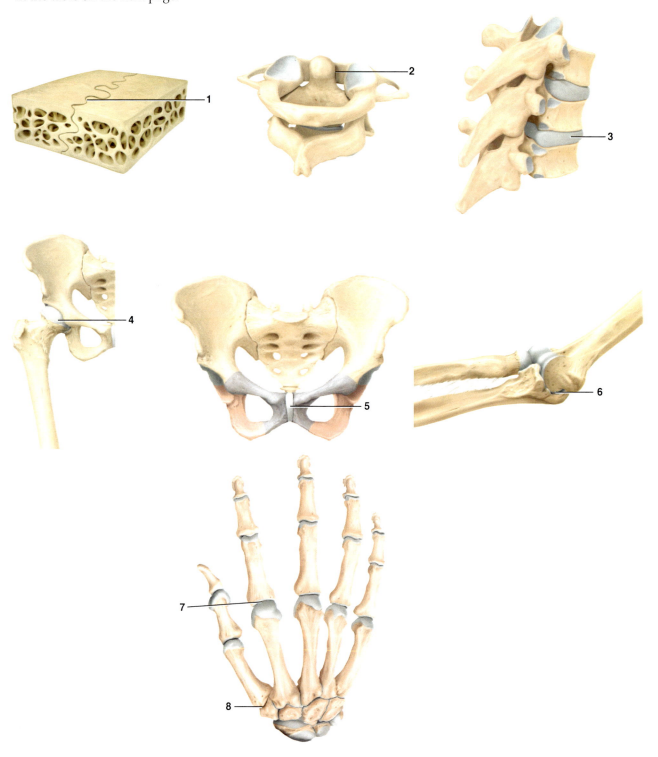

| | Classification | |
Joint Name	Structural	Functional
1.		
2.		
3.		
4.		
5.		
6.		
7.		
8.		

1. Name a hinge joint below the knee. _____

2. The intertarsals and intercarpals are classified as _____ synovial joints.

The Knee: A Special Synovial Joint

Identify the structures in the illustration below.

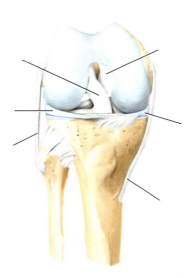

Types of Movements at Synovial Joints

Describe on the opposite page each numbered joint movement that appears below. Be sure to indicate the joint (or region) that moves. For example, "flexion of the hip joint (or thigh)".

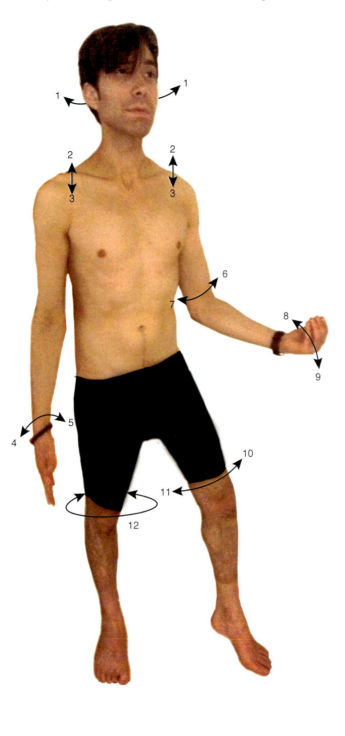

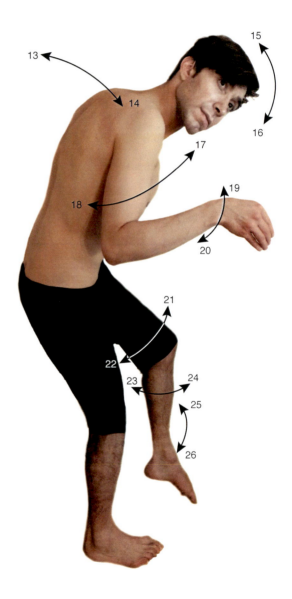

Answers to Synovial Joint Movements

1. _____

2. _____

3. _____

4. _____

5. _____

6. _____

7. _____

8. _____

9. _____

10. _____

11. _____

12. _____

13. _____

14. _____

15. _____

16. _____

17. _____

18. _____

19. _____

20. _____

21. _____

22. _____

23. _____

24. _____

25. _____

26. _____

Critical Thinking

1. Shrugging your shoulders is described as elevation of the scapulae. When the scapulae are brought closer to the midline of the back, as in a morning stretch, what would you call this action?

   _____

   _____

   _____

   _____

   _____

2. Why couldn't the sacroiliac joints have developed as synovial joints? (Refer to pages 132 or 174 if necessary.)

   _____

   _____

   _____

   _____

   _____

   _____

Microscopic Anatomy and Organization of Skeletal Muscle

Exercise 9

OBJECTIVES

1. Describe the functions of skeletal muscle.
2. Describe the anatomy of skeletal muscle fibers (cells).
3. Define *muscle fiber* and differentiate it from *myofibril*.
4. Describe how thick and thin *myofilaments* relate to the *sarcomere* of a myofibril and to each other.
5. Describe the structure of the *neuromuscular junction* and its role in initiating a muscle action potential.
6. Discuss how the *sarcolemma, transverse (T) tubules*, and *sarcoplasmic reticulum* link muscle cell excitation to a contraction.
7. Define *epimysium, perimysium*, and *endomysium*. Be specific regarding the place each of these connectives tissues holds in the gross and microscopic structure of an entire muscle.
8. Differentiate between a *tendon* and an *aponeurosis*.

MATERIALS

Skeletal muscle cell model
Slides of skeletal muscle tissue, intact and teased
Model of a neuromuscular junction

Slide of a neuromuscular junction
Comparison slides of smooth and cardiac muscle
Compound microscope
Video of skeletal muscle physiology (optional)

PRE-LAB QUIZ

1. The cell membrane of a muscle fiber is known as the _____.
2. True or False (Correct the statement if false.) Skeletal muscle fibers are multinucleate.
3. Where the axon of a motor neuron meets the cell membrane of a muscle fiber is called a
   _____.
4. Once a skeletal muscle fiber is stimulated to threshold, a series of events leads to the myofilaments _____ and _____
   sliding past one another.
5. Myofilaments are housed in contractile units known as_____.
6. Which of the following subunits of a skeletal muscle is the largest?
   a. a fascicle   c. a myofibril
   b. a muscle fiber   d. a myofilament
7. An entire skeletal muscle is enveloped by connective tissue known as the
   a. endomysium.   c. exomysium.
   b. perimysium.   d. epimysium.
8. True or False (Correct the statement if false.) At the junction between axon and muscle fiber, the nerve impulse directly stimulates the muscle to contract.
9. How is an aponeurosis different from a tendon?
10. True or False (Correct the statement if false.) Skeletal muscles are always under voluntary control.

173

Skeletal muscles produce a spectrum of body movements, such as running along a beach, chewing a burger, lifting weights at the gym, playing the piano, or smiling while embracing an old friend. All movements are based on a simple mechanical principle: *A contracting muscle generates a force that pulls on a bone or soft tissue.*

Skeletal muscles — which make up 40-50% of adult body weight — also maintain posture and generate body heat. Skeletal muscle is also known as *voluntary* muscle because it is under conscious control. However, skeletal muscles can contract automatically as when breathing, blinking, and maintaining posture. The study of muscles is known as **myology** (my-OL-uh-gee).

A skeletal muscle consists of thousands of individual muscle cells, also known as **muscle fibers**, accompanied by nervous tissue, blood vessels, and connective tissue. As a composite of these tissues, skeletal muscles can be properly called organs (Figure 9-1).

Organization of Skeletal Muscle Fibers into a Muscle

The relatively fragile skeletal muscle fibers are organized into a muscle by a family of supportive connective tissues. The connective tissues that bind skeletal muscle fibers together (Figure 9-1) are the:

- **endomysium** (en-doe-MIZE-ee-um), a delicate sheath of areolar and reticular connective tissue that surrounds each muscle fiber.

- **perimysium** (per-ih-MIZE-ee-um), a collagenous membrane that arranges 10 to 100 or more muscle fibers into a bundle called a **fascicle** (FAHS-ih-kul).

- **epimysium** (ep-ih-MIZE-ee-um), a coarse, dense connective tissue that envelops the entire muscle.

- **deep fascia** (FA-shuh), which is derived from epimysia, and surrounds and binds together muscles with similar functions.

Tendons and Aponeuroses

Connective tissues that connect muscles to bones are the:

- **tendons**, tough, ropelike connective tissues that extend from the epimysium. *Tendons attach a muscle to the periosteum of a bone.* Tendons must span a joint for movement to occur, and their thinness, especially in the limbs, conserves space. The mostly collagenous (and therefore durable and inelastic) makeup of a tendon is ideal for transmitting the force a of a muscle contraction to a bone. *Example*: The calcaneal tendon connects the calf muscles to the calcaneus (heel bone).

- **aponeuroses** (ap-oh-noo-ROE-seez), flat sheets of the same connective tissue found in tendons.

An aponeurosis is designed to link a bone to a broad, flat muscle whose shape it complements. *Example*: The latissimus dorsi muscle of the back is attached to the vertebral column by an aponeurosis.

Bottom Line: Various connective tissues — the endomysium, perimysium, and epimysium — organize skeletal muscle fibers within an entire muscle. Tendons and aponeuroses secure muscles to bones.

Beyond their role in binding muscle fibers together and strengthening the muscle as a unit, these supportive connective tissues provide channels for the entry and exit of blood vessels and nerves. Muscle tissue is extremely vascular because its high demand for ATP must be fueled by an efficient oxygen and nutrient delivery system.

Skeletal muscles require stimulation from the nervous system before they can contract. The somatic nerves that supply skeletal muscles contain **motor neurons** that deliver stimulation in the form of an electrical impulse, or **action potential**. These nerve impulses do not directly excite muscle fibers. Motor neuron action potentials provoke the release of a transmitter chemical from the terminal end of the neuron, which then crosses a tiny gap between neuron and muscle fiber. If the neuron action potential is strong enough to reach the excitation threshold of the muscle fiber, a muscle action potential is initiated and a contraction results.

The Microscopic Anatomy of Skeletal Muscle Fibers

The key components of skeletal muscle are the muscle fibers. These cells are much longer than those

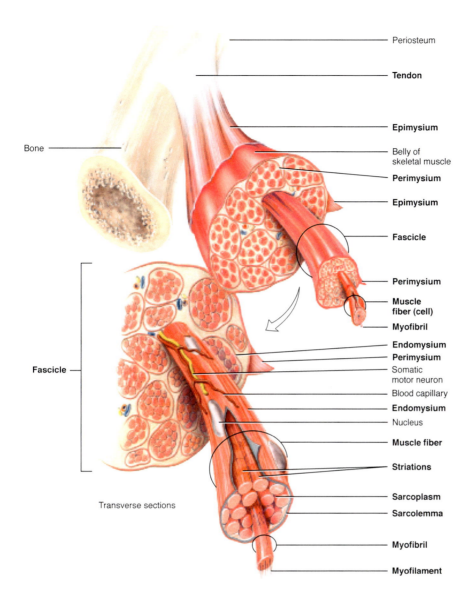

Periosteum

Tendon

Epimysium

Bone

Belly of skeletal muscle

Perimysium

Epimysium

Fascicle

Perimysium

Muscle fiber (cell)

Myofibril

Endomysium
Perimysium

Somatic motor neuron

Blood capillary

Endomysium

Nucleus

Muscle fiber

Striations

Sarcoplasm

Sarcolemma

Myofibril

Myofilament

Fascicle

Transverse sections

FIGURE 9-1. Components of a skeletal muscle.

of smooth and cardiac muscle, averaging about 10 cm (4 in) and sometimes reaching lengths of 30 cm (12 in). Their diameters range from 10 to 100 μm.

The Sarcolemma, Transverse Tubules, and Sarcoplasm

Skeletal muscle fibers are **multinucleate**. The many nuclei per cell result from the fusion of a hundred or more myoblasts during embryonic development (Figure 9-2a). Once fully formed as multinucleate cells, skeletal muscle fibers can no longer divide so the number of muscle fibers is determined by the time we are born. Growth of skeletal muscle tissue is by **hypertrophy**, increasing the size of individual muscle fibers, not by increasing their numbers. (See Clinical Application on page 181.)

The oval nuclei in a skeletal muscle fiber are located on the periphery of the cell, just beneath the plasma membrane This membrane is termed the **sarcolemma**, from *sarco*, flesh, and *lemma*, membrane. Along the length of the sarcolemma are thousands of tubelike indentations called **transverse tubules** (**T tubules**) (Figure 9-2c). The tubules provide a link to the inside of the muscle fiber, serving as conductors of muscle action potentials.

Inside the sarcolemma is the **sarcoplasm**, the cytoplasm of a skeletal muscle fiber. The sarcoplasm is almost completely filled with hundreds to thousands of **myofibrils** ("little muscle fibers"), rodlike subunits arranged longitudinally along the entire length of the muscle fiber (Figures 9-1 and 9-2c). Their cross banding makes them appear striped under the microscope. These stripes are called **striations** (Figure 9-1).

Each cylindrical myofibril is surrounded by a series of fluid-filled sacs, the smooth endoplasmic reticulum (ER). In myofibrils, the ER is known as **sarcoplasmic reticulum (SR)**. The dilated ends of the SR are called **terminal cisterns** and are located to either side of a T tubule. Together, a T tubule and its adjacent terminal cisterns are called a **triad** (Figure 9-2c).

Myofilaments and Sarcomeres

Within myofibrils are proteins called **myofilaments**.

Thin filaments, which are made of the protein **actin**, are smaller in diameter than **myosin**-containing **thick filaments** (8 nm vs. 10 nm). Where the filaments overlap, there are two thin for every thick filament. The myofilaments are contained within compartments known as **sarcomeres**. Each sarcomere is bounded on each side by a **Z disc**, so named for its zigzag pattern of dense proteins (Figure 9-3). *The extent to which the myofilaments overlap depends on whether a muscle is contracted or relaxed, which in turn determines the pattern of striations.*

The myofilament pattern at any given time creates zones and bands as follows (Figures 9-3 and 9-4):

- The **A band** is the dark midsection of the sarcomere. Its length equals the length of the thick filaments. Near each end of the A band is a region where thick and thin filaments lie adjacent to one another; this is the *zone of overlap.*

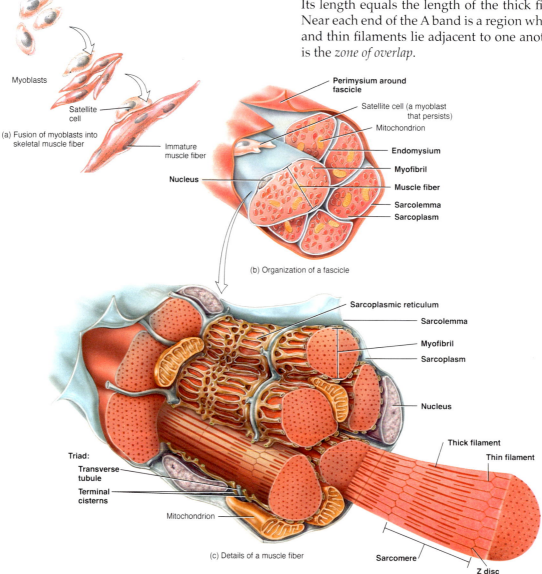

Myoblasts

Satellite cell

(a) Fusion of myoblasts into skeletal muscle fiber

Immature muscle fiber

Nucleus

Perimysium around fascicle

Satellite cell (a myoblast that persists)

Mitochondrion

Endomysium

Myofibril

Muscle fiber

Sarcolemma

Sarcoplasm

(b) Organization of a fascicle

Sarcoplasmic reticulum

Sarcolemma

Myofibril

Sarcoplasm

Nucleus

Thick filament

Thin filament

Triad:

Transverse tubule

Terminal cisterns

Mitochondrion

(c) Details of a muscle fiber

Sarcomere

Z disc

FIGURE 9-2. Microscope organization of skeletal muscle.

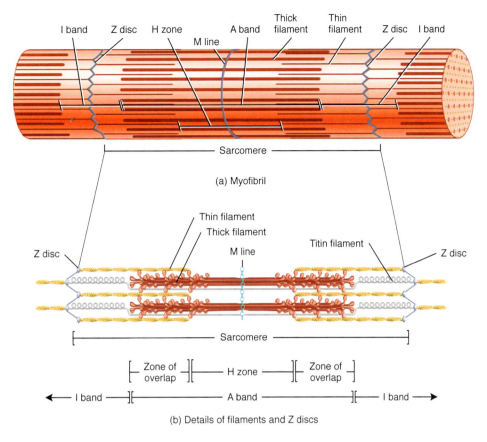

FIGURE 9-3. The arrangement of myofilaments within a sarcomere.

- The **I band** is a region found to either side of the Z disc. It appears lighter than the adjacent A bands because it includes only thin filaments.

- The **H zone** lies in the center of the A band and contains only thick filaments.
Mnemonic: The letter I is thin (thin filaments only) and the letter H is thick (thick filaments only).

- The **M line** is named for its position in the middle of the H zone. Supporting proteins along the M lines secure the thick filaments.

When a skeletal muscle fiber contracts, the thick filaments and thin filaments slide past one another toward the center of the sarcomeres of each myofibril. This is the *sliding filament mechanism*. As sarcomeres and myofibrils shorten, the muscle fiber shortens, thus producing the force of contraction. Note that at no time do the myofilaments change their length. (The changing pattern of striations from a state of contrac-

tion to one of relaxation was the key to discovering the sliding filament mechanism.)

During sarcomere shortening, the

- I bands decrease in length.

- H zone narrows during partial contraction and disappears during maximal contraction (Figure 9-4).

1. Why does the I band narrow as a skeletal muscle contracts?

_____

_____

_____

_____

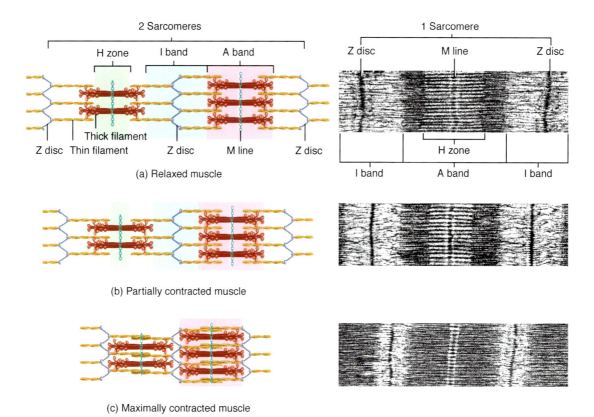

FIGURE 9-4. Sliding filament mechanism of muscle contraction.

2. Do the lengths of the thick or thin filaments change when a muscle contracts?

_____

_____

_____

_____

3. Does the A band change length during contraction? Justify your answer.

_____

_____

_____

_____

PROCEDURE 1

Examining Muscular Tissue Under the Microscope

1. On a three-dimensional model of a skeletal muscle fiber, identify the sarcolemma, nuclei, myofibrils, and light and dark striations.

2. Obtain a prepared slide of skeletal muscle tissue (Figure 9-5). In a longitudinal section, identify nuclei, and light and dark striations. In a cross section, identify nuclei, a fascicle, the perimysium surrounding a fascicle, and the endomysium surrounding a skeletal muscle fiber.

3. Observe a second slide of skeletal muscle tissue that had been teased apart to enable visualization of individual muscle fibers.

4. Compare slides and models of **smooth** and **cardiac muscle tissue** (Figure 4-6b and c) to skeletal muscle and to one another.

How do skeletal, smooth, and cardiac muscle tissue compare? Cite their structural characteristics with regard to:

Location and number of nuclei:

_____

_____

Cell length:

_____

_____

Presence or absence of striations:

_____

_____

Presence or absence of a branching pattern:

_____

_____

The Neuromuscular Junction

The axon of each somatic motor neuron subdivides into numerous terminal branches. Each branch of the axon serves a single muscle fiber at a **neuromuscular junction** (Figure 9-6). At the end of each branch is an **axon terminal**, which expands to form a **synaptic end bulb**. Within each end bulb are spherical sacs, the **synaptic vesicles,** containing the neurotransmitter *acetylcholine (ACh)*. A motor neuron and all the muscle fibers it innervates is a **motor unit**.

When a nerve impulse reaches the axon terminal, ACh is released from some of the vesicles and diffuses across a narrow space, the **synaptic cleft**, between the axon terminal membrane and the sarcolemma. The ACh molecules then bind to receptors within a specific region of the sarcolemma called the **motor end plate**.

The effect of ACh binding to its receptors is to increase the permeability of the sarcolemma to sodium ions by briefly opening the membrane's sodium channels. The positively charged sodium quickly diffuses through its channels into the sarcoplasm causing a reversal of the membrane's polarity, a physiologic change known as *depolarization*. Once stimulated, the muscle fiber con-

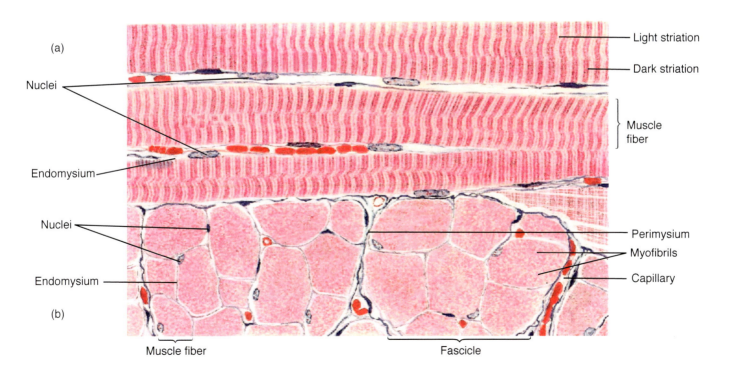

FIGURE 9-5. Skeletal muscle of the tongue at high magnification. (a) longitudinal section; (b) cross section.

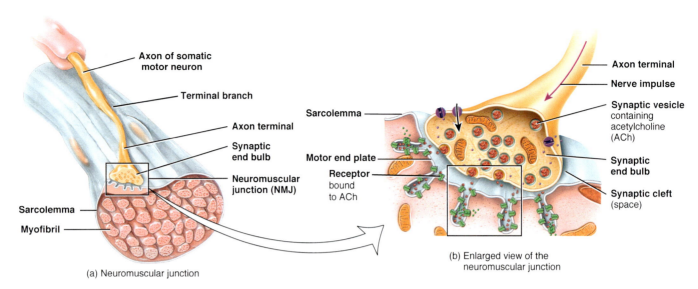

FIGURE 9-6. Structure of the neuromuscular junction.

(a) Neuromuscular junction

(b) Enlarged view of the neuromuscular junction

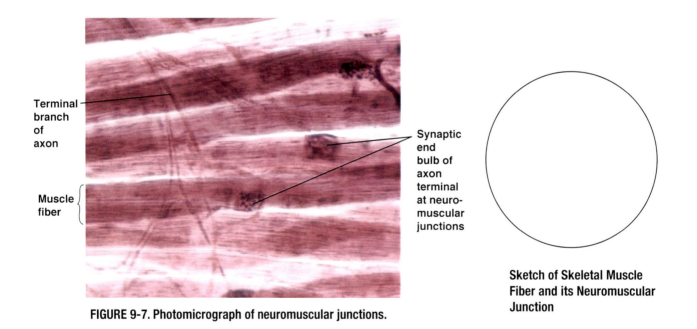

FIGURE 9-7. Photomicrograph of neuromuscular junctions.

Sketch of Skeletal Muscle Fiber and its Neuromuscular Junction

ducts a wave of depolarization across its entire length, a progression analogous to a lit fuse on a firecracker. This wave of depolarization is the action potential or **muscle impulse**. Within a millisecond, it is not only propagated along the sarcolemma, but down the T tubules as well. This action potential, once delivered to the sarcoplasmic reticulum by the T tubules, causes the SR's calcium ions to be released, an event which leads to contraction.

PROCEDURE 2

Examining the Anatomy of a Neuromuscular Junction

1. Locate a three-dimensional model of a neuromuscular junction on the demo table. Identify the axon terminal, synaptic end bulb, synaptic vesicles, synaptic cleft, and motor end plate of the sarcolemma.

2. Obtain a slide that shows the neuromuscular junctions of several muscle fibers. Under the high power objective of your microscope and using Figure 9-7 as a guide, follow the terminal branches to the axon terminals. Note the oval shape of the synaptic end bulb. In the circle, sketch a single muscle fiber and its neuromuscular junction. Label the terminal branch and axon terminal with its synaptic end bulb.

The Functional Anatomy of Skeletal Muscle

- *Skeletal muscles are composed of cells — the muscle fibers — organized into fascicles, bundles which are wrapped together to make an entire muscle.*

- *The functional subdivision of a skeletal muscle is the motor unit: a motor neuron and all the muscle fibers it innervates.*

- *A prerequisite for skeletal muscle contraction is stimulation by the nervous system. Muscle fibers are excited by nerve impulses from somatic motor neurons. These impulses are conducted along axons which split into terminal branches, each ending in an axon terminal.*

- *Each axon terminal meets the sarcolemma of a muscle fiber at a neuromuscular junction. The effect of a nerve impulse is to release the neurotransmitter acetylcholine (ACh) from vesicles within the synaptic end bulb of the axon terminal.*

- *Acetylcholine diffuses across the synaptic cleft of the neuromuscular junction and binds to receptors on the motor end plate region of the sarcolemma.*

- *The effect of ACh binding to its receptors is to increase the permeability of the sarcolemma to sodium ions by briefly opening the membrane's sodium channels. The sarcolemma depolarizes as sodium diffuses into the cell. The resulting action potential leads to contraction of the muscle fiber.*

- *How much force a muscle contraction generates depends on the strength of stimulation delivered by the muscle's motor nerve, a composite of many individual neurons. The greater the stimulus strength, the greater the number of motor units contracting simultaneously and the stronger the muscle contraction.*

Clinical Application
Muscular Hypertrophy and Fibrosis

We are born with a fixed number of skeletal muscle cells. From birth to adulthood, skeletal muscles grow by increasing the size of their muscle fibers — a type of growth called *hypertrophy*. This contrasts with growth in other tissues by *hyperplasia*, an increase in the number of cells.

As muscle tissue grows, the individual fibers produce more myofibrils and organelles such as mitochondria and sarcoplasmic reticulum. Thus, the dimensions of a muscle increase as a product of enlargement at the cellular level. The size a muscle reaches as it progresses to a mature adult is greatly influenced by growth hormone and testosterone.

Hypertrophy of skeletal muscle tissue also occurs in response to repetitive, forceful activity, such as weight training. This physiologic process is known as *adaptation*. Hypertrophy, whether natural or induced, leads to stronger muscle contractions. In simple terms, bigger muscles tend to be stronger muscles.

When damaged — as in a "pulled muscle", where muscle fibers are torn to varying degrees — some recovery of muscle tissue is possible. With the help of *satellite cells* — myoblasts that persist in mature skeletal muscle — new skeletal muscle fibers can be reformed. But if the damage is extensive, complete regeneration of functional muscle fibers may not be possible. Under these circumstances, scar tissue, a whitish, collagen-rich fibrous connective tissue, replaces the degenerated muscle tissue. This replacement of muscle tissue with nonfunctional fibrous connective tissue is known as *fibrosis*.

Notes

Microscopic Anatomy and Organization of Skeletal Muscle

NAME _____

LAB TIME/DATE _____

Organization of Skeletal Muscle Fibers into a Muscle

Matching

Match the description in Column A to its corresponding term in Column B.

Column A	Column B
_____1. Layer of connective tissue that surrounds a skeletal muscle.	a. endomysium
_____2. Layer of connective tissue that surrounds an individual muscle fiber.	b. fascia
_____3. Layer of connective tissue that binds muscle fibers together as a fascicle.	c. aponeurosis
_____4. Sheetlike connective tissue that connects flat muscles to bone.	d. epimysium
_____5. Cordlike connective tissue that connects slender muscles to bone.	e. perimysium
_____6. Connective tissue that binds together muscles with similar functions.	f. tendon

1. Besides binding muscle fibers together into an organized, functional whole muscle, what is another role played by connective tissue?

   _____

   _____

2. What is an advantage of a tendon connecting a muscle to a joint bone rather than the muscle attaching itself directly?

   _____

   _____

3. Add a label to each leader in the diagram below.

Key

a. fascicle

b. myofibril

c. tendon

d. epimysium

e. perimysium

f. muscle fiber

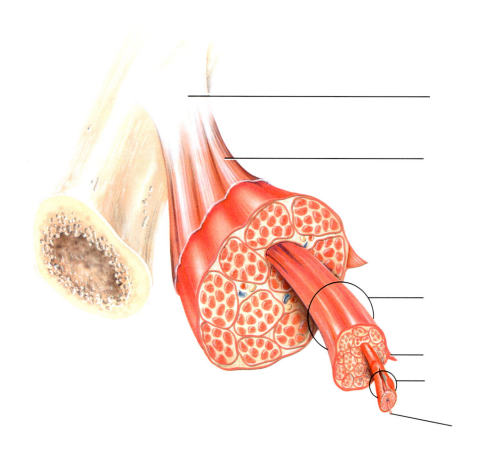

The Microscopic Anatomy of Skeletal Muscle Fibers

Matching

Match the description in Column A to its corresponding term in Column B.

Column A	Column B
_____1. Cell membrane of a muscle fiber	a. sarcomere
_____2. Saclike organelle that stores calcium ions	b. sarcoplasm
_____3. Membranous channels that tunnel inward from cell membrane	c. sarcoplasmic reticulum
_____4. Subunit with light and dark striations bounded by Z discs	d. sarcolemma
_____5. Cytoplasm of a muscle fiber	e. transverse tubules

1. Add a label to each leader in the muscle fiber diagram below. Your word list is:

Key

a. myofibril

b. nucleus

c. terminal cisterns

d. thin filament

e. thick filament

f. transverse tubule

g. sarcoplasmic reticulum

h. sarcolemma

i. sarcomere

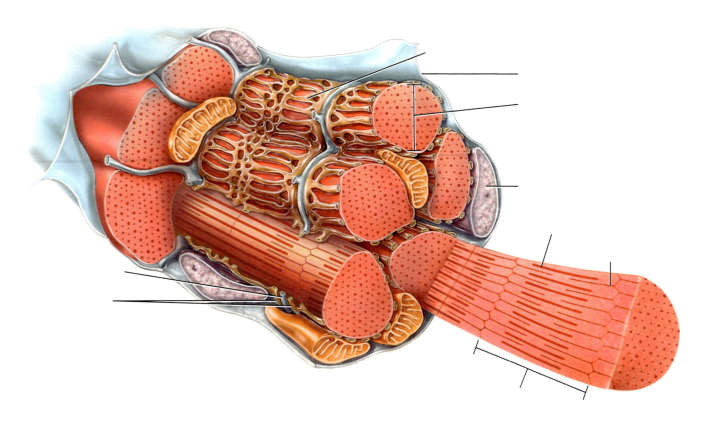

The Neuromuscular Junction

Complete the sentences in the following paragraph. The word list for the blanks are in the key accompanying the illustrations below. Label the illustrations using key words or their numbers.

Skeletal muscles require stimulation from somatic motor neurons before they can contract. The axon from each of these neurons subdivides into branches each of which serves a single muscle fiber. Each branch ends in an _____, which expands to form a _____. Within this expanded region are spherical sacs, the _____ containing the transmitter acetylcholine (ACh). When a nerve impulse reaches the end of the axon, ACh is released and diffuses across a narrow space, the _____. The ACh then binds to its receptors on the motor end plate of the_____, the cell membrane of the adjacent muscle fiber, leading to a muscle action potential. The action potential stimulates the release of calcium ions from the SR, causing sarcomeres within the cylindrical _____ of the muscle fiber to contract.

Key

1. sarcolemma (two places)

2. axon terminal (two places)

3. synaptic cleft

4. synaptic vesicles

5. synaptic end bulb (two places)

6. myofibrils

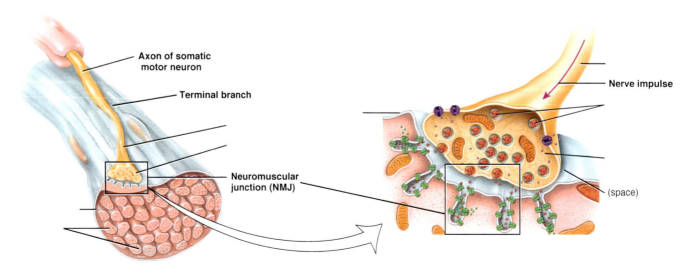

Axon of somatic motor neuron

Terminal branch

Neuromuscular junction (NMJ)

Nerve impulse

(space)

Critical Thinking

Is the bracketed sarcomere in a state of contraction or relaxation? Justify your answer.

_____

_____

_____

_____

_____

_____

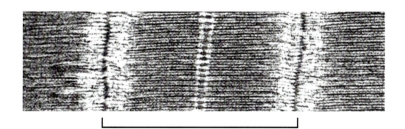

Notes

Skeletal Muscle Anatomy and Action

OBJECTIVES

1. To define the terms *origin, insertion, prime mover (agonist), antagonist, synergist,* and *fixator.*
2. To learn basic biomechanical principles as they pertain to musculoskeletal movement.
3. To list seven criteria for naming skeletal muscles.
4. To learn the locations and names of selected skeletal muscles.
5. To determine the actions of the selected skeletal muscles by deduction and palpation.

MATERIALS

Torso models
Models of the upper and lower limb muscles
Models of the head, neck and shoulder muscles
Anatomical chart of the muscular system

Human cadaveric musculoskeletal preparations (optional)
Skeleton painted to show muscle attachments
Video of the muscular system (optional)
Handheld mirrors
Cot or stretcher

PRE-LAB QUIZ

1. To produce body movements, skeletal muscles must span at least one joint and
   _____ on their origin/insertion bone. (Circle one.)

2. In the extremities, muscles lie proximal/distal (circle one) to the joint bones they move.

3. A muscle or muscle group that is mainly responsible for a body movement is called the
   _____.

4. Fixators that stabilize the wrist while muscles in the forearm are flexing the fingers into a power grip are the _____ in the forearm.

5. Cite two muscles named for their shape.

6. Most muscles insert onto a bone. Identify an exception to the rule.

Skeletal muscles make up the fleshy part of our anatomy and constitute 40 to 50% of body weight. They give the body its characteristic form and ability to move. Gross movements occur when skeletal muscles interact with our joint bones to form sophisticated musculoskeletal arrangements.

To appreciate the biomechanical basis for body movement, a few general concepts should be clearly understood.

- A skeletal muscle is made of two basic parts: the fleshy, contractile portion, or **belly,** and the connective tissue ends that attach to bones, the **tendons.** (Recall from Exercise 9 that tendons can be cord-like or sheet like; the latter are called aponeuroses.)

- The belly of a muscle exerts force on a tendon, which pulls on a bone to cause movement at a joint. For movement to occur, a tendon must span at least one joint.*

- The attachment of the muscle to the more fixed, proximal bone is the muscle's **origin**. The attachment to the more movable, distal bone is the muscle's **insertion** (Figure 10-1).

- The **action** of a muscle is the movement that occurs during contraction. *Example*: Flexion of the forearm.

- As a muscle contracts, it *pulls* on its insertion.

- As a rule, the insertion is pulled toward the more proximal origin.

As shown in Figure 10-1, the biceps brachii originates on the scapula, crosses over the elbow joint, and inserts on the radius. As the biceps contracts, its tendon pulls on the forearm and flexes it.

Analogy: Imagine a door with a spring that extends from the door's hinged side to its frame. When the door closes, the spring's frame side is stationary (the origin) while the part attached to the door is moving (the insertion).

Classification of Skeletal Muscles

Coordination of Movements by Muscle Groups

Muscles usually do not act alone to produce movement. In general, a muscle functions as part of a group. To move a particular part of the body, several muscles must be coordinated. Within a muscle group, a muscle may act as a:

- **prime mover (agonist)** — the principal muscle responsible for a particular movement.

- **antagonist** — a muscle whose action opposes that of the prime mover. The antagonist is relaxed during prime mover contraction and is usually located opposite the prime mover.

- **synergist** — a muscle whose contraction enhances the effectiveness of the prime mover. Synergists may be weaker muscles with the same action as the prime mover, or may act as **fixators** that stabilize a part of the body to make the prime mover more effective.

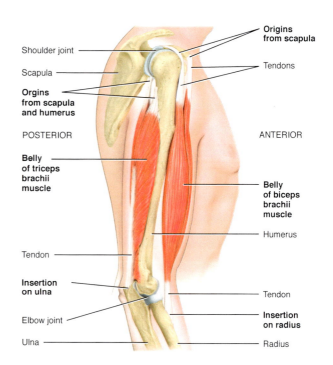

FIGURE 10-1. Origins and insertions of skeletal muscles of the arm. The biceps and triceps are antagonists and occupy opposite compartments.

* Muscles of facial expression are exceptions: they pull on skin or other muscles when mirroring our emotional state.

How Skeletal Muscles are Named

Learning the derivation of muscle names is an important step toward mastering these names and giving each muscle structural and functional context within the muscular system. There are hundreds of individual muscles, but most of their names can be traced to seven basic criteria. Table 10-1 lists those criteria, their translations, and examples of each.

Table 10-1. The Criteria Used to Name Skeletal Muscles		
Name	**Translation**	**Example**
1. SHAPE: The Relative Shape of the Muscle		
Trapezius	Trapezoidal	Trapezius
Orbicularis	Circular	Orbicularis oris
Platysma	Flat	Platysma
Deltoid	Triangular	Deltoid
Serratus	Saw-toothed	Serratus anterior
2. SIZE: The Relative Size of the Muscle		
Major	Larger	Teres major
Minor	Smaller	Teres minor
Maximus	Largest	Gluteus maximus
Minimus	Smallest	Gluteus minimus
Medius	Midsize	Gluteus medius
Longus	Long	Adductor longus
Latissimus	Widest	Latissimus dorsi
Vastus	Extremely large	Vastus lateralis
3. DIRECTION: The Direction of Muscle Fascicles Relative to the Midline		
Rectus	Straight; parallel to midline	Rectus abdominis
Oblique	Slanted; diagonal to midline	External oblique
Transversus	Perpendicular to midline	Transversus abdominis
4. ACTION: The Principal Action of the Muscle		
Flexor	Decreases joint angle	Flexor carpi radialis
Extensor	Increases joint angle	Extensor digitorum
Abductor	Moves limb away from midline	Abductor pollicis
Adductor	Moves limb toward midline	Adductor longus
Supinator	Turns palm anteriorly	Supinator
Pronator	Turns palm posteriorly	Pronator teres
5. NUMBER: The Number of Heads of Origin		
Biceps	Two heads	Biceps brachii
Triceps	Three heads	Triceps brachii
Quadriceps	Four heads	Quadriceps femoris
6. LOCATION: The Bone Where the Muscle Attaches (Originates)		
Example: The temporalis lies over the temporal bone.		
7. ORIGIN & INSERTION: The Bones Where the Muscle Originates and Inserts		
Example: The brachioradialis originates on the arm (*brachium*) and inserts on the radius.		

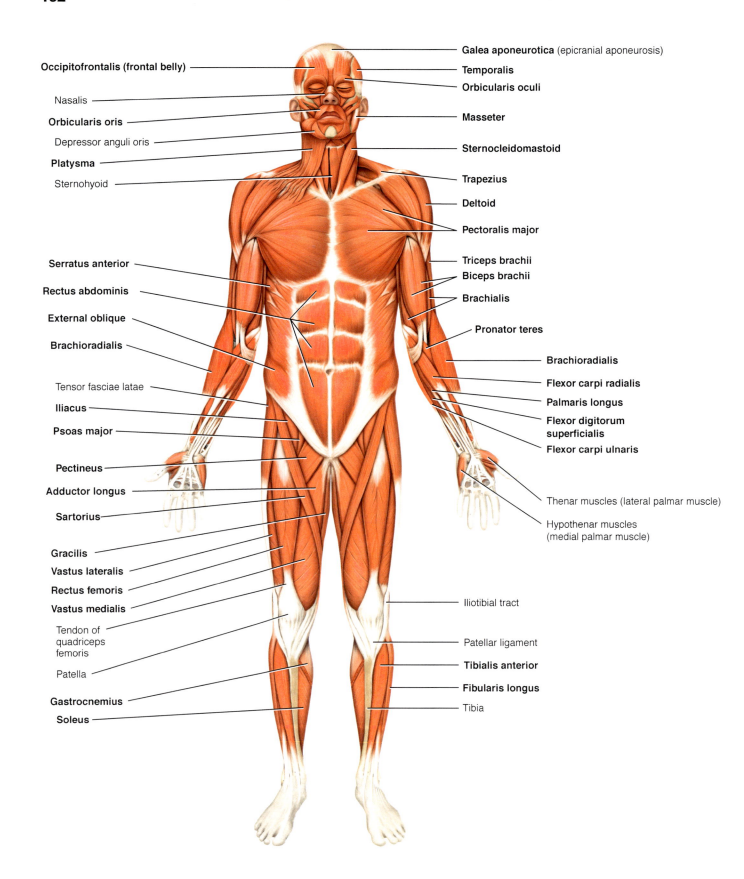

Galea aponeurotica (epicranial aponeurosis)

Occipitofrontalis (frontal belly)

Temporalis

Orbicularis oculi

Nasalis

Orbicularis oris

Masseter

Depressor anguli oris

Sternocleidomastoid

Platysma

Trapezius

Sternohyoid

Deltoid

Pectoralis major

Serratus anterior

Triceps brachii

Rectus abdominis

Biceps brachii

External oblique

Brachialis

Brachioradialis

Pronator teres

Tensor fasciae latae

Brachioradialis

Iliacus

Flexor carpi radialis

Psoas major

Palmaris longus

Flexor digitorum superficialis

Pectineus

Flexor carpi ulnaris

Adductor longus

Sartorius

Thenar muscles (lateral palmar muscle)

Gracilis

Hypothenar muscles (medial palmar muscle)

Vastus lateralis

Rectus femoris

Vastus medialis

Iliotibial tract

Tendon of quadriceps femoris

Patellar ligament

Patella

Tibialis anterior

Gastrocnemius

Fibularis longus

Soleus

Tibia

FIGURE 10-2. Principal superficial skeletal muscles, anterior view.

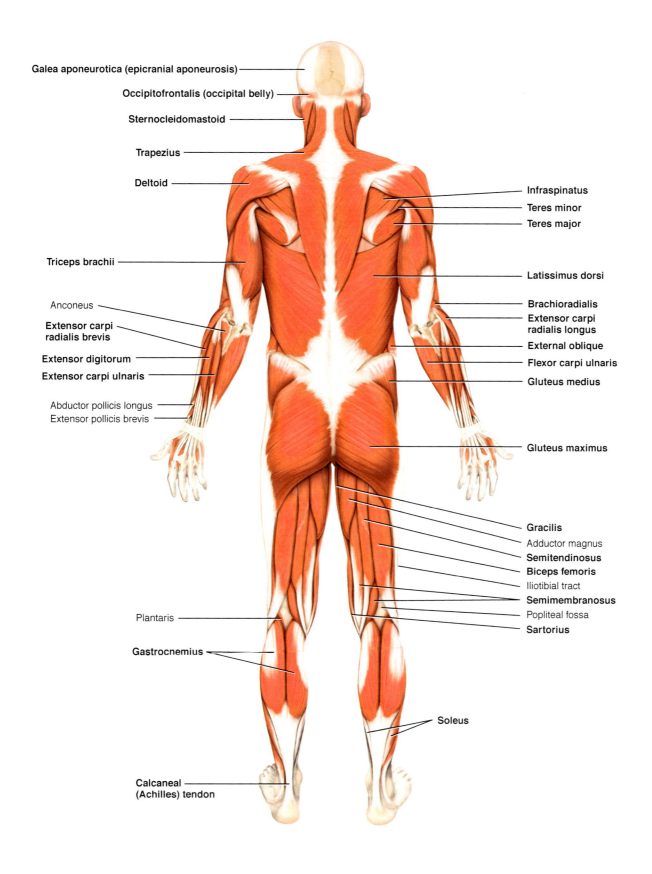

Galea aponeurotica (epicranial aponeurosis)

Occipitofrontalis (occipital belly)

Sternocleidomastoid

Trapezius

Deltoid

Triceps brachii

Anconeus

Extensor carpi radialis brevis

Extensor digitorum

Extensor carpi ulnaris

Abductor pollicis longus

Extensor pollicis brevis

Plantaris

Gastrocnemius

Calcaneal (Achilles) tendon

Infraspinatus

Teres minor

Teres major

Latissimus dorsi

Brachioradialis

Extensor carpi radialis longus

External oblique

Flexor carpi ulnaris

Gluteus medius

Gluteus maximus

Gracilis

Adductor magnus

Semitendinosus

Biceps femoris

Iliotibial tract

Semimembranosus

Popliteal fossa

Sartorius

Soleus

FIGURE 10-3. Principal superficial skeletal muscles, posterior view.

Identification of Human Muscles

Identify the skeletal muscles required for your class using the many resources in the laboratory. Take full advantage of the torso and limb models, cadaver specimens, painted skeleton, and charts.

In the limbs, muscles with a common action are grouped within the same **compartment**. They are held together by fascia and are supplied by the same nerves and blood vessels. *Example*: The flexor group in the anterior arm and the extensor group in the posterior forearm.

Most of the muscles on your checklist are **superficial** (Figures 10-2 and 10-3) and are easily palpated when they contract because they bulge, to varying degrees, just under the skin. The few **deep** muscles you will encounter will be identified as such.

Since muscles often have more than one action, the principal action of each muscle in the summary tables is written in blue type. Actions of synergists appear in black type.

Summary of Guiding Principles for Deducing Muscle Actions

Rather than rote memorizing muscle actions, pinpoint the location of a muscle, associate it with the joint it crosses, then deduce its action. Here is a summary of principles that will lead to muscle mastery by association and deduction.

- *Muscles generally do not lie directly over the joints and bones they move.* In the extremities, for example, the belly lies proximal to the joint at which the movement occurs.

- *Muscles become firm during their contraction phase.* Those that are superficially located can be palpated as they contract. This simple exercise will reinforce your sense of which muscle is tied to a particular action.

- *Muscles always pull on their insertion bones during contraction.*

- *Muscles operate as antagonistic groups.* Prime movers and their antagonists tend to lie on opposite sides of one another.

Muscles of the Head and Neck

Head and neck muscles include those involved in mastication (chewing), facial expression, movements of the head,

and eyeball and eyelid movements. Eye movements will be deferred to a later chapter.

Muscles of Facial Expression

Muscles of facial expression generally originate on skull bones and superficial fascia, and insert on the skin of the face. As such, they express emotions by pulling on our highly flexible facial skin.

PROCEDURE 1

Demonstrating Muscles of Facial Expression

Refer to Figures 10-4 and 10-5 and Table 10-2, locate the muscles below on the head and neck models. Perform the exercises in *green type* prescribed for each. Observe the change in facial appearance on your lab partner or on yourself using a mirror. Identify the:

- **occipitofrontalis** (ok-"sip-ih-toe-frun-TAY-lis), a "double" muscle comprised of a **frontal belly** that wrinkles the forehead and raises the eyebrows as when surprised. *Wrinkle your forehead by raising your eyebrows.* The second muscle is the **occipital belly,** which draws the scalp posteriorly. Between the muscles is the **galea aponeurotica**, which as the name implies, is an aponeurosis. (*Galea* is derived from its anatomical relationship to the cranium: it's Latin for helmet.)

- **orbicularis oculi**, a muscle encircling the eye that closes the eyelids. *Have your lab partner close both eyes or check out the effect of orbicularis oculi on yourself using a mirror while closing one eye.*

- **orbicularis oris,** a muscle encircling the mouth that closes the lips. *Purse your lips as if you're poised to kiss someone to see (and feel) the action of orbicularis oris.*

- **zygomaticus**, a paired muscle named for its origin on the zygomatic bone. It inserts on the skin at the corner of the mouth. *Flash the smile of someone who just aced the last lab practical and note how the two muscles pleasantly pull the angles of the mouth upward.*

- **buccinator** (BUK-suh-nay-tur), the principal muscle in each cheek. Its contraction compresses the cheek to ensure that food is directed between the teeth as we chew. *Purse the lips and blow on the back of your hand as if playing a trumpet. Palpate the cheeks near the corners of the mouth.*

Table 10-2. Muscles of Facial Expression.			
Muscle	**Origin**	**Insertion**	**Action**
Scalp Muscles			
Occipitofrontalis			
Frontal belly	Epicranial aponeurosis	Skin superior to supraorbital margin	Raises eyebrows, and wrinkles skin of forehead horizontally, as in a look of surprise; draws scalp anteriorly
Occipital belly	Occipital bone and mastoid process of temporal bone	Epicranial aponeurosis	Draws scalp posteriorly
Mouth Muscles			
Orbicularis oris	Muscle fibers surrounding opening of the mouth	Skin at corner of mouth	Closes and protrudes lips, as in kissing; compresses lips against teeth; and shapes lips during speech
Zygomaticus major	Zygomatic bone	Skin at angle of mouth and orbicularis oris	Draws angle of mouth superiorly and laterally, as in smiling
Buccinator	Alveolar processes (margins of tooth sockets) of maxilla and mandible	Orbicularis oris	Presses cheeks against teeth and lips as in whistling, blowing, and sucking; draws corner of mouth laterally; and assists in mastication by keeping food between the teeth
Orbit Muscle			
Orbicularis oculi	Medial wall of orbit	Circular path around orbit	Closes eye

Muscles of the Neck

Neck muscles generally flex, extend, and rotate the head. One of the two neck muscles listed below is an exception: it qualifies as a muscle of facial expression.

PROCEDURE 2

Demonstrating Muscles of the Neck

Refer to Figures 10-4 and 10-5 and Table 10-3 and identify the:

- **sternocleidomastoid** (SCM) (stir-no"-kly-doe-MASS-toyd), a paired muscle that connects the sternum

and clavicle ("sternocleido") to the mastoid process. When both SCMs contract simultaneously, the cervical spine and head are flexed. When an SCM contracts independently, it rotates the head toward the opposite shoulder. Alternately contracting each SCM signals "no". *Rotate your head to the right while palpating your left sternocleidomastoid.*

- **platysma** (pluh-TIZ-muh), a broad, thin muscle that spans the anterior aspect of the neck. It pulls down on the lower lip as it tenses the skin of the neck. *Place the index and middle fingers of each hand on either side of your larynx about an inch below your mandible. Forcibly push your mandible downward, as in a grimace, and note the tension in your neck.* (Be sure to observe a contracting platysma on your lab partner.)

Table 10-3. Muscles of the Neck			
Muscle	**Origin**	**Insertion**	**Action**
Sternocleidomastoid	Sternal head: manubrium of sternum; clavicular head: medial third of clavicle	Mastoid process of temporal bone (and lateral half of superior nuchal line of occipital bone)	Acting together (bilaterally), flex cervical portion of verterbral column; acting singly (unilaterally), rotate head to side opposite contracting muscle
Platysma	Fascia over deltoid and pectoralis major muscles	Mandible, muscles around angle of mouth, and skin of lower face	Draws outer part of lower lip inferiorly and posteriorly as in pouting; depresses mandible; tenses skin of neck

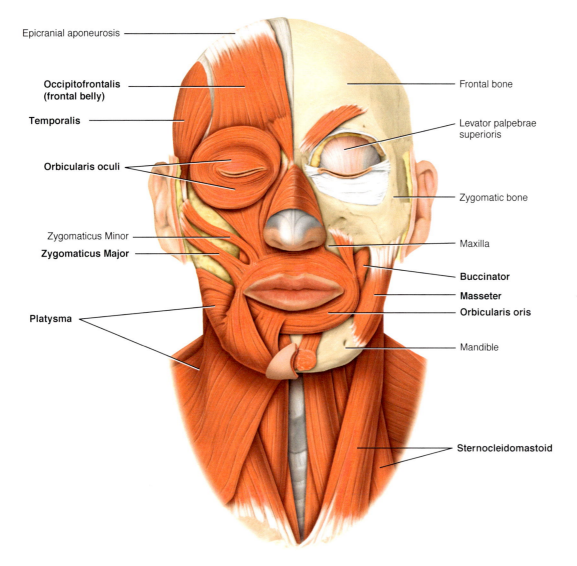

Epicranial aponeurosis

Occipitofrontalis
(frontal belly)

Temporalis

Orbicularis oculi

Zygomaticus Minor
Zygomaticus Major

Platysma

Frontal bone

Levator palpebrae
superioris

Zygomatic bone

Maxilla

Buccinator
Masseter
Orbicularis oris

Mandible

Sternocleidomastoid

FIGURE 10-4. Muscles of the head and neck, anterior view.

Muscles of Mastication

The muscles of mastication listed below enable chewing by elevating the mandible. (The medial and lateral pterygoids, which are referenced in your textbook, are responsible for side-to-side grinding movements of the teeth.)

PROCEDURE 3

Demonstrating Muscles of Mastication

Refer to Figures 10-4 and 10-5 and Table 10-4 and identify the:

- **masseter** (muh-SEE-tur), the prime mover of jaw closure. It derives its name from the Greek word for chewing. *Place your fingers near its insertion on the angle of the mandible while clenching your teeth.*

- **temporalis**, a fan-shaped muscle named for its origin on the temporal fossa. Like the masseter, it elevates the mandible. *Clench your teeth while palpating your temple.*

Table 10-4. Major Muscles of Mastication			
Muscle	**Origin**	**Insertion**	**Action**
Masseter	Maxilla and zygomatic arch	Angle and ramus of mandible	Elevates mandible, as in closing mouth
Temporalis	Temporal bone	Coronoid process and ramus of mandible	Elevates and retracts mandible

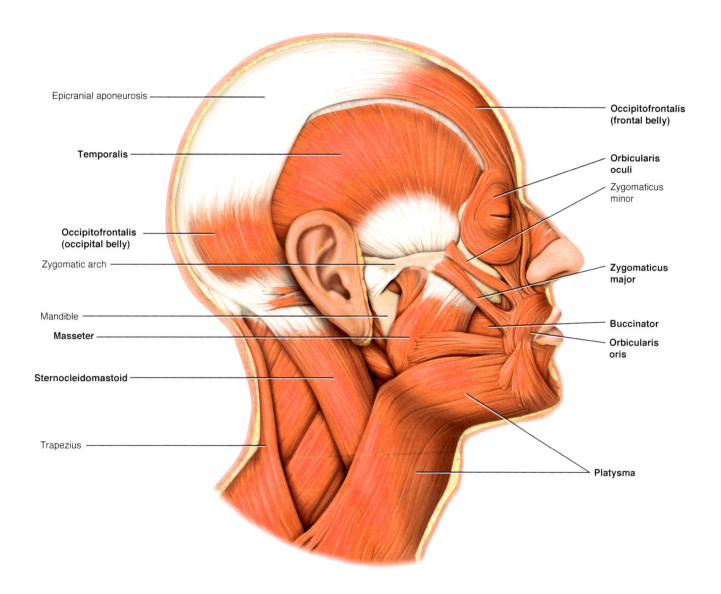

FIGURE 10-5. Muscles of the head and neck, right lateral view.

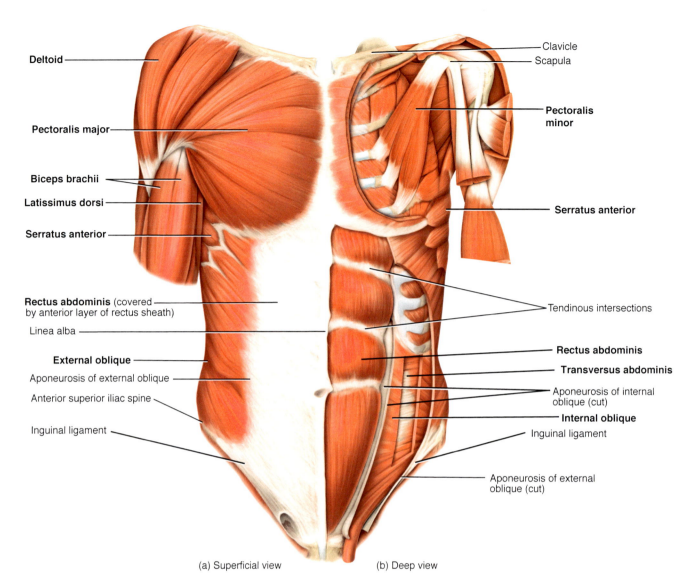

(a) Superficial view (b) Deep view

FIGURE 10-6. Muscles of the anterior trunk.

Muscles of the Trunk

Trunk musculature includes muscles of the thorax (chest), pectoral girdle, abdomen, and back. Thoracic, pectoral girdle, and back muscles move the arm, shoulder, and vertebral column while the abdominal muscles flex the trunk and "shore up" (compress) the abdominal wall.

Demonstrating Anterior Muscles of the Thorax and Shoulder

Once you have identified the muscles in this section, facilitate the association of a muscle to its action by applying resistance as directed in green type. Refer to Figures 10-6 and 10-7, Table 10-5, the torso model, and cadaver specimens, if available, and identify the:

- **pectoralis major**, a large, fan-shaped muscle of the chest wall that functions mainly as a powerful adductor of the arm. It also medially rotates and flexes the arm. *Have your lab partner adduct an arm while you oppose the movement by applying moderate resistance to the forearm. Palpate the upper portion of the muscle during the maneuver and note the firmness when the arm approaches the anatomical position. For a flexion-of-the-humerus exercise, sit at your lab station with hands under the tabletop and elbows almost fully extended. Pull upward as if to lift the table off the floor. Palpate the pectoral region.*

- **serratus anterior**, a fan-shaped muscle with a saw-toothed lateral edge lying inferior to the pectoral

Table 10-5. Anterior Muscles of the Thorax and Shoulder			
Muscle	**Origin**	**Insertion**	**Action**
Pectoralis major	Clavicle, sternum, costal cartilages of ribs 2-6, and aponeurosis of external oblique	Greater tubercle of humerus	Adducts, medially rotates, and flexes arm.
Serratus anterior	Superior eight or nine ribs	Vertebral border and inferior angle of scapula	Rotates scapula laterally (aiding arm abduction) and upward as arm is raised; pulls scapula forward when throwing and pushing
Deltoid	Lateral clavicle, acromion, and spine of scapula	Deltoid tuberosity of humerus	Prime mover of arm abduction; anterior fibers flex and medially rotate arm; posterior fibers extend and laterally rotate arm
Pectoralis minor	Anterior surface of ribs 3-5	Coracoid process of scapula	Rotates scapula laterally (abduction) and downward

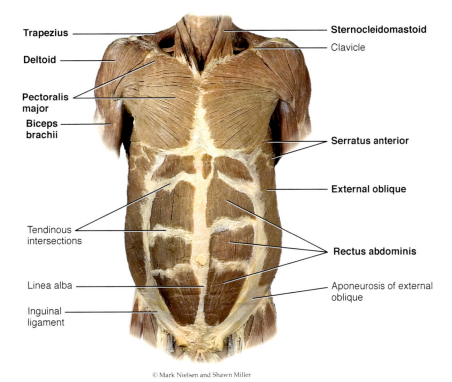

© Mark Nielsen and Shawn Miller

FIGURE 10-7. Anterior muscles of the trunk and shoulder in a cadaver.

muscles. When serratus rotates the scapula laterally, it helps to abduct the arm above the horizontal plane. It also pulls the scapula forward when throwing and pushing. It is nicknamed the "boxer's muscle" because it is essential for "throwing a punch".

The serratus anterior may be visible in a muscular classmate (a shirtless male) as both arms are abducted above the horizontal.

- **deltoid**, (DELL-toyd) a triangular muscle that gives the shoulder its roundness. Its posterior and middle (lateral) fibers strongly abduct the arm. The anterior fibers medially rotate and flex the arm; the posterior fibers extend and laterally rotate the arm. *Have your lab partner abduct an arm while you oppose the movement by applying moderate resistance to the proximal forearm. Palpate the "shoulder pad" during the maneuver and note the firmness when the arm approaches the horizontal.*

- **pectoralis minor** (pek-tuh-RAHL-iss), a thin flat muscle deep to the pectoralis major and hidden by it. It abducts the scapula and rotates it downward.

PROCEDURE 5

Demonstrating the Action of Abdominal Muscles

The abdominal muscles flex the vertebral column (trunk) and play a major role in compressing the abdominal wall. Abdominal compression increases intra-abdominal pressure and is thus an important aspect of defecation, urination, and forced exhalation. An increase in intra-abdominal pressure also shores up the spine and protects the back anatomy as one attempts lifting a heavy object. The four "abs" are the major support for the anterior aspect of the trunk between rib cage and pelvis. Their fibers are mutually perpendicular for greater strength.

On the torso model, Figures 10-6 and 10-7 and Table 10-6, locate the:

- **rectus abdominis** (REK-tus ab-DOM-in-iss), a muscle spanning the ventral midline from pubis to rib cage. The two recti are enclosed by aponeuroses of the oblique muscles and, once exposed, display four segments each. Rectus abdominis is the prime mover of trunk flexion, as in doing sit-ups or curls (also known as "crunches"). *Have the "subject" lie on the lab cot with legs bent at the knees, head on the cot, and index fingers on the forehead. The trunk is then elevated about 30 degrees off the horizontal with the neck held straight; hold for 5 seconds. Have the "observers" palpate the recti in this curl-up position.*

- **external oblique** (oh-BLEEK), a broad muscle whose fibers run downward and medially on either side of the abdominal wall lateral to the rectus abdominis. The external obliques are abdominal compressors when contracting together. Singly,

they laterally flex the vertebral column and aid back muscles in trunk rotation. *On the lab cot, with knees bent, the subject will tighten, that is, "suck in" the abdomen while the observers palpate external oblique. The side plank exercise also accentuates external oblique: On the lab bench (covered with examining-table paper), lie on your side. Lift your torso above the horizontal by resting on your elbow as you place your feet vertically side to side. Hold for 5 seconds and palpate the external oblique, which acts to stabilize the trunk in this position.*

- **internal oblique**, (oh-BLEEK) a broad muscle that is deep to external oblique and whose fibers run perpendicular to it. The action of internal oblique is the same as for external oblique, but it cannot be palpated directly.

- **transversus abdominis** (trans-VER-sus ab-DOM-in-iss), the deepest abdominal muscle. As its name suggests, its fibers run horizontally (and are perpendicular to rectus abdominis). Think of transversus abdominis as a natural girdle whose contraction compresses the abdomen. As with internal oblique, no direct palpation is possible.

Standing From a Sitting Position. *Sit at your lab station with your spine straight against the chair back and feet 6-8 inches apart. Try to stand with your back straight — DO NOT BEND AT THE WAIST. Difficult? Actually, the simple act of standing from a sitting position is impossible without trunk flexion via the abdominals.*
Mnemonic: A crunch contest can TIRE your abs: T = transversus abdominis; I = internal oblique; R = rectus abdominis; E = external oblique.

PROCEDURE 6

Demonstrating Posterior Muscles of the Thorax and Shoulder

Muscles of the posterior thorax and shoulder bring about movements of the pectoral girdle and humerus.

On the torso model, Figure 10-8, Table 10-7 and using cadaver specimens, if available, locate the:

- **trapezius**, (truh-PEE-zee-us) one of a pair of long, flat, triangular muscles whose superior fibers elevate the scapula, as in shrugging the shoulders. The middle fibers adduct the scapulae, as if doing a morning stretch, and the inferior fibers depress the scapulae, as

Table 10-6. Abdominal Muscles

Muscle	Origin	Insertion	Action
Superficial Abdominals			
Rectus abdominis	Pubic crest and pubic symphysis	Xiphoid process and cartilages of ribs 5-7	Flexes vertebral column; compresses abdomen; with trunk stabilized, flexes pelvis on vertebral column
External Oblique	Anterior surface of lower 8 ribs	Linea alba (ventral midline) and iliac crest	Acting together (bilaterally), compress abdomen and flex vertebral column; acting singly (unilaterally), laterally flex and rotate vertebral column.
Deep Abdominals			
Internal oblique	Iliac crest, inguinal ligament, and lumbar fascia	Linea alba, pubic crest, and cartilage of lower four ribs	Acting together (bilaterally), compress abdomen and flex vertebral column; acting singly (unilaterally), laterally flex and rotate vertebral column.
Transversus abdominis	Iliac crest, inguinal ligament, lumbar fascia, and cartilage of lower six ribs	Linea alba and pubic crest	Compresses abdomen

in pushing down to close a tightly packed suitcase. The trapezius muscles are the most superficial musculature of the back and together form a trapezoid, for which they are named. *Palpate the superior fibers while shrugging, the middle fibers while adducting the scapulae (moving them toward the midline), and the inferior fibers by pushing down hard on your lab bench with both hands.*

- **latissimus dorsi** (luh-TIH-suh-mus DOR-sye), literally the widest muscle of the back, it is the prime mover of arm extension. It is the muscle behind the power stroke in swimming, thus explaining the well-developed "lats" of accomplished swimmers. This power stroke also serves to deliver a hammer or ax to its destination. Latissimus dorsi also adducts and medially rotates the arm. *Palpate latissimus while the subject is medially rotating both arms simultaneously.*

- **infraspinatus** (in"-fruh-spih-NAY-tus), named for its location below the scapular spine. Its attachment to the lateral side of the humerus allows it to pull on the arm in a manner that rotates it laterally. Infraspinatus is a rotator cuff muscle. *Abduct the arm to the horizontal and flex the elbow joint to a right angle. While laterally rotating the arm against resistance, palpate the scapula region just below the spine.*

- **supraspinatus** (soo"-prah-spih-NAY-tus), a muscle named for its location above the scapular spine. It passes over the humeral head and pulls on the greater tubercle from above. It thus abducts the arm and is a synergist of deltoid. Supraspinatus is a rotator cuff muscle that cannot be directly palpated because it is obscured by trapezius.

- **teres major** (TERR-eez), a muscle named for its cross-sectional appearance. When dissected in the horizontal plane, its cut end is a nearly perfect circle (*teres* = round). Like infraspinatus, this is a scapula-to-humerus muscle. However, its insertion on the more medial lesser tubercle makes it a medial rotator of the arm. *Abduct the arm to the horizontal and flex the elbow joint to a right angle. While medially rotating the arm against resistance, palpate the scapula region at its inferior border.*

- **teres minor** (TERR-eez), a muscle located between infraspinatus and teres major whose insertion and action duplicates infraspinatus. It is a lateral rotator of the arm and is part of the rotator cuff as well. *Abduct the arm to the horizontal and flex the elbow joint to a right angle. Feel for the inferior angle of the scapula. While laterally rotating the arm against resistance, move your fingers toward the armpit about 2 cm (shy an inch) above the inferior border.*

Table 10-7. Posterior Muscles of the Thorax and Shoulder

Muscle	Origin	Insertion	Action
Trapezius	Occipital bone, spinous processes of seventh cervical and all thoracic vertebrae	Lateral clavicle, spine of scapula, acromion	Elevates, adducts, and depresses scapula (superior fibers elevate; middle fibers adduct; inferior fibers depress it); extends head
Latissimus dorsi	Spinous processes of T6-L5, sacrum, iliac crest (all via lumbodorsal fascia)	Intertubercular groove of humerus	Prime mover of arm extension; medially rotates and adducts arm
Infraspinatus	Infraspinous fossa of scapula	Greater tubercle of humerus	Laterally rotates arm; helps secure humeral head in glenoid cavity
Supraspinatus	Supraspinous fossa of scapula	Greater tubercle of humerus	Abducts arm; helps secure humeral head in glenoid cavity
Teres major	Dorsal surface at inferior angle of scapula	Lesser tubercle of humerus	Medially rotates, extends and adducts arm
Teres minor	Lateral border of scapula	Greater tubercle of humerus	Laterally rotates arm; helps secure humeral head in glenoid cavity.

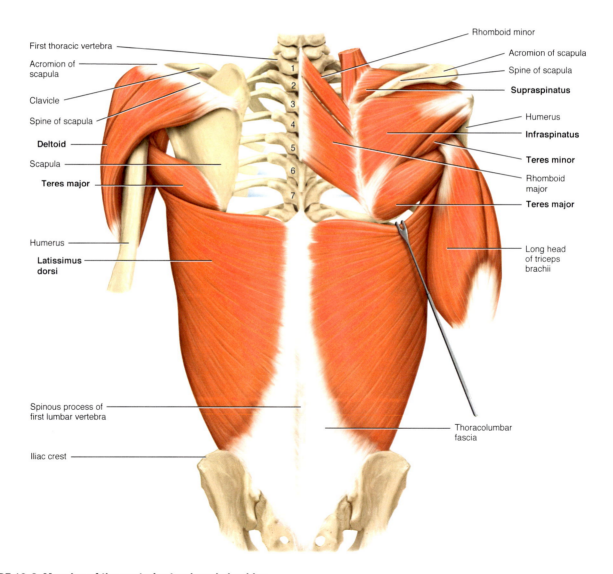

FIGURE 10-8. Muscles of the posterior trunk and shoulder.

Muscles of the Upper Limbs

In the extremities, a fundamental principle of biomechanics states that muscles lie proximal to the joints they move. In this and other limb exercises, note the location of the muscle proximal to its insertion and try to visualize its action.

PROCEDURE 7

Demonstrating Muscles That Act on the Forearm

For muscles that act on the forearm, refer to Figures 10-10, 10-11 and 10-12, the upper limb model, and cadaver specimens, if available, and identify the:

- **biceps brachii** (BY-seps BRAY-key-eye), a major flexor of the forearm within the anterior compartment of the arm. Biceps also supinates the forearm at the radioulnar joint. Mnemonic: "It turns the corkscrew (supinates) and pulls the cork (flexes)." *From the anatomical position, flex the forearm on your dominant side against resistance and note the bulging and firmness in the anterior arm. Palpate biceps and its tendon, which lies in the cubital fossa en route to its insertion on the radius.* (The cubital fossa is a shallow depression on the anterior aspect of the elbow just distal to the biceps belly; *cubitum* = elbow. See Figure 10-10.)

- **brachialis** (bray"-key-AL-us), the other major flexor of the forearm. Brachialis lies dorsal to (and mostly hidden by) the biceps brachii. Like biceps, it is an antagonist of triceps.

- **brachioradialis** (bray"-key-oh-ray-dee-AL-us), which is named for its origin and insertion. It is a synergist to biceps and brachialis during forearm flexion. *Flex the forearm to a right angle. Against resistance, continue to bring forearm toward arm and note the bulging brachioradialis where it forms a conspicuous contour on the lateral aspect of the forearm.*

- **triceps brachii** (TRY-seps BRAY-key-eye), the forearm extensor whose three heads are the sole occupants of the arm's posterior compartment. Because the common tendon of triceps inserts on the olecranon process of the ulna, it extends the forearm at the elbow joint and is therefore an antagonist of biceps and brachialis. *Starting with the fully flexed elbow joint of your dominant arm, extend the forearm against resistance and note the well-defined bellies of triceps as you palpate the posterior arm region. Imagine this straightening of the elbow joint as you are pushing an object or throwing a ball.*

- **pronator teres** (PRO-nate-ur TERR-eez), named for its action at the radioulnar joint. From its origin on the medial epicondyle of the humerus, pronator teres crosses over to the lateral forearm, inserting on the radius, and pulling it toward the ulna . The forearm is thus pronated and the palm of the hand now faces posteriorly (Figure 10-10).

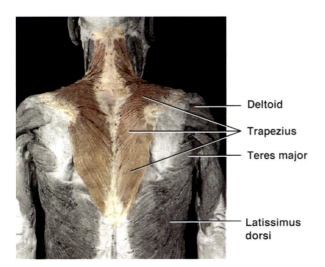

FIGURE 10-9. Muscles of the posterior trunk and shoulder in a cadaver. The superior, middle and inferior fibers of trapezius are highlighted.

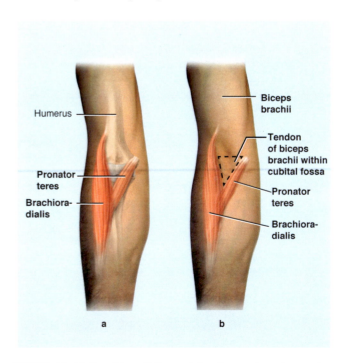

FIGURE 10-10. Brachioradialis, on lateral aspect, and pronator teres of the right upper limb. (a) The origins are on the humerus. (b) The cubital fossa (triangle) and its muscular borders. Note the location of the palpable biceps tendon.

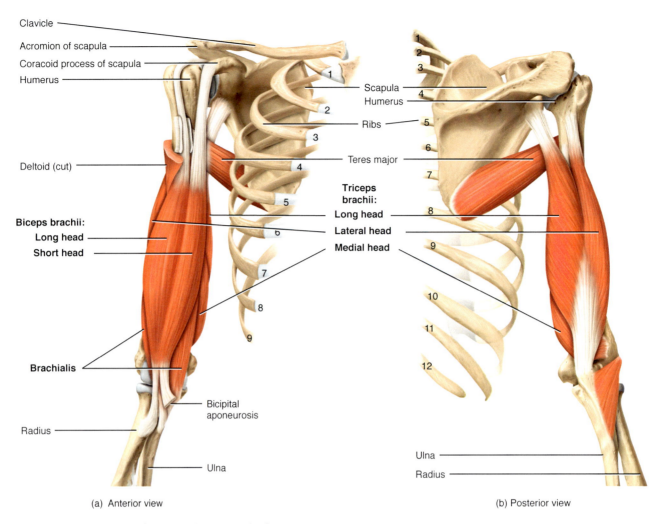

(a) Anterior view

(b) Posterior view

FIGURE 10-11. Muscles of the arm that move the forearm.

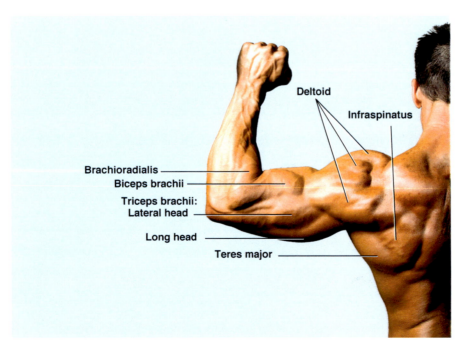

FIGURE 10-12. Surface anatomy of muscles that move the arm and forearm.

Table 10-8. Muscles That Act on the Forearm

Muscle	Origin	Insertion	Action
Forearm Flexors			
Biceps brachii	Long head originates from tubercle above glenoid cavity of scapula (supraglenoid tubercle). Short head originates from coracoid process of scapula.	Radial tuberosity and bicipital aponeurosis	Flexes forearm at elbow joint, supinates forearm at radioulnar joint
Brachialis	Distal, anterior surface of humerus	Coronoid process of ulna	Flexes forearm at elbow joint
Brachioradialis	Lateral border of distal end of humerus	Superior to styloid process of radius	Flexes forearm at elbow joint
Forearm Extensor			
Triceps brachii	Long head originates from infraglenoid tubercle, a projection inferior to glenoid cavity of scapula. Lateral head originates from lateral and posterior surface of humerus. Medial head originates from entire posterior surface of humerus inferior to a groove for the radial nerve.	Olecranon of ulna	Extends forearm at elbow joint and extends arm at shoulder joint
Pronator			
Pronator teres	Medial epicondyle of humerus and coronoid process of ulna	Midlateral surface of radius	Pronates forearm at radioulnar joint and weakly flexes forearm at elbow joint

PROCEDURE 8

Demonstrating Muscles of the Forearm That Act on the Wrist and Fingers

The muscles in the forearm originate, for the most part, on the epicondyles of the humerus. They are arranged such that their mass is centered in the forearm's proximal half. Strong, but lightweight tendons bridge the belly of these muscles to their insertion on bones of the wrist, hands and fingers. This anatomical arrangement ensures that the weight of each forearm is concentrated nearer the body's center of gravity. Try to visualize the actions of these muscles as they contract proximal to the wrist and finger joints. (These are *extrinsic* muscles of the hand because they originate outside the hand. *Intrinsic* muscles, which have their origin within the hand and abduct and adduct the fingers, are beyond the scope of this laboratory exercise.)

Anterior (Flexor) Compartment

Refer to Figures 10-13a and b, Table 10-9, the upper limb model, and cadaver specimens, if available. Identify the muscles of the anterior (flexor) compartment of the forearm, from lateral to medial, including the:

- **flexor carpi radialis** (FLEK-sor KAR-pye "ray-dee-AL-iss), whose name suggests a wrist flexor on the lateral side. Besides its role as a major wrist flexor, it also abducts the wrist and hand. *Make a fist, then slowly flex the wrist while palpating the ventral midline of your forearm just proximal to where the muscle's superficial tendon just disappears from view (Figure 10-14).*

- **palmaris longus** (pahl-MAR-iss LONG-us) a synergist to the flexor carpi muscles that crosses the wrist joint and inserts on the palmar aponeurosis. Its tendon can be seen just medial to that of flexor carpi radialis. *Make a fist, then slowly flex the wrist while palpating the ventral midline of your forearm just proximal to where the muscle's superficial tendon just disappears from view (Figure 10-14).*

* Palmaris longus is not universally present. The "prevalence of absence", as anatomy textbook authors describe it, is approximately 1% to 15% of the population, depending on ethnicity (*Journal of Hand Surgery*, British Volume, 2005). That some people are missing palmaris longus underscores its status as a secondary wrist flexor.

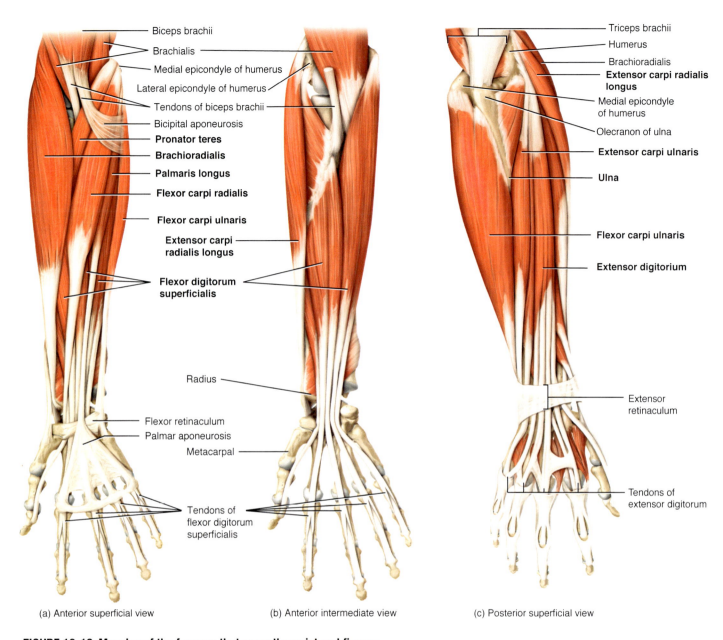

FIGURE 10-13. Muscles of the forearm that move the wrist and fingers.

- **flexor carpi ulnaris** (FLEK-sor KAR-pye ul-NAR-iss), the major wrist flexor on the medial side. It also adducts the wrist and hand. *Make a fist, then slowly flex and adduct the wrist while palpating the tendon near its insertion on the pisiform bone. Continue to palpate as you slide your fingers proximally toward the belly of flexor carpi ulnaris. Alternately flex and extend the wrist joint for greater effect.*

- **flexor digitorum superficialis** (FLEK-sor dih-jih-TOR-um soo"-per-fish-ee-AY-lus), which spans most of the width of the forearm and is just deep to the three flexors cited above. It flexes the wrist

as well as the fingers at the knuckles. After spanning the interphalangeal joints, the insertion of its four tendons on the middle phalanges (of digits 2-5) permits rapid finger movements, as in typing an e-mail message or playing the piano. (The "power grip" when making a fist occurs when flexor digitorum profundus, the deep finger flexor, contracts.)

When Flexor Tendons are Strained... Repetitive flexion of the wrist and fingers can strain the flexor tendons as they slide back and forth within the carpal tunnel on the anterior aspect of the wrist. Chronic irritation leads to inflammation, the

Table 10-9. Muscles of the Forearm That Act on the Wrist and Fingers			
Muscle	**Origin**	**Insertion**	**Action**
Anterior (Flexor) Compartment of the Forearm			
Flexor carpi radialis	Medial epicondyle of humerus	Second and third metacarpals	Flexes and abducts hand (radial deviation) at wrist joint
Palmaris longus	Medial epicondyle of humerus	Flexor retinaculum and palmar aponeurosis (fascial center of palm)	Weakly flexes hand at wrist joint
Flexor carpi ulnaris	Medial epicondyle of humerus and superior posterior border of ulna	Pisiform, hamate and base of fifth metacarpal	Flexes and adducts hand (ulnar deviation) at wrist joint
Flexor digitorum superficialis	Medial epicondyle of humerus, coronoid process of ulna, and ridge along lateral margin of anterior surface of radius	Middle phalanx of each finger (2-5)	Flexes middle phalanx of each finger at proxmal interphalangeal joint, and hand at wrist
Posterior (Extensor) Compartment of the Forearm			
Extensor carpi radialis longus	Lateral supracondylar ridge of humerus	Base of second metacarpal	Extends and abducts hand at wrist joint
Extensor carpi ulnaris	Lateral epicondyle of humerus and posterior border of ulna	Fifth metacarpal	Extends and adducts hand at wrist joint
Extensor digitorum	Lateral epicondyle of humerus	Distal and middle phalanges of each finger (2-5)	Extends distal and middle phalanges of each finger at interphalangeal joints, and hand at wrist joint

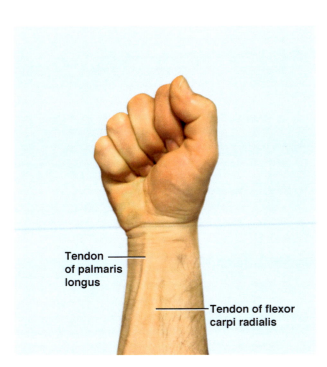

Tendon of palmaris longus

Tendon of flexor carpi radialis

FIGURE 10-14. Surface anatomy of flexed wrist illustrating wrist flexor tendons. (See Figure 10-13a.)

swelling from which compresses the median nerve. This is the cause of carpal tunnel syndrome. (See the *Carpal Tunnel Syndrome* Clinical Application, on page 132.)

Posterior (Extensor) Compartment

Refer to Figure 10-13, Table 10-9, the upper limb model, and cadaver specimens, if available. Identify the muscles of the posterior (extensor) compartment of the forearm, from lateral to medial, including the:

- **extensor carpi radialis longus** (ik-STEN-sor KAR-pye "ray-dee-AL-iss LONG-us), the longer of the two aptly named extensors of the wrist. From its origin on the distal humerus, this muscle crosses the wrist on its posterior aspect and inserts at the base of the second metacarpal. *Flex your thumb and place two fingers about a single finger width proximal to the dorsal wrist crease in line with your index finger. Fully extend your hand and note the bulge of this extensor.*

- **extensor carpi ulnaris** (ik-STEN-sor KAR-pye ul-NAR-iss), the other major wrist extensor. Its insertion at the base of the fifth metacarpal is a guide to its action and palpation. *About three finger widths proximal to head of the ulna (see page 129 for an ulnar landmark refresher), feel for a bulge as you fully extend the wrist.*

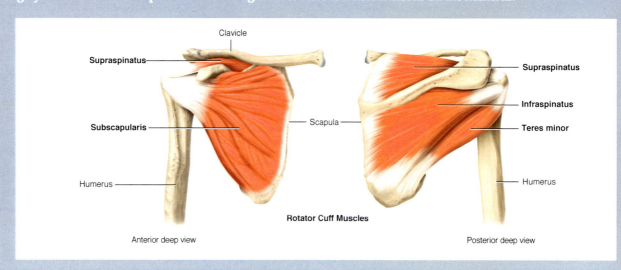

Rotator Cuff Muscles

Anterior deep view   Posterior deep view

- **extensor digitorum** (ik-STEN-sor dih-jih-TOR-um), which like its flexor digitorum antagonist, divides into four tendons that insert on the phalanges. In this case, the tendons attach to the posterior aspect of the phalanges after crossing the interphalangeal joints. Extensor digitorum, which occupies most of the posterior surface of the forearm, is the prime mover for finger extension.

Muscles of the Lower Limbs

Lower limb muscles originate mainly on the pelvic girdle, femur, and bones of the leg. (Recall that *leg* refers to the part of the lower extremity between the knee and ankle.) Movements of these muscles occur at the hip, knee, and ankle joints as well as joints within the foot. Once again, determine the actions by deduction: Muscles of the limbs have their origins proximal to the joints and bones they move (the insertions). Note that the stronger and more stable pelvic girdle does

not require the same degree of muscular support as the shoulder girdle, whose greater flexibility demands stabilizers, such as rotator cuff muscles.

PROCEDURE 9

Demonstrating Muscles of Pelvic Origin That Act on the Thigh's Anterior Aspect

The muscles that act on the anterior aspect of the thigh originate on the pelvic girdle and vertebral column and cross the front of the hip joint to insert on the femur. They are ideally positioned to flex the thigh.

Refer to Figure 10-15, Table 10-10, the lower limb model, and cadaver specimens, if available, and identify:

- **iliopsoas** (il-ee-oh-SO-us), two muscles that merge into a common tendon that inserts on the femur just below the hip joint. The prime mover of thigh flexion,

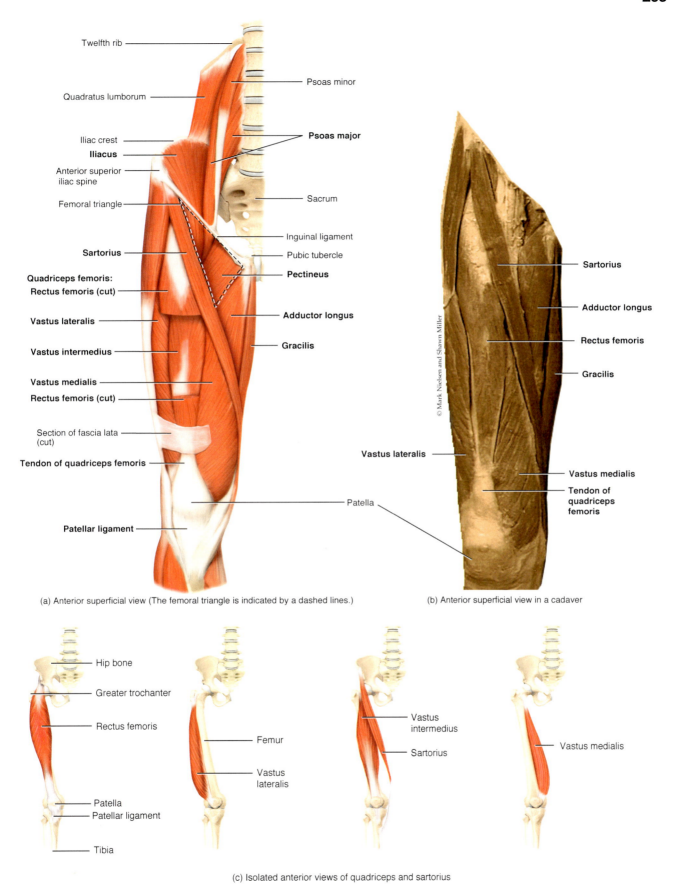

(a) Anterior superficial view (The femoral triangle is indicated by a dashed lines.)

(b) Anterior superficial view in a cadaver

(c) Isolated anterior views of quadriceps and sartorius

FIGURE 10-15. Muscles that act on the anterior aspect of the thigh and leg. (Iliacus and psoas major fuse into a common tendon and may be referred to as the iliopsoas muscle.)

Table 10-10. Muscles That Act on the Thigh and Leg: Anterior Aspect

Muscle	Origin	Insertion	Action
Origin on Pelvic Girdle and Vertebral Column Acting on Thigh (Femur)			
Iliopsoas			
	Transverse processes and bodies of lumbar vertebrae	With iliacus into lesser trochanter of femur	Psoas major and iliacus muscles acting together flex thigh at hip joint, and flex trunk on hip as in sitting up from supine position. Psoas alone laterally flexes vertebral column.
Psoas major			
Iliacus	Iliac fossa	With psoas major into lesser trochanter of femur	
Anterior (Extensor) Compartment of the Thigh Acting on Thigh (Femur) and Leg			
Quadriceps femoris			
Rectus femoris	Anterior inferior iliac spine	Patella via quadriceps tendon and then tibial tuberosity via patellar ligament	Extends leg and Flexes thigh
Vastus lateralis	Greater trochanter and linea aspera of femur		Extends leg
Vastus medialis	Linea aspera of femur		Extends leg
Vastus intermedius	Anterior and lateral surfaces of body of femur		Extends leg
Sartorius	Anterior superior iliac spine	Medial surface of tibia	Weakly flexes, abducts and laterally rotates thigh at hip joint; weakly flexes leg at knee joint

iliopsoas also flexes the trunk as when sitting up from a supine position.

- **psoas major** (SO-us), a "loin" muscle whose origin on the lumbar vertebrae allows it to laterally flex the vertebral column in addition to flexing the thigh.

- **iliacus** (il-ee-AH-kus), a muscle lateral to psoas major occupying a fossa on the medial side of its namesake, the iliac region of the pelvis. (Iliacus and psoas are deep muscles that cannot be palpated.)

Demonstrating Muscles of the Thigh's Anterior Compartment

The thigh's anterior aspect is comprised of four muscles, the **quadriceps femoris**, that all insert on the patella via the quadriceps tendon. Their collective action — extension of the leg — is predicted by their insertion on the tibial tuberosity via the patellar ligament. The quadriceps is the largest muscle in the body and a powerful leg extensor. The sartorius crosses the hip and knee joints and thus acts on both.

Refer to Figure 10-15, Table 10-10, the lower limb model, and cadaver specimens, if available, and identify the:

- **rectus femoris** (REK-tus FEM-ur-us), the lone member of quadriceps that originates on the pelvis and spans the hip joint. Here it acts as a synergist to the thigh-flexing iliopsoas.

- **vastus lateralis** (VAS-tuhs lah"-tur-AY-lis), the vastus muscle on the lateral side (*vastus* = large, as in vast).

- **vastus medialis** (VAS-tuhs mee-dee-AY-lis), the vastus on the medial side of the femur.

- **vastus intermedius** (VAS-tuhs in-tur-MEE-dee-us), the vastus deep to rectus femoris. It lies between vastus lateralis and vastus medialis.

Palpation of Quadriceps. All but vastus intermedius can be easily palpated. From a sitting position, bring your knee to almost full extension. Isometrically contract the quadriceps muscles. The rectus femoris can best be felt in the midline about halfway between the hip and knee joints. For vastus lateralis and vastus medialis, palpate a hand width proximal to the patella in line with its lateral and medial borders respectively.

- **sartorius** (sar-TOR-ee-us), the body's longest single muscle, originating on the ilium and spanning the hip and knee joints before inserting on the tibia's medial

Table 10-11. Muscles Act on The Thigh: Medial Aspect			
Muscle	**Origin**	**Insertion**	**Action**
Adductor longus	Pubic crest and pubic symphysis	Linea aspera of femur	Adducts and flexes thigh at hip joint and rotates thigh medially
Pectineus	Superior ramus of pubis	Pectineal line of femur, between lesser trochanter and linea aspera	Flexes and adducts thigh at hip joint
Gracilis	Body and inferior ramus of pubis	Medial surface of tibia	Adducts thigh at hip joint, medially rotates thigh, and flexes leg at knee joint

side. At the hip, it flexes, abducts, and laterally rotates the thigh. At the knee joint, it flexes the leg. The translation of *sartorius* is "tailor's muscle", a name coined because this muscle helps one sit cross-legged as would a tailor plying his trade.

Demonstrating Muscles of the Thigh's Medial (Adductor) Compartment

Muscles of the medial compartment of the thigh generally originate on the pubic region of the pelvic girdle and insert on the femur. They are adductors of the thigh at the hip joint. Most will also flex and medially rotate the thigh.

Refer to Figure 10-15, Table 10-11, the lower limb model, and cadaver specimens, if available, and identify the:

- **adductor longus** (uh-DUK-tur LONG-us), a muscle whose pubis-to-femur attachments permit it to adduct, flex, and medially rotate the thigh at the hip joint. *The tendon of origin near the pubic symphysis can be palpated as the hip joint is passively abducted. You will feel this tendon as a prominent cord as the thigh approaches full abduction. (Please be mindful that this exercise and those for the adductors that follow requires discreet palpation of the groin.)*

- **pectineus** (pek-TIN-ee-us), a muscle superior and lateral to adductor longus whose origin and insertion parallel those of its neighbor. The actions are therefore the same as adductor longus: adduction and flexion of the thigh. *Palpation of pectineus is rather difficult. Find the adductor longus tendon and move your fingers laterally.*

- **gracilis** (gruh-SIL-iss), a long, thin muscle (*gracilis* means slender) that crosses both the hip and knee joints. Owing to these insertions, gracilis adducts the thigh and flexes the leg. *The relatively flat tendon of origin can be palpated just medial to that of adductor longus. Since gracilis spans the knee joint, it is best*

to palpate this tendon while passively abducting the thigh and extending the knee joint.

PROCEDURE 10

Demonstrating Muscles That Act on the Thigh's Posterior Aspect

Muscles that act on the posterior aspect of the thigh originate on the posterior or lateral surface of the pelvis and insert on the posterior or lateral aspect of the femur. They are extensors and abductors of the thigh at the hip joint.

Refer to Figure 10-16, Table 10-12, the lower limb model, and cadaver specimens, if available, and identify the:

- **gluteus maximus** (GLU-tee-us MAK-sih-mus), the largest of the three gluteal muscles (*gluteus* is Latin for buttock). One of the body's strongest muscles, gluteus maximus extends the thigh — as when rearing back before kicking a ball. It is most active when climbing stairs or an incline, during which it counters the tendency to jackknife at the waist as the body ascends a staircase or hill. Note the anatomical basis for this stabilizing effect: gluteus maximus crosses the midsection from behind from its origin on the posterior pelvis to its insertion on the posterior femur. The tension it exerts on the pelvis prevents us from doubling over at the waist. *Walk up a short flight of stairs with your right palm over your right gluteus maximus. As your right foot hits the stair tread, the buttock will noticeably firm up.*

- **gluteus medius** (GLU-tee-us MEE-dee-us), the middle of the three gluteal muscles situated deep and lateral to gluteus maximus. Its insertion on the greater trochanter of the femur makes clear its action: abduction of the thigh. It also acts as a pelvic stabilizer to control pelvic sway while walking. *Place your fingers on the top of your thigh between the iliac crest and greater trochanter (the lateral bump*

Muscle	Origin	Insertion	Action
Table 10-12. Muscles That Act on the Femur: Posterior Aspect			
Origin on Pelvic Girdle and Vertebral Column			
Gluteus maximus	Iliac crest, sacrum, and coccyx	Gluteal tuberosity and iliotibial tract	Extends thigh at hip joint; stabilizes torso at waist when climbing stairs or an incline; not active when walking horizontally
Gluteus medius	Upper lateral surface of ilium	Greater trochanter of femur	Abducts thigh at hip joint and medially rotates thigh; stabilizes pelvis during walking
Posterior (Flexor) Compartment of the Thigh			
Hamstring Group			
Biceps femoris	Long head arises from ischial tuberosity; short head rises from linea aspera of femur	Head of fibula and lateral condyle of tibia	Flexes leg at knee joint and extends thigh at hip joint
Semitendinosus	Ischial tuberosity	Proximal part of medial surface of shaft of tibia	Flexes leg at knee joint and extends thigh at hip joint
Semimembranosus	Ischial tuberosity	Medial condyle of tibia	Flexes leg at knee joint and extends thigh at hip joint

near the top of the thigh). You can feel gluteus medius rhythmically contracting with each step to maintain a balanced gait.

Demonstrating Muscles of the Thigh's Posterior Compartment

The thigh's posterior compartment is comprised of three muscles, the **hamstring group**, that all insert on the proximal tibia and fibula. Their collective actions: extension of the thigh and flexion of the leg. (The name hamstrings was coined from an old butcher's practice of hanging the posterior thigh meat of animals by its prominent, string-like — and convenient — tendons.)

Refer to Figure 10-16, Table 10-12, the lower limb model, and cadaver specimens, if available, and identify the:

- **biceps femoris** (BY-seps FEM-uh-riss), named for its two heads, which originate on (1) the ischial tuberosity, the common origin of all three hamstrings, and (2) the back of the femur at its proximal end. All hamstrings insert on the back of the leg just below the knee joint and are the principal leg flexors at the knee joint. Because they also span the hip joint from behind, they are extensors of the thigh that complement gluteus maximus.

- **semitendinosus** (sem-ih-ten"-dih-NO-sus), the middle hamstring, named for its long tendon approximating half its overall length (*semi* = half).

- **semimembranosus** (sem-ih-mem"-bruh-NO-sus), named for the membrane-like connective tissue on its external surface for nearly half its length. The location of semimembranosus relative to the other hamstrings can be identified, of course, by its external anatomy once exposed. But there is also a memory tip known as the three Ms. Mnemonic: The semiMembranosus is Most Medial.

Palpation of Hamstrings. While standing, shift your weight to one leg and flex the knee of the other limb to a right (90 degree) angle. On the lateral aspect of the thigh just proximal to the flexed knee joint, feel for the prominent tendon of biceps femoris. As you slide your fingers medially, palpate the tendon of semitendinosus. Now increase the angle of flexion (to your maximum if not uncomfortable) and feel for the semimembranosus tendon about a finger width medial to semitendinosus. For each of the three muscles, the belly can be felt proximal to its corresponding tendon.

PROCEDURE 11

Demonstrating Muscles of the Anterior and Lateral Leg That Act on the Ankle and Toes

Muscles of the anterior and lateral leg that act on the ankle and toes originate on the tibia and fibula, and cross the ankle joint before inserting

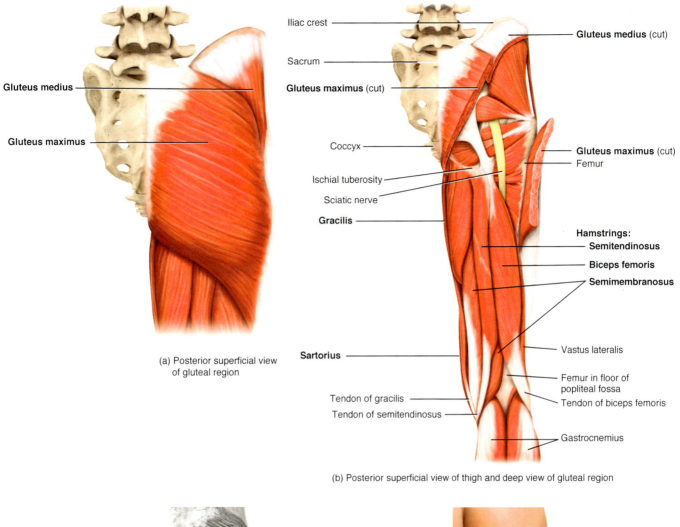

Iliac crest

Sacrum

Gluteus maximus (cut)

Coccyx

Ischial tuberosity

Sciatic nerve

Gracilis

Sartorius

Tendon of gracilis

Tendon of semitendinosus

Gluteus medius (cut)

Gluteus maximus (cut)

Femur

Hamstrings:
Semitendinosus
Biceps femoris
Semimembranosus

Vastus lateralis

Femur in floor of popliteal fossa

Tendon of biceps femoris

Gastrocnemius

Gluteus medius

Gluteus maximus

(a) Posterior superficial view of gluteal region

(b) Posterior superficial view of thigh and deep view of gluteal region

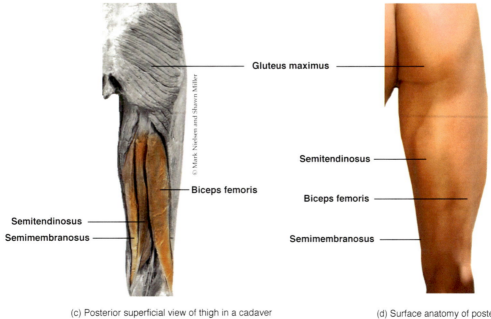

© Mark Nielsen and Shawn Miller

Gluteus maximus

Biceps femoris

Semitendinosus

Semimembranosus

Semitendinosus

Biceps femoris

Semimembranosus

(c) Posterior superficial view of thigh in a cadaver

(d) Surface anatomy of posterior thigh

FIGURE 10-16. Muscles that act on the posterior aspect of the thigh and leg.

Table 10-13. Muscle That Act on the Ankle and Toes

Muscle	Origin	Insertion	Action
Anterior Compartment of the Leg			
Tibialis anterior	Lateral condyle and body of tibia and interosseous membrane (sheet of fibrous tissue that holds shafts of tibia and fibula together)	First metatarsal and first (medial) cuneiform	Dorsiflexes foot at ankle joint and inverts (supinates) foot at intertarsal joints
Extensor digitorum longus	Lateral condyle of tibia, anterior surface of fibula and interosseous membrane	Middle and distal phalanges of toes 2-5	Dorisiflexes foot at ankle joint and extends distal and middle phalanges of each toe at interphalangeal joints and proximal phalanx of each toe at metatarsophalangeal joint
Lateral (Fibular) Compartment of the Leg			
Fibularis longus (peroneus)	Head and body of fibula	First metatarsal and first cuneiform	Plantar flexes foot at ankle joint and everts (pronates) foot at intertarsal joints
Superficial Posterior Compartment of the Leg			
Gastrocnemius	Lateral and medial condyles of femur	Calcaneus by way of calcaneal (Achilles) tendon	Plantar flexes foot at ankle joint and flexes leg at knee joint
Soleus	Head of fibula and medial border of tibia	Calcaneus by way of calcaneal (Achilles) tendon	Plantar flexes foot at ankle joint
Flexor digitorum longus	Middle third of posterior surface of tibia	Distal phalanges of toes 2-5	Plantar flexes foot at ankle joint; flexes distal and middle phalanges of each toe at interphalangeal joints and proximal phalanx of each toe at metatarsophalangeal joint

on bones of the ankle (tarsals), foot (metatarsals) and toes (phalanges). They move the foot at the ankle joint and extend the toes.

Refer to Figure 10-17, Table 10-13, the lower limb model, and cadaver specimens, if available, and identify:

- **tibialis anterior** (tib-ee-AL-us ann-TEER-ee-ur), a long prominent muscle that lies on the anterolateral surface of the tibia. Its termination at the medial base of the foot predicts dorsiflexion. *In a sitting position, bring one leg to near-complete extension and plantar flex the foot. Palpate the lateral aspect of that leg — about three finger widths from the tibial crest — then dorsiflex to feel tibialis anterior.*

- **extensor digitorum longus** (ik-STEN-sur dih-gih-TOR-um LONG-us, another inhabitant of the leg's anterior compartment whose name describes its function and long length from just below the knee to the dorsal aspect of the toes, excepting the big (great) toe. (This toe — the *hallux* — is extended by the extensor hallucis muscles.)
Extensor digitorum longus is also a doriflexor.

In a sitting position, bring one leg to near-complete extension and plantar flex the foot. Palpate the side of the leg just lateral to the tibialis anterior, then dorsiflex while extending the toes.

- **fibularis longus** (fib-yuh-LAR-us LONG-us), formerly the **peroneus** (from *perone*, Latin for fibula). This muscle is the longer version of two muscles in the lateral compartment of the leg that insert on the underside of the foot, plantar flexing it. *In a sitting position, bring one leg to near-complete extension. Feel for the origin of fibularis longus at the head of the fibula, which is a hand's width lateral to the base of the patella. Slide two fingers 10 cm (about 4 inches) inferior to the fibular head and notice a bulge as you plantar flex.*

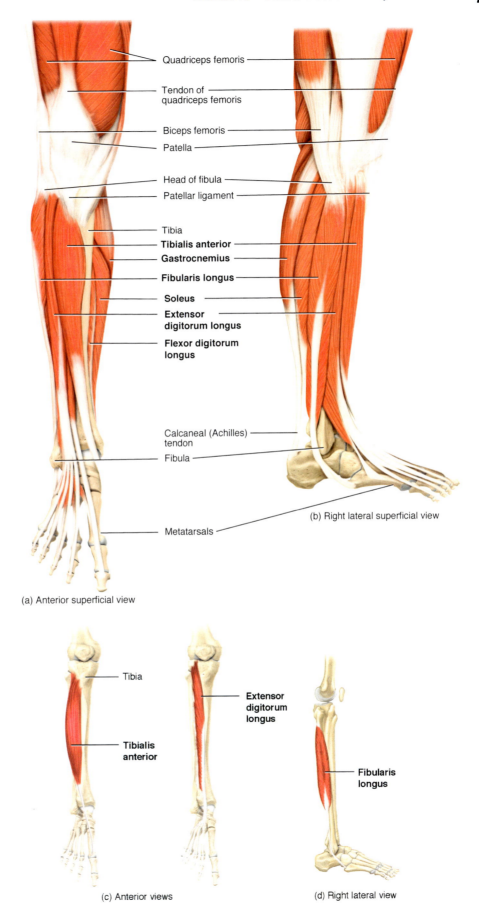

Quadriceps femoris

Tendon of quadriceps femoris

Biceps femoris

Patella

Head of fibula

Patellar ligament

Tibia

Tibialis anterior

Gastrocnemius

Fibularis longus

Soleus

Extensor digitorum longus

Flexor digitorum longus

Calcaneal (Achilles) tendon

Fibula

Metatarsals

(a) Anterior superficial view

(b) Right lateral superficial view

Tibia

Tibialis anterior

Extensor digitorum longus

Fibularis longus

(c) Anterior views

(d) Right lateral view

FIGURE 10-17. Muscles of the anterior and lateral leg that move the ankle and toes.

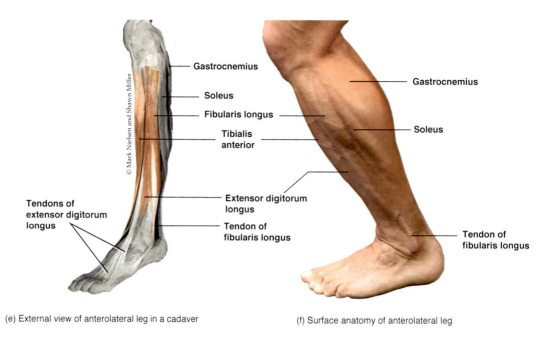

(e) External view of anterolateral leg in a cadaver

(f) Surface anatomy of anterolateral leg

FIGURE 10-17 (continued). Muscles of the leg that move the ankle and toes.

PROCEDURE 12

Demonstrating Muscles of the Posterior Leg That Act on the Ankle and Toes

Muscles of the posterior leg originate on the tibia, fibula, and distal femur. They generally cross the ankle joint from behind before inserting on the calcaneus, metatarsals, and toes. Most plantar flex the foot. The flexor digitorum muscle flexes the toes.

Refer to Figure 10-17, Figure 10-18 and Table 10-13, the lower limb model, and cadaver specimens, if available, and identify:

- **gastrocnemius** (gas"-troe-NEEM-ee-us*), the largest and most superficial of the calf muscles. It crosses the ankle via the calcaneal tendon and is a powerful plantar flexor, as in supporting your body weight when standing on your toes. Along with soleus, it provides the driving force behind basic human locomotion. (See Procedure 12.) Gastrocnemius, because it crosses the back of the knee joint from its origin on the femoral condyles, is a synergist to the hamstrings during knee flexion. *While standing, lean down and palpate the upper half of one your calves. Now stand on tiptoe and note the increased firmness and definition of gastrocnemius.*

* "Gastrocnemius", from the Greek, describes this muscle's shape (*gastro* translates as belly) and location (*kneme* = calf). The silent "k" (as in "knife") became a silent "c", which explains why the pronunciation cited above deletes the c. Nonetheless, the second syllable is often pronounced "trok".

- **soleus** (SO-lee-us), the calf muscle just deep to gastrocnemius, which obscures soleus on one's surface anatomy except for a rather limited view on the lateral aspect of the leg. Soleus shares the calcaneal tendon with gastrocnemius and thus is a co-prime mover in plantar flexion and locomotion. *While standing, lean down and palpate the calcaneal tendon just above the calcaneus (heel bone). Slide your fingers upward until the tendon is no longer felt. Move a finger width laterally from this midline location and stand on tiptoe to palpate soleus.*

- **flexor digitorum longus** (FLEK-sur dih-gih-TOR-um LONG-us), like its extensor counterpart, is a muscle that acts on all toes except the big toe. (This toe is flexed by flexor hallucis longus.) Besides flexing toes 2-5, flexor digitorum longus is a plantar flexor.

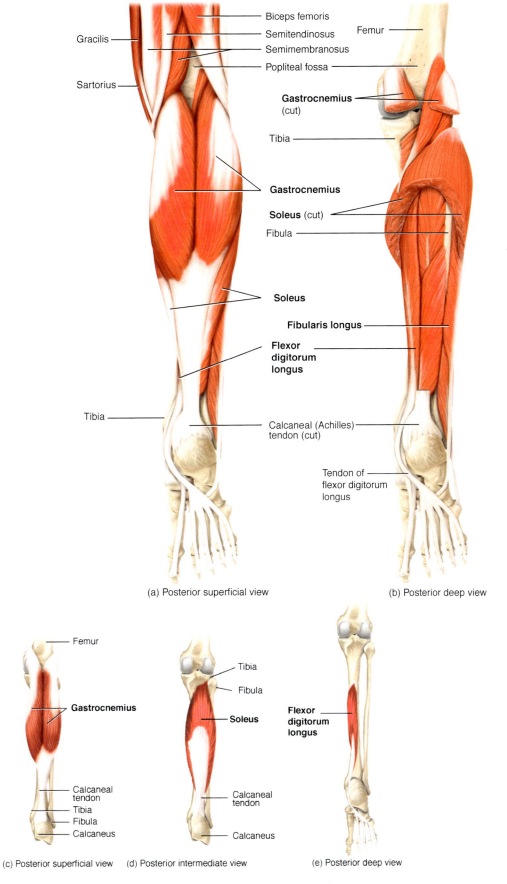

Gracilis

Biceps femoris

Semitendinosus

Semimembranosus

Popliteal fossa

Femur

Sartorius

Gastrocnemius
(cut)

Tibia

Gastrocnemius

Soleus (cut)

Fibula

Soleus

Fibularis longus

Flexor digitorum longus

Tibia

Calcaneal (Achilles) tendon (cut)

Tendon of flexor digitorum longus

(a) Posterior superficial view

(b) Posterior deep view

Femur

Gastrocnemius

Calcaneal tendon

Tibia

Fibula

Calcaneus

Tibia

Fibula

Soleus

Calcaneal tendon

Calcaneus

Flexor digitorum longus

(c) Posterior superficial view

(d) Posterior intermediate view

(e) Posterior deep view

FIGURE 10-18. Muscles of the posterior leg that move the ankle and toes.

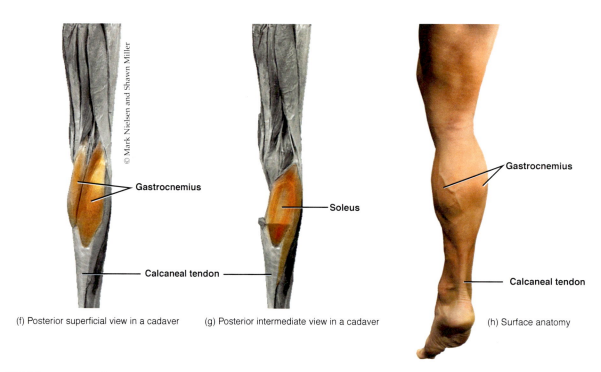

(f) Posterior superficial view in a cadaver   (g) Posterior intermediate view in a cadaver   (h) Surface anatomy

FIGURE 10-18 (continued). Muscles of the posterior leg that move the ankle and toes.

Gray Matter Matchup
Which Muscles Make You Jump?

Organize teams of four to six students each. Each team will be given a randomly assigned joint involved in the explosive phase of jumping off the floor by the instructor from the list below. Each team will then explain their answer to the other teams within ten minutes — and without consulting the textbook or flipping back through your laboratory manual. Anyone on another team may challenge an answer deemed inaccurate and provide a rebuttal. (Consult your instructor when a disagreement cannot be resolved.) Record all answers in the table below. (A jumpy lab partner may actually be an asset during this exercise.)

Explosive Phase of Jumping (springing upward after crouching)

Joints Involved	Muscles Involved	Actions
1. Hip		
2. Knee		
3. Ankle		

Human Locomotion

Walking is a complex pattern of neuromuscular activities that is actually a delicate balancing act. Bipedal (two-legged) walkers have a tendency to fall off balance with every step, an inclination that is countered by a series of highly coordinated mechanical compensations.

In the accompanying illustrations, the model starts from a standing posture and walks from right to left, leading with the right foot. The highlighted lower-limb muscles are those that show the most activity during each phase. Your objective for this procedure is to synthesize what you have learned about skeletal muscles into an integrated sequence that occurs while walking.

- When standing erect (Figure 10-19a), antigravity muscles are preventing flexion of the hip and knee joints and dorsiflexion of the ankle joints. (Flexion of these joints would lead to a vertical collapse, as occurs when a standing person faints and antigravity muscles quickly lose muscle tone.) These muscles include hip and knee extensors, and especially the plantar flexors of the ankle, *gastrocnemius* and *soleus*.

- The stride is begun by lifting the lead (right) foot off the ground (Figure 10-19b). This is immediately preceded by planting the weight of the body on the contralateral (opposite) foot, which becomes dorsiflexed by *tibialis anterior*. As the right foot (also dorsiflexed) leaves the ground, the right hip joint is flexed by *iliopsoas*, with an assist from *rectus femoris*. This starts the forward **swing phase** of the thigh.

- At the end of the swing phase, the right foot is planted, with the heel striking the ground first (Figure 10-19c). The *hamstrings*, extensors of the thigh (not shown), contract just before heel contact to oppose thigh flexion and bring the forward swing of the thigh to a halt. The plantar flexors of the ankle oppose dorsiflexion as weight is transmitted to the ground during this upright or **stance phase**. The weight-bearing right knee is extended during this phase by *quadriceps femoris*. This maintains stability of the knee joint as the body's center of gravity is shifted toward the supporting right foot.

- The stance phase is followed by plantar flexing the lead foot so that weight is concentrated on the right toes, especially on the big toe (Figure 10-19d). The right leg then propels the walker. This **push-off phase** is accomplished by our heel-raising gastrocnemius and soleus. *These two muscles supply the bulk of the propulsive force that thrusts the body forward during walking.* As a human pushes off, the contralateral knee is extended to support a transfer of weight to this side as the ankle is simultaneously dorsiflexed.*

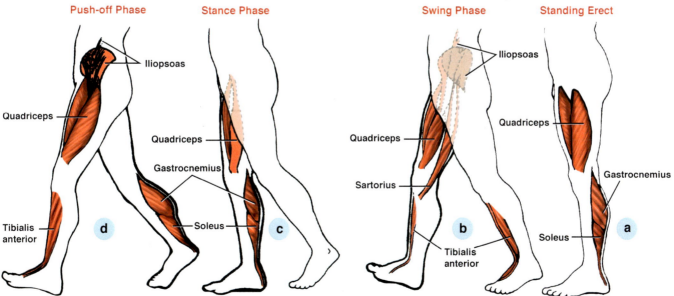

FIGURE 10-19. The principal muscles used in walking. The figure is walking from right to left.

* To prevent an exaggerated tilt of the pelvis during locomotion (which would significantly reduce walking efficiency), the gluteus medius contracts on the same side as the forward-stepping limb.

PROCEDURE 14

A Computer Simulation of Skeletal Muscle Anatomy and Action

Using the **Virtual Labs** software from McGraw-Hill Connect, complete the activities in the *Skeletal Muscle Anatomy and Action* section of the Laboratory Schedule.

Skeletal Muscle Anatomy and Action

NAME _____

LAB TIME/DATE _____

Naming of Skeletal Muscles

Match the criteria for naming skeletal muscles in column B to the muscle names in Column A.

Column A

_____1. rectus abdominis

_____2. temporalis

_____3. biceps brachii

_____4. brachioradialis

_____5. flexor digitorum

_____6. deltoid

_____7. gluteus maximus

Column B

a. shape of the muscle

b. action of the muscle

c. location of the muscle's origin

d. number of "heads" at origins

e. location of the origin and insertion of the muscle

f. direction of muscle fibers within fascicles

g. relative size of the muscle

Coordination of Muscles within Groups

Match the key term letters to the muscles below.

Key   a. prime mover (agonist)   b. antagonist   c. synergist   d. fixator

_____1. gastrocnemius during plantar flexion

_____2. triceps brachii during elbow extension

_____3. tibialis anterior during plantar flexion

_____4. brachioradialis during elbow flexion

_____5. biceps brachii during elbow extension

_____6. wrist extensors while fingers are flexed in a power grip

Biomechanics

1. In general, when a muscle of the extremities crosses a joint, it moves a bone located

    _____ to that joint (Use a directional term here).

2. Muscles located on the anterior arm that cross the elbow joint will

    _____ the _____ .

3. Muscles located on the anterior thigh cross the knee joint and

    _____ the leg.

4. If an anterior thigh muscle crossed the hip joint, its action would be

    _____ of the thigh.

5. From the anatomical position, touching the scapula on the same side of the body
    requires _____ of the
    forearm and _____ of the humerus.

6. An antagonist to the quadriceps group is the _____ .

7. An antagonist to the tibialis anterior is the _____ .

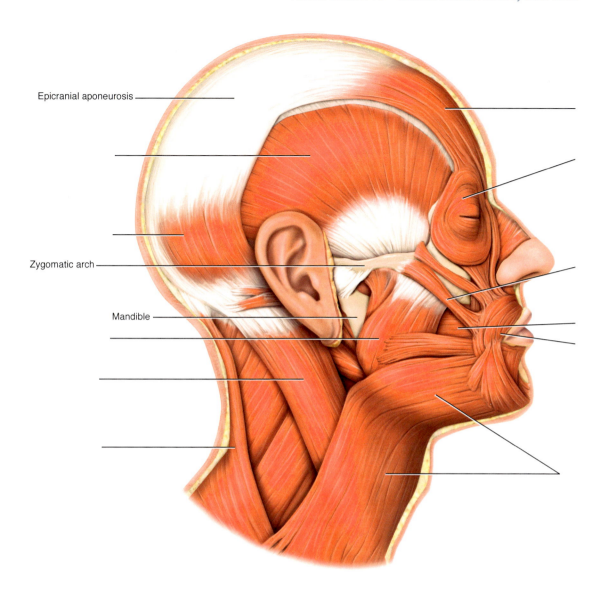

Epicranial aponeurosis ——————————

Zygomatic arch ——————

Mandible ——————

Muscles of the Head and Neck
Place the number of the corresponding key label next to the leader line.

Key

1. platysma

2. zygomaticus major

3. orbicularis oris

4. trapezius

5. occipitofrontalis: occipital belly

6. occipitofrontalis: frontal belly

7. temporalis

8. masseter

9. buccinator

10. orbicularis oculi

11. sternocleidomastoid

Muscles of the Trunk, Shoulder and Arm: Anterior View

Place the number of the corresponding key label next to the leader line.

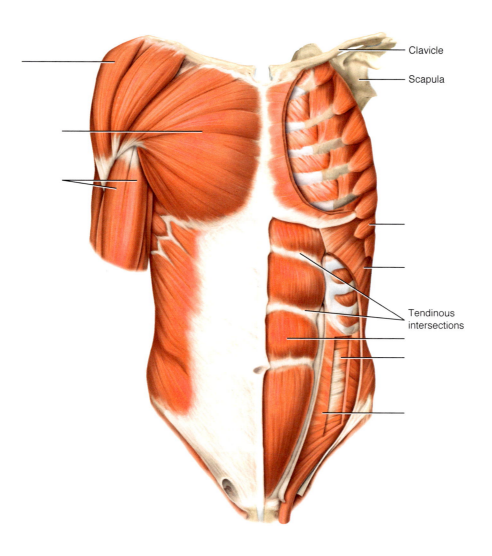

Clavicle

Scapula

Tendinous
intersections

Key

1. rectus abdominis

2. internal oblique

3. transversus abdominis

4. deltoid

5. external oblique

6. biceps brachii

7. pectoralis major

8. serratus anterior

Muscles of the Trunk, Shoulder and Arm: Posterior View

Place the number of the corresponding key label next to the leader line.

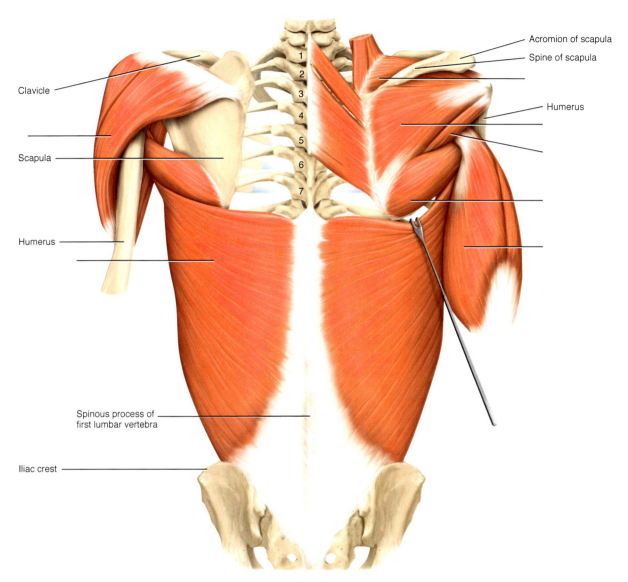

Acromion of scapula

Spine of scapula

Clavicle

Humerus

Scapula

Humerus

Spinous process of
first lumbar vertebra

Iliac crest

Key

1. deltoid

2. teres major

3. infraspinatus

4. supraspinatus

5. latissimus dorsi

6. teres minor

7. triceps brachii

Muscles that Move the Arm and Forearm

Place the number of the corresponding key label next to the leader line.

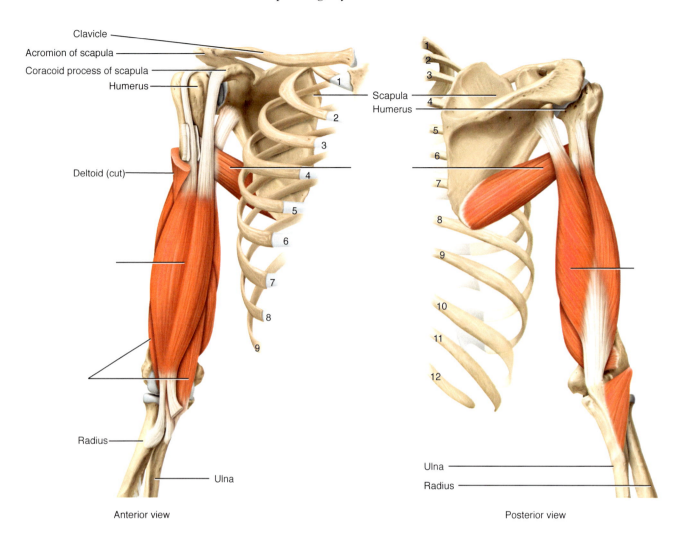

Anterior view

Posterior view

Key

1. biceps brachii

2. triceps brachii

3. brachialis

4. teres major

Muscles That Move the Thigh and Leg: Anterior View
Place the number of the corresponding key label next to the leader line.

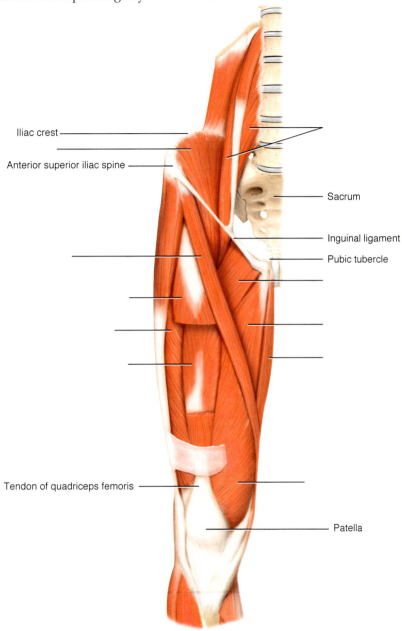

Iliac crest

Anterior superior iliac spine

Sacrum

Inguinal ligament

Pubic tubercle

Tendon of quadriceps femoris

Patella

Key

1. vastus lateralis

2. vastus medialis

3. vastus intermedius

4. rectus femoris

5. gracilis

6. iliacus

7. psoas major

8. sartorius

9. adductor longus

10. pectineus

Muscles That Move the Thigh and Leg: Posterior View

Place the number of the corresponding key label next to the leader line.

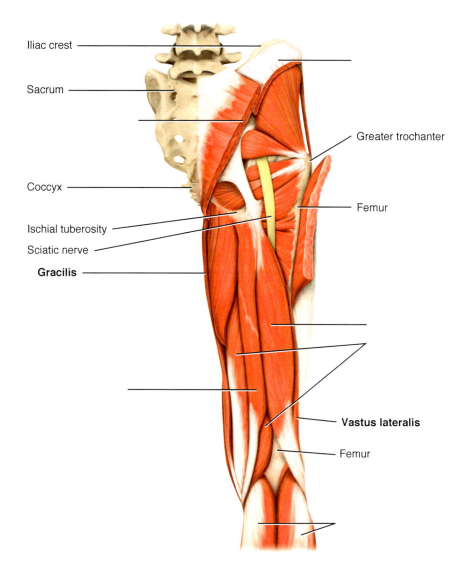

Iliac crest

Sacrum

Greater trochanter

Coccyx

Femur

Ischial tuberosity

Sciatic nerve

Gracilis

Vastus lateralis

Femur

Key

1. biceps femoris

2. semitendinosus

3. semimembranosus

4. gastrocnemius

5. gluteus maximus

6. gluteus medius

Summary of the Superficial Skeletal Muscles

Place the number of the corresponding key label next to the leader line.

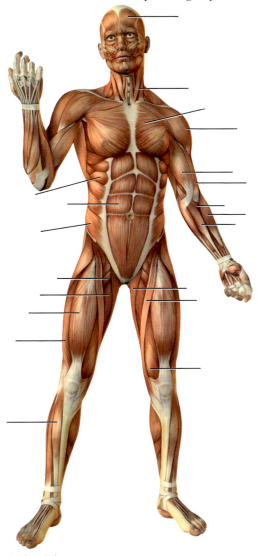 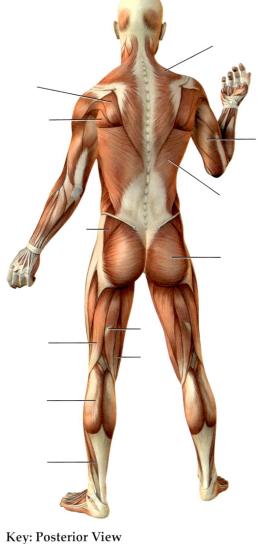

Key: Anterior View

1. vastus lateralis	11. flexor carpi radialis
2. vastus medialis	12. pectineus
3. pronator teres	13. epicranius: frontal belly
4. rectus femoris	14. tibialis anterior
5. gracilis	15. deltoid
6. sternocleidomastoid	16. biceps brachii
7. pectoralis major	17. brachialis
8. sartorius	18. serratus anterior
9. adductor longus	19. rectus abdominis
10. brachioradialis	20. external oblique

Key: Posterior View

1. biceps femoris	7. infraspinatus
2. semitendinosus	8. teres major
3. semimembranosus	9. latissimus dorsi
4. trapezius	10. gastrocnemius
5. gluteus maximus	11. triceps brachii
6. gluteus medius	12. soleus

Surface Anatomy Review: Anterior View
Place the number of the corresponding key label next to the leader line.

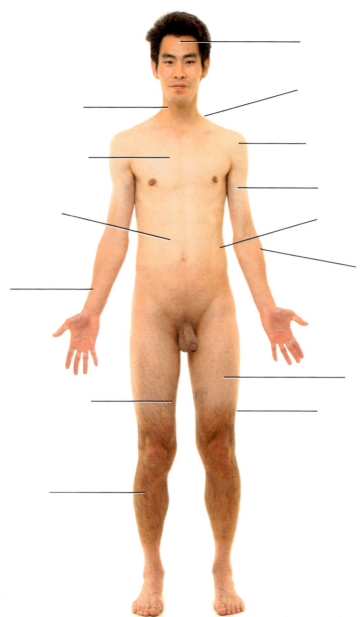

Key

1. trapezius

2. tibialis anterior

3. external oblique

4. rectus abdominis

5. deltoid

6. brachioradialis

7. biceps brachii

8. pectoralis major

9. rectus femoris

10. flexor carpi radialis

11. sternocleidomastoid

12. vastus lateralis

13. vastus medialis

14. occipitofrontalis: frontal belly

Surface Anatomy Review: Posterior View

Place the number of the corresponding key label next to the leader line.

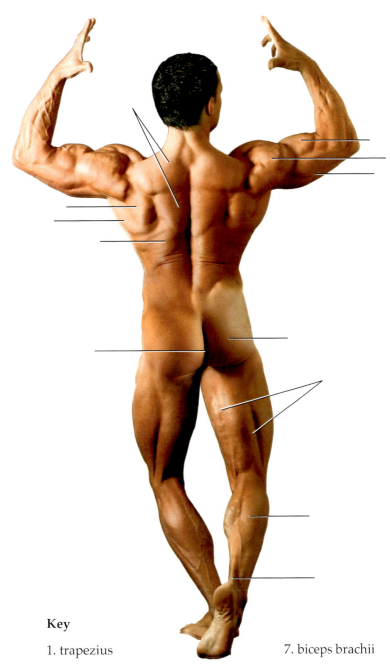

Key

1. trapezius

2. latissimus dorsi

3. infraspinatus

4. teres major

5. deltoid

6. gluteus maximus

7. biceps brachii

8. gastrocnemius

9. hamstrings

10. triceps brachii

11. calcaneal tendon

12. intergluteal cleft

Critical Thinking

1. Which muscles of the lower extremities are important in maintaining an upright posture? (Hint: Think of what these antigravity muscles must do at their respective joints.)

    _____

2. If both sternocleidomastoids were to contract at the same time, what would you predict their action to be? (What would pulling on the insertion — which is embedded in the muscle name — do to the head?)

    _____

3. Walk several feet with either hand straddling the upper buttock region on the same side. While walking, palpate this area such that the thumb is on the iliac crest and the little finger is just lateral to the intergluteal cleft. (See p. 105 to reveal this landmark if you cannot crack the translation of *intergluteal cleft.*) Which gluteal muscle contracts (as your lead foot hits the ground) to keep the hips level? (Note: This action stabilizes the pelvis to minimize sway and thus increase walking efficiency.)

    _____

4. Walk up a flight of stairs. Which gluteal muscle contracts to stabilize the hip joint and simultaneously limit the tendency to flex ("jack-knife") at the waist? Palpation will enlighten once again.

    _____

5. Human locomotion involves pushing off the ground, one foot at a time. Which muscles thrust us forward as we walk?

    _____

6. Note the figure in motion below. Which muscles that play a minor role in walking assume a major role in running?

    _____

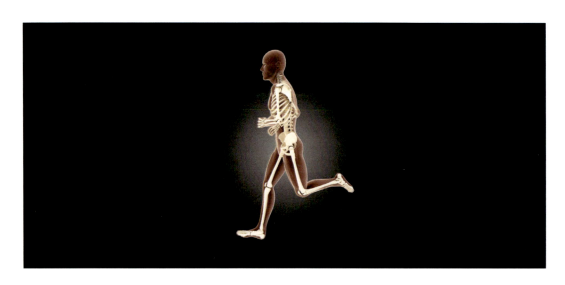

Human Locomotion: A Step-By-Step Analysis

Directions: Fill in the blanks with the names of the appropriate skeletal muscles. Use only those muscles on your required list for this laboratory session. Each blank represents a muscle or muscle group

Starting from the anatomical position, one begins to walk by flexing the thigh of the forward-

stepping limb. The prime movers for this swing phase are the_____

and _____. Simultaneously, the swing leg is flexed at the knee by the

force of gravity, aided somewhat by the _____ group and the strap-like

_____. As the lead foot approaches the ground, the knee joint is extended

by contraction of the _____group. The _____

dorsiflexes the ankle joint just before contact is made. The foot hits the ground heel first, but

momentum immediately shifts the weight to the ball, i.e. toward the distal ends of the metatarsals.

This is the stance phase. To lift the heel of the lead foot, the _____and

_____ muscles contract in the push-off phase, completing the step, thrusting

the body forward, and preparing the limb for its next lift-off.

Notes

Skeletal Muscle Physiology

OBJECTIVES

1. To review the terms depolarization and action potential and define repolarization, resting membrane potential, and refractory period.
2. To define and elicit a muscle twitch and describe its three components or phases.
3. To define and determine the threshold stimulus for eliciting a muscle contraction and define subthreshold stimulus and maximum stimulus.
4. To define recruitment (graded principle) and observe and understand the relationship between strength of stimulus and contractile force of muscle.
5. To define summation and tetanus (tetanic contraction) and observe how stimulus frequency affects muscle contraction.
6. To define and observe muscular fatigue.

MATERIALS

Laptop computer
PhysioEx software
Physiograph
Stimulator

Electrode gel
Exploratory and plate electrodes
Ergograph
Blood pressure cuff

PRE-LAB QUIZ

1. During the latent period, which is not occurring?
   a. diffusion of sodium ions into muscle fibers from the extracellular fluid
   b. depolarization of muscle fibers within a motor unit
   c. release of calcium ions from the sarcoplasmic reticulum
   d. sliding of myofilaments
2. True or False (Correct the statement if false.) A twitch is a series of quick, jerky contractions in response to a single stimulus.
3. About how long does a twitch contraction/relaxation cycle last on average?
   a. 1-2 msec   c. 10-20 msec
   b. 5-10 msec   d. 100-200 msec
4. True or False. (Correct the statement if false.) Depolarization/repolarization, the cycle of electrical events that precedes contraction of a muscle fiber, usually lasts no more than a couple milliseconds.
5. The principle that stronger stimuli delivered to a muscle will excite more motor units and generate more force than weaker stimuli is known as _____.
6. High-frequency stimulation to a skeletal muscle leads to smooth, sustained contractions during which the myograms show no evidence of relaxation. This phenomenon is known as
   a. complete tetanus   c. incomplete summation
   b. incomplete tetanus   d. isotonic contraction
7. Identify a chemical substance that accumulates in muscle tissue during muscular fatigue.

Prelude to a Contraction: The Action Potential

Exercise 9 summarized the events within skeletal muscle that lead to a contraction. We will now review the electrical and mechanical components of muscle physiology and add several key details that will facilitate your understanding of this laboratory exercise.

An unstimulated muscle fiber is *relaxed* in the mechanical sense and *resting* when measured electrically. More specifically, a resting muscle fiber has a distribution of ions such that negatively-charged ions outnumber positively-charged ions inside the cell. Conversely, positively-charged ions are more numerous outside the cell, mainly due to the relatively high concentration of extracellular sodium ions. This uneven distribution of ions creates a difference — called a *gradient* — across the plasma membrane, or sarcolemma.

When this elecrical gradient, or *potential*, is measured using tiny electrodes, it registers as roughly 70 millivolts (mv). It is written as "-70 mv inside" to reflect the greater negativity inside the cell compared to outside. The sarcolemma is said to be *polarized* since the distribution of ions on either side is not uniform.

This **resting membrane potential** is an important principle of muscle physiology because it is a pre-requisite for muscle excitability. That is, a muscle fiber cannot respond to a stimulus unless it re-establishes its resting membrane potential after each excitation–and–contraction cycle.

How a Skeletal Muscle Fiber is Connected to the Nervous System

Before a skeletal muscle can contract, an electrical stimulus must be applied to it. Stimulus strength is measured in volts. The **minimal** or **threshold stimulus** is the least voltage required for contraction. The stimulus is provided by the muscle's **motor nerve**.

Each of the neurons comprising a motor nerve innervates a **motor unit**, a group of muscle fibers whose numbers vary from several to a thousand or more. Each muscle fiber within the motor unit is supplied by an axon terminal that branches from its motor neuron. The axon terminal meets the sarcolemma of the muscle fiber at the **neuromuscular junction**.

All muscle fibers within a motor unit have the same threshold stimulus, a logical concept given their common neuron. *Within an entire muscle, however, different motor units exhibit different stimulus thresholds.* This allows the nervous system to regulate how many motor units need to contract at any given moment to perform a particular task. By increasing the strength of the stimulus, more motor units contract and more force is generated.

Summary of Events That Excite a Skeletal Muscle Fiber

Excitation of a resting muscle fiber occurs when stimulation by a motor neuron causes a change in the polarity of the sarcolemma. Here's a summary of electrical events that precede a muscle contraction.

- *A threshold stimulus reaches the neuromuscular junction (NMJ) of a muscle fiber within a motor unit.*

- *The transmitter acetylcholine is released, crosses the NMJ, and binds to its receptors on the sarcolemma.*

- *Sodium channels within the sarcolemma momentarily open, increasing permeability to sodium ions. This allows them to diffuse down their concentration gradient into the cell, an event called sodium influx. This quick burst of positively charged ions reverses the polarity across the membrane so that the inside of the cell is now positive, a phenomenon known as **depolarization**. The outside of the membrane becomes negative during this polarity shift. The depolarization of the sarcolemma has been likened to a wave of negativity that travels the length of the muscle fiber, beginning at the neuromuscular junction.*

- *To restore the resting membrane potential and enable the cell to respond to successive stimuli, sodium channels close and potassium channels open. Potassium ions are heavily concentrated inside the cell. The diffusion of potassium ions out of the cell at this point — potassium efflux — will "undo" the effect of sodium influx on the membrane potential. This return back to the resting state is called **repolarization**. The cycle of depolarization-repolarization is known as the **action potential**, or **muscle impulse**. The time frame for its propagation along the entire length of the sarcolemma from the stimulation point is 1 to 2 milliseconds.*

- *Before a muscle fiber has completely repolarized, it is unable to respond to a threshold stimulus. In this state, it is said to be **refractory**. The **refractory period** must be of short duration so that a muscle fiber can respond to the high-frequency stimulation normally delivered by the nervous system. Physiologic stimulus frequency (f) is order of magnitude 100 impulses per second. During the short interval between impulses (it would be*

10 msec at f = 100/sec), the depolarization-repolarization cycle must be completed, the resting membrane potential restored, and the refractory period terminated, within a couple milliseconds.
Analogy: The refractory period during which a muscle fiber is unresponsive to stimulation can be likened to flushing a household toilet. Once flushed, the toilet cannot be flushed again until it is no longer refractory.

- *To maintain the normal ionic concentrations on either side of the sarcolemma after sodium influx and potassium efflux, the **sodium-potassium pump** must continually move sodium out of the cell and potassium back in, against their diffusion gradients, by active transport.*

Excitation-Contraction Coupling

The depolarization wave along the sarcolemma rapidly descends into the cell via transverse extensions of the plasma membrane, the transverse tubules. This results in

- release of calcium ions from the sarcoplasmic reticulum (SR).

- binding of calcium ions to a regulatory protein (troponin) to remove inhibition between actin and myosin and enable these contractile proteins to engage one another.

- sliding of actin and myosin past each other such that the muscle fiber contracts (shortens) and muscle force, or *tension*, is generated. Multiplying this force by the number of muscle fibers within motor units simultaneously activated provides a measure of the whole muscle's force of contraction (usually expressed in grams or kilograms).

Linking the excitation of skeletal muscle fibers to their contraction is known as **excitation-contraction coupling**.

After the action potential, calcium ions are returned to the SR, inhibition between actin and myosin is restored, and muscle fibers re-enter their relaxation phase.

The Twitch

The basic subunit of a contraction in skeletal muscle is the **twitch**. It is recorded as a **myogram**, a mechanical record of a whole muscle's contraction-relaxation cycle. An isolated twitch does not constitute a muscle contraction in a practical sense. Picking up a pencil does not result from an individual twitch or two. Rather, as you will observe experimentally, a series of integrated twitches forms the basis of normal skeletal muscle contractions.

A twitch is defined as a quick, jerky contraction of skeletal muscle in response to a single stimulus. There are three stages to a twitch (Figure 11-1).

- The **latent period** is the time lag between stim-ulation of the muscle and its response. It is the prelude to contraction, representing the time necessary for a stimulus to depolarize muscle fibers within activated motor units. This time frame — fewer than 5 msec — corresponds to the excitation period (electrical events) prior to contraction (a mechanical event). Since the myogram is a written record of mechanical events, the latent period can be measured but cannot be seen.

- During the **contraction period**, muscle force increases. This is represented on a myogram by an upward sweeping line that extends from the baseline — a horizontal line representing zero force — to a peak representing maximum force developed.

- During the **relaxation period**, muscle force decreases. This is represented on a myogram by a downward curve back to the baseline.

PROCEDURE 1

Demonstrating a Twitch in a Human Subject
A stimulator can be used to deliver electrical impulses to forearm muscles to observe twitch contractions. *Stimulus strength*, also known as *stimulus intensity*, can be controlled by adjusting the VOLTS knob on the control panel.

Apply a thin layer of electrode gel to the back of the hand and to the anterior forearm from just distal to the

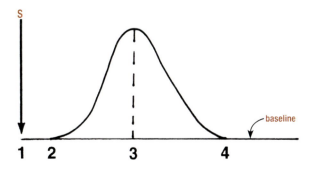

FIGURE 11-1. A twitch myogram. Key 1: time of stimulation (S); 1-2: latent period; 2-3: contraction period; 3-4: relaxation period. A contraction-relaxation cycle lasts 100-200 msec on average. For "fast-twitch" muscles, the cycle may be of 40-50 msec or less.

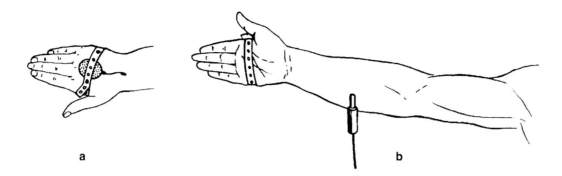

FIGURE 11-2. Stimulation of the human forearm to elicit muscle contractions. (a) Placement of the plate electrode on the hand with an elastic band; (b) positioning an exploratory electrode to locate a motor point on the forearm.

elbow joint to about halfway to the wrist. Connect the two electrodes to the stimulator. Attach the plate electrode as shown in Figure 11-2a. With an exploratory electrode pressed with moderate pressure to the skin (Figure 11-2b), stimuli can be applied singly — one stimulus at a time using a manually operated flip switch — or delivered continuously by the stimulator itself. In continuous mode, the frequency of stimulation can be varied, from one to 100 times a second.

1. With the impulse DURATION set at 1 millisecond (msec), and the impulse FREQUENCY knob set to 1 per second, set the stimulator to continuous mode (CONT knob) and the voltage to a subthreshold stimulus level, generally between 20 and 40 volts.

2. Probe the anterior aspect of the proximal half of the forearm (Figure 11-3) and raise the voltage in 5-volt increments until you get a response: flexion of one of the fingers. Mark the spot with the electrode tip by creating a shallow groove within the gel on both sides of this **motor point,** the region of greatest sensitivity to stimulation.*

What is the threshold stimulus?

_____ volts

Set the voltage knob 20 volts above threshold. With the stimulator in SINGLE mode, manually apply four or five single stimuli a few seconds apart with the toggle switch. Note the jerky contractions that are isolated twitches. These contractions are far from normal in appearance. (As we will see in a later experiment, twitches must fuse together to create a smooth contraction, a response that depends on high-frequency stimulation.)

* The motor point is the area where a motor nerve enters its corresponding muscle.

Muscle Recruitment

Individual muscle cells within a motor unit obey the **all-or-nothing law**. When a threshold stimulus is applied to a muscle cell, it contracts to the fullest extent. When stimuli above the threshold level are applied to *individual muscle cells*, the contraction elicited by a greater-than-threshold stimulus is no more forceful than that from a stimulus of minimal strength.

As the voltage applied to a *whole muscle* is increased, however, more individual muscle fibers reach their threshold and contract, and the total force generated is increased. This progressive increase in force due to activation of more motor units is known as **muscle recruitment**, or the **graded principle of contraction**.

The force of contraction of a twitch also depends on other physical variables, including the duration and frequency of stimulation. Certain physiologic changes, such as fatigue, can also modify the response of a muscle to electrical stimulation.

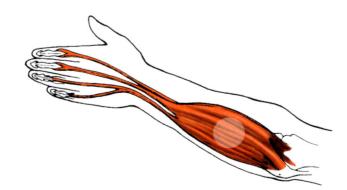

FIGURE 11-3. Location of the flexor digitorum superficialis in the forearm's anterior compartment. The motor point will be found within or near the circled area

PROCEDURE 2

Demonstrating Muscle Recruitment in a Human Subject

1. With the impulse duration set at 1 msec and the impulse frequency set to 1 per second, set the stimulator voltage to a suprathreshold (above-the-threshold) stimulus, 40 volts, in continuous mode.

2. Apply the electrode to the skin. To demonstrate muscle recruitment, increase stimulus strength in 5 volt increments. Head toward 70 volts, but terminate the experiment if the subject begins to experience even mild discomfort.

3. Note the visibly increased force of contraction as more motor units reach their threshold at progressively higher stimulus strength. This is recruitment in action.

Wave Summation and Tetanus

If a second stimulus is applied to a muscle before it has completed its contraction-relaxation cycle, a second more powerful contraction will occur. This fusion of twitches is known as **summation of twitches** or **wave summation**.

Motor neurons normally deliver a continuous volley of stimuli at summation-level frequencies to a skeletal muscle. When the muscle is stimulated so often that the *contraction period is interrupted*, the muscle is in **complete tetanic contraction,** or **complete tetanus,** and the top of the myogram appears as a straight line (Figure 11-4, far right). Tetanic contractions are essentially sustained summation and are the norm. They are smooth in appearance, not jerky. In the laboratory, continuous stimulation at *relaxation-interrupting frequencies* results in **incomplete tetanus** (Figure 11-4, middle). This phase of the experiment is for demonstration purposes and does not represent normal muscle physiology.

PROCEDURE 3

Demonstrating Wave Summation and Tetanus in a Human Subject

1. With the duration set at 1 msec, the frequency set to 2 per second, and the stimulator in continuous mode, set the stimulator voltage to 40 volts.

2. Place the exploratory electrode at the motor point. Gradually increase the stimulus frequency in 2 per second increments, until incomplete tetanic contraction occurs.

What is the frequency of stimulation at the first sign of summation (incomplete tetanus)?

frequency = _____ impulses / sec

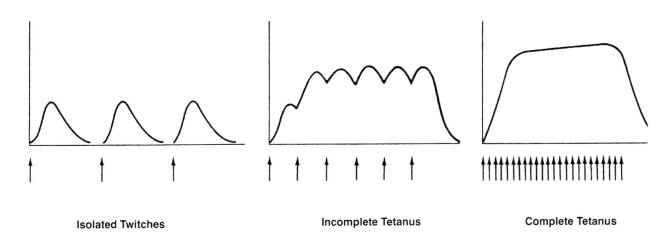

Isolated Twitches   Incomplete Tetanus   Complete Tetanus

FIGURE 11-4. Myograms of isolated twitches, incomplete tetanus, and complete tetanus. Arrows represent stimulus frequency.

What is the interval between stimuli when incomplete (relaxation-interrupting) tetanus is reached? _____ msec

Continue to increase the stimulus frequency in 2 per second increments, until complete tetanic contraction occurs.

What is the frequency of stimulation when complete tetanic contraction is reached?

frequency = _____ impulses/sec

What is the interval between stimuli when complete tetanic contraction is reached? _____ msec

How does the contraction-interrupting interval of complete tetanus compare with the time it takes to complete an isolated twitch?

complete tetanus interval = _____ msec

isolated twitch interval = _____ msec

From the complete tetanus data above, about how long is the contraction period of the subject's forearm muscle? (For the contraction period to be interrupted, its duration must be just greater than the complete tetanus interval.)

contraction period = > _____ msec

PROCEDURE 4

Muscular Fatigue

Fatigue in a working muscle is characterized by an accumulation of lactic acid while glucose, glycogen, and ATP concentrations are decreasing. In this condition, contractions become progressively weaker.

Demonstrating Muscular Fatigue

An ergometer (Figure 11-5) will be used to demonstrate the fatigue of muscles which move the index finger. Each student will:

1. Grasp the ergometer trigger with the index finger.

2. Record time zero.

3. Pull the trigger back at the rate of once per second. Use a stopwatch to keep the subject on pace.

4. Record the time at which the finger falters. As soon as the once-per-second pace slackens and cannot be resumed, calculate the interval from time zero to this end point as the **fatigue time**.

5. After 1 minute of rest, attach an inflatable cuff around the arm of the same finger, an inch or two above the elbow.

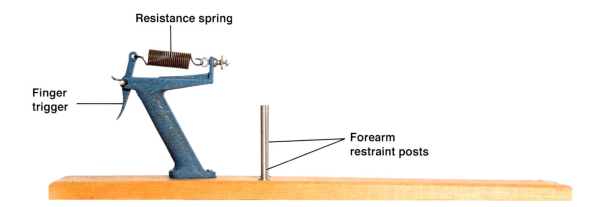

FIGURE 11-5. An ergometer for determining fatigue time.

6. Find the radial pulse (about a finger width proximal to the styloid process of the radius). Inflate the cuff to the point where the pulse can no longer be palpated. This signals that the circulation to the flexor digitorum muscles is temporarily blocked. At this time, stop inflating and start exercising. Once again, note the time interval from onset of finger flexion to fatigue.

Fatigue time, without cuff = _____ sec
Fatigue time, with cuff = _____ sec

The experimental data show a difference in fatigue time when blood flow to and from a working muscle is interrupted.

1. What accumulates faster in a muscle when the veins that drain it are blocked?

_____

_____

2. What energy-supplying nutrient commonly conveyed by the bloodstream cannot reach a muscle whose blood supply is cut off?

_____

3. What happens to fatigue time when blood flow is interrupted?

_____

4. Which molecule is most responsible for the observed change in fatigue time?

_____

PROCEDURE 5

A Computer Simulation of Skeletal Muscle Physiology

Using the **Virtual Labs** software from McGraw-Hill Connect, complete the activities in the *Skeletal Muscle Physiology* section of the Laboratory Schedule.

Clinical Application
Marathoners and Sprinters: Born or Made?

Marathoners and sprinters appear to have a genetic predisposition that supports their racing specialties.

Biopsies of their skeletal muscle reveal that accomplished marathoners have a higher percentage of motor units with *slow-oxidative* (SO) *fibers.* These fibers contract relatively slowly and are able to sustain mild to moderately strenuous physical activity for long periods without fatigue. An in-depth look at the inside of these muscle cells shows many mitochondria that provide ATP via oxidative pathways, hence the name of these fibers.

By contrast, sprinters' skeletal muscles lean toward *fast-glycolytic* (FG) *fibers.* These muscles are known for their quick bursts of speed and the ability to generate powerful contractions, both of which are necessary for sprints.

Can athletes train their genetically-endowed skeletal muscles to achieve greater feats of endurance as marathoners or speed as sprinters? The answer is a resounding yes. Aerobic capacity can be enhanced in marathoners through training as evidenced by a positive change in enzyme systems that support endurance activities.

In sprinters, anaerobic enzyme systems can likewise be optimized. In competitive weightlifters, where great strength over short periods of time underlies the sport, the fiber profile also tilts toward FG. Strength training enlarges these muscle fibers, which can be 50% larger than those of marathoners.

Notes

Skeletal Muscle Physiology

NAME _____

LAB TIME/DATE _____

Excitation and Contraction of Skeletal Muscle

Matching

Match the term in column B with its description in column A.

Column A

Column B

_____1. Stimulus that produces no
perceptible contraction.

a. wave summation

_____2. Increasingly stronger contractions
as a function of stimulus frequency.

b. threshold

_____3. Increasingly stronger contractions as
a function of stimulus strength.

c. subthreshold

_____4. Stimulus at which muscle first gives
evidence of contraction.

d. complete tetanus

_____5. Sustained contraction with no
indication of a relaxation period.

e. recruitment

1. How does increasing the strength of a stimulus cause a whole muscle to respond in a graded
fashion?

_____

_____

_____

2. Of what frequency are the contractions of normal body movements?
(Answer in contractions per second.)

_____

_____

Critical Thinking

1. Explain how increasing the stimulus frequency can increase the force generated within a single muscle fiber.

    _____

    _____

    _____

    _____

2. Are marathoners born or made? Explain the role of genetics and training with specific reference to skeletal muscle fiber types.

    _____

    _____

    _____

    _____

    _____

    _____

Notes

Notes

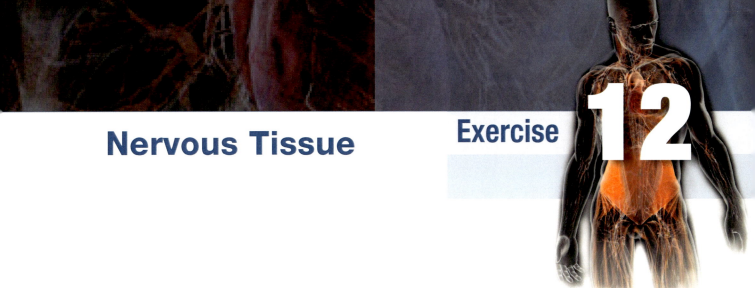

Nervous Tissue

Exercise **12**

OBJECTIVES

1. Identify the basic structures of a neuron and explain their function.
2. List the types of neuroglia and their functions.
3. Define synapse and explain the physiology of impulse transmission — or inhibition — at a synapse.
4. Discuss the function of the myelin sheath and explain the role of *Schwann cells* (*neurilemmocytes*) in myelin formation.
5. Define *nerve, tract, ganglion,* and *nucleus.*
6. Identify the *epineurium, perineurium*, and *endoneurium* as they relate to the anatomy of a nerve.

MATERIALS

Neuron model
Synapse model
Microscope

Prepared slides of spinal cord smear, nerve (c.s. and l.s.), teased myelinated nerve fibers, and cerebral pyramidal cells

PRE-LAB QUIZ

1. The functional unit of nervous tissue is the _____.
2. The CNS myelin-making cell is a neuron/glial cell. (Circle one.)
3. Highly branched regions of nerve cells whose surface area serves to receive input from other nerve cells are the _____.
4. Which term is *not* associated with the axon of a nerve cell?
   a. nerve fiber
   b. terminal
   c. myelin
   d. neurofibral node (of Ranvier)
   e. receptive region
5. Neuron-to-neuron communication zones at which a neurotransmitter determines whether a nerve impulse is generated is called a _____.
6. The connective tissue that envelops an entire nerve is the _____neurium.

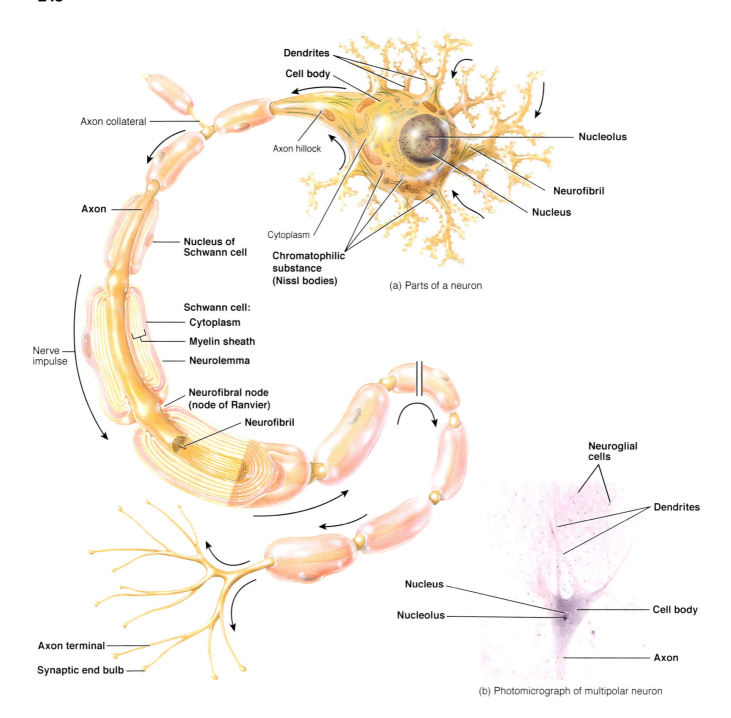

(a) Parts of a neuron

(b) Photomicrograph of multipolar neuron

FIGURE 12-1. Structure of a multipolar neuron.

The nervous system integrates our trillions of cells into a unified, functionally harmonious human. This formidable coordination task is carried out by two divisions: The **central nervous system (CNS)** and the **peripheral nervous system (PNS)**. The CNS is comprised of the brain and spinal cord. The PNS encompasses cranial and spinal nerves and includes **sensory receptors**, neurons that respond to stimuli, and **motor neurons** that link the CNS to **effectors**, our muscles and glands.

How we perceive the external world (and those who inhabit it), thoughts and actions that enrich our environment (or protect us from it), and *homeostasis* — maintaining the constancy of our internal environment — are products of *communication and control* by nervous tissues.

The functional unit of the nervous system is the **neuron**. Neurons are excitable cells that conduct impulses.

The Neuron

Neurons are highly specialized for conducting nerve impulses. While there are three anatomical variations, all share many features in common (Figure 12-1).

Examining Basic Neuron Structure

1. Using the neuron model, prepared slide of the multipolar neuron smear, and Figure 12-1, identify the:

- **cell body** or **soma**, the central part of a neuron that includes the nucleus and its nucleolus, and is surrounded by cytoplasm that contains organelles common to most cells. Neuron cell bodies make up the gray matter of the CNS and form clusters called **nuclei.** In the PNS, a cluster of cell bodies is termed a **ganglion**.

  The cell body serves two purposes: It is a center of anabolic metabolism and also a receptive region that interacts with other neurons. Its cytoplasm includes:

- **chromatophilic substance (Nissl bodies)**, rough endoplasmic reticulum that includes ribosomes that complement free ribosomes in the cytoplasm. The ribosomes synthesize proteins that support neuronal growth and allow regeneration in damaged peripheral neurons.

- **neurofibrils** (noo"-roe-FYE-bruls), cytoskeletal elements that provide structural support and aid in the transport of substances within the neuron.

- **dendrites** (DEN-drytes), the usually highly branched cytoplasmic processes that radiate from the cell body (*dendron* = tree, whose branches neuronal dendrites resemble). Dendrites are receiving processes whose plasma membranes, like those of the cell body, have receptors for neurotransmitters from adjacent neurons. Dendrites are thus *input* or *receptive regions. The large number of dendritic branches magnifies the receptive surface area and enhances cell-to-cell communication.*

- **axon**, also called a **nerve fiber**, the usually long and singular cytoplasmic process that conducts a **nerve impulse** from the cell body — beginning at the *trigger zone* (axon hillock) — to its branched terminals. The **axon terminals**, or **telodendria** (teel"-uh-DEN-dree-uh), release neurotransmitters from their expanded **synaptic end bulbs**. These neurotransmitters exert their influence where axon terminals form a synapse with another cell.

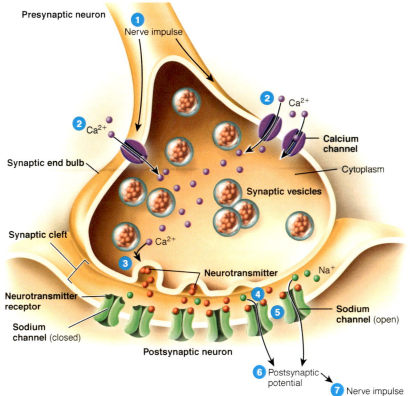

FIGURE 12-2. Synapse anatomy and physiology.

Summary of Synapse Physiology

1. A nerve impulse reaches the axon terminal of a presynaptic neuron.

2. Depolarization of the end bulb membrane opens calcium channels. Calcium ions diffuse inward.

3. The increase in intracellular calcium triggers exocytosis of the synaptic vesicles, releasing neurotransmitter molecules (●) into the synaptic cleft.

4. Neurotransmitter molecules diffuse across the synaptic cleft and bind to their receptors on the postsynaptic membrane.

5. Neurotransmitter molecules bind to their receptors opens ligand-gated ion channels.

6. When opening a sodium channel is opened (as shown), the influx of sodium ions (●) causes an excitatory postsynaptic potential that tends to depolarize the postsynaptic cell. (Depending on the neurotransmitter, other ion channels may open. Some channels will admit K^+ or Cl^-, both of which tend to inhibit or, hyperpolarize, the postsynaptic cell.)

7. If the nerve impulse in the presynaptic cell is of sufficient strength, a nerve impulse will be initiated in the postsynaptic cell.

A **synapse** (Figure 12-2) is a region where there is communication between two neurons or between a neuron and an effector cell. Effectors (muscles and glands) are so named because they respond to neurons by "effecting" an adaptive change. These responses are contractions by muscle cells and secretions from glandular cells.

Once a neurotransmitter is released from the axon terminal of a **presynaptic neuron**, it diffuses across a very narrow (0.02 μm) gap called the **synaptic cleft.** After a short synaptic delay (~1 msec), the neurotransmitter reaches the plasma membrane of another neuron or effector cell and binds to a specific membrane receptor. When a neuron is on the receiving end of a neurotransmitter, it is termed a **postsynaptic neuron.** The post-synaptic neuron may be *excited* (fire an impulse) or *inhibited* (remain in the resting state). The synapse between a neuron and skeletal muscle cells is called a **neuromuscular junction** (See Exercise 9).

Myelination

The axons of most neurons are enveloped in a whitish, fatty sheath known as **myelin**. These myelinated axons comprise the white matter of the central and peripheral nervous systems. The **myelin sheath** (Figure 12-3) is produced by glial cells: **oligodendrocytes** in the CNS and **Schwann cells (neurolemmocytes)** in the PNS. Myelin (1) insulates neurons, protecting them from cross stimulation, and (2) increases the speed of impulse transmission. On the model of a myelinated peripheral neuron, and referring to Figure 12-3, locate the:

- **neurolemma**, the plasma membrane of the Schwann cell. Many Schwann cells in series produce a myelin sheath. This process begins as Schwann cells envelop an axon, then rotate around it repeatedly like a jelly roll. Cytoplasm is squeezed to the periphery as the plasma membrane is wound tightly around the axon. *The neurolemma also makes possible the regeneration of injured peripheral neurons.*

- **neurofibral node (node of Ranvier)**, a gap in the myelin sheath between adjacent Schwann cells that enables the surrounding tissue fluid to interact with cytoplasm in the axon (axoplasm).

2. Obtain a slide of myelinated nerve fibers. Figure 12-4 shows these axons as they appear in a longitudinal section through a nerve.

In the space provided below, sketch a single myelinated nerve fiber. Label the axon (nerve fiber), myelin sheath, and neurofibral node.

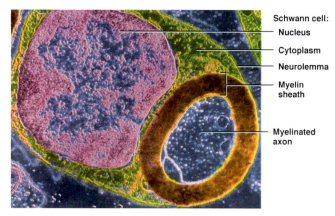

FIGURE 12-3. Transverse section of a myelinated axon.

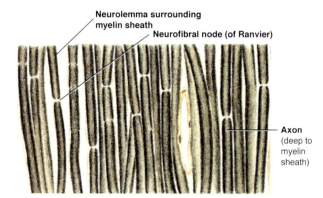

FIGURE 12-4. Photomicrograph-derived illustration of myelinated nerve fibers (axons) in longitudinal section. The nerve fibers have been separated slightly for greater visibility.

What is the significance of the gaps (neurofibral nodes) in the myelin sheath?

_____

_____

_____

Sketch of a Myelinated Nerve Fiber

Examining a Neuron from the Cerebral Cortex: A Pyramidal Cell

Obtain a prepared slide of the cerebral cortex of a human brain. Note the **pyramidal cells** (Figure 12-5), whose cell bodies are shaped like pyramids (triangles under the light microscope). In the cortex's frontal region, these neurons initiate all voluntary movement. Sketch a pyramidal cell on the next page and label the cell body, axon, and at least two dendrites.

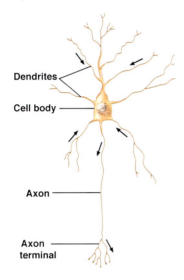

Pyramidal cell

FIGURE 12-5. A pyramidal cell from the cerebral cortex. Arrows indicate direction of impulse conduction.

The Classification of Neurons

Neurons are classified structurally and named depending on the number of processes emanating from the cell body (Figure 12-6). Note that nerve impulses are conducted from dendrites to axon.

Classification of Neurons by Structure

- **Multipolar neurons** (Figure 12-6a) have an axon and multiple highly branched dendrites extending from the cell body. Multipolar neurons are the most common neuron type and include all motor neurons (described shortly).

- **Bipolar neurons** (Figure 12-6b) have one axon and one dendrite. This is the least common neuron type. One location of bipolar neurons is the retina of the eye.

- **Unipolar neurons** (Figure 12-6c) are named for the single process that emerges from the cell body. A short distance from the cell body, this process branches like a **T**. Unipolar neurons begin as bipolar neurons in the embryo. During development, the two neuronal processes fuse into one. For this reason, they are also termed **pseudounipolar neurons**. Naming the processes of unipolar neurons is unconventional. The short, branched receptive endings are appropriately called dendrites. The axon begins at the convergence point of the dendrites. The portion of the axon from the dendrites to the cell body is the *peripheral process*. From the cell body to the axon terminals is the axon's *central process*, so named because it enters the CNS.

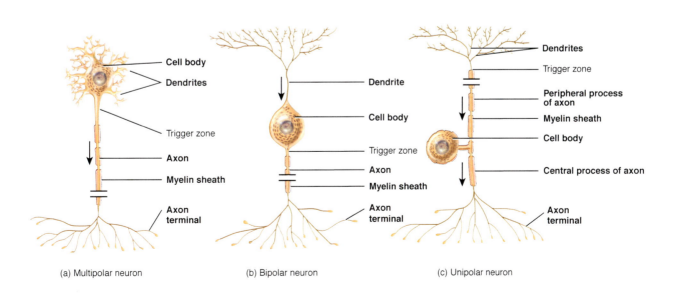

(a) Multipolar neuron   (b) Bipolar neuron   (c) Unipolar neuron

FIGURE 12-6. Structural classification of neurons. Arrows indicate direction of impulse conduction. (Breaks indicate that axons are longer than shown relative other to parts of the neuron.)

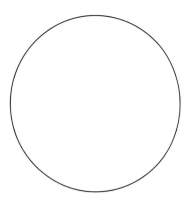

Sketch of Pyramidal Cell

Classification of Neurons by Function

Neurons are classified functionally as follows (See Figure 12-7.):

- Neurons that carry impulses from sensory receptors in the PNS, such as those in the skin and viscera (internal organs), are **sensory** or **afferent neurons**. These neurons are typically unipolar and their cell bodies are always clustered within a ganglion.

- Neurons that begin in the CNS and terminate in muscles or glands are called **motor** or **efferent neurons**. These are multipolar.

- **Interneurons**, or **association neurons**, comprise a third functional category. These nerve cells are located between sensory and motor neurons as an intermediate link in a neuronal circuit. They are multipolar and are always found within the CNS.

Neuroglia

Neuroglia, or **glial cells**, are the other cell type within nervous tissue. They are found in both the PNS and CNS and are nonexcitable; thus, they cannot transmit nerve impulses. Rather, neuroglia are the "supporting cast" that protect, insulate, and nourish the neuron population. Glial cells outnumber neurons by a wide margin, an anatomical fact hinted at in Figure 12-1(b) on page 248. In this smear of spinal cord multipolar neurons, note the number of glial cells (as indicated by their easily observed nuclei) in relation to the lone neuron in the field.

A PNS glial cell, the neurolemmocyte, or Schwann cell, is shown in Figure 12-3 (page 250) after it has directed the formation of a myelin sheath.

The Structure of a Nerve

A **nerve** (Figure 12-8) is a bundle of axons in the PNS arranged in similar fashion to a cable. In the CNS, axons are bundled as tracts (discussed shortly) and constitute white matter. Nerves are grossly visible, and like a skeletal muscle, are held together by connective tissue wrappings that encircle the neurons within on three levels:

- The **epineurium** (ep-ih-NOO-ree-um) is a tough dense connective tissue layer that envelops the entire nerve, providing protection and support.

- The **perineurium** (per-ih-NOO-ree-um) is a somewhat thinner layer of dense connective tissue that wraps around bundles of neurons termed **fascicles**. Blood vessels run through the perineurium and are supported by it.

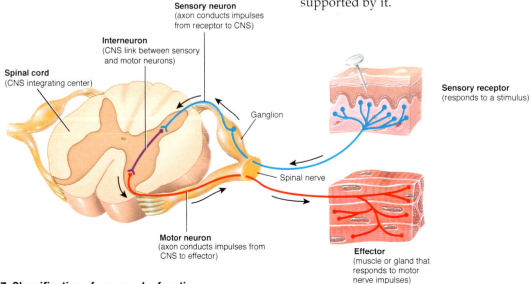

Sensory neuron
(axon conducts impulses from receptor to CNS)

Interneuron
(CNS link between sensory and motor neurons)

Spinal cord
(CNS integrating center)

Ganglion

Sensory receptor
(responds to a stimulus)

Spinal nerve

Motor neuron
(axon conducts impulses from CNS to effector)

Effector
(muscle or gland that responds to motor nerve impulses)

FIGURE 12-7. Classification of neurons by function.

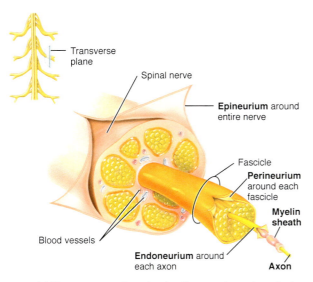

(a) Transverse section showing the coverings of a spinal nerve

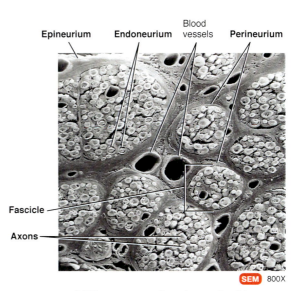

(b) Transverse section of nerve fascicles within a nerve.

FIGURE 12-8. Organization and connective tissue wrappings of a spinal nerve.

- The **endoneurium** (en-doe-NOO-ree-um) is a very thin connective tissue layer that surrounds individual neurons. In myelinated axons, the endoneurium is external to both the myelin and the neurilemma. Capillaries that service each axon are contained in this layer.

Analogies: (1) A nerve is to a neuron as a cable is to a single wire. (2) Endoneurium and myelin are to axons what electrical insulation is to bare wires.

PROCEDURE 3

Examining the Microscopic Structure of a Nerve

Obtain a prepared slide of a nerve that is sectioned in the transverse and longitudinal planes. In the transverse or cross section (c.s.) in Figure 12-9, locate the axon, myelin sheath, perineurium, endoneurium, and if possible, the epineurium.

Sketch a portion of the nerve c.s. in the space below.

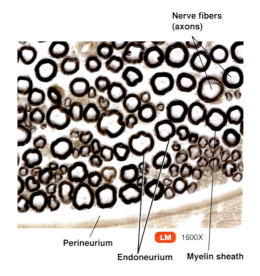

FIGURE 12-9. Nerve fascicle in transverse section under the light microscope.

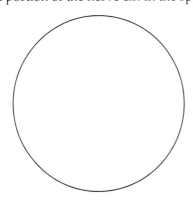

Sketch of Nerve in Transverse Section

Clinical Application
Multiple Sclerosis

Multiple sclerosis (MS) is an autoimmune disease that leads to destruction of myelin sheaths in CNS neurons. *Multiple* refers to the many brain and spinal cord regions affected by the disease. *Sclerosis* translates as "the condition of hardening", and refers to hardened tissue — scar-like *plaque* — that replaces the normal myelin sheath surrounding nerve fibers. The degenerative process leaves portions of the axon without myelin, a condition known as *demyelination*. The loss of myelin initially slows nerve impulse conduction velocity, then completely short-circuits impulse transmission in affected neurons.

Early symptoms of MS include premature fatigue, weakness of limb muscles or a feeling of heaviness, numbness or tingling sensations, and unfocused or double vision (diplopia). Onset of MS is usually between ages 20 and 50 and affects females twice as often as males. There are an estimated 350,000 cases in the U.S. and over 2 million worldwide.

The cause of MS has not been conclusively determined, but there is clear evidence of heritability (genetic susceptibility). Brothers and sisters of MS patients have a "sibling recurrence risk" that makes them over seven times more likely to contract the disease compared to the general population. Researchers have implicated environmental variables as well.

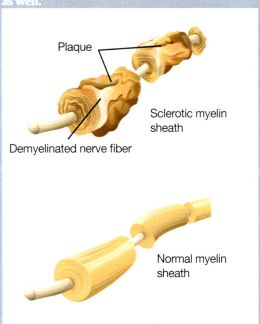

Plaque

Sclerotic myelin sheath

Demyelinated nerve fiber

Normal myelin sheath

Nervous Tissue

NAME _____

LAB TIME/DATE _____

Neuron Structure and Function

Matching
Match the term in Column B with its description in Column A. (A blank may contain more than one possible answer.)

Column A

_____1. functional term meaning "toward" the CNS

_____2. cells that support neurons

_____3. cluster of nerve cell bodies outside the CNS

_____4. functional classification of unipolar neuron

_____5. cluster of nerve cell bodies within the CNS

_____6. functional term meaning "away from" the CNS

_____7. junction between neurons

_____8. cell that facilitates transmission between sensory and motor neurons

_____9. PNS myelin maker

_____10. gap in myelin sheath

_____11. Schwann cell synonym

_____12. functional classification of multipolar neuron

Column B

a. ganglion

b. synapse

c. efferent

d. afferent

e. interneuron

f. sensory

g. motor

h. nucleus

i. neurolemmocyte

j. neurofibral node (of Ranvier)

k. Schwann cell

l. neuroglia

Label the neuron below using the following key terms:

Key

1. dendrite
2. cell body
3. axon
4. myelin sheath
5. neurofibral node

6. axon terminal
7. synaptic end bulb
8. nucleus
9. nucleolus
10. chromatophilic substance

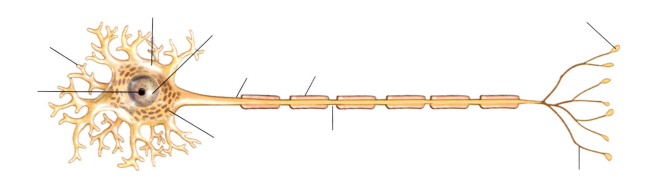

1. What capability does a neuron have that distinguishes it as the functional cell of the nervous system?

   _____

   _____

   _____

2. To what structural classification does the pyramidal cell belong?

   _____

   _____

3. A spinal nerve belongs to the_____ division of the nervous system.

4. What feature of a postsynaptic neuron's plasma membrane binds specifically with neurotransmitter molecules to influence the behavior of an ion channel?

_____

5. When ion channels open in response to a neurotransmitter, what are the two possible outcomes for the postsynaptic neuron?

_____

_____

_____

6. What structural feature of a neuron determines whether it is unipolar, bipolar, or multipolar?

_____

_____

Nerve Structure

Add a label or its number to each leader in the diagram below.

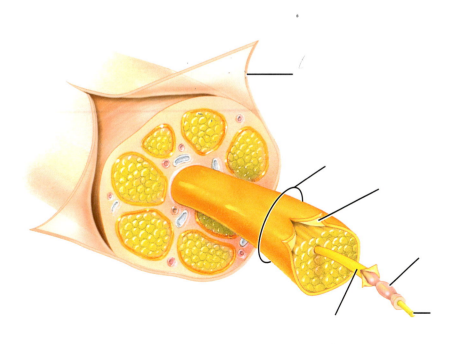

Key

1. endoneurium

2. fascicle

3. myelin sheath

4. epineurium

5. perineurium

6. axon

Notes

Anatomy and Physiology of the Spinal Cord

Exercise 13

OBJECTIVES

1. To observe the gross anatomical features of the spinal cord.
2. To observe the macroscopic and microscopic features of spinal cord cross sections.
3. To name the meninges that cover the spinal cord and describe their functions.
4. To cite two major functions of the spinal cord.
5. To describe the regional divisions of the paired spinal nerves.
6. To identify the components of sensory and motor spinal neurons.
7. To identify the components of a spinal reflex.
8. To evoke stretch reflexes in human subjects.
9. To locate the ascending and descending tracts of the spinal cord and describe their functions.
10. To define: *conus medullaris, cauda equina, dorsal (posterior) root, ventral (anterior) root, mixed nerve and reflex*.

MATERIALS

Spinal cord models
Nervous system chart
Preserved human spinal cord
   section

Prepared slide of spinal cord (c.s.)
Reflex hammers
Compound and dissecting microscopes

PRE-LAB QUIZ

1. What within the spinal cord — and in the central nervous system as a whole — links an incoming sensory impulse with an outgoing motor impulse?
   a. motor neuron
   b. receptor
   c. sensory neuron
   d. integrating center
   e. effector

2. Which term does not apply to a receptor in a spinal reflex?
   a. sensory
   b. peripheral
   c. afferent
   d. incoming
   e. efferent

3. True or False (Correct the statement if false.) Spinal reflexes are predictable and most are involuntary.

4. What region of the spinal cord contains motor neurons that direct the movement of skeletal muscles?
   a. ventral horn
   b. dorsal horn
   c. lateral horn
   d. dorsal column

5. A complex network of spinal nerves from which emerge nerves that innervate skin and skeletal muscles is called a _____.

One of the fundamental challenges in physiology is how to organize and unify millions upon millions of body cells into a functional being. The process of unifying body cells is known as **integration** and has two key requirements: *communication* and *control*.

Communication

Control

Integration

The nervous system is specialized for communication among tissues, using nerve impulses as its message code. Communication makes possible the precise control of cells, tissues, and organs. Control — regulating a function within specific limits — permits integration of all the body's functions and plays a vital role in homeostasis. The spinal cord and the brain comprise the **central nervous system**. The spinal cord is an extension of a region known as the brain stem. It serves two major functions: (1) It is a vital link between the brain and the peripheral nervous system, communicating via sensory and motor pathways with the brain's higher centers. (2) It is a reflex center that performs integrative functions independent of the brain.

Anatomy of the Spinal Cord

The adult spinal cord extends from its origin at the medulla oblongata of the brain on average 47 cm (18 inches) to the first or second lumbar vertebra. At its termination point, the cylindrical cord becomes the cone-shaped **conus medullaris**. For most of its length, the cord is about the width is of the pinky finger, but there are cervical and lumbar enlargements where upper and lower limb nerves enter and exit.

The spinal cord, whose consistency can be likened to firm jelly, has no rigid internal support structure. It therefore requires elaborate external protection. It is covered by bone as it passes through the vertebral foramina and is also surrounded by a trio of membranes, or **meninges**. Two of these membranes, the dura and arachnoid mater, extend beyond the conus to the S2 level. The third, the pia mater, extends into the coccygeal canal. The meninges in detail are the:

- **dura mater** (DOO-ruh MAYT-ur): a thick membrane of dense, fibrous connective tissue; the outermost of the three meninges.

- **arachnoid mater** (uh-RAK-noyd MAYT-ur): a translucent membrane below which are collagenous and elastic fibers, giving it the appearance of a spider's web; it is located just internal to the dura. Beneath the arachnoid is the **subarachnoid space**, a cavity filled with cerebrospinal fluid (CSF). The CSF is a watery shock absorber that also provides nourishment to surrounding tissues.

- **pia mater** (PEE-uh MAYT-ur): the innermost of the three membranes; a delicate, transparent membrane whose microcirculation provides nourishment for the spinal cord tissue immediately below. The pia, unlike the other meninges, follows

every contour of the cord surface. It will not be visible on a gross specimen.

External to the meninges, there is added support from other soft tissues, including a cushion of adipose tissue.

Spinal Nerves

Spinal nerves exit and enter the cord via **intervertebral foramina**. These nerves have the following characteristics:

- They occur in pairs and are positioned along the entire length of the vertebral column.

- There are 31 pairs: 8 **cervical**, 12 **thoracic**, 5 **lumbar**, 5 **sacral** and one **coccygeal**.

- All spinal nerves are mixed, that is, they contain both sensory and motor neurons. The **dorsal (posterior) root** carries sensory (afferent) impulses into the cord from receptors in the periphery. **The ventral (anterior) root** carries motor (efferent) impulses out of the cord to effectors in the periphery.

- Spinal nerves that extend beyond the end of the cord en route to their vertebral exit points assume the shape of a horsetail. In Latin, this is the **cauda equina**. The cauda equina includes nerves that pass through intervertebral foramina in the lumbar, sacral, and coccygeal regions.

Nerve Plexuses

Spinal nerves proper are only 1 to 2 cm in length. Soon after passing through an intervertebral foramen, each nerve splits into **dorsal** and **ventral rami** (RAY-my; RAY-mus, singular; *ramus* = branch). Like the nerves they emerge from, each ramus contains sensory and motor fibers.

- The smaller dorsal rami supply the skin and skeletal muscle of the trunk on its dorsal side. Where the rami originate approximates their level of distribution.

- The distribution of the ventral rami is more variable. Those of spinal nerves T2 to T12 go directly to the skin and muscles of the anterior and lateral trunk and to the muscles between the ribs (*intercostal nerves*). All other ventral rami form complex networks just lateral to their origin. These interwoven networks are called **plexuses** (from the Latin, "to braid") and give rise to peripheral nerves such that each nerve includes fibers from more than one spinal nerve. The four plexuses:

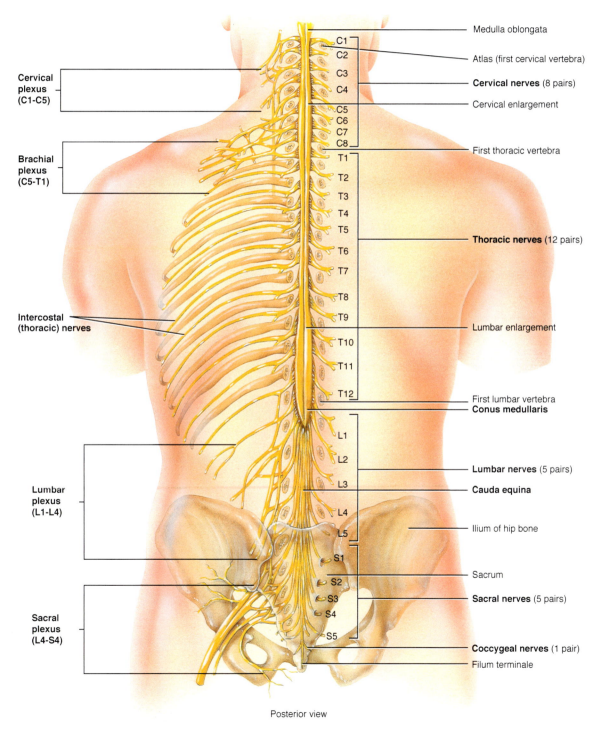

Posterior view

FIGURE 13-1. Gross structure of the spinal cord and the origin of spinal nerves and nerve plexuses.

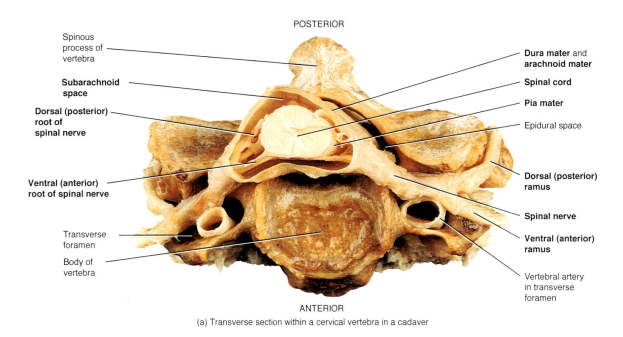

POSTERIOR

Spinous process of vertebra

Subarachnoid space

Dorsal (posterior) root of spinal nerve

Ventral (anterior) root of spinal nerve

Transverse foramen

Body of vertebra

Dura mater and arachnoid mater

Spinal cord

Pia mater

Epidural space

Dorsal (posterior) ramus

Spinal nerve

Ventral (anterior) ramus

Vertebral artery in transverse foramen

ANTERIOR

(a) Transverse section within a cervical vertebra in a cadaver

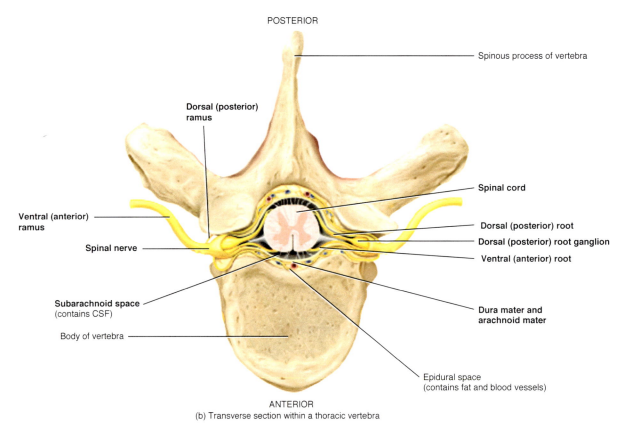

POSTERIOR

Spinous process of vertebra

Dorsal (posterior) ramus

Ventral (anterior) ramus

Spinal nerve

Subarachnoid space (contains CSF)

Body of vertebra

Spinal cord

Dorsal (posterior) root

Dorsal (posterior) root ganglion

Ventral (anterior) root

Dura mater and arachnoid mater

Epidural space (contains fat and blood vessels)

ANTERIOR

(b) Transverse section within a thoracic vertebra

FIGURE 13-2. Cross section of the spinal cord showing spinal nerves and rami.

cervical, **brachial**, **lumbar,** and **sacral**, innervate the upper and lower limb muscles and skin, principally, as well as the neck and pelvic anatomy. They are illustrated in Figure 13-1. Consult your textbook for further details.

PROCEDURE 1

Gross Examination of the Spinal Cord and Spinal Nerves

Using the spinal cord models, locate the structures called out in Figure 13-1 and 13-2.

Gray Matter

Gray matter is neuron anatomy in the CNS that is not myelinated. It includes unmyelinated nerve cell processes and cell bodies, which are never myelinated. In a spinal cord cross section, the gray matter bears resemblance to a butterfly, and schematically, an **H** (Figure 13-3).

- The two dorsal projections are the **dorsal (posterior) horns**. The dorsal horns contain interneurons and the central processes of sensory neurons. These neurons conduct impulses from their origin within receptors to the cord via the dorsal root. The cell bodies of these unipolar neurons create a bulge in the dorsal root known as the **dorsal root ganglion**.

- **Lateral horns** are lateral extensions of gray matter in the thoracic and lumbar regions of the cord. (They contain cell bodies of motor neurons of the autonomic nervous system's sympathetic division, also known as the thoracolumbar division.)

- The two ventral projections are the **ventral (anterior) horns**, which are larger and more rounded than dorsal horns. The ventral horns contain the cell bodies (and dendrites) of motor neurons. From this origin, these multipolar neurons exit the cord via the ventral root on their way to effectors.

- Spinal nerves are formed by the fusion of the dorsal and ventral roots. Spinal nerves therefore contain both sensory and motor fibers and are *mixed nerves*.

White Matter

White matter in the CNS is composed mostly of myelinated axons (nerve fibers) organized into bundles called **tracts**. The tracts are structurally divided into three **white columns** (Figures 13-3 and 13-6). Functionally, they are divided into:

- **ascending tracts** that carry sensory impulses from the spinal cord to the brain.

- **descending tracts** that carry motor impulses from the brain to the spinal cord.

PROCEDURE 2

Examining a Cross Section of the Spinal Cord Under the Microscope

Although the spinal cord's gray and white matter are grossly visible, viewing a cross section under the microscope reveals finer detail.

Obtain a slide of a human or mammalian spinal cord in cross section (Figure 13-3). Using the scanning objective on your microscope and after observing the dissecting microscope demonstration, identify: white matter, gray matter, dorsal horn, and ventral horn. With your high power objective, look for multipolar neurons within the ventral horns. (This gray matter is the source of the classic multipolar smear used to introduce neuron histology.)

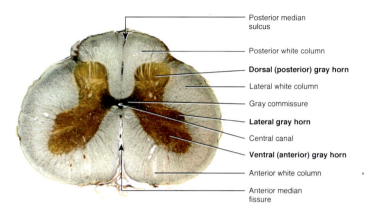

Posterior median sulcus
Posterior white column
Dorsal (posterior) gray horn
Lateral white column
Gray commissure
Lateral gray horn
Central canal
Ventral (anterior) gray horn
Anterior white column
Anterior median fissure

FIGURE 13-3. Transverse section of thoracic spinal cord (5X).

Spinal Cord Reflexes

The basic structural and functional unit of the nervous system is the **reflex**. A reflex is an automatic, predictable response to an internal or external stimulus. It therefore does not involve any higher cognitive ('thinking") centers of the brain. Reflexes are protective in nature, as in immediately retracting a limb from a potentially harmful stimulus, or when the pupil constricts to limit exposure of the retina of the eye to bright light.

A complete reflex is often referred to as a **reflex arc** (Figure 13-4) owing to the shape of the neuronal pathways that form the circuit. A reflex arc has five components:

1. Excitation of sensory receptors (hyperexcitable sensory nerve endings in the periphery).

2. Conduction over sensory (afferent) nerve fibers.

3. Coordination of incoming and outgoing impulses by a central nervous system integrating center.

4. Conduction over motor (efferent) nerve fibers.

5. Excitation of an effector (a muscle or gland).

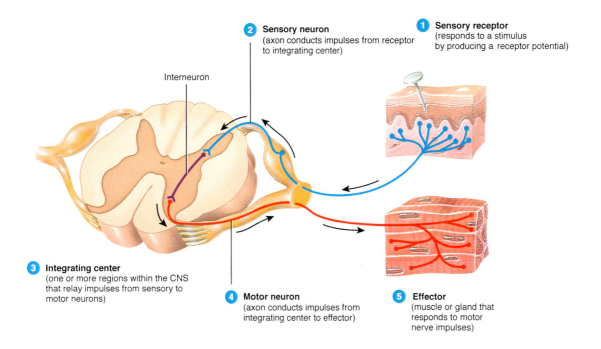

FIGURE 13-4. General components of a human reflex arc. Pictured is a pathway for a withdrawal (flexor) reflex, which pulls a limb away from a painful stimulus.

Evoking spinal reflexes in a clinical setting provides information about the integrity of the spinal cord and the peripheral nerves to and from the cord. Problems involving the central or peripheral components of the reflex arc — such as may be due to injury or disease — are mirrored in the reflex response, making the reflex test a standard diagnostic tool.

• The **stretch reflex** is the simplest of spinal cord reflexes since only incoming sensory neurons and outgoing motor neurons are involved. Stretch reflexes are initiated when **stretch receptors** a class of **proprioceptors*** are excited by a reflex hammer. These receptors are located within the belly of skeletal muscles. A tap of the hammer on the muscle tendon causes the belly to stretch. The stretch receptors are excited, causing contraction of the muscle. This contraction is a logical response to overstretching.

Stretch reflexes within skeletal muscles also maintain posture. In this case, gravity acts as the stimulus, exerting a constant pull on the stretch receptors. The

result is a steady, partial state of contraction known as **muscle tone** or **tonus**.

• The **withdrawal reflex** exemplifies the more common reflex circuitry: an interneuron is positioned between the sensory and motor neurons (Figure 13-4). A withdrawal reflex is also known as a **flexor reflex** because flexor muscles pull the limb away from the stimulus.

The stimulus in a withdrawal reflex is harmful or unpleasant, such as a hot object from which a hand is drawn away. The speed of the reflex arc (~ 50 msec or 1/20 sec) prevents tissue damage.

In both stretch and withdrawal reflexes, sensory impulses influence many motor neurons simultaneously, causing contraction of some muscles and inhibition of other muscles to produce a coordinated response.

---

* Proprioceptors are receptors that respond to stimuli arising within the body. These *interoceptors* are exemplified by receptors of the stretch reflex (muscle spindles) and those that signal abdominal cramps. *Exteroceptors*, by contrast, are excited by external stimuli, such as intense rays of the sun on the skin or in the eyes.

PROCEDURE 3

Evoking Stretch Reflexes

The patellar ("knee-jerk") and calcaneal (Achilles) stretch reflexes can be easily evoked with a reflex hammer. Because all stretch reflexes involve sensory neurons synapsing directly with motor neurons, they are often described as **monosynaptic reflexes**.

Patellar Reflex

1. With the subject sitting on a laboratory bench, the experimenter taps the quadriceps tendon (patellar ligament) with either side of a reflex hammer. The tap is delivered just distal to the patella and proximal to the tibial tuberosity as in Figure 13-5. (Palpate for soft tissue between these two bony landmarks, if necessary, to pinpoint the target area.)

2. Repeat the experiment with the subject facilitating the response by interlocking the fingers and pulling forcefully as if to separate them (*Jendrassik's maneuver*). This maneuver increases the excitability of motor neurons at their synapses with sensory neurons in the spinal cord. For a given stimulus strength, more motor neurons will reach their threshold for generating an impulse.

How was the response of the effector, the quadriceps, different during the Jendrassik maneuver?

_____

_____

If more motor neurons fire during the Jendrassik maneuver, how would you explain the before-and-after difference in the behavior of quadriceps?

_____

_____

Calcaneal Reflex

Have the subject kneel on a chair with both feet hanging freely over the edge. Tap one of the calcaneal tendons lightly with the broad end of the reflex hammer. Repeat while the subject performs the Jendrassik maneuver. Record your observations in the data table below.

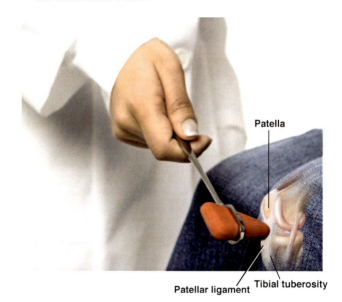

Patella

Patellar ligament   Tibial tuberosity

FIGURE 13-5. Procedure for evoking the patellar reflex.

Table 13-1. Summary of Patellar and Calcaneal Reflexes		
Reflex	**Effector**	**Response Evoked**
Patellar		
Calcaneal		

Spinal Cord Tracts

The ascending (sensory) and descending (motor) tracts of the spinal cord are illustrated in Figure 13-6. Consult your textbook to learn the functions of each tract and then complete Table 13-2.

Table 13-2. Ascending and Descending Spinal Tracts and their Functions	
Tract	**Function**
ASCENDING	
Posterior Columns (Gracile & Cuneate Fasciculi)	
Spinocerebellar	
Spinothalamic	
DESCENDING	
Direct Pathways *	
Corticospinal (Pyramidal)	
Indirect Pathways	
Rubrospinal Tectospinal Vestibulospinal Reticulospinal	

* Direct pathways originate in the cerebral cortex and convey voluntary information. Indirect pathways originate in the brain stem and convey information that is processed automatically.

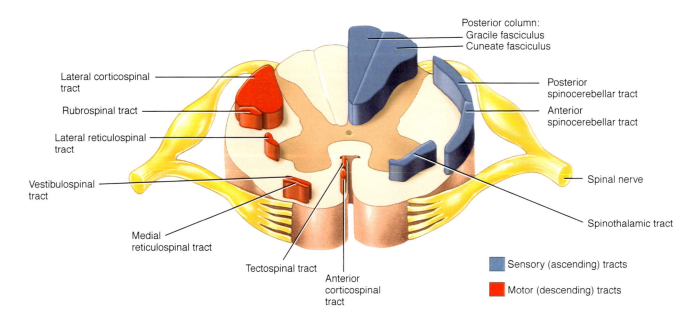

FIGURE 13-6. Ascending and descending tracts in the spinal cord.

The Lumbar Puncture: Sampling Cerebrospinal Fluid

The fluid-filled subarachnoid space that envelops the spinal cord is safely accessible for diagnostic testing in the lumbar region. The cord ends at the L1 or L2 level, permitting aspiration of cerebrospinal fluid between L3-L4 without risk of cord injury. This is a *lumbar puncture* or *spinal tap*.

Although only a relatively small volume of subarachnoid CSF is aspirated (7-8 ml or about ¼ fluid ounce), it is enough to impact the subarachnoid compartment surrounding the brain, which is continuous with that of the spinal cord. The loss of fluid volume allows the brain to sit somewhat lower in the cranial cavity when standing or sitting up. The exaggerated pressure that the base of the brain places on the meninges can lead to a severe headache upon standing. After the procedure, patients are advised to lie on their back or in a prone position for most or all of the next 24 hours. To help replenish the CSF as rapidly as possible, it is advisable to drink extra fluids for the next two days.

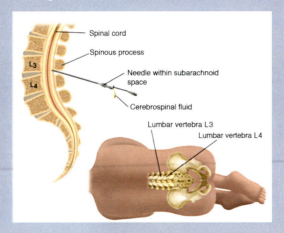

Spinal cord

Spinous process

L3

L4

Needle within subarachnoid space

Cerebrospinal fluid

Lumbar vertebra L3

Lumbar vertebra L4

Notes

Anatomy and Physiology of the Spinal Cord

NAME _____

LAB TIME / DATE _____

Anatomy of the Spinal Cord and Spinal Nerves

Matching

Match the term in Column B with its description in Column A.

Column A

_____1. spray of spinal nerves inferior to L2

____c____2. region with five pairs of spinal nerves

____b____3. region with eight pairs of spinal nerves

____a____4. region with twelve pairs of spinal nerves

_____5. tough external covering of spinal cord composed of dense fibrous connective tissue

_____6. spinal cord terminus

_____7. innermost, transparently thin connective tissue covering the spinal cord

_____8. translucent middle connective tissue covering the spinal cord

_____9. component of spinal nerve that carries sensory information into spinal cord

_____10. component of spinal nerve that carries motor information from spinal cord

_____11. spinal nerve branch that serves muscles of upper and lower limbs

_____12. spinal nerve branch that serves muscles of posterior trunk

Column B

a. thoracic

b. cervical

c. sacral

d. cauda equina

e. ventral root

f. dorsal root

g. pia mater

h. dura mater

i. arachnoid mater

j. dorsal ramus

k. ventral ramus

l. conus medullaris

1. A collection of sensory nerve cell bodies just lateral to the cord is the dorsal root

    _____ .

2. The _____ horns of gray matter contain the cell bodies of
    motor neurons destined for skeletal muscles.

3. Spaces between adjacent bones of the vertebral column that are passageways for spinal nerves are the

    _____ foramina.

4. What is the distinction between the white and gray matter of the spinal cord?

    _____

    _____

    _____

    _____

4. Place the number of the corresponding key label next to the leader line.

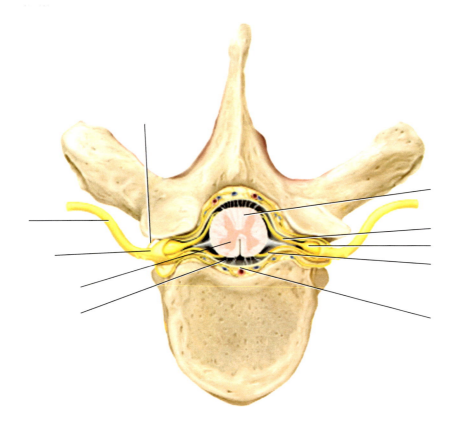

Key

1. white matter
2. gray matter
3. dorsal root
4. ventral root
5. dorsal ramus
6. ventral ramus
7. subarachnoid space
8. spinal nerve
9. dorsal root ganglion
10. dura and arachnoid
    mater

Spinal Reflexes

Label the parts of the withdrawal reflex.

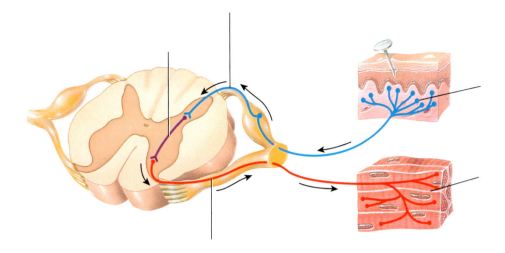

1. What function do reflexes generally serve?

   _____

   _____

   _____

2. The stimulus in the patellar reflex is the _____.

3. The effector in the patellar reflex is the _____.

4. The withdrawal reflex arc is a three-neuron, polysynaptic circuit. What is the synonym for this reflex?

5. What is the diagnostic significance of an abnormal stretch reflex? (Refer specifically to components of the reflex arc.)

   _____

   _____

   _____

   _____

Critical Thinking

1. A man was admitted to the emergency room with an injury to the spinal cord. A neurologic assessment determined that the patient had no paralysis, but could not walk. He responded to skin stimulation, but could not accurately describe the position of his limbs with his eyes closed. Which of the spinal tracts were damaged? (Hint: Awareness of limb position is described as conscious proprioception. Consult your textbook as needed.)

   _____

   _____

2. What is wrong with this picture? (One of the two anatomical errors relates to the fact that the lumbar puncture patient is an adult.)

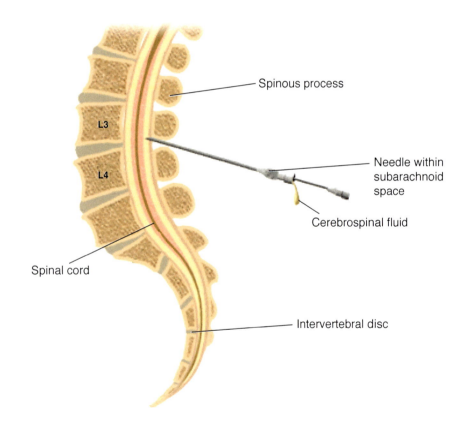

Spinous process

L3

Needle within
subarachnoid
space

L4

Cerebrospinal fluid

Spinal cord

Intervertebral disc

Anatomy and Physiology of the Brain

Exercise **14**

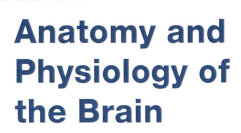

OBJECTIVES

1. To identify the three meninges which cover the brain and describe their functions.
2. To observe the gross anatomy of the brain and identify required structures within the four major subdivisions.
3. To observe a histological section of the cerebral cortex.
4. To identify the cranial nerves by name, number, and origin, and to describe their functions.
5. To define *gyrus*, *sulcus*, *fissure*, *ventricle* and *aqueduct*.
6. To review major ascending and descending pathways to and from the brain

MATERIALS

Human brain model, dissectible
Preserved human brain and meninges
Human brain slices, frontal and sagittal
   sections (preserved in alcohol or in plastic)

Chart of brain histology
Microscope
Slide of cerebral cortex

PRE-LAB QUIZ

1. A sulcus is a _____ within the brain.
   a. fold
   b. convolution
   c. deep groove
   d. shallow groove

2. The diencephalon includes the
   a. midbrain.
   b. pons.
   c. medulla oblongata.
   d. thalamus.

3. What advantage is conferred by a "wrinkled" cerebral cortex?

4. Voluntary movement is initiated by motor neurons in the
   a. basal nuclei.
   b. parietal cortex.
   c. frontal cortex.
   d. cerebellum.

5. The only cranial nerve whose distribution is not limited to the head and neck is the

   _____.

The Human Brain

The human brain is the pinnacle of nervous system development. While it retains the primitive reflex centers in the brain stem as in lower animals, its cerebral cortex can be considered the "crown of evolution." It is cerebral cortical neurons that allow humans to perform delicate movements, learn to speak and write a language, call upon memory and judgment to make rational decisions, and to imagine.

Gross Anatomy of the Brain: External Structures

Among the various schemes for organizing brain anatomy, most neuroanatomists subdivide the brain into four principal regions:

1. cerebrum
2. diencephalon
3. brain stem
4. cerebellum

PROCEDURE 1

Identifying External Brain Anatomy

On a brain model and human brain and referring to the illustrations in this section, locate the external structures where indicated.

The Cerebrum

The **cerebrum** (Figure 14-1) is the largest subdivision of the brain, housing 10 to 12 billion neurons and comprising 80% of its mass. It is divided into two cerebral hemispheres. Identify the:

- **cerebral cortex**, the gray outer surface (4-6 mm thick). The **nuclei** (groups of nerve cell bodies) in the cortex form the basis for voluntary movement and for higher intellectual functions, such as learning, judgment and language. The many external folds of cerebral tissue create substantial cortical surface area within a relatively compact cranial cavity. These folds, and the grooves that separate them, are named as follows:

  - **gyrus** (JYE-russ), plural **gyri** (JYE-rye): a fold of cerebral cortex; also known as a **convolution**.

  - **sulcus** (SULL-kuss), plural **sulci** (SULL-sye): a shallow groove between folds of cerebral cortex.

  - **fissure** (FIH-shur), a deep groove. Fissures and many grooves are named and represent important anatomical landmarks on the brain's surface.

- **cerebral hemispheres**, the left and right halves of the cerebrum, and the brain's most superior region. They are separated by the **longitudinal fissure**. The **corpus callosum** is a thick band of connecting nerve fibers that transmits impulses between the hemispheres. Each hemisphere is subdivided by sulci into lobes whose names correspond to adjacent cranial bones.

- The **frontal** and **parietal lobes** are separated by the **central sulcus**; the **lateral sulcus** separates the **temporal lobe** from the frontal and parietal lobes. The **occipital lobe** is offset from the parietal lobe by the parieto-occipital sulcus, which is not externally visible . (The insula, a fifth lobe of each cerebral hemisphere, is also not visible externally.)

- Within each hemisphere is a **ventricle**, a cavity filled with **cerebrospinal fluid (CSF)**. Located below these **lateral ventricles** is the **third ventricle** in the midsagittal plane. The **fourth ventricle** lies between the brain stem and cerebellum. The third and fourth ventricles are interconnected by a CSF-filled **cerebral aqueduct**. (See Figures 14-5 and 14-6.)

Locate two important gyri in each hemisphere: the **precentral gyrus** (frontal lobe) and the **postcentral gyrus** (parietal lobe) in Figures 14-1 and 14-2.

- The **precentral gyrus** includes the **primary motor cortex**, whose pyramidal cells initiate voluntary (conscious) movement of skeletal muscles. The neurons that convey impulses to skeletal muscles are designated as **somatic motor neurons**. Those originating in the primary motor cortex are the first of a two-neuron circuit and begin the pyramidal (corticospinal) tracts. These *upper motor neurons* comprise descending spinal tracts that synapse with *lower motor neurons* in the ventral horns of the spinal cord. Lower motor neurons bridge the cord to the skeletal muscles.

- Anterior to the motor area in the frontal lobe is a region called the **prefrontal cortex**, which is oddly named given its location. This is one of several **association areas**, aptly named because they interconnect nerve fibers throughout the cerebral cortex.

- The **postcentral gyrus** is the **primary somatosensory cortex**. It is here that impulses from sensory receptors from the skin (for stimuli like touch pressure, and pain) are localized. ("I feel something on my back.") In the **somatosensory association cortex**, just posterior to the postcentral gyrus, there is a more specific translation of the stimulus. ("I was just stung on my back by that bee!")

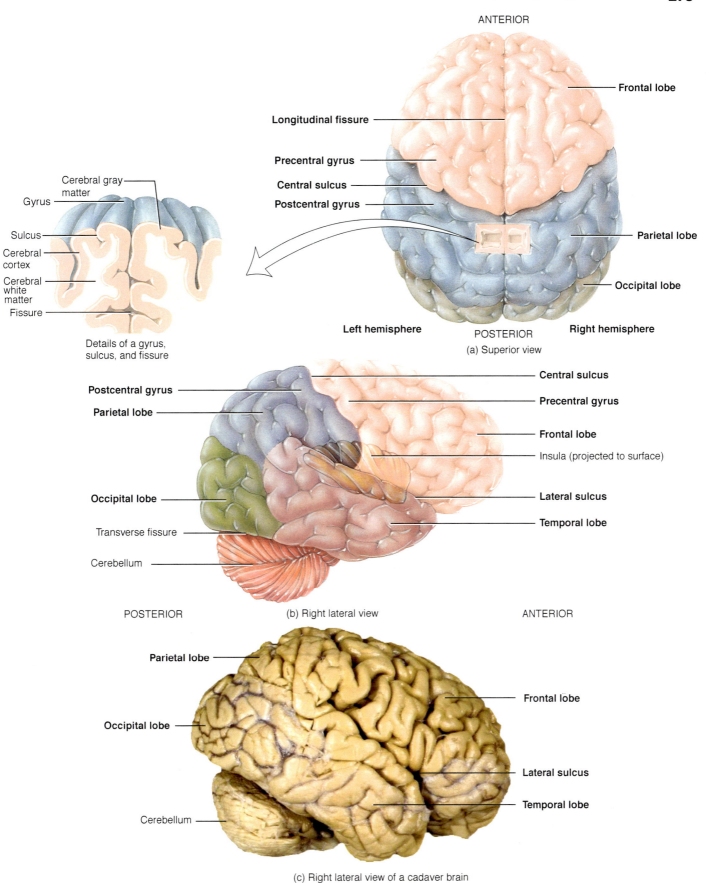

ANTERIOR

Frontal lobe

Longitudinal fissure

Precentral gyrus

Central sulcus

Postcentral gyrus

Parietal lobe

Occipital lobe

Left hemisphere

POSTERIOR

Right hemisphere

(a) Superior view

Cerebral gray matter

Gyrus

Sulcus

Cerebral cortex

Cerebral white matter

Fissure

Details of a gyrus, sulcus, and fissure

Central sulcus

Postcentral gyrus

Precentral gyrus

Parietal lobe

Frontal lobe

Insula (projected to surface)

Occipital lobe

Lateral sulcus

Transverse fissure

Temporal lobe

Cerebellum

POSTERIOR

(b) Right lateral view

ANTERIOR

Parietal lobe

Frontal lobe

Occipital lobe

Lateral sulcus

Temporal lobe

Cerebellum

(c) Right lateral view of a cadaver brain

FIGURE 14-1. External anatomy of the cerebrum. Inset: Frontal section illustrating cerebral cortical gray matter and underlying white matter.

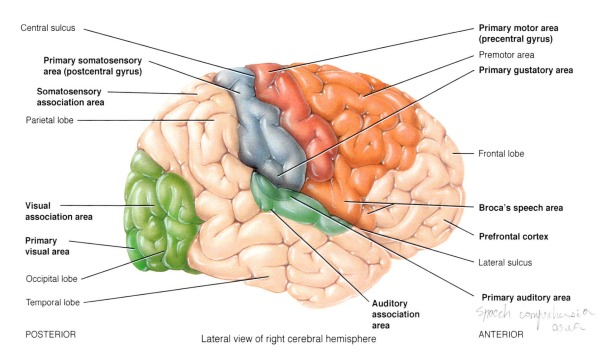

Central sulcus

Primary somatosensory
area (postcentral gyrus)

Somatosensory
association area

Parietal lobe

Visual
association area

Primary
visual area

Occipital lobe

Temporal lobe

POSTERIOR

**Primary motor area
(precentral gyrus)**

Premotor area

Primary gustatory area

Frontal lobe

Broca's speech area

Prefrontal cortex

Lateral sulcus

Primary auditory area

Auditory
association
area

Speech comprehension area

Lateral view of right cerebral hemisphere

ANTERIOR

FIGURE 14-2. External anatomy of cerebrum showing functional areas of the cerebral cortex.

The circuit enabling conscious awareness of a stimulus from skin (cutaneous) receptors involves three sensory neurons and two synapses:

(I) a somatosensory neuron from a sensory receptor to the spinal cord;

(II) a long interneuron within an ascending tract to the thalamus of the diencephalon; and

(III) a neuron connecting the thalamus with the primary somatosensory cortex in the postcentral gyrus.

The interpretation of impulses from visceral (non-somatic) receptors — the special sense organs — occurs in the following lobes of the cerebral cortex:

• olfactory and auditory areas: temporal lobe
• gustatory (taste) area: parietal lobe
• visual area: occipital lobe

The Association Cortex

The association cortex occupies the lateral surfaces of the temporal, parietal, and occipital lobes, and the frontal lobe anterior to the primary motor cortex (Figure 14-2). *The purpose of the association cortex is to integrate sensory experiences encoded in memory and thereby coordinate learning and reasoning.* The associative domain also enables imagination, creativity and planning for the future.

Association neurons further serve to link a memory-evoking stimulus with an appropriate — and often, advantageous — response. *Example*: Your A&P instructor asks a question (the *stimulus*).

AWARENESS:
1. You *hear* the question (this involves the primary auditory area of the temporal cortex.): "What is the action of the superior portion of the trapezius?"

PERCEPTION:
2. You then *interpret* the question using your association cortex. This requires that you tap into your auditory association area (also in the temporal lobe).

RESPONSE:
3. You now *respond* to the question, either physically, or verbally.

A physical response might be shrugging your shoulders, which may (a) reflect true knowledge of the fact that trapezius pulls up your shoulder blades, or (b) be a lucky expression of doubt that is totally in your favor.

A verbal reply might sound like this: "The superior fibers of the trapezius muscle elevate the scapulae."

Either response requires linking thought with action: The association cortex instructs the pyramidal cells in the primary motor cortex to shrug the shoulders OR the frontal lobe's speech (Broca's) area to direct the mouth and tongue to articulate the appropriate spoken words. In this example, the association cortex enables completion of a recall task within a conscious stimulus-response scenario.

Bottom Line: The association cortex coordinates the use of several higher intellectual resources, housed in several regions of the cerebral cortex, to learn, recall, and act on input channeled through our senses.

The cerebrum contains the nuclei of origin of the olfactory (I) and optic (II) cranial nerves.

The Diencephalon

The thalamus and hypothalamus (discussed shortly) reside in the diencephalon. On the underside of a brain model, note the following structures that occupy, or emanate from, the floor of the diencephalon (Figures 14-3 and 14-4). Identify the:

- **olfactory bulbs**, where cranial nerve I synapses with olfactory neurons originating in the nasal cavity.

- **olfactory tracts**, which convey olfactory impulses to the olfactory area of the temporal lobe.

- **optic nerves**, cranial nerves II.

- **optic chiasma** (KY-as-muh), where some of the optic nerve axons cross to the opposite side of the brain.

- **optic tracts**, which convey optic impulses to the primary visual area of the occipital lobe.

- **pituitary gland** (**hypophysis)**, which attaches to a stalk that emanates from the hypothalamus. (If you are examining a cadaver brain, this gland is invariably missing. Like the cranial nerves, the stalk is cut to facilitate removal of the brain from the cranial cavity.)

The Brain Stem

Inferior to the diencephalon is the brain stem. On the model, and referring to Figures 14-3 and 14-4, note the:

- **midbrain**, a short intermediary region that conducts impulses to and from the cerebrum and hindbrain (pons, medulla oblongata, and cerebellum). The midbrain contains the origin of cranial nerves III and IV.

- **pons** (literally, "bridge"), which consists primarily of sensory and motor tracts that functionally link the cerebrum with the other hindbrain structures. The pons contains the origins of cranial nerves V, VI, VII, and VIII.

- **medulla oblongata** (muh-DUH-luh or muh-DOO-luh ah-blong-GAH-tuh), the most inferior part of the brain. It is superior to, and continuous with, the spinal cord. The medulla consists primarily of sensory and motor tracts, but also contains vital reflex centers, nuclei that regulate heart rate, blood pressure, and breathing. The medulla oblongata contains the origins of cranial nerves IX, X, XI, and XII.

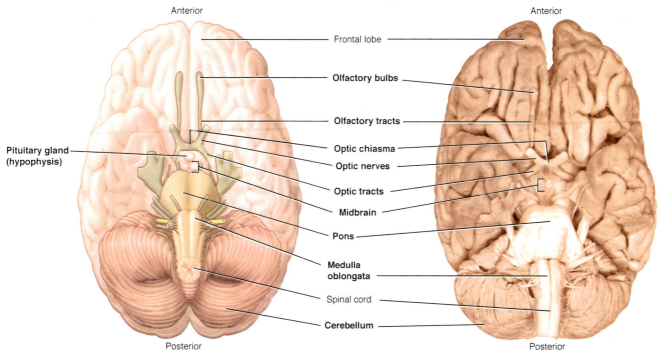

FIGURE 14-3. Inferior surface of the human brain. A cadaver brain (minus the pituitary gland) is to the right.

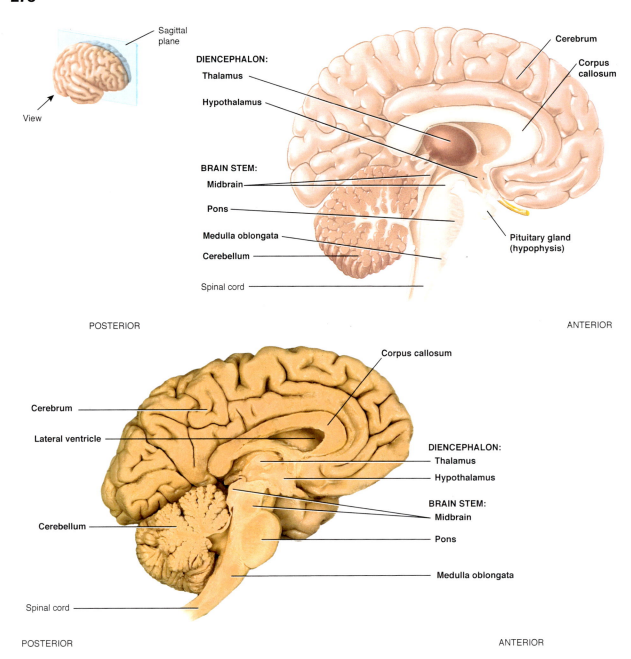

FIGURE 14-4. The brain in midsagittal section, viewed from the medial aspect. Lower figure is a cadaver specimen.

The Cerebellum

The **cerebellum** is named for its external resemblance to the cerebrum. Note its anatomy in both dorsal and ventral views of the brain model and human brain (Figures 14-1, 14-3 and 14-4). It is subdivided, like the cerebrum, into two hemispheres, and has a folded gray-matter cortex that features gyri and sulci, and that overlies white matter. It is connected to the brain stem by three paired bundles of fibers called the cerebellar peduncles.

PROCEDURE 2

Identifying Internal Brain Anatomy

Your study of the internal brain anatomy will focus on the same four major regions outlined in Procedure 1. Use the dissectible models and the sectioned human brains along with relevant illustrations in this section as guides.

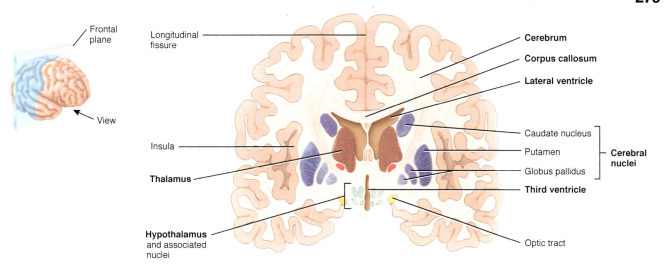

FIGURE 14-5. Anterior view of frontal section of the brain showing basal nuclei and diencephalon anatomy.

The Cerebrum

Dissect a brain model in the midsagittal plane to reveal the medial aspects of the two cerebral hemispheres (Figure 14-4). Locate the:

- **corpus callosum**, a large band of white matter (fiber tracts) that connects the two hemispheres. (Tracts that link hemispheres are generically known as *commissures*.)

- **lateral ventricles**, one in each hemisphere.

- **cerebral nuclei.** Obtain a brain model sectioned in the frontal plane. Observe the white matter internal to the gray matter of the cortex. Deep within the white matter is gray matter known as cerebral nuclei. Within these clusters of cell bodies are the basal nuclei (formerly **basal ganglia***), paired masses of gray matter, one in each hemisphere (Figure 14-5).

Function: The cerebral nuclei are part of the indirect (extrapyramidal) motor pathways (see page 266) and control movements initiated by pyramidal neurons of the direct pathway. They also help regulate skeletal muscle tone required for particular body movements. The basal nuclei control subconscious actions of skeletal muscles, such as gesticulating and swinging the arms while walking. Another example is spontaneous ("burst-out") laughter as opposed to polite (conscious) laughter to acknowledge a so-so attempt at humor.

Note the various nuclei in the frontal section pictured in Figure 14-5 in blue. (You will be required to know the basal nuclei as a collective group of gray-matter subdivisions within the cerebrum, not by their individual names.)

* "Basal ganglia" is a misnomer. Ganglia are clusters of neuronal cell bodies outside the CNS.

The Diencephalon

With particular reference to Figures 14-4 and 14-5, locate the:

- **thalamus** (THAL-uh-mus), two large, paired oval masses of primarily gray matter. In a frontal section, note the corpus callosum and lateral ventricles and their relationship to the thalamus.

Function: The thalamus is an important relay and integrating center for all sensory impulses bound for the cortical sensory areas except olfaction. Once in the cerebral cortex, we can now localize the stimulus and interpret its significance.

- **hypothalamus** (hi-poe-THAL-uh-mus), named for its location beneath the thalamus, it occupies the floor and lower lateral walls of the third ventricle.

Function: As the major controller of autonomic (visceral) activities, the hypothalamus regulates temperature, appetite, and water/electrolyte balance. It also bears an important functional relationship to the pituitary gland (hypophysis), which is attached to its inferior surface by a stalk known as the **infundibulum**.

The Brain Stem

1. Find the short **midbrain** between the mammillary body (an olfactory relay station just posterior to the pituitary gland shown in Figure 14-6) and the pons below (Figure 14-3). In a midsagittal section, you will see one of two **superior colliculi** and one of two **inferior colliculi** (Figure 14-6). Trace the cerebral aqueduct as it passes through the midbrain to the fourth ventricle of the hindbrain.

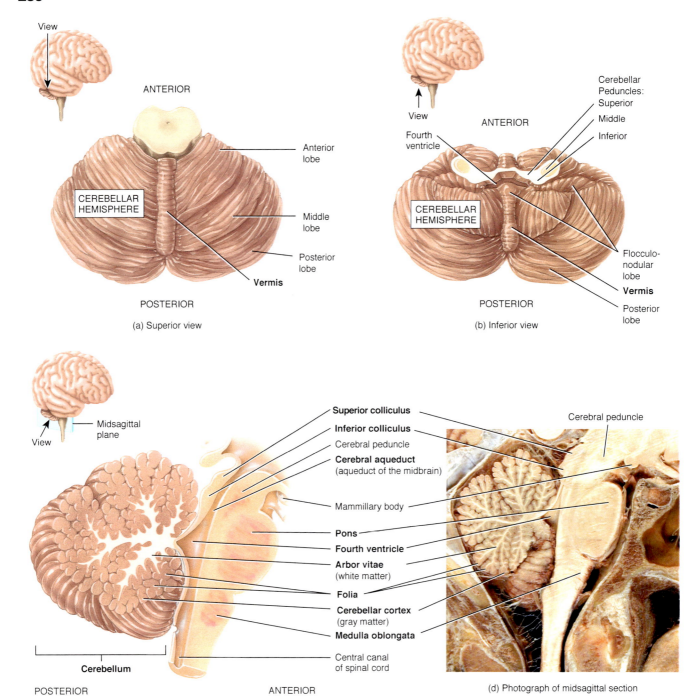

View

ANTERIOR

Anterior
lobe

CEREBELLAR
HEMISPHERE

Middle
lobe

Posterior
lobe

Vermis

POSTERIOR

(a) Superior view

View

ANTERIOR

Cerebellar
Peduncles:
Superior

Middle

Inferior

Fourth
ventricle

CEREBELLAR
HEMISPHERE

Flocculo-
nodular
lobe

Vermis

POSTERIOR

Posterior
lobe

(b) Inferior view

Midsagittal
plane

View

Superior colliculus

Inferior colliculus

Cerebral peduncle

Cerebral aqueduct
(aqueduct of the midbrain)

Mammillary body

Pons

Fourth ventricle

Arbor vitae
(white matter)

Folia

Cerebellar cortex
(gray matter)

Medulla oblongata

Central canal
of spinal cord

Cerebral peduncle

Cerebellum

POSTERIOR

ANTERIOR

(c) Midsagittal section of cerebellum and brain stem

(d) Photograph of midsagittal section

FIGURE 14-6. The brain stem and cerebellum.

Function: The midbrain contains reflex centers (gray matter nuclei): the superior colliculi for visual reflexes and the inferior colliculi for auditory reflexes. Besides these centers, the midbrain is a thoroughfare for sensory and motor impulses (via white matter tracts).

2. Observe the rounded **pons**, a region about 4 cm (1.5 inches) long between the midbrain and medulla oblongata. Identify the fourth ventricle posteriorly.

Function: The pons has (1) tracts that convey sensory and motor impulses to and from higher and lower brain regions, and (2) centers that regulate breathing.

3. The **medulla oblongata** is the terminal region of the brain stem, about 2.5 cm (1 inch) in length, that joins the spinal cord. *Oblongata* derives from "oblong", another word for rectangular, which describes the medulla's shape in an inferior view.

It is noteworthy that 80% of corticospinal (pyramidal) neurons cross over to the contralateral (opposite) side of the body in the medulla oblongata. (The remaining axons cross over in the spinal cord.) Thus, brain damage from a stroke, or *cerebral vascular accident (CVA)*, in the left cerebral hemisphere will have consequences on the right side of the body and vice versa.

Function: The medulla oblongata is (1) a thoroughfare between the brain and spinal cord, and (2) an integrating center for vital reflexes, including those that control heart rate, blood vessel diameter, and breathing.

The Cerebellum

In sagittal section, note a cerebellar hemisphere (Figure 14-6). Each of its two hemispheres contains three lobes that are connected by a smaller lobe in the midline called the **vermis**. As in the cerebrum, there is cortical gray matter and deeper white matter. The white matter here is arranged like branches of a tree. Closely examine the **arbor vitae** ("tree of life") as the branches are known.

Function: The cerebellum receives sensory input from skeletal muscles and the vestibular apparatus (the organ of balance of the inner ear). By interpreting this information, it maintains balance (equilibrium) and muscle tone via motor impulses to the somatic musculature. The cerebellum also coordinates muscle movement initiated by the motor cortex by its effect on prime movers and antagonists. The result is smooth and precise voluntary movements.

The Meninges of the Brain

As with the spinal cord, the brain is covered by a series of protective membranes known as meninges (Figure 14-7). On a preserved human brain observe the:

- **dura mater:** a thick membrane of dense, fibrous connective tissue and the outermost of the three meninges. The brain dura, unlike that of the spinal cord, is a double membrane: its external portion is the *periosteal layer*, which adheres to the inner aspect of the cranium; the internal membrane is the *meningeal layer*. The two layers are fused together except where they separate to enclose venous sinuses that route blood from the brain to the internal jugular vein.

The three extensions of the dura are the (1) *falx cerebri* (FALKS SER-ih-bry), which separates the two cerebral hemispheres; (2) *falx cerebelli* (FALKS ser-ih-BEL-eye), which separates the two cerebellar hemispheres; and (3) *tentorium cerebelli* (ten-TOR-ee-um ser-ih-BEL-eye), which partitions the cerebellum from the cerebrum.

- **arachnoid mater:** a translucent membrane beneath

which are prominent blood vessels; it is located just internal to the dura.

- **pia mater:** the innermost of the three membranes. The pia is a fine, transparent membrane which unlike the other meninges, follows every contour of the brain surface. It covers tiny blood vessels as they course along the surface of the brain. Because of its thinness and transparency, the pia will not be visible on a gross specimen.

As with the spinal cord, there is a **subarachnoid space** containing cerebrospinal fluid (CSF). The CSF is an effective shock absorber and plays a role in nourishing brain tissue as well. There is no epidural space surrounding the brain.

Selective Attention: The Stroop Test (Optional)

The Stroop effect, named for the American psychologist John Ridley Stroop (1897-1973), refers to a type of mental interference that occurs when the brain attempts to process conflicting information. When, for example, someone is engaging you in conversation while you are trying to concentrate on a short-term memory task, your focused attention on the task is challenged.

The Stroop effect can be used as a test of *selective attention*. The test challenges you to work through a conflict between the meaning of words and the recognition of colors.

PROCEDURE 3

Taking the Stroop Test

1. Assign a classmate the role of official timer. This requires a timing device or a watch with a second hand.

2. Have the timer turn to page 283 and cover the Test B panel. At time zero, read aloud the colors of the words in Test A. The clock will stop when you have finished.
   How long did Test A take to complete?

   _____ sec

3. Uncover the Test B panel. At time zero, read aloud the c o l o r s of the words in Test B — *not the words themselves*.

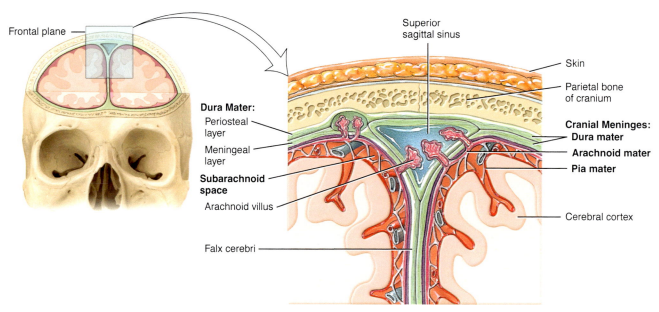

(a) Anterior view of frontal section through skull showing the cranial meninges

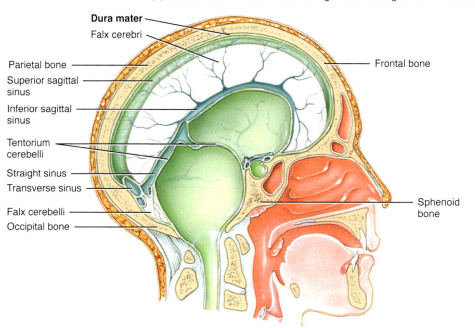

(b) Sagittal section of extensions of the dura mater

FIGURE 14-7. The meninges of the brain.

How long did Test B take to complete?

_____ sec

(Stroop test times for average 40-year olds are: Test A ~10 sec and for Test B ~20 sec. Test times increase with age, especially those for Test B.)

Localizing the Stroop Effect

Brain scans show that the frontal lobe is active — especially in the prefrontal cortex — when processing conflicting information. In a clinical setting, using Stroop test norms as a frame of reference, the test is sometimes used to diagnose attention deficit/hyperactivity disorder (ADHD).

The epidemic of auto accidents while texting or talking sharply illustrates the limits of selective attention.

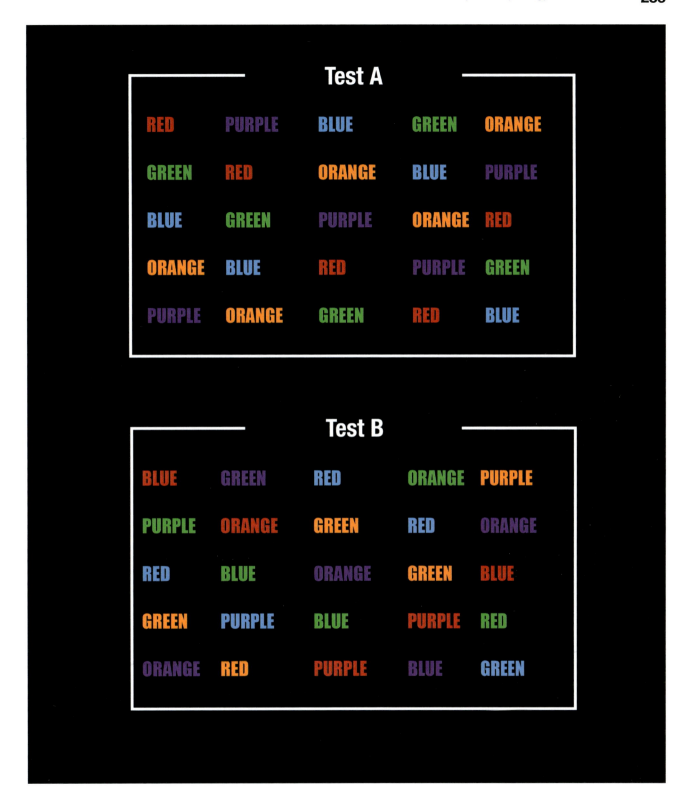

FIGURE 14-8. The Stroop Test. Determine how long it take, in seconds, to (A) read aloud the words as written, and to (B) read aloud the colors of the words, not the words themselves.

Sensory or Motor Event	Pathway Involved
1. Feeling your eyes covered as someone comes from behind, whispering "Guess who?" (*Touch* is the stimulus.)	
2. Swinging a baseball bat after you decide a pitch is to your liking. (*Engaging muscles with conscious effort* is the outcome.)	
3. A person strutting down Main Street, swinging their arms. *(There is no conscious effort during arm movement.)*	
4. Walking down a staircase, sensing each step without looking at your feet. (This is *kinesthesia*, or conscious muscle sense.)	

The Cranial Nerves

The cranial nerves arise from the base of the brain and pass through the foramina of cranial bones. They, along with spinal nerves, are the major subdivisions of the peripheral nervous system.

There are 12 pairs of cranial nerves whose names, in most cases, reflect their distribution (such as the *facial* nerve) or function (as in the *abducens*, which innervates an eyeball abductor). All are distributed to the head and neck except for the vagus, which innervates the throat and the thoracic and abdominopelvic cavities. (*Vagus* is Latin for "wandering".)

Each cranial nerve is assigned a Roman numeral. The sequence of numbers indicates the anterior-to-posterior order in which the nerves arise from the brain. In contrast to the spinal nerves, all of which are mixed (containing both sensory and motor fibers), the cranial nerves may be mixed, sensory, or motor:

Three cranial nerves, I, II, and VIII, are special sensory nerves because their axons carry impulses for the special senses: smell, vision, and hearing.

Five cranial nerves, III, IV, VI, XI, and XII, are designated motor nerves since they are composed of axons of motor neurons. *Autonomic motor nerves* innervate cardiac muscle, smooth muscle, and glands and are parasympathetic by classification. Those motor nerves whose effectors are skeletal muscles are classified as *somatic motor nerves*.

Four cranial nerves, V, VII, IX, and X, are mixed.

Mnemonic for remembering the cranial nerves as sensory (S), motor (M), or mixed (B, for both):
Some **S**ay **M**arry **M**oney **B**ut **M**y **B**rother **S**ays **B**rilliant **B**rains **M**atter **M**ore.

PROCEDURE 4

Locate the 12 cranial nerves on the brain models. Table 14-1 summarizes cranial nerve components and principal functions. Figures 14-9 to 14-18 highlight each cranial nerve's origin and destination.

Table 14-1. Summary of Cranial Nerves.		
Cranial Nerve	**Components**	**Principal Functions**
Olfactory (I)	Special sensory	Olfaction (smell)
Optic (II)	Special sensory	Vision (sight)
Oculomotor (III)	Motor (somatic) Motor (autonomic)	Movement of eyeballs and upper eyelid Adjusts lens for near vision (accommodation) Constriction of pupil
Trochlear (IV)	Motor (somatic)	Movement of eyeballs
Trigeminal (V)	Mixed: Sensory Motor (branchial*)	Touch, pain, and thermal sensations from scalp, face, and oral cavity (including teeth and anterior two-thirds of tongue) Chewing
Abducens (VI)	Motor (somatic)	Movement of eyeballs
Facial (VII)	Mixed: Sensory Motor (branchial) Motor (autonomic)	Taste from anterior two-thirds of tongue Control of muscles of facial expression Secretion of tears and saliva
Vestibulocochlear (VIII)	Special sensory	Hearing and equilibrium.
Glossopharyngeal (IX)	Mixed: Sensory Motor (branchial) Motor (autonomic)	Taste from posterior one-third of tongue Proprioception in some swallowing muscles Monitors blood pressure and oxygen and carbon dioxide levels in blood. Touch, pain, and thermal sensations from upper pharynx Assists in swallowing Secretion of saliva
Vagus (X)	Mixed: Sensory Motor (branchial) Motor (autonomic)	Proprioception from throat and laryngeal (voice box) muscles Monitors blood pressure and oxygen and carbon dioxide levels in blood Sensations from thoracic and abdominal organs Swallowing, vocalization, and coughing Motility and secretion of gastrointestinal organs Constriction of respiratory passageways Decreases heart rate
Accessory (XI)	Motor (branchial)	Movement of head and pectoral girdle
Hypoglossal (XII)	Motor (somatic)	Speech, manipulation of food, and swallowing

Mnemonic for Cranial Nerves

Oh	Oh	Oh	To	Touch	And
Olfactory	Optic	Oculomotor	Trochlear	Trigeminal	Abducens
Feel	Very	Green	Vegetables	At	Home
Facial	Vestibulocochlear	Glossopharyngeal	Vagus	Accessory	Hypoglossal

* *Branchial* motor nerves innervate skeletal muscles that develop from embryonic pharyngeal (branchial) arches. In adults, these muscles are in the head, neck and throat and include chewing and swallowing musculature.

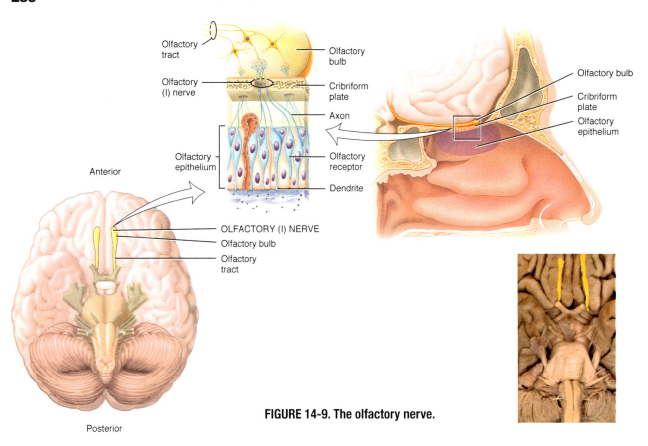

FIGURE 14-9. The olfactory nerve.

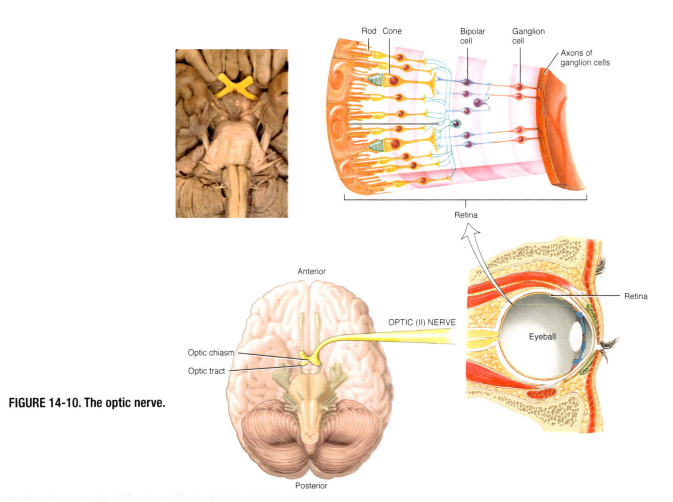

FIGURE 14-10. The optic nerve.

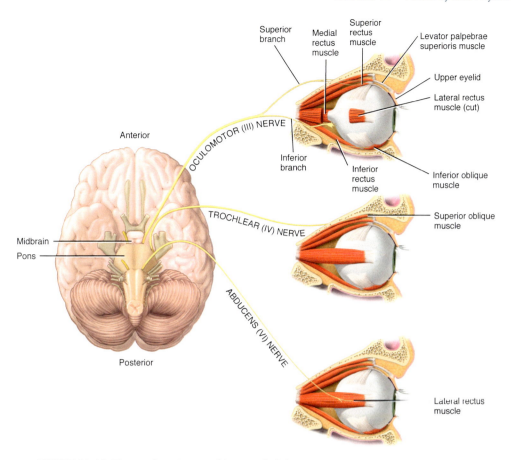

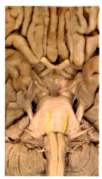

FIGURE 14-11. The oculomotor, trochlear and abducens nerves.

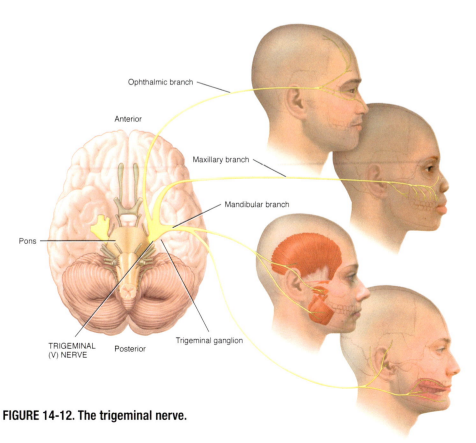
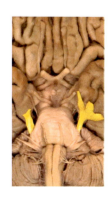

FIGURE 14-12. The trigeminal nerve.

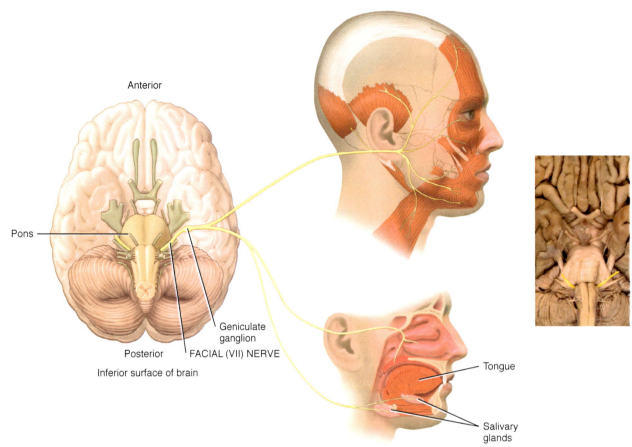

FIGURE 14-13. The facial nerve.

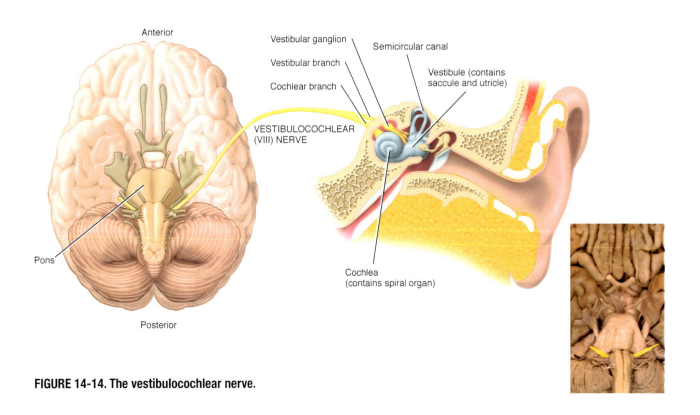

FIGURE 14-14. The vestibulocochlear nerve.

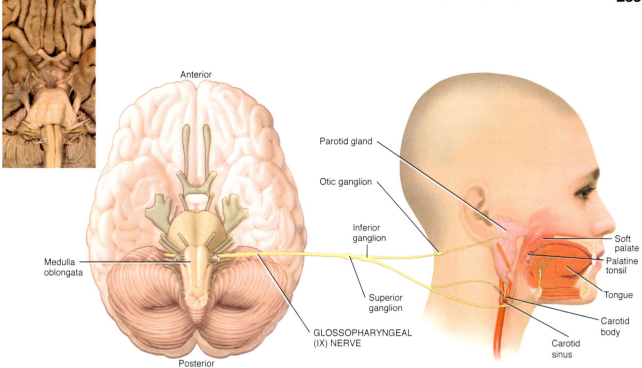

FIGURE 14-15. The glossopharygeal nerve.

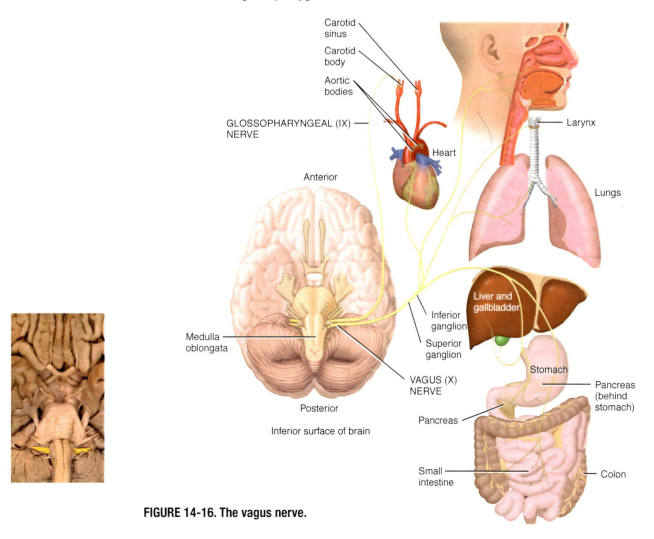

FIGURE 14-16. The vagus nerve.

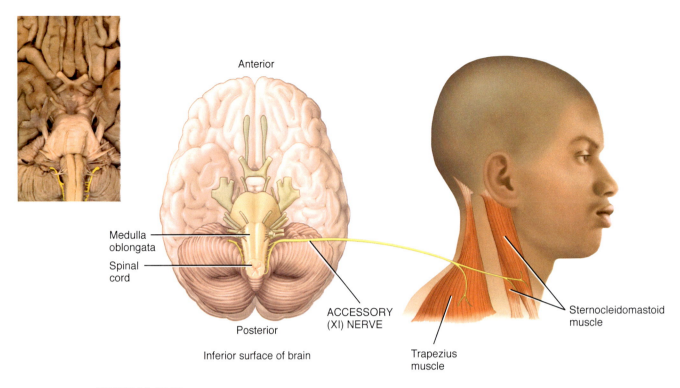

Anterior

Medulla
oblongata

Spinal
cord

Posterior

ACCESSORY
(XI) NERVE

Inferior surface of brain

Trapezius
muscle

Sternocleidomastoid
muscle

FIGURE 14-17. The accessory nerve.

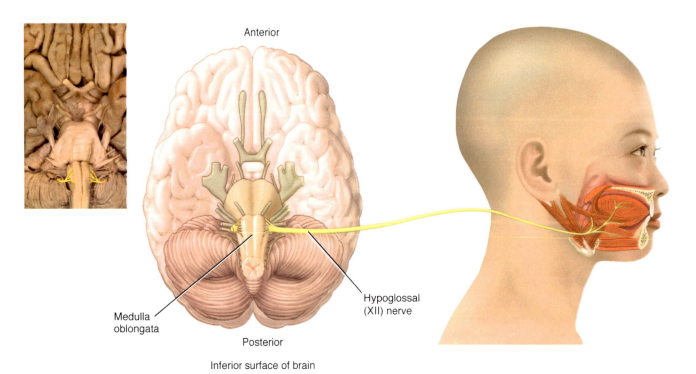

Anterior

Medulla
oblongata

Posterior

Hypoglossal
(XII) nerve

Inferior surface of brain

FIGURE 14-18. The hypoglossal nerve.

Histology of the Cerebral Cortex

PROCEDURE 5

Obtain a slide of the cerebral cortex from the demo table, and under high power, identify the pyramidal neurons that are at the origin of the corticospinal tracts.

Clinical Application

Ecstasy or Addiction: A Pleasure Center in the Midbrain

The ventral tegmental area (VTA) in the floor of the midbrain is the origin of neurons that project to the frontal association area, forming a major part of our "reward circuitry". The reward neurotransmitter is dopamine.

Food, alcohol, drugs, gambling, love, sex, cellphones — even charitable giving — all stimulate the VTA and cause pleasurable sensations. All of these pleasurable stimuli (with the possible exception of charitable giving) have been prefaced by the words "addicted to". Webster's defines *addiction* as an unusually great need — and sometimes a strong and harmful need — to have something (such as a drug) or to do something (such as gambling).

The frontal association area in the prefrontal cortex has been localized as a region that exercises judgment and exerts control over human behavior. Compromising the normal functioning of this area — as in repeated drug use — creates an imbalance that can lead to unreasonable behavior, including addiction, characterized by rash actions without due regard for the consequences.

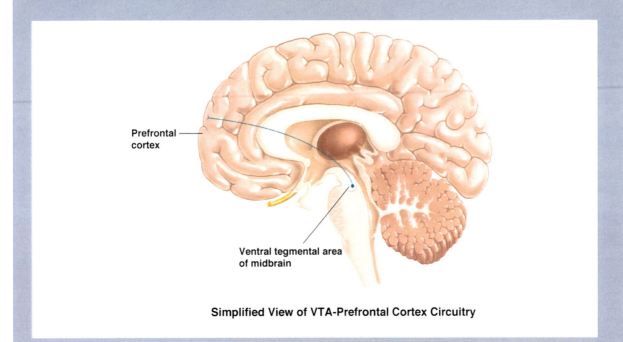

Prefrontal cortex

Ventral tegmental area of midbrain

Simplified View of VTA-Prefrontal Cortex Circuitry

Notes

Anatomy and Physiology of the Brain

NAME _____

LAB TIME / DATE _____

Gross Anatomy of the Brain

Matching

Match the brain region in column B to function in Column A.

Column A		Column B
_____1. cardiovascular center		a. cerebral cortex
_____2. sensory relay center		b. cerebral nuclei
_____3. contains primary motor and somatosensory areas		c. medulla oblongata
		d. hypothalamus
_____4. regulates involuntary movements such as gesticulating		e. midbrain
		f. pons
_____5. bridge that connects brain regions with one another		g. thalamus
_____6. controls appetite and body temperature		h. cerebellum
		i. association areas
_____7. connects cerebral hemispheres		j. corpus callosum
_____8. site of visual and auditory reflexes		
_____9. coordinates prime movers and antagonists		
_____10. links sensory experiences to learning and knowledge		

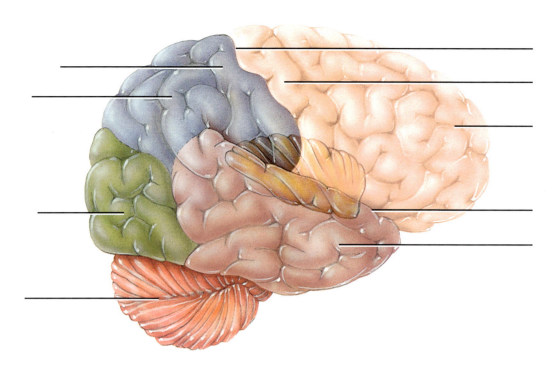

Place the number of the corresponding key label next to the leader line.

Key

1. occipital lobe

2. lateral sulcus

3. temporal lobe

4. parietal lobe

5. frontal lobe

6. precentral gyrus

7. postcentral gyrus

8. cerebellum

9. central sulcus

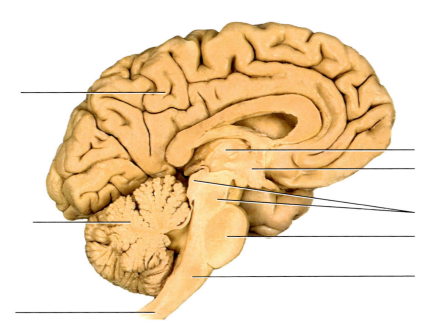

Place the number of the corresponding key label next to the leader line.

Key

1. thalamus

2. hypothalamus

3. cerebellum

4. midbrain

5. medulla oblongata

6. cerebrum

7. pons

8. spinal cord

Key

1. cerebellum

2. fourth ventricle

3. arbor vitae

4. cerebellar cortex

5. superior colliculus

6. inferior colliculus

7. cerebral aqueduct

8. medulla oblongata

9. pons

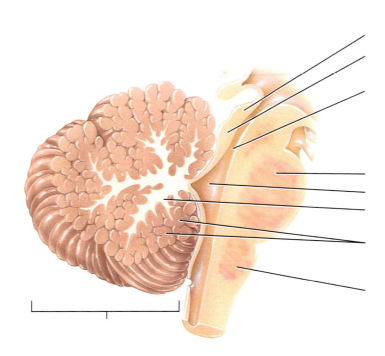

The Cranial Nerves

Matching

Match the cranial nerve in Column B with its name or function in Column A. (Some answers may be used more than once.)

Column A	Column B
_____1. vestibulocochlear	a. cranial nerve II
_____2. glossopharyngeal	b. cranial nerve X
_____3. facial	c. cranial nerve VII
_____4. vagus	d. cranial nerve IX
_____5. hypoglossal	e. cranial nerve I
_____6. trochlear	f. cranial nerve III
_____7. accessory	g. cranial nerve IV
_____8. abducens	h. cranial nerve VIII
_____9. trigeminal	i. cranial nerve V
_____10. optic	j. cranial nerve XI
_____11. oculomotor	k. cranial nerve VI
_____12. olfactory	l. cranial nerve XII

_____13. enables distinction between vanilla and garlic aromas

_____14. controls extrinsic eye muscles as you gaze panoramically at the Grand Canyon

_____15. enables tongue movements as you explain your study strategies to a classmate

_____16. makes chewing a pizza slice possible

_____17. aids in swallowing that pizza slice

_____18. enables you to hear Beethoven's Fifth

_____19. slows down your heart rate after a jog around campus

_____20. the nerve behind the shoulder-shrugging muscles

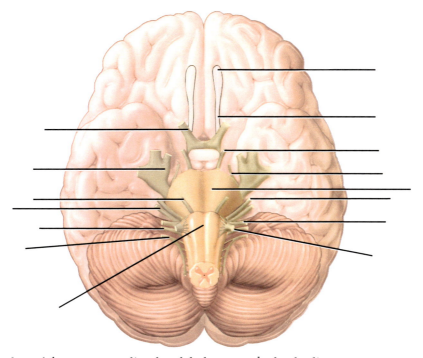

Place the number of the corresponding key label next to the leader line.

Key

1. optic nerve
2. abducens nerve
3. olfactory bulb
4. olfactory tract
5. pons
6. medulla oblongata
7. trigeminal nerve
8. vagus nerve

9. facial nerve
10. accessory nerve
11. oculomotor nerve
12. trochlear nerve
13. vestibulocochlear nerve
14. glossopharyngeal nerve
15. hypoglossal nerve

1. The _____ of the midbrain are involved with visual and auditory reflexes.

2. The control of water and electrolyte balance is effected by neurons of the _____.

3. The cleft that separates the two cerebral hemispheres is the _____.

4. Nuclei and ganglia are groups of neuron _____.

5. A fold on the surface of the cerebrum or cerebellum is called a _____.

6. What is the function of the meninges that surround the brain and spinal cord?

    _____

    _____

    _____

7. Name a body cavity innervated by the vagus nerve.

    _____

8. (a) Which neurons initiate voluntary movement?

    _____

    _____

    (b) Where do the cell bodies of these neurons originate?

    _____

    (c) When might you depend on these neurons in a college classroom?

    _____

    _____

    _____

    _____

    _____

Critical Thinking

1. A skull fracture may lead to a hematoma, a large area of clotted blood on the brain surface that may place excessive pressure on cerebral cortical neurons. If a hematoma caused visual impairment, on what lobe would it be impinging?

    _____

    _____

2. Explain why a stroke on the left side of the brain may cause motor problems on the right side of the body.

    _____

    _____

    _____

    _____

Notes

General Sensation

Exercise 15

PRE-LAB QUIZ

1. Converting the energy of a stimulus to a nerve impulse is known as
   a. adaptation.
   b. transduction.
   c. localization.
   d. conduction.

2. Which among the following skin locations will be *not* tested for sensitivity to touch in this lab session?
   a. back of leg
   b. palm of hand
   c. fingertip
   d. lips
   e. back of neck

3. Adaptation occurs when _____ to the somatosensory cortex.
   a. sensory receptors fire less frequently
   b. sensory receptors stop firing
   c. impulses are blocked en route
   d. a gradually weaker stimulus slows impulses

4. Which stimulus does not have a corresponding receptor in the skin?
   a. light pressure
   b. touch
   c. deep pressure
   d. stretch
   e. proprioceptive

5. Define *tactile localization*.

Our survival depends upon continually adjusting to the internal and external environments. Changes in these environments are called *stimuli.* **Sensory receptors** are nerve cells specialized for the detection of stimuli. Receptors convey a multitude of sensory messages to the central nervous system, which can then interpret the messages and react accordingly. It is the brain that makes possible *awareness* (sensation of a stimulus) and *perception* (interpretation of what the stimulus means).

Receptors of the general senses are widely distributed and are relatively simple structures. They respond to stimuli such as touch — the *tactile* sense — pressure, heat, cold, and pain. By contrast, receptors for the spe-cial senses — vision, hearing, equilibrium (balance), olfaction (smell), and gustation (taste) — are housed in more complex sense organs. (Special senses are covered in Exercise 16.)

The classification of receptors is based on (1) *location* (such as an external or internal part of the body), (2) *structure* (pain receptors are free nerve endings while many others are encapsulated), and (3) the types of *stimuli* that excite them (such as tactile: a tap on the shoulder, visual: a Monet painting, or auditory: a boom of thunder).

Exteroceptors, as their name implies, respond to stimuli in the external environment, such as a sudden temperature change, or the sensation of a

wind gust. They are of necessity close to the body surface and include cutaneous (skin), visual, and auditory receptors.

Interoceptors are located internally within the viscera, hence their synonym *visceroreceptors*. Some respond to stretch in the wall of hollow organs, as would occur during swallowing or stomach expansion. Interoceptors also include chemoreceptors on the tongue for taste perception and olfactory receptors in the nose for smell.

Proprioceptors detect internal stimuli arising in skeletal muscles and their tendons, and in joints and their ligaments. An example of proprioception is sensing limb position while walking. Sensing body movements via interoceptors is known as **kinesthesia**.

At the heart of sensory receptors are the *dendritic endings of sensory neurons*. In their simplest form, these are **free (nonencapsulated) nerve endings**. Free nerve endings respond mainly to temperature and pain stimuli.*

*Different types of receptors can respond to similar stimuli (such as intense pressure applied to the skin triggering a response from both pressure and touch receptors), but receptors typically tend to be specialists for which there is a preferred, or *adequate,* stimulus (for example, light rays for the retina of the eye). Overstimulation of receptors regardless of type can cause pain.

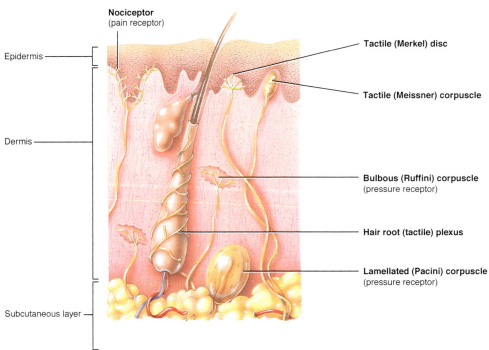

FIGURE 15-1. Structure and location of sensory receptors in the skin and subcutaneous layer.

Pain signals the potential for injury, making pain receptors — our **nociceptors** (Figure 15-1) — an indispensible part of the exteroceptor and interoceptor population.

Tactile (Merkel) discs are free nerve endings associated with epidermal cells. **Hair root (tactile) plexuses** are wound around the roots of hairs and fire impulses when the hairs are bent. Both types respond to light touch (Figure 15-1).

The **encapsulated nerve endings** (Figure 15-1) are enclosed by connective tissue and include:

- **tactile (Meissner) corpuscles** or **corpuscles of touch**, which are located in the dermis of hairless skin. These receptors respond to touch and also to vibrations, as when a car travels over a bumpy road. Vibrations are sensed when touch receptors fire rapid, repetitive impulses.

- **bulbous (Ruffini) corpuscles**, which are dermal receptors that respond to stretch (as when spreading the fingers apart) and deep pressure.

- **lamellated (Pacini) corpuscles** are named for the multilayered, onion-like connective tissue surrounding the dendrites (*lamella* = layer). They are found in the deepest region of the dermis and respond to deep pressure and vibrations.

Receptor Physiology

All sensory receptors convert stimulus energy to electrical impulses — a process known as **transduction**. As transducers, receptors enable information signaled by stimuli to be communicated within the nervous system. Awareness of the these stimuli provokes a response mediated by our effectors.

Comparing the Density of Cutaneous Receptors

Cutaneous receptors are distributed in pinpoint, or **punctiform**, fashion (Figure 15-2). Each receptor type creates a degree of sensitivity that varies with the density of the receptor population.

Each receptor's dendrites represents a **receptive field** (Figure 15-2). The receptive field of a cutaneous receptor is that particular part of the skin surface that when stimulated to threshold initiates a nerve impulse. The impulses from cutaneous receptors terminate in the primary somatosensory cortex, giving us awareness of the stimulus. This region of the brain (the postcentral gyrus) is organized into a body map so that we can feel from which skin area the stimulus originated. The somatosensory association cortex enables perception of the stimulus by interpreting its meaning.

Cutaneous Sensations

The sensory receptors of the skin convey information from *mechanical* stimuli (touch, pressure, and stretch), *thermal* stimuli (heat and cold), and *painful* stimuli. The density of these cutaneous receptors varies in two ways:

1. There are differences in the number of receptor types. For example, nociceptors for pain are the most numerous (averaging about 200 per cm^2).

2. There are regional differences for a given receptor. As an example, the skin of the sole of the foot is sparsely populated with touch receptors whereas the external genitalia have the highest density of touch receptors.

PROCEDURE 1

This experiment compares the density of cutaneous receptors for tactile and thermal receptors.

1. The subject should be seated comfortably with eyes closed.

2. The experimenter should be as noncommittal as possible, giving no indication of what stimulus is to be applied.

3. A rubber stamp is provided to mark a grid on the anterior aspect of the subject's forearm, just proximal to the wrist. Care should be taken to choose a site with as few hairs as possible.

4. Apply touch stimuli with a bristle, cold stimuli with a probe immersed in ice water, and heat stimuli with a probe from a warm (45°C) water bath. Alternately apply the stimuli (in no particular order) to a square within the grid. Be sure to wipe the immersed probes dry just prior to stimulation. The total number of touch, heat and cold stimuli applied should be the same.

5. In the data grid on the next page, use a "T" for a positive response to touch, and "C" and "H" for positive responses to the cold and heat stimuli respectively. Because receptors are randomly distributed, exciting these sensory neurons is a hit-or-miss proposition. It is therefore unlikely that all 36 squares will show positive responses to all three stimuli given their low intensity.

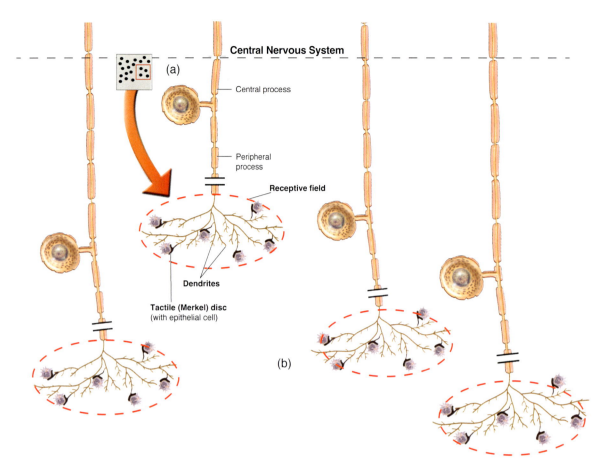

Central Nervous System

(a)

Central process

Peripheral process

Receptive field

Dendrites

Tactile (Merkel) disc
(with epithelial cell)

(b)

FIGURE 15-2. Punctiform distribution of sensory receptors in the skin. (a) A square centimeter of skin showing the average number of tactile (Merkel) discs, about 25 per cm². (b) A magnified view, showing several tactile discs and their receptive fields. Note that the receptor neuron's central process extends into the central nervous system, carrying information to the somatosensory cortex directly or via the spinal cord.

Data Grid for Cutaneous Receptors

proximal

distal

Which stimulus produced the highest number of responses? _____

Which stimulus produced the lowest number of responses? _____

PROCEDURE 2

Distribution of Skin Receptors for Touch

As noted, receptors for touch are not uniformly distributed on the body surface. Some areas of skin have a higher density of touch receptors than others and are therefore more sensitive to a particular touch stimulus. For example, the hand has a relatively high density of touch receptors and a sensitivity which is of obvious practical importance.

Two-Point Discrimination Test

The **two-point discrimination test** compares the sensitivity to touch across several body areas: palm of hand, back of hand, fingertip, calf, ventral forearm, and back of neck. Here's the protocol:

1. Seat the subject with eyes closed.

2. The experimenter will use a caliper or esthesiometer to apply a two-point stimulus to the subject's skin at various locations. For each location, start with the points completely together, and then increase their distance apart until the subject feels two distinct points. This is the **two-point threshold**. Be sure that the points are applied simultaneously. (To ensure objectivity, the experimenter should occasionally apply only one point.)

3. This test demonstrates that the more sensitive the area, the closer the compass points can be placed and still be felt as separate contacts. In the chart below, record the least distance in millimeters when the subject discriminates two separate sensations.

Two-Point Discrimination Test	
Skin Area Tested	**Two-Point Threshold (mm)**
Palm of hand	
Back of hand	
Fingertip	
Calf	
Ventral forearm	
Back of neck	

PROCEDURE 3

Tactile Localization

Tactile localization is determining where on the skin a tactile stimulus is applied. Areas with a high density of tactile receptors correlate well with accurate tactile localization. To test for tactile localization:

1. Seat the subject with eyes closed.

2. For each area cited in the tactile localization test table, the experimenter will begin the test by touching the skin with a fine-point black felt-tip marker.

3. The subject then attempts to match the point where the initial stimulus was applied using a red marker. Record the **localization error** by measuring the distance between the two markers in millimeters.

4. Repeat the test a second, then a third time. Average the errors of localization for each area and record this distance in the Testing Tactile Localization table.

Testing Tactile Localization	
Body Area Tested	**Average Error (mm)**
Palm of hand	
Fingertip	
Ventral forearm	
Back of hand	
Back of neck	

Does the error of localization diminish when the test is repeated? _____

Explain your answer.

_____

_____

_____

Which area had the smallest error of localization?

_____

Adaptation of Sensory Receptors

A sensory receptor is excited when a stimulus causes some alteration of its structure or physiology. When the applied stimulus remains constant over a period of time, the degree of change, and consequently the _frequency of action potentials fired by the receptor, gradually diminishes._ This results in a corresponding decrease in the intensity of the sensation, often to the point where the stimulus is no longer sensed at all. This phenomenon is known as **adaptation**.

Touch receptors are **mechanoreceptors**, that is, they are excited when a mechanical stimulus causes a deformation (change in shape) of the sensory neuron. If the initial application of the stimulus excites a sufficient number of receptors, a sensation of touch will be felt. When the stimulus that elicits a sensation is of low strength and is kept constant, adaptation of receptors may cause the sensation to disappear. (Note that adaptation is generalized across all receptors with one significant exception: For reasons of self-preservation, pain receptors are non-adapting.)

As you will see in the next procedure, receptors for touch adapt rather rapidly, a feature that limits the distraction of wearing a watch, jewelry, and clothing. Clothes that are lightweight and comfortable become hardly more noticeable to your tactile receptors than wearing nothing at all.

PROCEDURE 4

Adaptation of Touch Receptors

With the subject's eyes closed, the experimenter will place a penny on the anterior aspect of the forearm. Record how long the sensation persists. Once it has disappeared, add three more pennies on top of the first. Note how long the latter sensation persists.

Adaptation time for one coin   = _____ sec

Adaptation time for four coins   = _____ sec

Notes

Notes

General Sensation

NAME _____

LAB TIME / DATE _____

Receptor Physiology

Matching

Match the receptors in column B to their description in Column A.
(A letter may be used more than once.)

Column A

_____1. encapsulated touch receptor found in dermal layer of hairless skin

_____2. receptors that detect tastes in the mouth and aromas in the nose

_____3. receptors found in the viscera

_____4. cutaneous mechanoreceptors for touch that link to epidermal cells

_____5. free nerve endings throughout the body

_____6. general term for receptors located on or near the surface of the body

_____7. receptors that respond to physical damage to tissues

_____8. receptors in limbs that sense body position

Column B

a. kinesthetic receptors

b. tactile (Merkel) discs

c. interoceptors

d. exteroceptors

e. proprioceptors

f. tactile (Meissner) corpuscles

g. nociceptors

h. chemoreceptors

Cutaneous Receptors

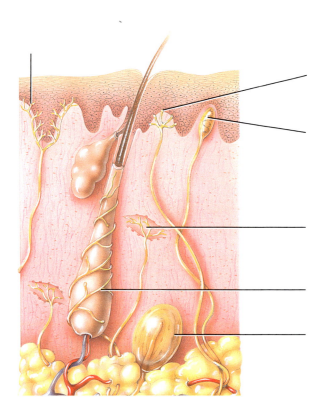

Place the number of the corresponding key label next to the leader line

Key

1. nociceptor

2. tactile (Merkel) disc

3. lamellated (Pacini) corpuscle

4. bulbous (Ruffini) corpuscle

5. tactile (Meissner) corpuscle

6. hair root plexus

1. What condition in a sensory receptor leads to adaptation?

   _____

   _____

2. Why are nociceptors non-adapting?

    _____

    _____

    _____

3a. Which of the tested areas had the lowest two-point threshold?

    _____

b. Why does this experimental finding make perfect functional sense?

    _____

    _____

4. Compare chemoreceptors with mechanoreceptors with regard to location and the stimuli to which they respond.

    _____

    _____

    _____

    _____

Critical Thinking

1. Why is the density of pain receptors the highest among sensory receptors?

    _____

    _____

    _____

2. Cold receptors are more numerous than those for heat. What do you think might be the evolutionary significance of this?

    _____

    _____

    _____

Notes

Special Senses

Exercise 16

OBJECTIVES

1. To identify the external and internal anatomy of the eye.
2. To explain the distinction between rods and cones regarding their location within the retina and visual perception.
3. To test for *visual acuity*.
4. To define *astigmatism* and test for it.
5. To test for *color blindness*.
6. To define *accommodation* and determine the *near point of vision*.
7. To observe *pupillary reflexes*.
8. To identify the external, middle, and internal anatomy of the ear.
9. To explain the function of the *spiral organ* of the *cochlea*.
10. To define *cataract, glaucoma, conjunctivitis, presbyopia* and *macular degeneration*.
11. To determine the prerequisites for taste reception by the tongue.
12. To determine which regions of the tongue are most responsive to the four primary tastes.
13. To define *sensorineural deafness* and *conduction deafness* and distinguish between them via the Weber and Rinne tests.
14. To determine reaction time to auditory and visual stimuli.
15. To describe the diagnostic advantage of the ophthalmoscope.

MATERIALS

Eye models
Eye anatomy chart
Snellen chart for visual acuity test

Color blindness plates
Penlights
Ophthalmoscope

(continued on next page)

PRE-LAB QUIZ

1. The eyeball layer that becomes the cornea anteriorly is the
   a. sclera.
   b. choroid.
   c. retina.
   d. zonule.
2. Adjusting the curvature of the lens for near viewing distances is known as
   _____.
3. Sound waves entering the external auditory meatus cause the _____ membrane to vibrate at the same frequency.
4. The transducers for hearing are the hair cells found
   a. in the oval window.
   b. in the cochlea.
   c. within the eighth cranial nerve.
   d. lining the middle ear.
5. Taste buds are found within _____, extensions of the tongue's mucosa.

MATERIALS (continued)

Ear models
Ear anatomy chart
Tuning forks
Cotton balls
Laboratory tissues
Sucrose granules
Acetic acid solution (1%)

Cotton swabs
Sodium chloride solution (10%)
Quinine sulfate solution (0.1%)
Sucrose solution (10%)
Reaction time equipment
Assorted raw foods, cubed

Functional Anatomy of the Eye

Receptors for light — our **photoreceptors** — are known as rods and cones. These sensory neurons, which are named for their shape, transduce (convert) light energy to nerve impulses. The impulses are conducted to the brain's occipital lobe where awareness and perception of visual images occurs. Refer to Figures 16-1 and 16-2 during your tour of eye anatomy:

- **Rods** allow us to see in dim light, distinguish shades of darkness, and recognize shapes and movement.

- **Cones** respond to bright light, allow us to see colors, and are responsible for sharpness of vision, or **visual acuity**.

Both rods and cones are found within the **retina**, the inner layer of the eyeball There are many more rods than there are cones to optimize photoreception when light is limited. Cones are most densely concentrated in the **fovea centralis**, the central area of the retina's **macula lutea** (MAK-yoo-luh LOO-tee-uh), which is itself centrally located within the retina. This concentration of cones makes the fovea the area of sharpest vision.

Macular degeneration, also known as **age-related macular disease (AMD)**, results in a loss of central vision, but not peripheral vision. Objects straight ahead cannot be seen clearly. Macular disease is a major cause of blindness in the elderly.

Both rods and cones are absent from the **optic disc**, or **blind spot**. This is the region where the nerve fibers of the photoreceptors meet the **optic nerve**, which conveys the visual impulses to the primary visual cortex. Covering and nourishing the retina is the highly vascular **choroid**, a thin, dark membrane which absorbs light rays so they cannot be reflected. (If the internal eyeball were reflective, light could not be properly focused onto the retina and vision would be blurred.)

The anterior portion of the choroid is the **ciliary body**, consisting mostly of smooth muscle that changes the shape of the lens to adjust for near and far vision. The

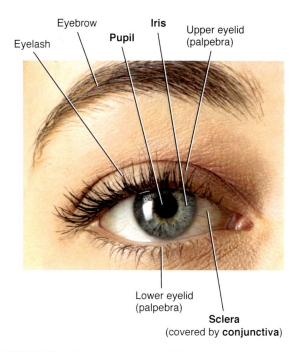

FIGURE 16-1. Surface anatomy of the right eye.

outermost layer of the eyeball is the **sclera**, a white fibrous tissue (the white of the eye). It covers all of the eye except for the anterior portion, the **cornea**. The transparent cornea allows light to enter and *refracts* (bends) it onto the retina. The mucous membrane covering the sclera, but not the cornea, is the **conjunctiva** (con-junk-TYE-vuh). Inflammation of the conjunctiva, from physical, chemical, or microbial causes, is **conjunctivitis**, in which the white of the eye becomes reddened and sore. A highly contagious form of conjunctivitis is called *pinkeye*.

Before reaching the photoreceptors on the retina, light must pass through several other structures:

- The **aqueous humor**, within the anterior chamber, is a watery fluid that bathes the eye, providing transport for nutrients and waste, and maintaining intraocular pressure. When the draining of fluid lags behind the production rate, fluid pressure increases. A critically high — and potentially damaging — intraocular pressure is known as **glaucoma**.

- The **pupil** is the black hole in the center of the **iris**, the colored portion of the external eye anatomy. The iris contains circular muscle fibers that dilate or constrict the pupil, and so controls the amount of light reaching the retina.

- Behind the iris and the pupil is the transparent **lens**. The lens is biconvex in shape and resembles a lentil. (The resemblance to this legume is embodied in *lenticular*, the adjective meaning "pertaining to the lens".) It is the eye's most refractive structure. The lens is comprised of flexible crystalline proteins attached to the processes of the ciliary body by **suspensory ligaments** (also known as *zonular fibers* or the *ciliary zonule*).

When the ciliary muscle relaxes, the suspensory ligaments pull the lens flatter, enabling it to focus light from distant objects.

When the ciliary muscle contracts, it pulls the choroid layer forward, lessening the tension on the suspensory ligaments and the lens. The lens curves outward, becoming more convex, and is able to sharply focus light from near objects. This process of the lens changing shape to compensate for near viewing distances is known as **accommodation**. (Figure 16-3).

Aging of the lens leads to deterioration of its proteins and progressive opacity, a condition known as **cataracts**. This cloudiness can ultimately obstruct vision to the point of blindness. Cataracts can only be treated by surgical replacement of the lens.

- The **vitreous humor** is a jellylike substance that fills the cavity between the lens and the retina. It helps maintain pressure and shape and keeps the retina in place.

PROCEDURE 1

Examining the Anatomy of the Eye
Study the eye models to acquaint yourself with the eye's internal and external anatomy. If available on the demo table, examine a human eye specimen.

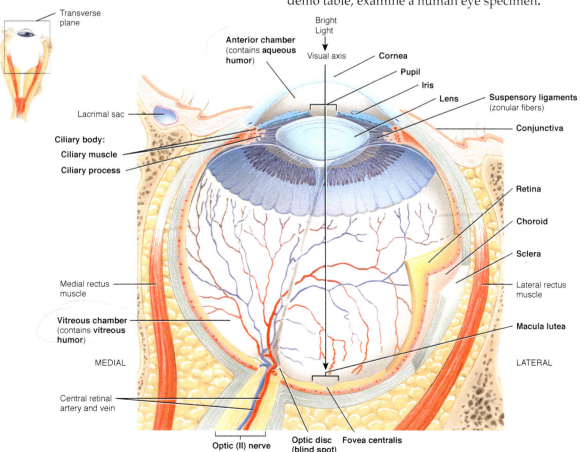

Superior view of transverse section of right eyeball

FIGURE 16-2. Anatomy of the eyeball.

Visual Acuity

To visualize an object, receptors in the photosensitive layer of the eye must transduce light energy from that object into electrical impulses and convey these impulses to the visual center of the brain. Whether this brain image is clear or blurred depends on the eye's ability to focus light onto its photoreceptors. In normal vision, **emmetropia**, the refractive (light-bending) surfaces of the eye focus light directly onto the photoreceptors (Figure 16-4a).

In nearsightedness, **myopia**, the optical image falls short of the receptors (Figure 16-4b). In farsightedness, **hyperopia**, an individual focuses beyond the normal focal point (Figure 16-4d). The familiar Snellen chart used by ophthalmologists is designed to present different sized letters for viewing at a given distance. The purpose is to compare the distance at which a normal eye sees that letter to the distance the individual being examined sees that letter. For instance, a normal eye sharply focuses the letter **E** shown below at a distance of 20 feet.

Visual acuity is expressed as the distance at which the individual sees a given letter clearly divided by the distance at which a normal eye can read the letter. An acuity of 20/100 indicates below normal vision — what a normal eye sees clearly at 100 feet can only be seen clearly by the person being examined at 20 feet. A ratio of 20/10, on the other hand, indicates above normal acuity.

E

Visual Acuity	
Corrected	**Uncorrected**

Left eye

Right eye

PROCEDURE 2

Measuring Visual Acuity: The Snellen Test

1. Stand at the floor marker 20 feet from the Snellen eye chart and cover one eye.

2. Guided line by line by a classmate, read down the chart as far as you can, calling out each letter. *Record the acuity ratio of the last letter line you can correctly identify in the Visual Acuity data table on this page.*

3. Repeat with the other eye and record.

4. If you wear glasses or contacts, repeat the test with your corrective lenses and record the corrected acuity for each eye.

Astigmatism and Color Blindness

Astigmatism is a common refractive defect of the eye caused by an irregularly shaped cornea or lens. As a result, light rays spread out over the retina instead of converging at a specific focal point.

Color blindness is the inherited inability to distinguish certain colors from one another. At the cellular level, one of the three types of cones is either absent or functions abnormally. The most common form is red-green color blindness, which can be traced to defective red or green cones. These individuals cannot distinguish between red and green. The incidence of color blindness is 1% for females and 4% of the male population.

PROCEDURE 3

Testing for Astigmatism

Put your own eyes to the test by examining an astigmatism chart (Figure 16-5). An astigmatic individual will see some of the radiating lines indistinctly while others appear sharply focused.

Testing for Color Blindness

To evaluate color perception, your instructor will provide Ishihara or other color test plates.

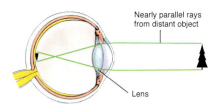

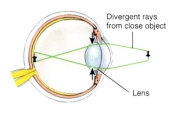

FIGURE 16-3. (a) The cornea and lens refract parallel light rays from distant objects so the image is focused on the retina. (b) In accommodation, the lens becomes more spherical, which increases the refraction of divergent light rays entering the eye.

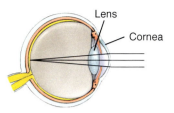

(a) Normal (emmetropic) eye

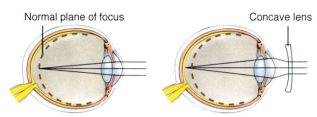

(b) Nearsighted (myopic) eye, uncorrected   (c) Nearsighted (myopic) eye, corrected

(d) Farsighted (hyperopic)   (e) Farsighted (hyperopic) eye, corrected

FIGURE 16-4. Refraction abnormalities in the eyeball and their correction.

PROCEDURE 4

Near Point Determination

To function effectively, the eye has to make rapid adjustments to changes in viewing distance. As shown in Figure 16-3, light rays reaching the eyeball from a far object are parallel. By contrast, light rays from objects viewed nearby tend to be divergent. These differences in the orientation of incoming light rays necessitate a change in lens curvature to keep the retinal image sharp. Changes in lens contour are made possible by the elasticity of the lens proteins and the interaction of ciliary muscle and suspensory ligaments. Recall that accommodation is the increase in lens curvature to sharply focus light rays from near objects.

The **near point of vision** is the minimum distance from the eye at which an image can be clearly focused with maximum accommodation. Test for your near point as follows:

1. Close the right eye. With the open eye, focus on a printed letter held out at arm's distance. (The **E** on page 316 may be used for this test.)

2. Gradually bring the letter closer to the eye until the clarity of the image just begins to fade.

3. Record the distance between letter and eye as the near point of that eye.

   Near point of left eye = _____ cm

4. Repeat the procedure with the other eye.

   Near point of right eye = _____ cm

5. Compare your results with the expected near point for your age in Table 16-1.

One explanation for the tendency toward farsightedness with progressing age is a loss in lens elasticity. Older eyes are therefore less able to accommodate for near vision. This condition is known as **presbyopia**.

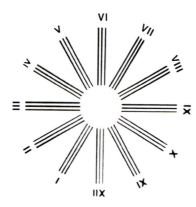

FIGURE 16-5. Chart for detecting astigmatism.

Age (years)	Near Point (cm)
10	9
20	10
30	12
40	18
50	53
60	83
70	100

TABLE 16-1. Correlation of Age and Normal Near Point Values

What change occurred in pupillary diameter?

_____

PROCEDURE 5

Pupillary Reflexes

As you have seen in Procedure 4, the photoreceptors of the eye initiate an accommodation reflex response to viewing distance. There is also a reflex adjustment to light intensity. Both reflexes are designed to adjust the light that enters the pupil to an optimal level. This is accomplished by the smooth muscle of the iris constricting or dilating the pupil.

Light (Photopupillary) Reflex

1. Note the approximate size of the subject's pupillary diameter under ambient lighting.

2. Use an index card to shield one of the subject's eyes. Then, shine a light beam from a penlight into the other eye at a distance of about 15 centimeters (6 inches).

What change occurred in pupillary diameter?

_____

Near (Accommodation Pupillary) Reflex

1. Have the subject focus on an object across the room. Note the approximate size of the subject's pupillary diameter.

2. Hold an object about 15 centimeters away from the subject and ask the subject to focus on it. Observe the pupillary diameter. This pupillary response and convergence of the eyeballs accompany accommodation of the lens to near objects.

Examining the Retina with an Ophthalmoscope (Optional)

The **ophthalmoscope** is an instrument that enables visualization of the **fundus**, the part of the eye's interior opposite the pupil. Examination of the fundus can reveal abnormalities of the optic nerve and disc, retina (such as detachment), and retinal blood vessels (as would occur in diabetics).

The ophthalmoscope (Figure 16-6) consists of two lenses, one on the subject's side and another on the opposite for the examiner. A thumb-operated **focusing wheel** sharpens the retinal image. An **aperture dial** allows the viewer to vary the opening through which light passes into the eye. The light intensity can be adjusted by a **rheostat control** at the top of the handle.

PROCEDURE 6

Conducting an Examination with an Ophthalmoscope

Note: Use the ophthalmoscope only under the supervision of your instructor.

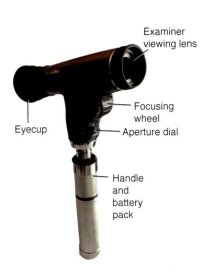

FIGURE 16-6. The Welch Allyn PanOptic ophthalmoscope. *a fundoscope.*

- Examiner viewing lens
- Focusing wheel
- Aperture dial
- Eyecup
- Handle and battery pack

FIGURE 16-7. Examination of a subject's left eye. A cell phone can be used to record an image of the fundus.

1. Set the aperture dial to the green line (small aperture) position. The subject should be seated and looking straight ahead at a distant object in the room. Begin examining the subject's left eye by standing or sitting on the subject's left side.

2. Look through the ophthalmoscope with your thumb on the focusing wheel and focus on an object 10-15 feet away.

3. Turn on the illuminator by depressing the green button on the rheostat control and rotating the dial 90 degrees clockwise.

4. Position the ophthalmoscope about 15 cm (6 inches) from the subject's eye. Direct the light into the pupil at a 10-15 degree angle, on the temporal side, *not directly into the pupil*. Once illuminated, you will see the fundus as a red circle. *The subject should continue to look straight ahead and not into the ophthalmoscope.*

5. Slowly follow the red circle and advance the ophthalmoscope toward the subject until the eyecup makes contact with the subject's brow. Compress the eyecup to about half its length to optimize the view (Figure 16-7). (It may help to steady the instrument by placing your hand on the subject's forehead.)

6. Once you have a view of the fundus, rotate the focusing wheel until you have a sharp image of the optic disc, a light-colored circle with blood vessels radiating from the center (Figure 16-8).

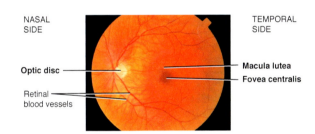

NASAL SIDE — TEMPORAL SIDE — Optic disc — Macula lutea — Fovea centralis — Retinal blood vessels

FIGURE 16-8. The fundus of the left eye as seen through an ophthalmoscope.

7. Observe the macula by directing the light beam about one optic disc diameter to the temporal side of the fundus. Alternatively, having the subject look directly into the scope will mimic the normal bright light path to the macula and illuminate it. (See Figure 16-2.) The macula is a darker area to the temporal side of the optic disc and is without visible blood vessels. Note the fovea centralis at the center of the macula.

SAFETY PRECAUTION
Do not examine the macula for more than a second at a time. Limit total viewing time to 30 seconds.

8. Switch places with your lab partner and have your left retina examined. After the procedure, shut off the rheostat control by rotating the dial counterclockwise until the green button pops up.

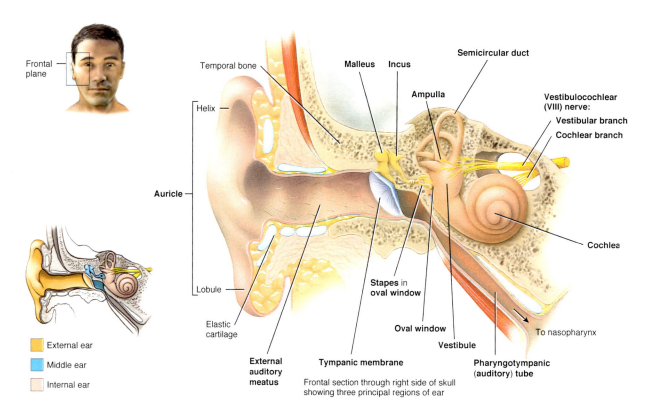

Frontal plane

Temporal bone
Malleus   Incus
Semicircular duct
Ampulla
Vestibulocochlear (VIII) nerve:
Vestibular branch
Cochlear branch
Helix
Auricle
Cochlea
Lobule
Elastic cartilage
Stapes in oval window
Oval window
Vestibule
To nasopharynx
External auditory meatus
Tympanic membrane
Pharyngotympanic (auditory) tube

Frontal section through right side of skull showing three principal regions of ear

External ear
Middle ear
Internal ear

FIGURE 16-9. Anatomy of the ear.

Anatomy of the Ear

Hearing receptors are located in the **internal ear**. The ear is structured so that sound waves are directed through the **external auditory meatus** of the **external ear** to the **tympanic membrane**, or **eardrum**, causing it to vibrate at the same frequency. This in turn sets off vibrations of the three tiny bones of the **middle ear**.

- The first of these bones, the **malleus**, is attached to the tympanic membrane.

- The middle bone is the **incus**.

- The innermost bone, the **stapes**, presses against a flexible membrane, the **oval window**, separating the middle ear from the fluid-filled tubes and chambers of the internal ear. Sound vibrations are in this manner transmitted from the air-filled middle ear cavity to the fluid-filled internal ear.

PROCEDURE 7

The middle ear is connected to the nose and nasopharynx by the **pharyngotympanic** (**auditory** or **Eustachian**) **tube**. By equalizing air pressure on both sides

of the tympanic membrane, this tube prevents abrupt changes in air pressure from rupturing the eardrum or dampening volume.

The **cochlea** is shaped like a snail's shell and contains the sensory receptors for hearing within the **spiral organ**. Sound vibrations from the stapes cause pressure waves within the fluid medium of this organ and movements of its **hair cell**s. The hair cells transduce mechanical vibrations into electrical signals and nerve impulses are then communicated to the brain via the **cochlear branch** of the vestibulocochlear nerve. The two branches of the vestibulocochlear nerve or cranial nerve VIII, pass through the temporal bone surrounding the internal and middle ear.

Pitch, or frequency, of a sound is discriminated by the spiral organ: certain pitches, for example the bass notes on a piano keyboard, stimulate particular hair cells and not others.
Loudness, or amplitude is discriminated by the primary auditory cortex of the temporal lobe. Loud sounds send more impulses per second to the brain than soft sounds. The auditory association area thus perceives an explosion as loud and a shushing librarian as soft.

The **vestibule** of the internal ear branches off into three **semicircular ducts**. Sensory receptors, tiny hair cells within the vestibule and the **ampulla** (the enlarged portion) of each of the semicircular ducts, provide the sense of *equilibrium* or balance. Sensory fibers leading from these receptor cells form the **vestibular branch** of the **vestibulocochlear nerve**.

PROCEDURE 8

Examining the Anatomy of the Ear
Study the ear models and chart and in particular the structures indicated in Figure 16-9 in the review section.

Tests for Sensorineural and Conduction Deafness
Hearing loss can be attributed to either a (1) malfunction of structures that conduct sound vibrations to the internal ear: **conduction deafness**, or (2) a problem with sensory structures that transduce sound vibrations or carry nerve impulses to the brain: **sensorineural deafness**.

PROCEDURE 9

The following tests are used to determine whether there is a sensory or conductive abnormality in the hearing apparatus. *Deafness* in this context means partial hearing loss.

The Weber Test
1. Strike a tuning fork against the hard rubber device provided on the demo table to produce vibrations.

2. Having the subject hold the tuning fork against the *glabella*, the area between the bridge of the nose and the forehead, and ask the subject where the sound seems to be coming from.

A person with normal hearing will localize the sound as coming from the midline of the face. A person with middle ear dysfunction — conduction deafness — will perceive the sound better in the defective ear because the ambient room noise interferes with the perception of sound in the normal ear, but not in the dysfunctional ear. To simulate middle ear deafness, plug one ear with cotton before conducting the Weber Test. See Table 16-2 for a summary of Weber Test interpretations.

The Rinne Test

1. Have the subject plug with cotton the ear that will not be tested.

2. Once again strike a tuning fork against the hard rubber and place the handle of the vibrating tuning fork on the subject's mastoid process at the level of the upper portion of the ear canal.

3. Hold the tuning fork there until it is no longer heard by the subject. Then place it in front of the auditory meatus, with the U-shaped side of the fork perpendicular to the subject's skull, and ask the subject if a sound is still audible.

A person with normal hearing will hear the sound conducted through air a few seconds after it is no longer audible through bone. A person with conduction deafness, however, will hear the sound as long or in some cases longer, by bone conduction. Although a person with nerve deafness will hear sound longer by air conduction, the sound must be louder for any

Condition	Finding	
	Weber Test	**Rinne Test**
No hearing loss	No lateralization	Sound perceived longer by air than by bone conduction
Conduction deafness	Lateralization to the poorer ear	Sound perceived as long or longer by bone conduction
Sensorineural	Lateralization to the better ear	Sound perceived longer by air than by bone conduction

TABLE 16-2. Interpretation of the Weber and Rinne Tests.

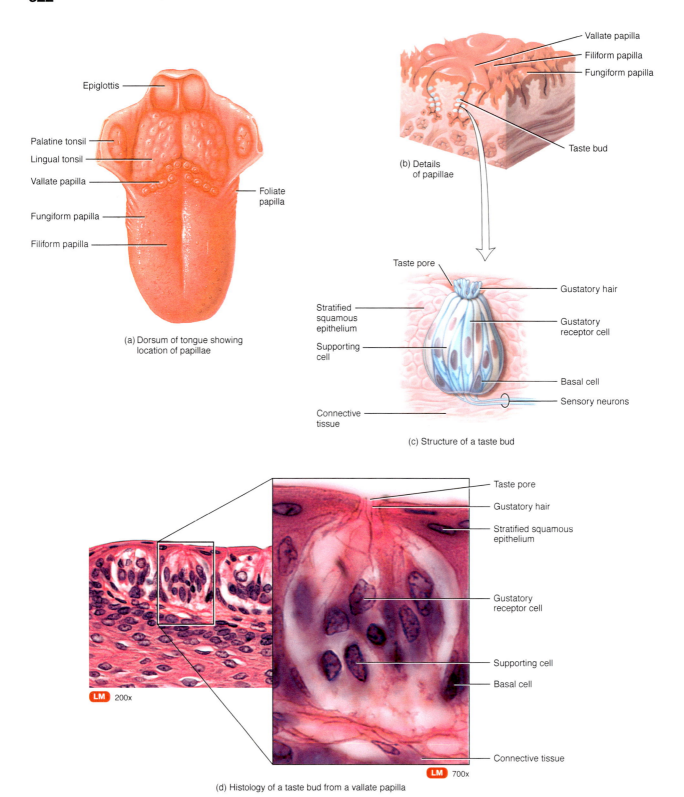

(a) Dorsum of tongue showing location of papillae

(b) Details of papillae

(c) Structure of a taste bud

(d) Histology of a taste bud from a vallate papilla

FIGURE 16-10. The relationship of gustatory receptor cells in taste buds to tongue papillae. The names assigned to the papillae are based on their shape: *vallate* **= a raised edge surrounding a depression;** *fungiform* **= shaped like a mushroom;** *filiform* **= shaped like a filament, and** *foliate* **= shaped like a leaf.**

hearing to occur at all. Refer again to Table 16-2 for a summary of Rinne Test interpretations.

Gustation (Taste)

The chemoreceptors specialized for transducing the chemical stimuli that enter the mouth are the **taste buds** (Figure 16-10). Most of our taste buds are found on the tongue within elevations called **papillae** (puh-PILL-ee; singular: **papilla**). In this experiment, you will discover why tasting is impossible on a dry tongue, and where on the tongue chemoreception for each of the four basic, or primary, tastes is most acute. Note: Charting a distinct "tongue map" is not a feasible objective because all taste buds respond to all primary tastes to some degree.

In the early 20th century, gustation science postulated *umami* as a fifth basic taste. Umami, a loanword from the Japanese meaning "pleasant savory taste", is related to the compound glutamate and excites glutamate receptors within taste buds. Foods high in glutamate, and therefore high on the umami index, include tomatoes and mushrooms.

PROCEDURE 10

Determining the Distribution of Taste Receptors (Optional)

1. Dry the subject's tongue with a clean tissue and separate a few granules of sucrose (table sugar) on it. Note the latent period needed before the sugar can be tasted.

2. Have the subject rinse the mouth and once again dry the tongue with a tissue. Moisten the tip of a cotton applicator with one of the four solutions listed below and apply the solution lightly to the tip, sides, back, and middle of the tongue. Record with a check mark where each taste is perceived greatest by the subject in the chart below. After each test, rinse the mouth with water and repeat with another solution until all four have been tested.

   (a)   quinine sulfate: bitter
   (b)   sucrose: sweet
   (c)   acetic acid: sour
   (d)   sodium chloride: salty

TABLE 16-3. The Distribution of Taste Receptors

Tongue Regions Where Basic Taste Sensations are Greatest				
	Bitter	Sweet	Sour	Salty
Tip				
Sides				
Back				
Middle				

Examining the Combined Effects of Texture and Smell on Taste Perception

1. The volunteers for this experiment will sit with eyes closed and nostrils pinched shut with the fingers or a nose clip.

2. The subject will now be served an assortment of cubed raw or minimally processed foods by a waitperson du jour. The server should wear disposable lab gloves and gently bring each food sample to the subject's mouth with a toothpick. Do not in any way hint at the identity of these samples.

3. The subject will proceed to identify the cube by manipulating the sample in the following sequence:

   - FIRST: Roll the food in the mouth with the tongue to ascertain its texture.

   - SECOND: Chew the food sample. Identify the food if possible.

   - THIRD: If the subject cannot identify the food to this point, unblock the nostrils and continue chewing to attempt an identification of the sample.

Record your results in Table 16-4.

With which food was the sense of smell most critical for an identification?

_____

Reaction Time

The protocols detailed below use a reaction time recorder to measure a subject's response time to visual and auditory stimuli in milliseconds.

Visual Reaction Time

1. Instruct the subject to watch for a randomly delivered red light stimulus and to press the disc-

TABLE 16-4. The Combined Effects of Texture and Smell on Taste Perception

Food Identification by Texture and Smell				
Food tested	Texture only	Chewing with nostrils closed	Chewing with nostrils open	Food Identification Unsuccessful

shaped response pad as soon as the light appears. This stops the timer; the reaction time in milliseconds will appear on the display. (Note The instructor must place the stimulus trigger out of sight.)

2. Complete ten time trials and record the average reaction time in Table 16-5.

Auditory Reaction Time

1. Instruct the subject to listen for a randomly delivered buzzer tone and to press the response pad as soon as the tone is heard. Once again, pressing the pad will stop the timer and the reaction time will appear.

2. Complete ten time trials and record the average reaction time in Table 16-5.

The Effect of Caffeine on Reaction Time

Caffeine can increase the speed of information processing in the nervous system and thereby decrease reaction time. (See the Clinical Application, *Caffeine: How Does It Work*?)

1. The subject for this procedure must complete the visual and auditory reaction time experiments in the section above with *no prior caffeine consumption for at least eight hours.*

2. After recording the un-caffeinated time trials, the subject drinks a 12-ounce cup of brewed coffee. [Table sugar (sucrose) and milk sugar (lactose) should be minimized since they may be uncontrolled variables in the experiment.] Wait 20-30 minutes if the subject has an empty stomach or 45 minutes if the subject has recently eaten. Repeat the reaction time procedures and record all data in the Reaction Times chart below (Table 16-5).

What was the percentage change in visual reaction time? (Preface the percentage by a plus sign for an increase or a minus sign for a decrease.)_____%

What was the percentage change in auditory reaction time?_____%

Which pathway — visual or auditory — was faster?

_____

Explain your answer.

_____

_____

_____

TABLE 16-5. Visual and Auditory Reaction Times Before and After Caffeine

Reaction Times (milliseconds)				
	Light		Sound	
Stimulus	Before Caffeine	After Caffeine	Before Caffeine	After Caffeine
1				
2				
3				
4				
5				
6				
7				
8				
9				
10				
Average				

Clinical Application
Caffeine: How Does It Work?

Caffeine is the most widely consumed central nervous system stimulant. Its name is derived from *café*, the French word for coffee. Its effects on brain chemistry make us more alert and cognitively sharper, which helps explain why it is consumed on a daily basis by an estimated 90% of all adults in the U.S.

Caffeine's most important mechanism of action is to blunt the effect of *adenosine*, a breakdown product of ATP that makes us mentally and physically sluggish. Adenosine acts like an inhibitory neurotransmitter to suppress neuronal activity.

When we are awake, brain neurons and glial cells consume large amounts of ATP, causing adenosine to accumulate faster than it is metabolized. By the end of a long day, prolonged wakefulness has raised its concentration, and as adenosine levels increase, we become progressively more sleepy. During sleep, the metabolism of adenosine gets ahead of its production. After a good night's sleep, the decline in adenosine concentration signals that we are rested.

Caffeine works by blocking membrane receptors for adenosine. The molecular structure of caffeine is similar to that of adenosine, allowing caffeine to "lock in" to the adenosine receptors, but without activating them and triggering adenosine's inhibitory effects. Caffeine, on the contrary, blocks the inhibitory action of adenosine at synapses. This synaptic interference allows excitatory neurotransmitters to facilitate impulse transmission in circuits related to wakefulness and cognition. Its action as an adenosine antagonist is the key to its stimulant effects.

The effects of caffeine vary from person to person. Especially sensitive individuals may experience caffeine's stimulant effects at lower doses, for a longer time, and more demonstrably (as in "coffee jitters"). The response to caffeine also depends greatly on how much sleep one has had. When sleep deprived, say from a long night studying A&P, caffeine can counteract the relatively high adenosine levels still in your brain and bring you to a state of wakefulness approaching normal. After many hours of blissful slumber, however, that *grande* from Starbucks may put some of us into overdrive.

Special Senses

NAME _____

LAB TIME/DATE _____

Functional Anatomy of the Eye

Matching
Match the term in Column B with its description in Column A.

Column A

_____1. contains muscle of accommodation

_____2. the protective white of the eye

_____3. nourishing fluid in anterior chamber

_____4. photoreceptive layer

_____5. area of greatest visual acuity

_____6. the eye's most refractive structure

_____7. blind spot

_____8. colored structure surrounding pupil

_____9. convex anterior refractive structure

_____10. pigmented vascular layer

Column B

a. choroid

b. lens

c. fovea centralis

d. sclera

e. iris

f. optic disc

g. cornea

h. ciliary body

i. aqueous humor

j. retina

Anatomy of the Eye

Place the number of the corresponding key label next to the leader line.

Key

1. cornea

2. optic nerve

3. suspensory ligaments

4. ciliary muscle

5. lens

6. aqueous humor
   (within anterior chamber)

7. vitreous humor

8. iris

9. fovea centralis

10. retina

11. sclera

12. choroid

13. pupil

14. macula lutea

15. conjunctiva

16. optic disc

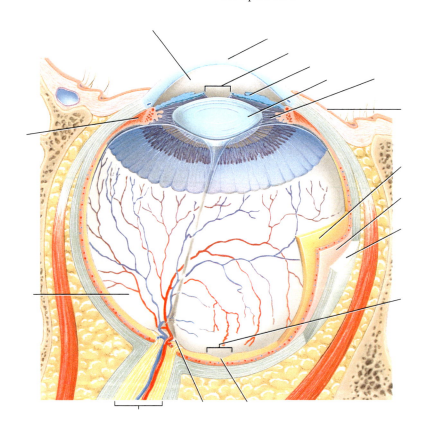

The Lens and Refraction of Light

Place the key word in the appropriate blank.

Key

1. increased
2. decreased
3. loose
4. taut
5. contracted
6. relaxed

During distant vision, the ciliary muscle is _____ , the suspensory ligaments are

_____ , the convexity of the lens is _____ , and light

refraction is _____ .

During near vision, the ciliary muscle is _____ , the suspensory ligaments

are _____ , the convexity of the lens is _____ , and

light refraction is _____ .

Trace the path of a beam of bright light through the eye, naming all structures it passes through en route to its destination in the retina.

_____

_____

_____

Anatomy of the Ear

Matching

Match the term in Column B with its description in Column A.

Column A

_____1. transmits vibrational energy from an ossicle to fluid of internal ear

_____2. middle ossicle

_____3. canal within external ear that conducts sound waves to middle ear

_____4. vibrates sympathetically with sound waves from external ear

_____5. organ of equilibrium that maintains balance

_____6. passageway between throat and middle ear cavity that equalizes air pressure on both sides of eardrum

_____7. ossicle that attaches to eardrum

_____8. ossicle that attaches to membrane of internal ear

_____9. the ear's most external structure

_____10. organ containing hair cells that transmit auditory impulses to eighth cranial nerve

Column B

a. cochlea

b. malleus

c. stapes

d. incus

e. auricle

f. external auditory meatus

g. semicircular canals

h. oval window

i. tympanic membrane

j. pharyngotympanic (auditory) tube

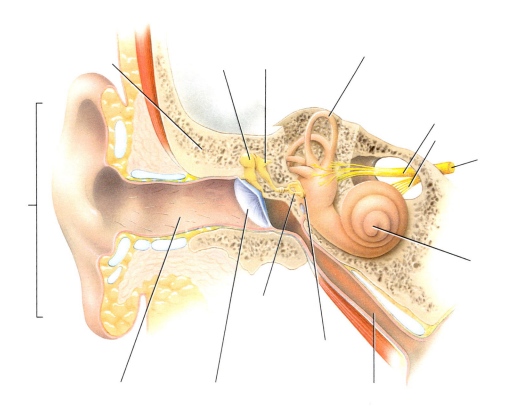

Anatomy of the Ear

Place the number of the corresponding key label next to the leader line.

Key

1. cochlea
2. temporal bone
3. tympanic membrane
4. incus
5. stapes
6. malleus
7. semicircular duct

8. cochlear branch of CN VIII
9. external auditory meatus
10. pharyngotympanic tube
11. vestibular branch of CN VIII
12. oval window
13. auricle
14. vestibulocochlear nerve

Trace the path of a sound vibration from the external auditory meatus to the vestibulocochlear nerve.

_____

_____

_____

_____

_____

Critical Thinking

1. Why would reading continuously for several hours lead to an "eyestrain" headache? (Hint: Consider the status of the ciliary muscle.)

_____

_____

_____

_____

_____

2. Auditory reaction time is theoretically faster than visual reaction time. The experimental data support this premise in almost every case.

Why is auditory reaction time faster? (Compare the auditory and visual pathways from sensory receptors to destination in the cerebral cortex. Use your textbook if necessary.)

_____

_____

_____

_____

_____

_____

_____

_____

Glossary

The glossary has been designed as reference and pronunciation guide keyed to the technical words encountered in this manual. A phonetic guide to pronunciation follows all but the most familiar words. Diacritical marks have been eliminated and replaced by syllables that are self-pronouncing. The syllable where the major accent falls is written in CAPITAL letters; the minor accent, if there is one, is signified by two apostrophe marks side-by-side (").

When scientific terms are sensibly constructed, convey a reasonable amount of information, and are in widespread use, they are worth the trouble to learn. In many cases, they are actually a shortcut to expressing or understanding an idea. However, learning scientific words can be exceedingly difficult (and downright boring) if one attempts rote memorization and overlooks the patterns and similarities within the English language.

The task is greatly simplified by keeping an eye out for common prefixes, suffixes, and root words. Many such fragments make repeat appearances and thus provide keys to recognizing old words and deciphering new ones.

As an example, consider the prefix *peri*, which translates as "around." Placed before *kardia*, the Greek root for heart, the term pericardium (the protective sac around the heart) is coined. In combination with *os*, the Latin root for bone, periosteum (a membrane surrounding bone tissue) is derived. Everyday words very often reflect their European ancestry, as in periscope and perimeter. The majority of words used to describe human form and function are of Greek and Latin origin.

In each of the preceding examples, a compound structure is evident. Generally speaking, a root (often in a combining form ending with a vowel) is linked to a prefix and/or suffix to produce a word not as mysterious as it may first appear.

A Pronouncing Glossary for Anatomy and Physiology

abdomen (AB-doe-mun or ab-DOE-mun) The region between the diaphragm and pelvis.

abdominopelvic (ab-dom"-ih-noe-PEL-vik) **cavity** The cavity inferior to the diaphragm that is subdivided into a superior abdominal cavity and an inferior pelvic cavity.

abduction (ab-DUK-shun) Movement away from the midline of the body.

absorption (ub-SORP-shun or ub-ZORP-shun) In physiology, the transport of fluid across cell membranes and into the circulation.

accommodation (uh-com-ih-DAY-shun) A change in the shape of the eye lens so that vision is more acute; an adjustment of the lens to changes in the distance between eye and object from distant to near.

acetabulum ("ass-ih-TAB-yoo-lum) The rounded cavity on the external surface of the coxal (hip) bone that receives the head of the femur.

acetylcholine (uh-"seat-ul-KOE-leen) A peripheral and central nervous system neurotransmitter. In the PNS, it stimulates skeletal muscle contraction by initiating an action potential at the neuromuscular junction; abbreviated ACh.

Achilles (uh-KIL-eez) **reflex**. See CALCANEAL REFLEX

acid Any substance which releases free hydrogen ions in a solution or which reacts with a base to form a salt. In the latter reaction, the hydrogen of the acid is replaced by a positive ion.

acid-base balance A state of equilibrium between acidic and basic substances in the blood and other body fluids.

acidosis (as-uh-DOE-sus). A condition of abnormally high acidity of the blood and tissues.

acinus (A-suh-nus). One of the small sacs lined with secretory cells found within an exocrine gland; plural: acini (A-suh-nye)

acoustic (uh-KOOS-stik). See AUDITORY.

acromion (uh-KROE-mee-un). The lateral triangular projection of the spine of the scapula, forming the point of the shoulder and articulation with the clavicle.

action potential The change in electrical potential of a nerve or muscle cell membrane following excitation by a threshold-level stimulus. It is an electrical signal propagated along a the plasma membrane.

acuity (uh-KYOO-uh-tee) Clearness of sharpness of hearing or vision.

adaptation (ad"-ap-TAY-shun) 1. A decline in the frequency of sensory nerve action potentials when a receptor is stimulated continuously. 2. The adjustment of the pupil of the eye to variations in light intensity.

adduction (uh-DUK-shun) Movement toward the midline of the body.

adipocyte (AD-dih-po-site) A fat cell.

adipose (AD-dih-pose) **tissue** Connective tissue that stores fat within adipocytes.

adenohypophysis ("ad-un-oh-hy-POF-uh-sus) The anterior portion of the pituitary gland (hypophysis) and the source of the hormones GH, TSH, LH, FSH, and ACTH.

adventitia (ad-vun-TISH-uh) The outermost connective tissue covering a structure.

aerobic (air-OH-bik) Living, active, or occurring only in the presence of oxygen.

afferent (AF-uh-runt) Designating nerves or blood vessels leading inward to a central part.

alimentary (al-uh-MENT-uh-ree) Pertaining to nutrition or the digestive organs.

alkalosis (al-kuh-LOE-sus) A condition of abnormally high alkalinity of the blood and tissues.

angstrom (ANG-strum) One tenth of a millimicrometer or about one two hundred fifty millionth of an inch.

anion (AN-eye-un) An ion carrying a negative charge.

antagonist (an-TA-guh-nist) A muscle that acts in opposition to a prime mover (agonist).

anterior (an-TIR-ee-ur) In front of; pertaining to the front side of the body; ventral.

apex (AY-peks) The narrowed or pointed end of a structure.

apical (AY-pih-kul) 1. Relating to the apex of a structure. 2. Situated at the distal (free) end of a cell; compare BASAL.

aponeurosis (ap-uh-noo-ROE-sus) A sheet-like, tendinous connective tissue enclosing a muscle, or joining a muscle to a part of the skeleton.

appendicular skeleton (ap-un-DIK-kyoo-lur) The bones of the upper and lower extremities (limbs), and the shoulder and pelvic girdles.

aqueous (AY-kwee-us) **humor** The transparent, watery fluid that fills the anterior cavity of the eye between the cornea and lens.

arachnoid mater (uh-RAK-noyd MAYT-ur) Literally, web-like mother; specifically, the middle of the three membranes (meninges) which cover the brain and spinal cord; also called ARACHNOID.

areolar (uh-REE-uh-lur) **tissue** A type of loose connective tissue that attaches the skin to underlying tissues and which serves as a supportive packing material around various organs.

arm The region of the upper extremity from the shoulder to the forearm.

articular (ar-TIK-kyoo-lur) Pertaining to joints of the skeleton.

articulation (ar-tik-kyuh-LAY-shun) A joint between bones or cartilages in the skeleton.

aspect Facing in a certain direction. *Example:* The dorsal aspect of the thoracic spine has a convex curvature.

astigmatism (uh-STIG-muh-tiz-um) A defect of the refractive system of the eye (usually the cornea), the result of which is a blurred image due to the failure of light rays to meet at a focal point.

auditory (AUH-duh-tor-ee) Pertaining to sound or the sense of hearing; also: ACOUSTIC.

autonomic ("awt-uh-NOM-ik) **nervous system** A part of the nervous system that innervates smooth and cardiac muscle and glandular tissues and which exerts involuntary control over these structures.

axilla (ag-ZIL-uh or ak-SIL-uh) The armpit.

axial (AKS-ee-ul) **skeleton** The bones of the head and trunk: the skull, vertebral column and thoracic cage.

axon (AKS-on) The branch of a nerve cell through which impulses are carried away from the cell body; the conducting portion of a nerve cell.

basal (BAY- zul) 1. Relating to the base of a structure. 2. Relating to the proximal end of a cell; compare APICAL. 3. Pertaining to the lower layers of a stratified tissue.

basal ganglia (BAY-zul GANG-glee-uh) See BASAL NUCLEI.

basal nuclei (BAY-zul NOO-klee-eye) Four masses of gray matter located deep in the cerebral hemispheres which control involuntary skeletal muscle movements.

basement membrane A thin layer of modified connective tissue that anchors epithelial cells to underlying connective tissue.

biceps (BY-ceps) A muscle having two heads of origin; See BICEPS BRACHII and BICEPS FEMORIS.

biceps brachii (BY-ceps BRAY-kee-eye) A muscle of the anterior arm that flexes the forearm.

biceps femoris (BY-ceps FEM-or-iss) One of the hamstring muscles lying on the posterolateral aspect of the femur; it extends the thigh and flexes the leg.

biconcave (by-kon-CAVE) Curved inwardly on both sides.

biconvex (by-con-VEKS) Bulging outwardly on both sides; used especially to describe the shape of the eye's lens.

brachial (BRAY-kee-ul) Pertaining to the arm (from shoulder to elbow).

brachialis (bray-kee-AL-us) A muscle of the anterior arm, deep to the biceps, that flexes the forearm.

buccal (BUK-ul) Pertaining to the cheek or mouth.

buccinator (BUK-sih-nay-tor) A facial muscle that compresses the cheek.

buffer (BUF-er) A chemical that tends to resist changes in pH.

calcaneus (kal-KAY-nee-us) The heel bone.

calcaneal (kal-KAY-nee-ul) **reflex** Contraction of calf muscles and plantar flexion of the foot following a tap on the calcaneal tendon.

calibration (kal-ih-BRAY-shun) The standardization of a measuring instrument so that unknown values may be accurately determined.

canal A narrow tube, channel, or passageway.

canaliculus (can-ul-IK-yoo-lus) A tiny tubular channel found in osseus tissue that supplies intercellular fluid to bone cells.

cancellous (KAN-sel-us) **bone** See SPONGY BONE.

carpal (KAR-pul) Pertaining to the wrist (carpus).

cartilage (KART-ul-ij) A white, translucent, semirigid connective tissue which lends support to the skeletal and respiratory systems.

catabolism (kuh-TAB-uh-liz-um) Destructive metabolism; chemical reactions involving the breakdown of organic molecules.

catalyst (KAT-ul-ust) Any substance, such as an enzyme,

that increases the rate of a chemical reaction without itself undergoing chemical change.

cation (KAT-eye-un) An ion with a positive charge.

caudal (CAW-dul) Inferior in position.

cell body The nucleus-containing central part of a neuron exclusive of its axons and dendrites.

Celsius (SEL-see-us) A unit of measurement consisting of 100 gradations between the boiling and freezing points.

centigrade See CELSIUS.

central canal A minute canal within the osteons of bone tissue; it contains blood vessels and nerves; formerly Haversian canal.

centriole (SEN-tree-ole) An organelle that organizes the spindle fibers during mitosis.

cephalic (suh-FAL-ik) Pertaining to the head; superior.

cerebellum (ser-uh-BEL-um) A large, dorsally projecting part of the hindbrain concerned especially with muscle coordination and maintaining equilibrium. It is situated anterior to and above the medulla oblongata and consists of two hemispheres and a central portion (vermis).

cerebral (suh-REE-brul or SER-uh-brul) Pertaining to the cerebrum.

cerebral cortex (suh-REE-brul or SER-uh-brul KOR-teks) The convoluted outer layer of the cerebrum.

cerebral nuclei (suh-REE-brul or SER-uh-brul NOO-klee-eye) Four masses of gray matter located deep in the cerebral hemispheres that control involuntary skeletal muscle movements; bassal nuclei.

cerebrum (suh-REE-brum or SER-uh-brum) The largest part of the brain, consisting of hemispheres separated by a deep longitudinal fissure and connected by bands of nerve fibers. The surface of each hemisphere is thrown into numerous folds or convolutions (gyri) separated by furrows (sulci).

cervical (SER-vih-kul) Of or relating to the vertebral column in the neck.

chondrocyte (KON-droe-site) A mature cartilage cell.

cilia (SIL-ee-uh) Tiny, hairlike projections on certain cells in the respiratory and reproductive systems that move in a wavelike manner; they are designed to move substances across the free surface of the tissue; singular: cilium.

collagen (KOL-uh-jen) A tough insoluble fibrous protein that is the chief constituent of connective tissue fibers.

collagenous (kuh-LAJ-uh-nus) Relating to connective tissue fibers that contain collagen.

colliculus (kuh-LIK-yoo-lus) Literally; small hill; a small elevation of tissue; in the brain, one of four such projections in the midbrain.

colloid (KOL-oyd) Solute particles of such a size as to form a suspension in the body fluids (that is, the particles do not readily settle out) and which cannot pass across cell membranes. Example: most proteins.

color blindness An inability to distinguish colors normally.

columnar (kol-UM-nar) Relating to an epithelial cell that is taller than it is wide.

compact bone A dense form of bone tissue comprising the shaft of long bones and as a shell covering bones in general; compare SPONGY BONE.

compound 1. noun: a substance composed of two or, more different elements. 2. adjective: describing a microscope utilizing more than one lens system.

concave (kon-CAVE) Having a depressed, curved surface.

conduction (kun-DUK-shun) **deafness** Complete or partial hearing loss caused by a mechanical defect which impedes the conduction of sound vibrations from the middle ear to the internal ear.

condyle (KON-dile) A rounded projection at the end of a bone that articulates with another bone.

cones One of two types of photosensitive cells in the retina of the eye; they make possible color vision and visual acuity.

connective tissue One of the four primary tissues; its functions include support, storage, and the interconnection of body parts. *Examples*: bone, cartilage, blood, tendons, and adipose tissue.

contractility (kun-trak-TIL-ih-tee) Contractile force; the magnitude of force developed by a muscular organ.

contraction (kun-TRAK-shun) The active process of generating a force in muscle.

convoluted (kon-vuh-LOO-tud) Twisted or coiled.

convolution ("kon-vuh-LOO-shun) An elevation on the surface of a structure caused by an infolding of the structure upon itself; see also GYRUS.

coracoid (KOR-uh-koyd) Literally, shaped like a crow's beak; a bony projection of the scapula for muscle attachment.

cornea (KOR-nee-uh) The transparent anterior portion of the outer layer of the eyeball.

coronal ((KOR-uh-nul or kuh-ROE-nul) Of or relating to the frontal plane that passes through the long axis of the body.

corpus (KOR-pus) Literally, body; the major portion of an organ.

corpus callosum (KOR-pus kuh-LOE-sum) The large, white band of connecting nerve fibers that unites the cerebral hemispheres.

cortex (KOR-teks) The outer, surface layer of an organ.

corticospinal ("kor-tih-koe-SPY-nul) Relating to nerve pathways running from the brain's cerebral cortex to the spinal cord; especially, the large tract of white fibers carrying motor impulses from the frontal cortex to the spinal cord's ventral horns.

costal (KAHS-tul) Pertaining to the ribs.

coxal (KOKS-ul) **bone** The hip bone; the coxal bones make up the pelvic girdle; also called os coxa.

cranial (KRAY-nee-ul) 1. Of or relating to the skull or cranium. 2. Cephalic or superior.

crest A ridgelike projection of a bone.

cubital (KYOO-buh-tul) Pertaining to the space on the anterior forearm at the elbow joint.

cutaneous (kyoo-TAY-nee-us) Pertaining to the skin.

cytokinesis ("sy-toe-ky-NEE-sus) The apportioning of the cytoplasm to the daughter cells during cell division.

cytology (sy-TOL-uh-gee) The study of cells.

cytoplasm (SY-toe-plaz-um) The protoplasm of a cell other than that of the nucleus.

deltoid (DEL-toyd) A large triangular muscle that covers the shoulder joint and serves to abduct the arm.

dendrite (DEN-drite) A branching neuronal process that transmits the nerve impulse to the cell body; the receptive portion of a nerve cell.

dens (denz) A process on the body of the second cervical vertebra (axis) that serves as a pivot for the rotation of the atlas; also known as the **odontoid** (uh-DON-toyd) **process.**

depolarization (dee-"poe-lar-ih-ZAY-shun) Of nerve and muscle cell membranes: moving away from a polarized (resting) state toward a nonpolarized state; this change is caused by a migration of positively charged ions into the cell; the result is an electrical impulse that is propagated along the surface of the cell.

dialysis (dy-AH-uh-sis) The separation of small solutes from larger ones owing to their different diffusion characteristics across a semipermeable membrane.

diaphragm (DY-uh-fram) The partition of muscle and connective tissue that separates the thoracic and abdominal cavities.

diaphysis (dy-AF-uh-sus) The shaft of a long bone.

diarthrodial (dy-ar-THROE-dee-ul) Pertaining to a synovial joint (diarthrosis).

diarthrosis (dy-ar-THROE-sus) A freely moving joint; a synovial joint.

diffusion (dih-FYOO-zhun) The spreading of a solid, liquid, or gas toward a uniformdistribution of particles as the result of their spontaneous movement; the particles move from a region of higher to one of lower concentration.

distal (DISS-tul) Farther from the point of origin of a limb structure; compare PROXIMAL.

dorsal (DOR-sul) Pertaining to the back; posterior.

dorsal (DOR-sul) **root** One of two roots of a spinal nerve that passes dorsally to the spinal cord; it consists of sensory fibers, also known as **posterior root.**

dorsal (DOR-sul) **root ganglion** (GANG-lee-un) A collection of nerve cell bodies that forms a visible bulge within a dorsal root.

dorsiflexion (DOR-sih-"flek-shun) Flexion of the foot at the ankle joint.

duct A canal or passageway.

dura mater (DUR-uh MAYT-ur) Literally, "hard mother"; the tough, fibrous membrane that envelops the brain and spinal cord external to the arachnoid and pia mater.

effector (ih-FEK-tur or ih-FEK-tawr) A gland or muscle activated in response to neural stimulation.

efferent (EF-ur-unt) Designating nerves or blood vessels leading away from a central part.

elastic fibers Nonliving threadlike structures found in connective tissue and containing the protein elastin; they provide elasticity in organs such as blood vessels and the skin.

electrolyte (ih-LEK-troe-lite) Any compound that separates into ions when dissolved in water.

endoplasmic reticulum ("en-duh-PLAZ-mik ruh-TIK-yoo-lum) A membranous network of tubular or saclike interconnecting channels within the cytoplasm; it functions especially in the transport of materials within the cell and may be associated with ribosomes; abbreviated ER.

epiphysis (ih-PIF-uh-sus) An end of a long bone.

epithelium (ep-uh-THEE-lee-um) A type of primary tissue which covers the surface of the body and lines cavities, ducts and blood vessels; it serves to protect, absorb, and produce secretions and excretions.

ergometer (ur-GOM-et-ur) In muscle physiology: an apparatus for measuring the work performed by a group of muscles.

extension (ik-STEN-shun) A movement which increases the angle between two bones.

extensor (ik-STEN-sur) A muscle that widens the angle between two bones.

external oblique (oe-BLEEK) One of a pair of broad, superficial muscles of the abdomen that compresses the abdominal wall.

extracellular Outside a cell.

extrapyramidal ("ek-struh-puh-RAM-ud-ul) Literally, outside of the pyramidal tracts; pertaining to bundles of nerve fibers which exert involuntary control over skeletal muscle function.

facet (FAS-ut) A smooth, nearly flat surface on a bone for articulation

fascia (FASH-uh) A sheet of connective tissue covering or binding together body structures.

fasciculi cuneatus See POSTERIOR COLUMNS.

fasciculi gracilis See POSTERIOR COLUMNS.

fasciculus (fuh-SIK-yuh-lus) A bundle of nerve, muscle, or tendon fibers; plural: **fasciculi** (fuh-SIK-yuh-lye).

fat 1. A class of neutral, water-insoluble organic molecules composed of three fatty acids and glycerol; 2. Tissue consisting chiefly of cells distended with triglyceride; also called adipose tissue.
femur (FEE-mur) The proximal bone of the lower limb; thighbone.

fibroblast (FY-bro-blast) A cell that produces fibers and other intercellular materials in connective tissue.

fibula (FIB-yuh-luh) The more lateral and smaller of the two leg bones.

fissure (FISH-ur) Generally, a narrow groove or cleft: in the brain, a deep linear depression.

flagellum (fluh-JEL-um) A hairlike projection form a spermatozoon which propels the cell in whiplike fashion.

flexion (FLEK-shun) Bending; the movement that decreases the angle between two bones.

flexor (FLEKS-or) A muscle that produces flexion; compare EXTENSOR.

focal (FOE-kul) **point** The point at which light rays converge behind the lens of the eye.

foramen (for-AY-mun) An opening in a bone passage of vessels and nerves; plural foramina or foramens.

forearm The region of the upper extremity from the elbow to the wrist.

forebrain The anterior portion of the brain consisting of the telencephalon (cerebral hemispheres) and the diencephalon (which includes the thalamus and hypothalamus).

fossa (FOSS-uh) A shallow depression; plural: fossae (FOSS-ee)

fovea centralis (FOE-vee-uh sen-TRAL-iss) The region of the retina, consisting of densely packed cones, that is responsible for the greatest visual acuity.

free surface In histology, the side of an epithelial tissue which borders directly on empty space, such as a lumen or other open area

frequency In muscle physiology, the variable that defines how often a muscle receives electricalstimulation; expressed in units of impulses per second.

frontalis (frun-TAL-iss) See OCCIPTOFRONTALIS. The muscle of the forehead; it alters facial expression by raising the eyebrows and wrinkling the skin of the forehead.

frontal (FRUN-tul) Pertaining to the forehead region.

frontal (FRUN-tul) **lobe** That part of the brain represented by four main convolutions in front of the central sulcus of the cerebrum.

frontal (FRUN-tul) **plane** A longitudinal section which divides the body (or an organ) into anterior and posterior parts; also called coronal plane.

ganglion (GAN-glee-un) A group of nerve cell bodies located in the peripheral nervous system.

gastrocnemius ("gas-troe-NEEM-ee-us or gas"-trok-NEEM-ee-us) The large superficial muscle of the calf region; it plantar flexes the foot and aids in flexing the knee.

glia (GLEE-uh) See NEUROGLIA.

gluteal (GLOO-tee-ul) Pertaining to the buttocks.

gluteus maximus (GLOO-tee-us MAX-ih-mus) The large superficial muscle in the buttock region; it extends and laterally rotates the thigh.

gluteus medius (GLOO-tee-us MEED-ee-us) A muscle of the buttock region which abducts and medially rotates the thigh.

glycogen (GLY-kuh-jin) A polysaccharide whose subunits are glucose molecules; the major storage form of carbohydrate in the body.

goblet cell A modified columnar epithelial cell specialized for mucus production; it is found in the respiratory and gastrointestinal mucosa.

Golgi (GOAL-gee) **body** An organelle consisting of a concentric series of curved membranous sacs; it functions to concentrate and package cell secretions within membrane-bound vesicles; also known as **Golgi complex** or **Golgi apparatus**.

gray matter Nervous tissue of a grayish color containing large numbers of nerve cell bodies as well as unmyelinated axons; the term is applied to central nervous structures, including the cerebral cortex, basal and other nuclei, and the dorsal and ventral horns of the spinal cord.

groove A shallow linear depression.

gyrus (JIY-rus) One of the convolutions of the cerebral hemispheres of the brain. The gyri (plural; JY-rye) are separated by shallow grooves (sulci) or deeper grooves (fissures).

hamstring One of the tendons of the posterior thigh muscles.

hamstring group Three muscles on the posterior aspect of the thigh: the semimembranosus, semitendinosus, and biceps femoris; they flex the leg and extend the thigh.

Haversian (huh-VER-zhun) **canal** See CENTRAL CANAL.
Haversian (huh-VER-zhun) **system** See OSTEON.

hemisphere Either half of the cerebrum or cerebellum.

hindbrain The most inferior region of the brain; it contains the cerebellum, pons, and medulla oblongata.

histiocyte (HISS-tee-oe-site) See MACROPHAGE.

histology (hiss-TOL-uh-jee) The branch of anatomy dealing with the microscopic structure of tissues.

homeostasis (hoe-mee-oe-STAY-sis) The maintenance of a relatively constant internal environment.

horn In neurology: a projection of gray matter within the spinal cord.

humerus (HYOO-mer-us) The bone of the upper limb which articulates with the scapula at the shoulder joint and the ulna and radius in the elbow region.

hyaline (HY-uh-lun) Glassy and transparent. In histology, a translucent cartilage found at articulations and in the rib cage and respiratory anatomy.

hypertonic (hy-per-TAHN-ik) 1. Of a solution: having a higher solute concentration than a reference solution. 2. Of a muscle: having above normal tone or tension.

hypophysis (hy-POF-uh-sus) The pituitary gland; a small oval endocrine gland that is attached by a stalk to the hypothalamus; it consists of an epithelial anterior lobe and a posterior lobe of nervous origin.

hypothalamus (hy-poe-THAL-uh-muss) The part of the brain that lies beneath the thalamus on each side, forms the floor of the third ventricle, and contains vital autonomic regulatory centers.

hypotonic (hy-poe-TAHN-ik) 1. Of a solution: having a lower solute concentration than a reference solution. 2. Of a muscle; having below normal tone or tension.

iliac (IL-ee-ak) Pertaining to the superior pelvic region.

iliopsoas (il-ee-oe-SO-us) A powerful flexor of the thigh composed of the psoas major and iliacus muscles.

impulse An action potential transmitted along a nerve or muscle cell.

inferior Relatively farther from the head or upper part of the body; lower.

infraspinatus (in"-fruh-spih-NAY-tus) A shoulder muscle which originates on the scapula and rotates the arm laterally.

inguinal (IN-gwun-ul) Pertaining to the groin area.

innervate (IN-ur-vayt) To supply with nerves.

insertion The distal, more moveable attachment site of a skeletal muscle.

intercellular ("in-tur-SEL-yoo-lur) Between cells.

intercellular ("in-tur-SEL-yoo-lur) **fluid** See TISSUE FLUID.

interstitial ("in-tur-STISH-ul) Pertaining to the fluid-filled space between cells.

interstitial ("in-tur-STISH-ul) **fluid** See TISSUE FLUID.

intracellular ("in-truh-SEL-yoo-lur) Within a cell.

in vitro (VEE-troe) Literally, within glass; used to denote a biologic phenomenon occurring in the laboratory.

in vivo (VEE-voe) Within the living body.

ion (EYE-un) An atom with a positive or negative electric charge.

iris (EYE-russ) The pigmented, circular structure in front of the eye's lens; it regulates the intensity of light reaching the retina.

isometric ("eye-suh-MET-rik) The same length; in muscle physiology, a contraction during which the length of the muscle stays the same as the tension (force) increases.

isotonic (eye-suh-TAHN-ik) 1. Of a solution: having the same solute concentration as a reference solution. 2. Of a muscle: having uniform tension (force) during a contraction.

intervertebral ("in-tur-VERT-uh-brul) Between adjacent vertebrae.

intervertebral ("in-tur-VERT-uh-brul) **disc** A fibrocartilaginous pad between adjacent vertebrae.

intervertebral foramen ("in-tur-VERT-uh-brul fur-AYE-mun) The space between adjacent vertebrae that allows the passage of spinal nerves.

kinetic (kuh-NET-ik) **energy** The energy of motion.

lacuna (luh-COO-nuh) A small cavity within the intercellular material of bone and cartilage in which cells reside.

latent (LAYT-unt**) period** In skeletal muscle physiology: the period between stimulus and response.

lateral (LAT-ur-ul) Toward the side; away from the midline of the body.

latissimus dorsi (lat-ISS-ih-mus DOR-sye) A large muscle of the back which adducts, extends, and medially rotates the arm.

lens The elastic, biconvex structure behind the pupil of the eye which focuses entering light onto the retina.

ligament (LIG-uh-munt) A band or sheet of fibrous connective tissue that connects bones where they form joints, or that supports the viscera.

linea alba (LIN-ee-uh AL-buh) A narrow band of tendinous connective tissue in the midline of the abdominal wall.

lumbar (LUM-bar) Pertaining to the portion of the back between the thorax and pelvis.

lymph (limf) **node** A rounded mass of lymphoid tissue.

lysosomes (LYE-so-somes) Organelles containing digestive (hydrolytic) enzymes that recycle worn out cellular parts and, in immune cells, digest microbes intracellularly.

marrow See RED MARROW and YELLOW MARROW.

marrow cavity The space in the shaft of long bones which houses yellow marrow.

masseter (muh-SEET-ur) A large facial muscle that raises the lower jaw and assists in mastication.

mastication ("mas-tih-KAY-shun) The act of chewing.

matrix (MAY-triks) The intercellular substances in which the cells and fibers of connective tissue are imbedded.

meatus (mee-AY-tus) An opening or passageway.

medial (MEE-dee-ul) Toward the middle; toward the body midline.

medulla oblongata (muh-DULL-uh "ob-long-GOT-uh). The most posterior part of the hindbrain; it is continuous posteriorly with the spinal cord.

meninges (muh-NIN-jeez) A group of three membranes that covers the brain and spinal cord; singular: meninx (MEN-inks).

microvilli (my"-kro-VIL-eye) The tiny projections of certain epithelial cell membranes designed to enhance absorptive surface area.

midbrain That portion of the brain which includes the inferior and superior colliculi and connects the pons and cerebellum with the cerebral hemispheres.

mitochondria (my-toe-KON-dree-uh) Sausage-shaped organelles (0.5 micrometer in diameter) which contain oxidative enzymes and are the primary source of energy in the cell; singular: mitochondrion (my-toe-KON-dree-un)

mitosis (my-TOE-sus) The division of the cell nucleus; also called karyokinesis; it is usually followed by division of the cytoplasm.

mixed nerve A nerve that includes both sensory and motor nerve fibers.

motor In neurology: pertaining to neurons carrying impulses away from the central nervous system and toward an effector; **efferent**.

motor fibers Axons of motor neurons which innervate skeletal muscles.

motor nerve A nerve composed entirely of motor fibers.

motor neuron (NOOR-on) A neuron that innervates muscle tissue.

motor point A region within a muscle where its nerve enters and where visible contraction can be elicited with minimal external stimulation.

motor unit A functional unit in muscle tissue consisting of a motor neuron and all the muscle cells it innervates.

multipolar neuron (mul″-tih-POE-lur NOOR-on) A motor neuron that has one long axon and numerous dendrites.

myelin (MY-uh-lin) A fatlike substance forming the principal component of the sheath which surrounds nerve fibers.

myelinated (MY-uh-lih-nay-ted) **nerve fibers** Axons covered with a sheath of myelin.

myogram (MY-uh-gram) A recording of a muscular contraction.

myograph (MY-uh-graf) A transducer which enables the force of a muscle contraction to be recorded.

nerve fiber The axon portion of a nerve cell together with its coverings.

neural (NOOR-ul) Pertaining to the nervous system.

neurofibral (″noor-uh-FY-brul) **node** A constriction in the myelin sheath of a nerve fiber that enables a neuron to communicate metabolically with the intercellular fluid; also known as a node of Ranvier.

neuroglia (noor-uh-GLEE-uh or noo-RAHG-lee-uh) The tissue of the nervous system that supports the functional nerve cells. Compare NEURON.

neuron (NOOR-on) A nerve cell: the functional unit of the nervous system. It consists of a cell body and its processes: an axon and one or more dendrites.

node of Ranvier (RON-vee-ay) See NEUROFIBRAL NODE.

notch In skeletal anatomy: an indentation or depression, especially on the ledge of a bone.

nuclear (NOO-klee-ur) Pertaining to the nucleus of a cell.

nuclear (NOO-klee-ur) **membrane** A membrane surrounding the cell nucleus.

nucleolus (noo-KLEE-uh-lus) An RNA-containing spherical body within the cell nucleus.

nucleus (NOO-klee-us) 1. An organelle which contains a relatively large quantity of DNA. 2. The dense core of an atom composed of protons and neutrons. 3. A group of nerve cell bodies within the central nervous system.

occipital (ok-SIP-uh-tul) Pertaining to the posterior side of the skull.

odontoid (uh-DON-toyd) **process** See DENS.

olecranon (uh-LEK-ruh-non) **process** A large process on the posterior aspect of the ulna that forms the bony prominence of the elbow.

olfactory (ohl-FAK-tuh-ree) Pertaining to the sense of smell.

optic disc The region of the retina where nerve fibers leave to become part of the optic nerve; because no photoreceptors exist here, it is known as the **blind spot**.

oral (OR-ul) Pertaining to the mouth.

orbicularis oculi (or-bik-yoo-LAR-iss OK-yoo-lye) A circular muscle surrounding each eye that closes the eyelids.

orbicularis oris (or-bik-yoo-LAR-iss OR-iss) A circular muscle surrounding the mouth that closes and purses the lips.

orbit The bony cavity of the skull that holds the eyeball.

organ A group of tissues that functions as a unit to perform a specialized function.

organelle (or-gun-EL) A specialized structure within a cell that performs a definite function. *Examples*: mitochondria, the Golgi body, lysosomes, and the nucleus.

orifice (OR-uh-fiss) An opening.

origin The attachment site of a muscle that remains relatively fixed during the contraction of that muscle.

os coxa (ahss KOKS-uh) The coxal bone; either of the two hip bones; the single adult hip bone represents the fusion of three separate bones in the child: the pubis, ilium, and ischium;

plural: os **coxae** (ahss-KOKS-ee), see also PELVIC GIRDLE.

osmometer (oz-MOM-uh-tur) An apparatus that measures the osmotic pressure of a solution.

osmosis (oz-MOE-sus) The diffusion of water through a selectively permeable membrane.

osmotic (oz-MOT-ik**) pressure** The force with which a solution bounded by a selectively permeable membrane attracts water molecules across that membrane by osmosis; the osmotic pressure of a solution varies directly with its concentration and is especially influenced by nondiffusible solute particles.

osseus (AHSS-ee-us) Bony; pertaining to bone tissue.

ossicle (AHSS-ih-kul) Any small bone, but especially one of the three tiny bones of the middle ear.

osteocyte (OS-tee-uh-site) A cell that is characteristic of mature bone and is isolated within a lacuna of the bone matrix.

osteon (OS-tee-on) An organized system of microscopic interconnecting canals in mature compact bone; formerly Haversian system.

palate (PAL-at) The roof of the mouth.

palatine (PAL-uh-tine) Pertaining to the palate.

palmar (PAHL-mar) Pertaining to the palm of the hand.

palpation (pal-PAY-shun) Examination by touch.

parfocal (par-FOE-kul) Having microscope lenses with the corresponding focal points all in the same plane.

parietal (par-EYE-ih-tul) 1. Pertaining to the walls of a cavity. 2. Pertaining to the paired bones that comprise much of the lateral wall of the cranium.

patella (puh-TEL-uh) The kneecap.

patellar (puh-TEL-ar) **reflex** Extension of the leg resulting from tapping the patellar ligament and the subsequent stretching and contraction of the quadriceps muscle; also known as the knee-jerk reflex.

pectoral (PEK-tur-ul) Pertaining to the chest.

pectoralis (pek-tuh-RA-liss) **major** A large triangular muscle of the anterior upper portion of the chest; it adducts and flexes the humerus and rotates it medially.

pelvic (PEL-vik) Pertaining to the pelvis.

pelvic (PEL-vik) **girdle** The portion of the skeleton to which the lower extremities are attached; it consists of the two coxal (hip) bones.

pelvis (PEL-viss) A basin-shaped structure; the lower portion of the trunk. In the skeleton, the hip bones, sacrum, and coccyx.

perichondrium (per-uh-KON-dree-um) The membrane of fibrous connective tissue which envelops cartilage (except at the joints).

periosteum (per-ee-OS-tee-um) A double-layered membranous connective tissue that surrounds a bone, except at its joint surface.

peripheral (per-IF-ur-ul) **nervous system** The nervous system exclusive of the brain and spinal cord; the cranial and spinal nerves; abbreviated PNS.

phalanges (fuh-LAN-jeez) The bones of the fingers and toes; singular; **phalanx** (FA-lanks).

pharynx (FA-rinks) The throat.

photoreceptor (foe"-toe-ruh-SEP-tur) A receptor, a rod or cone cell, in the retina that converts light energy into nerve impulses.

pia mater (PEE-uh MAYT-ur) The thin vascular membrane covering the brain and spinal cord internal to the arachnoid and dura mater.

pituitary (pih-TOO-ih-tare-ee) **gland** See HYPOPHYSIS.

plantar (PLAN-tar) Pertaining to the sole of the foot.

plantar flexion (PLAN-tar FLEK-shun) Extension of the foot at the ankle joint; also written as plantarflexion.

plasma membrane The selectively permeable membrane that encloses a cell's cytoplasm.

platysma (pluh-TIZ-muh) The broad, thin muscle that extends from the neck to the area around the inferior aspect of the mouth. It acts to wrinkle the skin of the neck and depress the jaw and the corners of the mouth.

pons (ponz) Literally, a bridge; the structure connecting the cerebellum with the brain stem and providing a link between the upper and lower levels of the central nervous system.

posterior (poe-STEER-ee-ur) Near or toward the back of the body; **dorsal**.

posterior (poe-STEER-ee-ur) **columns** Bundles of nerve fibers lying near the midline on the dorsal side of the spinal cord; they convey sensory impulses from the periphery to the medulla oblongata.

presbyopia (prez-bee-OH-pee-uh) A condition of defective elasticity of the lens of the eye, usually as a consequence of aging; the result is difficulty of accommodation and inability to attain a sharp focus for near vision.

prime mover A muscle whose contraction is primarily responsible for a particular movement; also known as the **agonist**.

process A projection or outgrowth of bone or other tissue.

prominence [PROM-ih-nun(t)s] A projection or protrusion, usually of bone or cartilage.

pronation (proe-NAY-shun) 1. The inward rotation of the forearm causing the palms to face posteriorly. 2. In walking, inward movement of the foot so that it tends to come down on its inner margin.

protraction (proe-TRAK-shun) Forward movement of a body part.

protuberance [proe-TOO-buh-run(t)s] A bulge or projection.

proximal (PROKS-ih-mul) Toward the attached end of a limb or the origin of a structure.

pseudostratified epithelium (soo"-doe-STRAT-ih-fyed ep-ih-THEE-lee-um) Single-layered epithelium in which the basal ends of all cells rest on the basement membrane, but whose apical ends may or may not reach the free surface. Because the cells' nuclei lie at different levels, they give the tissue a stratified appearance.

psoas (SOE-us) **major** A muscle extending from the lumbar spine to the femur; it is a powerful flexor of the thigh.

pupil (PYOO-pil) The opening in the center of the iris through which light enters the eye.

pupillary (PYOO-pil-air-ee) **reflex** The constriction of the pupil when a beam of intense light strikes the retina.

pyramidal (pih-RAM-ih-dul) **tract** One of three descending tracts from the brain through the spinal cord. It arises from pyramidal cells in the cerebral cortex; also known as a **corticospinal tract**.

quadriceps (KWOD-rih-seps) **group** A large muscle on the anterior surface of the thigh composed of four parts: rectus femoris, vastus lateralis, vastus medialis, and vastus intermedius. These muscles insert by a common tendon on the tibia and act to extend the leg.

radius (RAY-dee-us) The shorter and more lateral bone of the forearm which revolves partially around the ulna.

reaction time The time elapsing between application of a stimulus and the response to it.

receptor (rih-SEP-tur) 1. A protein molecule on the plasma membrane that binds specifically to a chemical from the intercellular fluid. 2. A specialized peripheral nerve ending

that generates impulses in response to a particular type of stimulus.

rectus (REK-tus) Any of several straight muscles (as the rectus abdominis); a muscle with fibers organized into bundles whose gross appearance is straight.

rectus abdominis (REK-tus ab-DOM-ih-nis) An abdominal muscle that spans the pubis and rib cage on either side of the ventral midline; it flexes the trunk and helps compress the abdominal wall.

rectus femoris (REK-tus FEM-uh-ris) See QUADRICEPS GROUP.

red marrow A type of connective tissue found in the spaces of spongy bone that specializes in the production of blood cells.

reflex (REE-fleks) A predictable, involuntary response to a stimulus that is protective in nature.

retina (RET-ih-nuh) The photosensitive layer of the eyeball; see also CONES and RODS.

retraction (rih-TRAK-shun) The act of drawing backward. *Example*: bringing a protruded lower jaw to its normal position.

ribosome (RYE-buh-sohm) A submicroscopic RNA-containing organelle that functions to synthesize proteins. Ribosomes may be single units (free ribosomes) or occur as clusters called polyribosomes (polysomes).

refraction (rih-FRAK-shun) The deflection of light rays as they pass through the light-bending structures of the eye.

rods Long, slender photoreceptors in the retina of the eye; they permit vision in dim light.

rotation (roe-TAY-shun) The process of turning on an axis.

sagittal (SAJ-ih-tul) **plane** A section that divides the body (or an organ) into left and right portions.

sartorius (sar-TOR-ee-us) A slender muscle of the thigh with the distinction of being the longest in the body; it rotates the thigh laterally and aids in knee flexion.

scapula (SKAP-yoo-luh) The shoulder blade; a large, triangular bone that forms the posterior part of the shoulder.

sclera (SKLER-uh) The firm, white, fibrous outer layer of the eyeball that protects the eye and maintains its shape.
secretory vesicle (SEE-kruh-tor-ree or sih-KREET-uh-ree VES-ih-kul) A membrane-bound sac that shuttles secretions from the Golgi body to the plasma membrane for export.

selectively permeable (PER-mee-uh-bul) A membrane

that allows fluid but not all dissolved substances to pass through it.

semicircular canals A series of three fluid-filled ducts (superior, posterior and inferior) forming part of the internal ear. The expanded end of each canal -- the ampulla -- contains a receptor which detects rotational (angular) acceleration or deceleration of the head. The canals are positioned so that at least one of them is stimulated by an appropriate movement (such as turning the head to one side).

semimembranosus (sem-ih-mem-bran-OE-sus) See HAMSTRINGS.

semipermeable (sem-ih-PER-mee-uh-bul) See SELECTIVELY PERMEABLE.

semitendinosus (sem-ih-ten"-din-OE-sus) See HAMSTRINGS.

sensory In neurology: pertaining to neurons carrying impulses toward the central nervous system; afferent.

sensory nerve A nerve composed of sensory nerve fibers.

sensory neuron A neuron which carries sensory information from a receptor to (or within) the central nervous system.

septum (SEP-tum) A dividing partition.

shoulder girdle See PECTORAL GIRDLE.

simple In histology: an epithelial tissue composed of a single layer of cells.

sinus (SY-nus) In skeletal anatomy: a cavity within a bone (especially within the skull).

skeletal muscle Muscle that (with few exceptions) attaches to parts of the skeleton and is involved primarily with bodily movements; also known as voluntary muscle and striated muscle (due to its striped appearance under the microscope). It consists of long, cylindrical, multinucleated cells.

smooth muscle Involuntary muscle found within the internal organs (except the heart), that consists of spindle-shaped, nonstriated fibers; also known as **visceral muscle**.

soleus (SOE-lee-us) A flat muscle of the calf that plantar flexes the foot.

solution A homogeneous mixture of a solid, liquid, or gaseous substance with a liquid.

spinal nerves Nerves arising from the spinal cord: 31 pairs, consisting of 8 cervical, 12 thoracic, 5 lumbar, 5 sacral, and 1 coccygeal. Each spinal nerve is attached to the cord by two roots: a dorsal (posterior) sensory root and a ventral (anterior) motor root.

spine 1. A sharp process of a bone. 2. The spinal column, consisting of 26 vertebrae: 7 cervical, 12 thoracic, 5 lumbar, 1 sacral, and 1 coccygeal. The multiple bones of the sacrum and coccyx are fused in the adult and are counted as one each.

spinocerebellar ("spy-noe-ser-uh-BEL-ur) Related to the spinal cord and cerebellum, specifically, to the ascending tracts connecting these structures.

spinothalamic ("spy-noe-THAL-uh-mik or spy"-noe-THAL-mik) Related to the spinal cord and thalamus, specifically, to the ascending tracts connecting these structures.

spongy bone Bone tissue with an open organization resembling latticework; compare COMPACT BONE.

sternocleidomastoid ("stir-noe-kly"-doe-MAS-toyd) One of two superficial muscles along the side of the neck that rotate the head (when contracted singly) and flex it (when contracted together); also known as sternomastoid.

sternomastoid ("stir-noe-MAS-toyd) See STERNOCLEIDOMASTOID.

stimulator In muscle and nerve physiology, an instrument that provides electrical stimulation whose strength, frequency, and duration can be precisely controlled.

stimulus An alteration in the environment of a cell that produces a response. *Example*: A nerve impulse is a stimulus that excites a muscle cell, causing it to contract.

striated (STRY-ay-ted) Characterized by a striped appearance; in muscle histology, muscle whose cells have prominent crossbands.

striated (STRY-ay-ted) **border** In epithelial tissue: the appearance of a brush-like outer surface when cells lining the intestine or kidney tubules are viewed under high magnification under the light microscope. What appear to be striations are actually highly folded projections of the plasma membrane known as **microvilli**.

striated muscle See SKELETAL MUSCLE.

striation (stry-AY-shun) One of a series of stripes or streaks.

subarachnoid ("sub-uh-RAK-noyd) **space** The space between the arachnoid and pia mater; it contains cerebrospinal fluid.

subcutaneous (sub-kyoo-TAY-nee-us) Being, used, or made under the skin.

sulcus (SUL-kus) A furrow or linear groove; on the brain, a depression more shallow than a fissure.

summation (suh-MAY-shun) Generally, the accumulated effects of electrical stimuli applied in rapid succession. Summated contractions are based on the concept that stimuli delivered at relatively high frequency will interrupt the contraction cycle of individual twitches, causing them to "fuse" together and develop greater force than that which results from stimuli given singly; see also TETANUS.

superficial Located close to or on the body surface; external.

superior Pertaining to the head or upper part of the body; in relative terms, higher.

supination (soo-pih-NAY-shun) 1.The outward rotation of the forearm causing the palms to face anteriorly. 2. The outward movement (eversion) of the foot.

suture (SOO-chur) An immovable joint that connects the bones of the adult skull.

synergist (SIN-ur-jist) A muscle whose contraction enhances the effectiveness of the prime mover.

tarsals (TAR-suls) The seven bones that form the ankle.

temporal (TEM-por-ul) Related to the temples or temporal bones of the skull.

temporal (TEM-por-ul) **bone** A bone on both sides of the skull at its base; it encloses the organ of hearing.

temporalis (tem-por-AL-is) A muscle originating on the lateral aspect of the cranium and inserting on the mandible. Its function is to close the jaw as in chewing.

tendon (TEN-dun) Fibrous connective tissue serving to attach muscles to bone and other tissues.

tendon of insertion A tendon that secures a muscle to its point of insertion.

tendon of origin A tendon that secures a muscle to its point of origin.

tension In muscle physiology: the force developed during contraction.

teres (TEH-reez) Literally, round; of a muscle, cylindrical in shape (round in cross section).

teres (TEH-reez) **major** A muscle of the shoulder that adducts, extends, and medially rotates the arm.

teres (TEH-reez) **minor** A muscle of the shoulder that laterally rotates the arm.

tetanic (teh-TAN-ik) **contraction** See TETANUS.
tetanus (TET-uh-nus) In muscle physiology; a state of sustained contraction produced by a succession of stimuli whose frequency is sufficient to cause summation; normal contractions are tetanic in nature; compare TWITCH.

thalamus (THAL-uh-mus) The mass of gray matter at the base of the forebrain; it serves as a relay center for incoming sensory information.

thermoreceptor ("ther-moe-rih-SEP-tur) A receptor sensitive to temperature changes.

thoracic (thor-A-sik) Pertaining to the chest (thorax).

thorax (THOR-aks) The part of the body between the neck and the abdomen. It encompasses the pleural, pericardial, and mediastinal cavities.

threshold stimulus In muscle physiology: the weakest stimulus capable of eliciting a contraction. In neurons and muscle cells, the weakest stimulus capable of eliciting an action potential.

tibia (TIB-ee-uh) The shinbone; the larger and more medial of the two bones of the leg; it articulates with the femur proximally and talus distally.

tibialis (tib-ee-AL-us) **anterior** A muscle on the front of the shin that dorsiflexes and inverts the foot.

tissue A group of similar cells which form a distinct structure and serve a particular function.

tissue fluid The extracellular fluid that bathes cells and provides a medium for nutrient and waste exchange; also known as **interstitial fluid** or **intercellular fluid**.

trabecula (truh-BEH-kyuh-luh) One of many small bars within the lattice-like framework of spongy bone; plural: **trabeculae** (truh-BEH-kyuh-lee).

tract A collection of nerve fibers in the central nervous system having the same origin, termination, and function.

transducer (trans-DOO-sur) An instrument or neural structure that converts one form of energy into another. *Example*: The organ of hearing converts sound waves into nerve impulses.

transverse (tranz-VERS) **plane** A crosswise plane. In histology, a section through a tissue that is perpendicular to the longitudinal axis. In body planes, a section that is horizontal, dividing the body into upper and lower portions.

transversus abdominis (tranz-VER-sus ab-DOM-ih-niss) A thin muscle whose transverse fibers encircle the abdominal cavity deep to all other abdominal muscles; it compresses the abdominal wall.

triceps (TRY-ceps) A muscle having three heads of origin with a single insertion.
triceps brachii (TRY-ceps BRAY-key-eye) The large muscle occupying the posterior side of the arm; it extends the elbow joint and helps to extend the arm.

trochanter (troe-KAN-tur) Either of two large bony processes below the neck of the femur.

tubercle (TOO-bur-kul) A small, rounded bony process.

tuberosity (too-bur-OSS-ih-tee) A bony process larger and broader than a tubercle.

twitch A brief, jerky contraction of muscle in response to a single stimulus.

tympanic (tim-PAN-ik) **membrane** The eardrum; a thin membrane that forms the lateral boundary of the middle ear and functions in the mechanical reception of sound waves and in their transmission toward the site of sensory reception in the internal ear; also known as **tympanum**.

ulna (UL-nuh) The larger and more medial bone of the forearm. With the humerus, it forms the elbow joint.

vascular (VAS-kyoo-lur) Pertaining to blood vessels.

vasti (VAS-tye) A group of three large muscles on the anterior thigh. See also QUADRICEPS GROUP.

ventral (VEN-trul) See ANTERIOR.

ventral (VEN-trul) **root** One of the two roots of a spinal nerve that passes ventrally to the spinal cord; it consists of motor fibers; also known as **anterior root**.

ventricle (VEN-tri-kul) In neurology: one of four small, fluid-filled cavities within the brain.

vertebra (VER-tuh-bruh) Any of the bony segments of the spinal column. A typical vertebra consists of a ventral body (centrum) and a dorsal arch. The arch encloses the vertebral foramen and bears seven processes: a dorsal spinous process, two lateral transverse processes, and four articular processes; plural: **vertebrae** (VER-tuh-bree).

vesicle (VES-ih-kul) A small liquid-filled sac.

vestibular (ves-TIB-yuh-lur) **apparatus** A collective term for the semicircular canals, utricle and saccule of the internal ear; their receptors respond to changes in head position, acceleration, and in the direction of movement.

villus (VIL-us) A projection, often fingerlike in appearance, found on the surface of certain membranes; plural: **villi** (VIL-eye). *Example*: The arachnoid villi of the brain and the intestinal villi of the small bowel.

viscera (VIS-uh-ruh) The internal organs; singular: viscus.

visceral (VIS-ur-ul) Pertaining to the internal organs or to the internal part of a structure (such as a membrane).

visceral muscle See SMOOTH MUSCLE.

visual acuity (uh-KYOO-ih-tee) The ability of the eye to distinguish detail.

white fibers 1. Myelinated nerve fibers. 2. Collagenous fibers in connective tissue.

white matter Nervous tissue of whitish color containing larger numbers of myelinated nerve fibers; the term is applied to central nervous system structures; see also TRACT.

xiphoid (ZY-foyd) **process** The pointed segment at the lower end of the sternum.

yellow fibers Elastic fibers in connective tissue.

yellow marrow (MA-roe) Marrow found in the shaft of adult long bones and containing principally fat tissue.

Z disc A zigzag pattern of dense proteins that separates neighboring sarcomeres and defines the width of a single sarcomere.

Appendix A
Significant Figures

Digits that arise as a result of a measurement are termed significant. These numbers are placed into two categories: exact and inexact. An exact number is a value obtained as the result of a count, for example, 13 cars or from a definition, 12 inches = 1 foot. An inexact number is a value obtained when a measuring device is used, such as a ruler, balance or thermometer. Because of design limitations on instruments, the number of digits obtained from a particular measurement is restricted. For example, if you were reading the temperature from a thermometer calibrated to the units place, you would estimate and record the value obtained to the tenths place, as in 100.1 C. The last digit is an estimate, but it is significant and must be recorded. When using this particular thermometer, you would always record temperatures to the tenths place. If you used a different thermometer, calibrated to tenths, then you would record your readings to the hundredths place. In general, when reading an instrument, you determine how it is calibrated and always estimate your value to one more place.

Significant Figures in Results of Calculations
How many figures can be properly recorded in a calculated result? There are two rules for this procedure.

Addition or Subtraction
The result should be rounded off so that is has as many decimal places as the measurement with the fewest decimal places.

Multiplication or Division
The calculated result should be rounded off to the same number of significant figures as the measurement with the fewest number of significant figures.

Note: Exact numbers are never used to limit the number of significant figures in a calculated result.

Rounding Off Numbers

When we drop figures that are not significant, we say we have rounded off the number. There are rules for properly rounding off numbers.

1. If the digit being dropped is less than 5, the last remaining digit remains the same. Thus, 7.5447 rounded off to three significant figures would be 7.54.

2. If the digit being dropped is greater than 5, the last remaining digit is increased by 1. Thus, 3.271 rounded off to two significant figures would be 3.3.

3. If the digit being dropped is 5
    a) and it is the last number in the figure (e.g. 7.45) or is only followed by zeros (e.g. 7.4500), then the last remaining digit remains the same if it is even and is increased by 1 if it is odd. Thus 7.45 or 7.4500 rounded off to two significant figures would by 7.4; 7.15 or 7.1500 would be 7.2.

    b) and it is followed by any other number or numbers other than zero (as in 7.451) then the last remaining digit is increased by 1. Thus 7.451 rounded off to two significant figures would be 7.5 and 7.1510 would be 7.2.

Examples of Rounding off Rules			
Rule	Figure	Number of Significant Figures	Answer
2	15.4773	4	15.48
2	14.9991	3	15.0
1	39.1574	5	39.157
1	100.1	3	100
3a	27.475	4	27.48
3b	41.25000	3	41.2
3b	41.35001	3	41.4

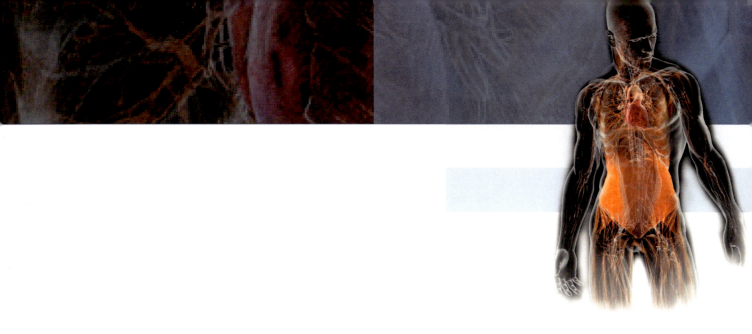

Appendix B
Graphing Technique

Graphs are used in many ways in scientific work. They can show a general trend in a set of measurements or be used to find relationships and predict information. It is therefore worthwhile to learn how to prepare a well-designed graph.

In general, a graph is constructed on a set of perpendicular axes. The horizontal axis (x-axis) is called the abscissa and the vertical axis (Y-axis) is called the ordinate. The place where the axes cross is called the origin. The simple algebraic equation $Y = 2x + 1$ produces a straight line when plotted. For each numerical value of x, there is a corresponding value of y. For example, if $x - 2$, $y - 5$; if $x = 3$, $y = 7$ and so on. Because the variation in y depends upon the value of x, the letter y is called the *dependent variable* and x the *independent variable*. The numeral 1 is called a constant and the multiplier of x is called a coefficient. The constant is the intercept on the y-axis when x is equal to 0 and the coefficient is the slope. The slope measures the change in the value of y with respect to the change in x. The coefficient 2 and the constant 1 are usually referred to as parameters of the equation. When we deal with mathematical equations (and graphs), we have to recognize the dependent variable (the quantity we intend to measure in our experiment), the independent variable (the quantity we can vary) and the parameters. By convention, we plot the dependent variable along the y-axis and the independent variable along the x-axis. From the resultant graph we can estimate the numerical quantities of the parameters; this is the purpose of a graph. These parameters represent very important physical meanings. The following guidelines should be used for best results.

1. Use a scale large enough to cover as much as possible of the graph paper. Therefore, choose scales for the x and y axes that cover the range of the experimental data. For example, if the measured volumes range from 55 ml to 275 ml, choose a volume scale that ranges from 0 to 300 ml. This covers the entire data range and allows you to choose divisions at intervals of 100 ml. This simplifies the plotting of data and the reading of the graph.

2. Label the graph. Place a descriptive title centered on top. Make sure both axes have been labeled with the proper variables and units.

3. Place a dot for each point at the appropriate place on the graph.

4. Draw a smooth curve or straight line, as the case may be, that best represents all the points. Such a line may not necessarily pass through any of the points, but it should pass as closely as possible through all of them. A connect-the-dot type line should not be drawn between consecutive points unless there is reason to believe that such discontinuities do in fact really occur at the experimental points. Such reasons almost never exist.

5. Refer to check list below before considering your work complete.

- Is there a title?

- Are axes labeled with units?

- Have graduations been chosen to make maximum use of paper?

- Are data points properly located?

- Has a "best fit" line been drawn?

Appendix C
Units of Measurement Commonly Used in Anatomy and Physiology

Mass

1 gram (g)	=	0.035 ounce (1 ounce = 28.35 g)
1 kilogram (kg)	=	1000 g = 2.2 pounds
1 milligram (mg)	=	1/1000 g = 0.001 g (1 pound = 454 g)
1 microgram (μg)	=	1/1,000,000 g = 0.000001 g = 10^{-6} g

Length

1 meter (m)	=	39.37 inches
1 centimeter (cm)	=	1/100 m = 0.01 m = 0.4 inch
1 millimeter (mm)	=	1/1000 m = 0.001 m
1 micrometer (μm)	=	1/1000,000 m = 0.000001 m = 10^{-6} m = 1 micron (μ)
1 nanometer (nm)	=	1/1,000,000,000 m = 0.000000001 m = 10^{-9} m = 1 millimicron (mμ)

Volume

1 liter (l)	=	1000 milliliters = 100 cubic centimeters (cc or cm^3) = 1.06 quart
1 deciliter (dl)	=	100 milliliters = 100 cc
1 milliliter (ml)	=	1/1000 l = 0.001 l = 1 cc = 0.03 fluid ounce (1 fluid ounce = 29.58 ml)

Temperature

To convert degrees Fahrenheit (°F) to degrees Celsius (centigrade) (°C): 5/9 (°F - 32)
To convert degrees Celsius to degrees Fahrenheit: 9/5 (°C) + 32

Notes

Index